International
Afro Mass Media

International
Afro Mass Media

A REFERENCE GUIDE

James Phillip Jeter, Kuldip R. Rampal,
Vibert C. Cambridge, and Cornelius B. Pratt

GREENWOOD PRESS
Westport, Connecticut • London

P 94.5
B 55 I 57

Library of Congress Cataloging-in-Publication Data

International Afro mass media : a reference guide / James Phillip
  Jeter . . . [et al.].
       p.   cm.
    Includes bibliographical references and index.
    ISBN 0–313–28400–8 (alk. paper)
    1. Black mass media.   I. Jeter, James Phillip.
  P94.5.B55I57   1996
  302.23'08996—dc20   95–9304

British Library Cataloguing in Publication Data is available.

Copyright © 1996 by James Phillip Jeter, Kuldip R. Rampal,
Vibert C. Cambridge, and Cornelius B. Pratt

Library of Congress Catalog Card Number: 95–9304
ISBN: 0–313–28400–8

First published in 1996

Greenwood Press, 88 Post Road West, Westport, CT 06881
An imprint of Greenwood Publishing Group, Inc.

Printed in the United States of America

The paper used in this book complies with the
Permanent Paper Standard issued by the National
Information Standards Organization (Z39.48–1984).

10 9 8 7 6 5 4 3 2 1

Contents

IV. Afro-America
   James Phillip Jeter

Illustrations

TABLES

FIGURE

Acknowledgments

The author of the section on North Africa is grateful to many individuals connected with the information ministries, media industries, and media education and/or training institutes in Morocco, Tunisia, Algeria, Libya, and the Sudan for providing information used in the preparation of this work. It is not possible to mention all the names here, but the author would be remiss if the individuals who were particularly helpful were not acknowleged. They include Chakib Laroussi, director of communication at the Ministry of Information in Rabat, Morocco; Amina Tadili, press liaison in the Ministry of Information, Rabat; A.M. Abdesslam, journalist at the Maghreb Arabe Presse in Rabat; the staff of the English service of RTM in Rabat; Ezzeddine Besbes, director of the Tunisian External Communication Agency; Ridha Methnani, dean of the Institute of Press and Information Sciences in Tunis; Ridha Najar, director of the African Center for the Improvement of Journalists and Communicators in Tunis; Abdelhafidh Herguem, director-general of Radiodiffusion Television Tunisienne in Tunis; Mounir Adhoum, deputy director, Tunisian Information Office, Washington, D.C.; Jalila Kara, news and sports coordinator of the Arab States Broadcasting Union in Tunis; Nawaf Adwan, director of research at ASBU; Mustapha Masmoudi, chairman, Mass Media Institute in Tunis; and Hedi Zaouchi, journalist at the Tunis Afrique Presse in Tunis. Gratitude is also due to the Office of Sponsored Research and Projects at Central Missouri State University, which awarded a research grant to the author for field research in North Africa.

Introduction

This reference guide examines and assesses the relationships between peoples in Africa and of African descent and "Afro" mass media around the world. It focuses on the media systems of four major audiences: sub-Saharan Africans, North Africans, Caribbeans, and African-Americans. It is not a survey of media facilities in those regions. Rather, the authors provide a four-pronged analysis of the media: their settings and philosophical contexts, their development and government relations, the education and training of their personnel, and the challenges in the use of new technologies.

Much of the human dilemma results from the external differences among people. Race and national origin are two constructs through which people may differentiate themselves. Thus, the word "Afro" in the title of this work is intended to be a global term used to refer to people who trace their ancestors to Africa and people who live in certain countries on the continent.

As one of the first great civilizations of the world, Africa was noted for its powerful kingdoms for nearly 6,500 years. Africa's racial purity changed over the centuries as the continent attracted imperialists nearly 700 years before the birth of Christ. The Assyrians (670 B.C.), the Persians (525 B.C.), the Greeks (332 B.C.), the Romans (30 B.C.), and the Arabs (642 A.D.) each took their turns as conquerors, bringing a variety of cultural influences to northern Africa.

The media audiences in the four geographically distinct regions that are the focus of this guide have had extensive historical and cultural contacts and have been subject to external influences.

For example, long before the earliest Portuguese set foot on Africa and before the onset of the scramble for Africa, Africans had coastal trading posts and trans-Saharan caravan networks through which they became involved in commercial and cultural relations with the rest of the world. Thus, when the

Portuguese arrived in West Africa in the 1400s, there was an extensive commercial infrastructure by which they explored and developed further trading posts and commercial centers for trafficking in black slaves and in commodities such as kola nuts, gold, iron, and leather goods.

Although the first slaves were sent to Europe, the establishment of European plantations in North and South America created a new market for their human cargo. This diaspora accounts for the presence of people of African descent in the Caribbean and the United States of America. By the 1800s, an estimated ten million slaves had been exported from western Africa to the Americas. At various points, Belgium, France, Germany, Great Britain, Italy, the Netherlands, Portugal, and Spain established colonies/empires on the African continent as a result of an intensive period of exploration to the interior African continent in the late 1700s.

The European influence in Africa south of the Sahara was not strictly economic. Africans had established religious traditions when the missionaries arrived and the missionaries brought with them Christianity and values that initially shaped the moral thinking of the media. The early presses in a number of African colonies were established and run by missionaries. The missionaries also set up schools and agricultural facilities through which they engendered their own set of moral values, work ethic, and political institutions. While it was obvious that these European religious and political values were sometimes at cross-purposes with those of indigenous religions and governments, these values left traditions that influenced the media systems in independent African nation-states. For example, the media in such states were still largely government-owned, even after much of the continent had become independent. Beyond government ownership, Africa's mass media were subject to other Western influences such as those regarding the concept of news and the use of communication technologies in social and economic development. The resulting clash of media values puts Africa's modern mass media at loggerheads with African governments, which have resorted to adopting stricter media policies to cow the media.

The domination of the African peoples of the world by men of European descent continued into the twentieth century and was virtually total. As late as 1921, the African continent only had two independent countries (Ethiopia and Liberia). Americans of visible African descent lived in a legally "separate but equal" society until 1954. Demands for freedom and equal rights by blacks in America coincided with demands for independence in the Caribbean and on the African continent. Between the 1950s and the 1980s, the visible vestiges of colonial rule and second-class citizenship began to disappear.

The political history of sub-Saharan Africa is different from the Arabic North. Consequently, this book treats media developments on the continent in separate sections. In this work, the authors explore how more than 500 million people in Africa and of African descent communicate within their countries and regions and on a worldwide basis.

This comparative study of "Afro" mass media and the impact of social and political systems, of culture and ideology, of different communication mechanisms, and of special technical and other problems is designed for a broad audience. However, it should be special interest to students, teachers, and professionals in all areas of communications and mass media, government, sociology, economics, and African and African-American studies.

1 AFRICA SOUTH OF THE SAHARA

_____ Cornelius B. Pratt

1 Setting and Philosophical Contexts

This chapter provides an overview of Africa south of the Sahara and details the contexts of its media philosophy. The history and politics of the region are remarkably different from those of North Africa. It is daunting to present an overview of a region that stretches from the Sudan to the Cape of Good Hope—almost three times the size of the United States of America, about the size of Argentina, China, Europe, India, and New Zealand combined. Moreover, Africa south of the Sahara is a hodgepodge of some 50 culturally, politically, and historically diverse countries whose political landscape, created mostly by colonists, spawned, as recently as May 1993, yet a new nation of about 4 million people: Eritrea. That landscape had been influenced by political systems and practices reflective of the intrusion of foreign powers on the continent: the Belgians in Congo and Ruanda-Urundi (which, after 1962, became the separate countries of Rwanda and Burundi); the French and the British in much of western and subequatorial Africa; and the Germans in what was then South West Africa and what was then Tanganyika; the English, French, Italians, and Ethiopians in Somalia; the freed black slaves from the southern United States of America in Liberia; the Dutch settlers in South Africa; the Portuguese in Angola, Mozambique, and in São Tomé and Príncipe; and the Italians in Somalia and Eritrea.

That same landscape had spawned anticolonial movements for independence, which peaked in the 1960s, when 31 sub-Saharan nations attained independence, with 17 doing so in 1960. (Cameroon was the first in that year, on January 1, 1960; Mauritania the last, on November 28, 1960.) That same landscape had created intermittent democracies in Burkina Faso, Ethiopia, Ghana, Liberia, Nigeria, Sierra Leone, Somalia, Togo, and Uganda. And it had resulted in civil strife in Angola, Ethiopia, Rwanda, Burundi, Nigeria, Liberia, Mozambique, and Somalia.

The economic landscape, on the one hand, shows a continent endowed with natural resources, with South Africa, Zambia, Zaire, and Zimbabwe having some of the world's richest minerals and Nigeria the world's lightest, lowest-sulphur crude oil. The economic landscape, on the other hand, is dominated by low-income economies, with fewer than 10 countries of the region's 50 countries classified by the World Bank as having middle-income economies (World Bank, 1993). The region has the following seven characteristics:

1. an annual percentage growth rate of −1.1 for its gross domestic product between 1980 and 1990;
2. a life expectancy of 51 years;
3. a population of 570 million spread over some 25 million square kilometers;
4. an average annual population growth rate of 3.1 percent (Even though the region has the world's highest fertility, secondary-school enrollment rates have stagnated since the mid-1980s, perpetuating high birth rates and poor education [World Resources Institute, 1994]);
5. an infant mortality rate of 51 per 1,000 live births;
6. a poverty rate that will make the region's share of the developing world's poor increase from 16 percent in 1985 to 30 percent by the end of the century (Ake, 1991); and
7. a per capita gross national product of $330.

Its economic landscape has also made it lose its ability to feed itself: In 1974 it imported 3.9 million metric tons of cereals; by 1989, the figure was 7.4 million.

How can an author draw a broad portrait of the successes and failures of the region; of the region's media, whose development and growth have been stagnated for years by heavy-handed government policies; of a wide array of fledgling nation-states with few media resources (see Table 1.1); and of a region where history is continually and rapidly being unfolded? The commonalities immanent on the continent make that possible, as Diamond (1993) writes, "Independently, in some 50 African states . . . authoritarian regimes of widely different structures, ideologies and leaderships have broadly similar consequences with respect to economic development, social justice and accountability, and individual and group rights" (p. 8).

Even with such obvious commonalities, keeping up with the occasional rapid-fire changes in the region is as daunting as confronting the Africanist's extant research barriers: "We don't have that kind of information"; and "we need authorization for that information to be made public." Conducting research about or on Africa presents its unique set of challenges. For one thing, research in the region is not data-driven. Reliance may be placed on secondary data

Table 1.1
Mass Media Profile for Africa South of the Sahara

Mass Media

Country	Estimated Population (in millions)	Radio Receivers ('000 in use)	Television Receivers ('000 in use)	Number of Daily Newspapers (and daily circulation, in '000)
Angola	11.3	540	57	4 (115)
Benin	5.2	415	23	1 (12)
Botswana	1.5	1,100	20	1 (48)
Burkina Faso	10.0	235	48	3 (17)
Burundi	6.0	500	5	1 (20)
Cameroon	13.0	2,100	20	2 (80)
Cape Verde	.361	100	5	None
Central African Republic	3.07	550	13	1 (2)
Chad	6.5	1,350	7	1 (2)
The Comoros	.53	60	.002	None
The Congo	2.9	250	13	5 (17)
Côte d'Ivoire	14.0	1,700	810	5 (150)
Djibouti	.57	40	20	None
Equatorial Guinea	.42	150	3	2 (2)
Eritrea	3.8	NA	NA	None
Ethiopia	54.0	9,400	115	3 (107)
Gabon	1.3	250	43	1 (20)
The Gambia	1.1	182	NA	2 (2)
Ghana	16.4	4,000	255	3 (240)
Guinea	6.5	140	65	1 (13)
Guinea-Bissau	1.1	40	NA	1 (6)
Kenya	28.2	4,300	265	5 (350)
Lesotho	2.0	425	50	6 (36)
Liberia	2.7	600	47	8 (40)

Table 1.1 (continued)

Mass Media

Country	Estimated Population (in millions)	Radio Receivers ('000 in use)	Television Receivers ('000 in use)	Number of Daily Newspapers (and daily circulation, in '000)	
Madagascar	13.7	1,500	140	5	(53)
Malaŵi	9.8	2,200	NA	1	(21)
Mali	9.0	400	10	1	(40)
Mauritania	2.2	300	1.2	1	(10)
Mauritius	1.2	385	163	7	(96)
Mozambique	17.4	650	40	2	(81)
Namibia	1.8	240	40	6	(50)
Niger	8.8	460	35	1	(5)
Nigeria	94.0	15,000	4,800	31	(1,600)
Réunion	.65	150	92	3	(55)
Rwanda	7.9	650	None	None	
Saint Helena	.006	3	None	None	
São Tomé and Príncipe	.28	32	None	None	
Senegal	8.1	850	62	3	(50)
Seychelles	.72	30	8.2	1	(4)
Sierra Leone	4.7	1,000	25	1	(10)
Somalia	7.0	400	105	1	(10)
South Africa	42.0	12,000	3,600	22	(1,400)
The Sudan	26.0	7,000	250	3	(30)
Swaziland	.89	122	16	3	(20)
Tanzania	28.0	4,000	80	3	(220)
Togo	4.0	750	150	2	(16)
Uganda	18.4	3,500	115	4	(55)
Zaire	44.0	3,500	23	5	(80)
Zambia	9.1	1,660	250	2	(110)
Zimbabwe	11.4	622	140	2	(210)

NA = Publications, service or data not available

sources, such as UNESCO's *Statistical Yearbook* and *Europa World Yearbook*. For another, research procedures that researchers in the West may take for granted, for example, conducting telephone or mail interviews, are not easily applicable to the African research environment.

These circumstances explain, in part, some of the frustration of international journalists who attempt to report the continent. They are blindsided by the fast-evolving events that seem to defy rational thought. How, for instance, can a region that was, until the mid-1970s, a net exporter of agricultural products be a major importer 10 years later? Abbott (1993) proffers answers: Growth in population has exceeded growth in food production; exploitation of the region's enormous agricultural potential has not occurred; the emergence of a period of deindustrialization from which the region has not recovered; the precipitous decline in the manufacturing sector.

How could a region that has some of the world's choicest resources have become overrun by debt crises since the mid-1970s, with Nigeria, Côte d'Ivoire, and Zaire accounting for about one-half of the sub-Sahara's total scheduled debt service? (Nafziger, 1993) Some of the reasons are the high export concentration associated with volatile export prices and earnings, international price instability, and deteriorating commodity terms of trade (Nafziger, 1993).

These scenarios have created political and economic obstacles for Africa south of the Sahara. From the perspective of international media audiences, Africa is a continent fraught with disasters and with the problems of inept administrations. The international media have been major pipelines for perceptions that tend not to acknowledge the struggles and occasional progress of the continent. Granted, much of today's authoritarian Africa is an atavist product of the colonial experience. Because colonial interests took precedence over domestic interests, the colonial governments maintained authoritarian styles of administration, which subsequent indigenous governments later adopted. Perhaps African governments' relatively brief experiences with self-government make them, as Sesay (1987) observed, susceptible to foreign government interventions in civil liberties, political/military, humanitarian, economic, secret service, and mass media matters. Land (1992) argues, for example, that Western programming on Ivoirien television results from the politicization of the medium by the nation's president and from the imposition of a cultural policy that favors the importation of Western culture.

Granted, bureaucratic corruption has been rife on the continent (e.g., Ayittey, 1992; Dumont, 1979; Greenstone, 1979; Levine, 1975). There have been numerous cases of official abuse of civil rights, including those of journalists. Ayittey (1992) documents such abuses in 27 sub-Saharan African countries from 1986 through 1991. There have been cases of wanton administrative ineptitude. And, granted, as put by Ayittey (1992) in blunt, hard-hitting terms:

Africa has been betrayed. Freedom from colonial rule has evolved into ghastly tyranny, arbitrary rule, denial of civil liberties, brutal suppression of dissent, and the wanton slaughter of peasants. This malicious betrayal drives the deep sense of disillusionment, despair, and anger pervasive among Africans. (p. 10)

These harsh realities expressed in the media resulted in a recurrence of negative images about the region among international audiences. In some instances, it is not the fault of international journalists who contend with inadequate, obsolete infrastructure while gathering the news (Brice, 1992; Fitzgerald, 1989; Strieker, 1986). However, the emphasis of the media has, almost always, been one-sided. So pervasive are these images that the National Broadcasting Corporation in the United States, beginning November 13, 1992, ran a weeklong series titled '' 'Today' in Africa.'' Its intent was to provide a comprehensive coverage of the continent, in light of recurring concerns that had been expressed about imbalanced Western media coverage of the region (Dahlgren, 1982; Fair, 1993; Ibelema & Onwudiwe, 1994; Ogundimu, 1994; Pratt, 1980; Stokke, 1971; Weaver & Wilhoit, 1983).

Africa continues to be the least understood among U.S. nationals (Abdolfathi, 1971; Mudimbe, 1988; Staniland, 1991). Most people know very little about the sub-Saharan region and ascribe to it the extreme image of the movie "The Gods Must Be Crazy" (Gordon & Gordon, 1992). The rest of this chapter and the next three attempt to put Africa's continuing challenges within the media context, charting developments and influences that shape media behavior and their social implications. An understanding of this behavior is critical to mapping out strategies for confronting Africa's problems: "Without a [*sic*] free media," writes Ayittey (1992), "respect for freedom of expression and a climate that admits intellectual pluralism, Africa will never solve its problems" (p. 229). This fitting testimony underscores the importance both of the media in Africa's development and of the direct interest of Africa's governments in having more than a passing interest in them. And it also underscores the importance of the discourse presented in this and in the next three chapters.

PHILOSOPHICAL CONTEXTS

Africa's governing juntas have used the media to avert further strife and to promote their own version of national interests. The continuing pattern of economic and political challenges of sub-Saharan Africa have rung resounding bells worldwide—and they should. The scenarios in the region are telling: the ethnic conflicts in Liberia and Rwanda since 1992; the Ethiopian famine at its height in the mid-1980s and a similar occurrence in Somalia; the plunder and economic decimation of Uganda by Idi Amin and Milton Obote, of Liberia by William Tolbert and Samuel Doe, of Somalia by Siad Barre, of Ethiopia by Mengistu Haile Mariam, and of Zaire by Mobutu Sese Seko; the precipitous decline in the economies of Kenya, Nigeria, and Sierra Leone, following their mismanagement by Daniel arap Moi of Kenya and by the military in both Nigeria and Sierra Leone. Given the worsening economy in much of Africa, the media have been used as institutions of hope as much as they have been used as targets of governments' ever-changing media policies.

As targets of governments' changing media policies, the media are used as institutions for cutting the losses of the ruling elite. These two outcomes of government–press relations underlie the philosophical contexts of Africa's mass media. This chapter outlines developments in media philosophies in Africa south of the Sahara. Even though the region is not culturally and politically homogeneous, one can discern four forms of media philosophies.

Two possibilities engender such philosophies. The first is that a nation's political system dictates its relationships with the mass media (e.g., Weaver, Buddenbaum, & Fair, 1985). Military governments, now an enduring reality in Africa, tend to develop authoritarian media policies. Widely known country cases are Ethiopia, Ghana, Liberia, Nigeria, Somalia, Sudan, and Uganda. The second is that, as a consequence of the first, the media assume development roles on behalf of a nation's development agencies.

Politically stable governments are able to establish social and economic institutions whose activities converge to nurture viable social institutions, among which are the media. So important are the influences of a nation's political system on its institutions that one must, at the outset, consider the relationships between politics and the media in understanding the media philosophy that is emerging in sub-Saharan Africa. In recognition of the social impact of indigenous precolonial political systems and practices, such a discourse must highlight the precolonial experience.

Indigenous, precolonial African governments had institutional structures that were complex and efficient. In most cultures, for example, hierarchy was the overriding concept, with day-to-day duties conducted by chiefs and their councils of elders who revered kingship and its trappings and abhorred blatant opposition to authority. This translated into traditional systems and domestically constituted authorities that created wide public acceptance of local governments, which functioned efficiently. For example, Lord Frederick Lugard introduced indirect rule into Nigeria, by which the traditional emirs of northern Nigeria and the *obas* (or kings) of western Nigeria formed the bases for British rule in parts of Nigeria and in other British African colonies. Attempts to apply the system to the Igbos of southeastern Nigeria in 1928 hit a roadblock. The appointment of "warrant" chiefs to act as liaisons between the British and the people led to suspicion and hostility that culminated in the Aba women's riots of 1929; the "warrant" chiefs were attacked, the native courts destroyed.

Among stateless societies such as those of the Igbo of Nigeria, the Kru of Liberia, and the Konkomba of Togo, respect for others is based on kinship rather than on kingship. Yet, societal matters are handled evenhandedly, with elders expressing free-speech rights by voicing opinions prior to reaching a consensus. Even though such people were largely individualistic, governance was still democratic in the African scheme of things.

The arrival of colonialism weakened the bases of African governments: public acceptance and reverence. The political concept of apartheid in South Africa, for example, was so reprehensible to the indigenous South African that it was an anathema to political expediency. Because it created rigid social and political boundaries and distributed the spoils of apartheid by using heinous criteria, governmental authority was questioned consistently and media philosophies were shaped in line with political leanings. The underground press saw nothing commendable in Pretoria's policies; the pro-government press created a facade of popular government endorsement.

The widespread occurrence, beginning in the 1960s, of military governments in sub-Saharan Africa, quickly saw the emergence of actions that were inimical to journalistic interests. In Equatorial Guinea, for example, there was governmental opposition toward democratic traditions even though a November 17, 1992, referendum resulted in a 98 percent popular support for multiparty politics. This trend was also reflected in Malawi, in opposition to the single-party rule of former President Kamuzu Banda. Such political systems, imposed, as it were, on the disenfranchised, resulted in a backlash on the miniscule freedoms that the media had.

Prior to independence, a number of sub-Saharan African nations adopted constitutional freedoms of the colonial governments. The handing over of the reins of government to the indigenous political parties, however, created schisms in the relations between teetering governments and an initially virile mass media system. The irony of this outcome is that the deepening roots of indigenous leaders in the "modern" governance of their countries saw a reaffirmation of new realities: The media were to succumb to the wishes of the powers that be of the newly independent nations.

The emergence of Africa's media philosophy is contingent upon its political systems. The failure of Angola's President José Eduardo dos Santos to include Jonas Savimbi, leader of the National Union for the Total Independence of Angola (UNITA), in a national government resulted in a stalemate in a peaceful establishment of a nationally elected government and the resumption of hostilities by UNITA. The lack of a government acceptable to all sides threatens the environment in which viable media can be nurtured. The outcome: Angola's media are just as fragmented and politically aligned according to the biases of the media lords. Thus, there has been speculation that Angola's postelection political divisions may rub off on Mozambique, which held its first multiparty elections in late October 1994, after 16 years of civil war. Charges about possible foreign interference in the elections and debates on the sharing of national power between the ruling Frelimo party and the South African–backed Renamo revolutionaries have created political divisions that are likely to deepen, even after the national elections. For one thing, the administrative style of the Frelimo government has been repressive; for another, the Renamo group is still chafing from its loss of both the presidency and a majority of the seats in parliament.

Perhaps nowhere is government interference more pronounced in sub-Saharan Africa than in Nigeria, where democratic traditions are less embedded in the country's authoritarian military traditions than in its political character. The country has had nine years of indigenous democratic rule, but it has been governed by the military for more than 20 years. Skirmishes between the military and the press resulted in the 1994 closure of *The Guardian,* perceived by the military elite as perhaps Nigeria's most rapacious independent daily newspaper. Even Kenya, whose government professes democratic traditions and free media, has subjected its media to overt censorship (Hachten, 1993; Heath, 1992; Maja-Pearce, 1992). Some Africanists are increasingly leery of the prospects for sustainable, Western-type democratic institutions and for enduring popularly elected governments in the region.

Faringer (1991) suggests three historical reasons for the legacy of press restrictions in Africa: (1) even though British press laws were applied to much of Africa, their enforcement was left to local authorities; (2) the British colonists did not provide adequate training to local journalists, leaving political dissidence to be met with prosecution and restriction; and (3) the political climate in the former British African countries did not nurture debate and tolerance, the absence of which led to rebellion and political turbulence. Even so, Faringer (1991) described the media systems in three British territories—Nigeria, Ghana, and Kenya—as among the best developed on the continent.

Kenya's Mau Mau movement in the 1950s and the clamor for independence in a number of other colonies prior to the 1960s saw the nurturing of newspapers such as the *African Morning Post* (Ghana); the *West African Pilot* and the *Daily Service* (Nigeria); the *Daily Nation* (Kenya); and the *Voice of UNIP, Zambia Spark, Zambia Pilot,* and the *Voice of Zambia* (Zambia). Such newspapers were, first, instruments for establishing indigenous forms of government, tools of political parties or of nationalist movements. Second, they were instruments for legitimizing the indigenous governments whenever they were in place. Third, they were instruments for demonstrating the disapproval of indigenous, repressive political systems that departed from the broad-based expectations of a nation. These three evolving roles determine, in large measure, the philosophical contexts of Africa's mass media.

DEFINING MEDIA ROLES

For the African region, we delineate the following four approaches by which we may define media roles.

Rural Development: The Philosophy of the Relevance of Communication

Even though rural media operations tend to be limited, they have the potential to contribute to rural development and to reach large audiences.

Africa's rural and nonrural media are governed by a philosophy that makes them subservient to local governments and constituted authorities. The framework for this subservience is partly cultural, which means that traditional African thought has major implications for the journalistic handling and reporting of the news. Nnaemeka (1990) concludes that even though such subservience is tantamount to projecting colonialism, communication has been cast within an interpretive system of thought familiar mainly to the native population. A characteristic of the rural media is their limited reach, even though a majority of Africa's population lives in the nonurban areas.

There are really three types of media that must be taken into account in identifying a rural media philosophy: the literacy- /technology-based urban media used for communicating with the urban elites; the integrated, urban-rural media for communicating with the urban nonelites; and the nontraditional and traditional media for communicating with rural audiences. Prima facie, all three types are rooted in the ideology of the relevance of news, information, and entertainment to the everyday activities of the audience.

There are examples of government use of nontraditional mass media to promote the welfare of rural residents. In the Mhondoro and Save North communal areas of Zimbabwe, where small-scale communal agriculture is common, major improvements in agricultural practices and crop production levels have occurred since the country attained independence in 1980 (Zinyama, 1992). A distinguishing feature of the agricultural systems in both these areas is self-management: mutual-help, farmer-training, and agricultural-marketing groups (Zinyama, 1992). Local voluntary farmer organizations have used nontraditional media to communicate in a variety of ways and to provide grass-roots support for overcoming difficulties identified by the farmers themselves. In Kenya, the Woodfuel Development Program relied on the mass media for disseminating information on its tree-raising activities (Chavangi, 1992). Ungar (1989) reported developments in rural Ngecha, a Kikuyu village to the north of Nairobi, where living in the 1960s was a constant struggle for survival and for basic necessities. Today, skills are being taught local residents and commerce is being transformed by the use of the mass media, particularly radio.

However, mass media use in developing countries, and in Africa in particular, is, at least in principle, largely an urban phenomenon. Thus, to the extent that any media are effective in reaching rural residents, it is likely to be traditional channels such as folklore, drama, and oral narratives that most effectively deliver development information in rural areas.

Moemeka's (1981) survey of residents in Obamkpa, a village in Nigeria's Delta state, found that they preferred traditional media to modern media for exposure to three development projects because the use of traditional media tends not to require the same literacy skills that are required for the use of newspapers or magazines. Even so, "[t]he use of the rural newspaper would increase the chances of the illiterate population learning how to read and write; it would also facilitate the desire of the newly literate to acquire the ability of reading to learn and write" (Moemeka, 1994, p. 16).

Thus, the emerging philosophy of the media that are directed at rural audiences is one that creates opportunity to develop basic literacy and to develop messages relevant to development projects. In fact, most of the early rural news-papers in Africa were linked to a literacy program (Ansah, Fall, Kouleu, & Mwaura, 1981). Radio is the most widely used medium for accomplishing both literacy and development goals. Television, still relatively scarce in rural Africa, has a much wider reach and a much better receivership than newspapers.

Nationalism: The Philosophy of the Offensive

The establishment of private newspapers in much of Africa symbolized the beginnings of nationalism. In South Africa, for example, the alternative press had its genesis and grounding in the extraparliamentary movement; it also served as a voice for the political cause that gave it birth (Jackson, 1993).

In the Sudan, the semiofficial newspaper, *Hadarat al-Sudan,* and nationalist newspapers, *Al-Fajr* and *Al-Nil,* were channels for promoting sentiments reflec-tive of the motto ''the Sudan for the Sudanese,'' which was geared toward giving the Sudan a distinct identity (Babiker, 1985). While *Hadarat al-Sudan* was ambivalent about its stand on self-governance, the latter two took issue with the condominium structure by which the Sudan was governed jointly by the British and Egyptians. (Even though most of the Sudan lies south of the Sahara, its cultural affinity with countries largely in and to the north of the Sahara suggests that it be discussed in more detail in Part II of this book, which focuses on North Africa.)

In Côte d'Ivoire, colonial publications such as *Le Trait d'Union, L'Indépen-dant Colonial, Deci Dela,* the African-owned *L'Eclaireur,* and *Le Flambeau de la Côte d'Ivoire* had an incendiary cause: to criticize both the French adminis-tration and local powerhouses. The motivation among Africans and some co-lonial settlers to set up shop was that newspaper ownership provided good strategy for organizing politically (Wilcox, 1975). The media were the guardians of the people's rights and the primary political tools to effect a change from a colonial administration to an indigenous government. Such a press role is similar to that in the U.S. colonies, where revolutionaries like Samuel Adams, Isaiah Thomas, and Thomas Paine used persuasion, coercion, the platform, the press, vigilante tactics, and propaganda to foment a revolt against Great Britain.

In South Africa, since 1948, when apartheid was enunciated as a national policy, the country's press, particularly the English newspapers, has played an extensive opposition role that compensates for the inaudible voices of the Eng-lish-speaking opposition members of parliament.

In a few countries where the press did not become embroiled in political causes, there seemed to exist a high level of media independence and freedom. Botswana provides an appropriate illustration. The press was not the main vehicle for the in-dependence struggle; in fact, the private press was born out of commercial neces-sity (Zaffiro, 1988). Consequently, the media were more vigorous than those elsewhere in Africa in fulfilling nontraditional functions (as agents of accultura-tion and as points of reference for the public's evaluation of official policies) (Zaf-firo, 1988). However, sociopolitical and economic forces in Southern Africa continue to shape changes in the hitherto auspicious relationships between the ruling Botswana Democratic Party and the once-virile press.

The early newspapers in Africa were owned by indigenous business interests; others by several missionary organizations or by colonial settlers. In fact, newspaper shops were among the first indigenous businesses on the continent. For news dissemination, colonial governments published a few newspapers; daily bulletins were also published by the government printer.

The general editorial policy of the early, privately owned newspapers was based on the reasoning that, in the absence of popularly elected governments, the press was the most effective channel for airing grievances, for reporting indigenous news, and for influencing the course of events. Such private media had one key target: the government. The media did not merely report the news as objectively as they should—or could. Objectivity, in a strict journalistic sense, was not the guiding principle. Effectiveness in placing issues strategically on the public agenda was the watchword. Thus, much of Africa's preindependent press, as was the case in the U.S. colonies, was highly partisan and sensational. Press-agentry techniques were used to exploit the passion of Africans. Africa's liberation movements provided opportunities for the media to focus on the excesses of a foreign government and to tweak the consciences of the disenfranchised indigenes. The clash between indigenous journalists and colonial government bureaucrats provided opportunities to focus the attention of Africans on discussing their political future. An extensive study of international and national news on print and broadcast media in 15 African countries indicated, for example, that psychopolitical security, community of interests, national politics, and the personality of the head of government were the overriding criteria for their selection (Da Costa, 1980).

A study of two Afrikaans newspapers—*Beeld* and *The Citizen*—and one black newspaper—*The Sowetan*—showed significant differences in the number of lead stories on international news and on black-white issues, suggesting that apartheid values had an influence on the news (Claassen, 1989).

The editorial philosophy of Africa's early press parallels that of the early U.S. press; however, there is a key difference between it and that in Africa. While the prerevoluntionary press in the United States criticized both the government and business, the press in Africa concentrated its activities on colonial politics, with only a passive interest in the way colonial governments developed the economies. The underlying factor for this press philosophy was that political reforms, which resulted in the increased participation of Africans in the administration of their countries, were the most important factors that affected the social and economic conditions of their countries in the preindependent era. Such arguments have been made in other political systems, in which journalists have been seen as advocates for changes in the status quo (Altschull, 1984; Greenberg, 1980; Tuchman, 1978a).

In much of the then-British West Africa, for example, British government efforts were directed at establishing good and orderly government rather than improving the region's economic climate. The colonial government's development policy focused on nurturing a stable political environment.

Such political goals were at odds with the political ambitions of the indigenous elites, some of whom used the press to attain political goals. Omu (1968) noted four reasons for the political interest of the African press: (1) Africans did not constitute an alternative government in the British democratic tradition; (2) public attention was almost exclusively directed toward politics; (3) some prestige was attached to severe criticism of government; and (4) criticism of the government boosted newspaper sales and political influence.

These reasons dictated the very nature of press coverage and shaped its philosophy. This media philosophy was pervasive in both Anglophone and Francophone Africa. However, because Francophone Africa had policies of cultural assimilation and association that created évolués out of Africans, the French used stricter press controls than were apparent in Anglophone Africa. Therefore, conflicts between indigenous and colonial influences were less severe than those in Anglophone Africa.

Africa's early press was more of a tool for nationalism than were the broadcast media. Nonetheless, at least in the subequatorial region, private, clandestine radio stations played precisely the nationalistic role undertaken by the press. In fact, because radio had always had a wider reach and had always posed fewer challenges than the press, nationalist movements saw it as a quick, direct method for reaching audiences in areas far from the radio stations. Four such stations were Radio Freedom, the Voice of Namibia, the Voice of Zimbabwe, and the Voice of the Revolution, all of which opposed white minority regimes and aired programs from stations outside the countries in which they had their primary target audiences (Mosia, Riddle, & Zaffiro, 1994).

For 28 years, Radio Freedom, set up by the African National Congress, broadcast antiapartheid messages from transmitters in Zambia, Luanda, Ethiopia, Zimbabwe, Madagascar, Ghana, and Egypt. The Voice of Namibia (VON) was established by the South West Africa People's Organization to challenge the propaganda of the Namibia-based, South African–controlled South West African Broadcasting Corporation. VON also broadcast from radio stations outside Namibia. The Voice of Zimbabwe, established by the Zimbabwe African National Union, and the Voice of the Revolution, established by the Zimbabwe African Peoples' Union, mobilized Zimbabweans against colonial regimes. So effective were these four stations in fomenting independence that after independence a number of their staffers were co-opted into the emerging, state-run national broadcasting services. This development had two outcomes: (1) the nationalists found themselves working side-by-side with staffs who had vested interests in former colonial governments, resulting in strained working relationships; and (2) for the most part, the broadcast system eventually came under the full control of newly independent governments, enabling the emergence of a philosophy of endorsement. In the subequatorial region, as in much of Africa, radio and television are virtually government owned. The national governments in Nigeria and Uganda have, since the early 1990s, granted several licenses to private groups to establish private broadcasting, a phenomenon that is looked upon increasingly in Africa as a step toward ending government monopoly on the airwaves.

National Development: The Philosophy of Endorsement

With the passing of the colonial experience, the African press developed a philosophy that was consistent with the new realities of the region. Perhaps no one described this change better than Jose (in Wilcox, 1975), an African journalist, who wrote:

in the new nations and traditional societies of Africa, . . . a journalist has additional responsibilities to help in building a nation out of the multilingual, multicultured societies in countries where economic resources are inadequate to meet the expectations of the people. (p. 25)

The evolving philosophy was one by which Africa's press endorsed institutional policies, criticizing and evaluating, within limits, their relevance and significance to an emerging economy. Sometimes such a media role was limited to encouraging behaviors conducive to development by creating an enabling environment for other sectors of African economies to implement development programs. Jose (1975) described this philosophical change in these terms:

In many African societies, the press was used as a weapon in the fight against colonial rule. . . . in the name of press freedom and nationalism we deliberately wrote seditious chapters against colonial governments. Today, . . . many African journalists still believe that a good press is one that is in constant state of war with the government; that a progressive journalist is one who is in and out of prison for sedition. My own strong view is that African press cannot use the strategy and weapons we used against our own government whether elected or in uniform. It would be self-destructive. (p. 259)

This view is consistent with Hachten's (1987) development concept of the press, which holds that the media in the Third World assume major nation-building roles. While government-operated media are usually in the forefront of development programs, the private media have demonstrated similar obligations to the national interest. As noted elsewhere (Pratt, 1994), even the private sectors of African economies have been involved in supporting national development programs. Such support from the press is not limited to Africa; studies have also reported cooperative relationships between the press and government in the West (e.g., Paletz, Reichert, & McIntyre, 1971; Tuchman, 1978a, 1978b; Tunstall, 1971).

There is, however, mounting evidence that the development philosophy of Africa's media has been called into serious question because of the continuing failures of the communications in attaining development goals (Pratt, 1994). Even though development programs have been prevalent in sub-Saharan Africa, there is, at best, only a soupçon of economic development. The never-ending search for development has, therefore, pitted one group of development specialists against another, with each group formulating strategies that are supposedly better than those of competing groups. Three broad areas illustrate differences among the development mind-sets of such specialists.

First, development specialists disagree on the importance of communication technologies to national development. Success stories and statistical evidence indicate that, when used effectively, such technologies bring more than a soupçon of development to their host nations. Yet, it has been argued, for example, that the Satellite Instructional Television Experiment (SITE) in India holds limited promise for the country's development. Have the living standards of the rural Indian family improved significantly since its exposure to SITE?

Second, development specialists disagree on the criteria that could determine the success of development programs. The top-down approach has been assailed as ineffective, condescending, and patronizing; the participatory, bottom-up approach has been touted as a viable, community-sensitive alternative to meaningful development. Yet, the latter approach has been criticized as essentially perpetuating the status quo, leaving development to be formulated by people with little willingness or resources to break from the past.

Third, development specialists understand that accurate evaluation criteria should oftentimes be culture-bound; that is, different societies require different criteria for assessing development trends that are often not subject to simplistic quantification. This means that, while some quantitative indices (e.g., gross national product, growth and structure of production, inflation, infant mortality rates) become reified, particularly within nations, as conventional measures of national development, qualitative indices (e.g., cultural heritage, family values) that might just as well affect development positively are usually ignored. Yet, the international donor agencies are more impressed by quantitative indices than by the qualitative types. The World Bank and International Monetary Fund programs are largely data-driven.

In light of these differences, development specialists should take a hard look at the development philosophies of the media by first identifying that, empirically, the link between communication and development is difficult under the best of circumstances, and second, recognizing that, even though communication alone cannot solve Africa's problems, "it is a tool, a part of the effort, a piece of the solution, and we should pay more attention to it" (Stevenson, 1993, p. 113).

The need to better understand the immanent development problems of the development support philosophy of the media suggests that we pay attention to the continuing communication-for-development discourse by addressing two questions: (1) Cast against the backcloth of the pervasive use of communication for development in Africa south of the Sahara, to what extent has the region developed sustainable economies? (2) Within the context of question number 1, what two management-related factors explain the limited success of the region's efforts in building sustainable economies?

To answer the first question, we find that Africa's strategic modifications, adopted to avert failures and limitations of existing paradigms for development, have not rescued its economies from the verge of collapse. Admittedly, the outcomes of some of those adjustments are justified by pockets of development on the continent. Governments, with an eye for improved results, have made piecemeal adjustments in their communication-for-development programs. But even such programs tend to hold little promise for the continent. Beyond that, a number of recommendations are tantamount to the pontifications of critics who make little or no significant contribution to the continuing discourse on development. So severe is the region's economic crisis that Oxfam, the United Kingdom–based international relief organization, called for a Marshall-type plan for Africa. The failure of extant development strategies suggests an answer to the second question: Getting financial or other forms of aid is one thing; getting the staff to manage effectively the disbursement of that aid is another. To cut their loses in the field, and, thereby, improve the chances for the success of communication-for-development programs, development specialists should consider two management-related factors.

The first factor is ineffective and corrupt leadership. Since the 1960s, a wave of military dictatorships has threatened democratic traditions on the continent. Even the handful of countries with truly elected democratic governments have administrations that face grave and daunting problems.

Mobutu Sese Seko's government in Zaire may be an aberration on the continent, but it reflects a growing pattern of the zero-sum game that a number of African governments play with their citizens. The election of Ghana's Jerry Rawlings and the political stalemate that followed the 1993 presidential election in Nigeria both point to the reluctance of the military, following its ascendancy to the helm of affairs, to relinquish power fully to democratically elected officials.

Africa's civilian and military governments are, for the most part, mismanaged. Such governments boast a number of multimillionaires whose incomes, not to mention their on-the-side, part-time businesses, cannot justify even a miniscule portion of their wealth. Government officials concoct schemes to loot the national treasury. Even the monetary values of exports are underreported; operational costs are padded. It has been estimated, for example, that Zaire's Mobutu Sese Seko has looted between 10 and 18 percent of the national budget; in contrast, that country's public health sector was allocated a miniscule 3.5 percent of the budget (Misser, 1993). Additionally, the president was asked early in 1993 to refund $50 million in rents received in 1976 and 1977 for leasing a part of the country to German investors (Misser, 1993).

Further, given the circumstances of their ascendancy to power and the instability of their administrations, the ruling elites' accountability to the nation is a rare occurrence. This administrative incompetence rubs off on almost every facet of governments' activities: the formulation of development plans, the award and extension of contracts, the evaluation of programs, the expenditures of governments, and the reporting of basic statistics that form the bases for governments' resource or revenue allocation. The economic and social systems are starved of administrative and financial support, leading to the eventual collapse of even the best-thought-out development programs.

The second factor is related to the strategic development plans for the region. A number of African countries, soon after attaining political independence, created five-year development plans. (Ghana's 10-year-old Economic Recovery Program, an extensive program of economic reconstruction, is an exception; it has helped that country halt the tide of a plummeting economy.) Further, African governments have adopted, or responded favorably to, continentwide plans: Africa's Priority Program for Economic Recovery, 1986–1990; the United Nations Program of Action for African Economic Recovery and Development, 1986–1990; the March 1988 Khartoum Declaration of the Khartoum Conference on the Human Dimension of Africa's Economic Recovery and Development.

In general, these plans—unarguably well-conceived—have at least four major weaknesses.

First, they are a medium of ethnic and political leverage. It is common for an African head of state to ensure that, within the first year or so in office, his (*all* sub-Saharan African heads of state have so far been men) hometown has paved roads, pipe-borne water, and electricity, regardless of the economic expediency of such projects. A relatively affluent or an economically inconsequential region becomes an element, if not the focus, of a plan, not because of the economic, but because of the political, expediency of doing so. Plans easily become platforms for sales pitches to achieve resource allocation. And there is no shortage of pretentious rationalizations for siting a manufacturing plant or project in one location, in preference to another.

Cameroon is a recent case in point. Part of the aid it once received from the European Community was reallocated to building a controversial road between Yaoundé and Ayos, a low-population-density town in President Paul Biya's home region. The granting agency even admitted the difficulty in demonstrating that the project would make a direct contribution to solving the country's fiscal crisis.

Second, development plans are drawn usually because they are de rigueur. Most sub-Saharan African countries have one form of development plan or another. The national interest, as formulated by the planning board, is indicated more in plans per se than in their implementation. Thus, the national commitment to the success of those plans is occasionally questionable.

Third, the planning process itself tends to be skewed by its dependence on unreliable data. For example, census data in Africa are instruments of political and ethnic leverage. When plans are based on politically charged indices such as those on state, regional, and national population figures, ethnic composition, and literacy levels, they are just as suspect as the indices on which they are based. Inviting international agencies to collect sociological, demographic, nutrition, and health data does not preclude the possibility of gathering spurious data and shaping a nation's future on them.

Finally, development plans run their courses without systematic, timely interventions. This means that evaluation, if at all done, is carried out occasionally as a summative exercise, not as an intermediate impact assessment. The usual five-year plan is a constant challenge to the momentum that members of planning committees bring initially to the drawing board. Beyond that, it is difficult to get all key members' input during the implementation and the final stages of the plan. Therefore, when a plan is implemented, the goals and directions set by the planning committee may undergo midcourse changes, unknown, in large measure, to members of the initial planning committee.

Media Role in Development: The Extant Philosophy of Dissent

The media's endorsement philosophy was fraught with limitations. The media's earlier philosophy of the offensive was effective in wresting the political destinies of their countries from colonial interests. However, there is now growing evidence that the expectations and dreams that drove Africa's indigenous political parties to the helm of governance have not come true. Since independence, expectations have been raised; and such expectations have been compromised. There is a strong, pervasive sense of discontent on the continent.

Even though the 1970s were generally an economic-boom period for the region, the 1980s and the 1990s have been periods of economic collapse. Davidson (1992) argues that, even though there are pockets of continuing economic development on the continent, the "dreadful 1980s" have left many countries actually worse off now than they were during colonialism. Zambia, for example, was the richest sub-Saharan country in 1964–the year it attained independence. Today, it is among the poorest, following a 30 percent decline in its per capita income and a doubling of its infant-mortality rate. The continent has been ravaged by civil and ethnic strife, by natural environmental disasters, by overpopulation, poverty, homelessness, and by a growing number of refugees. With the exception of countries such as Ghana, Côte d'Ivoire, and Cameroon that are on the verge of recouping their economies, much of the continent is wallowing in economic decline.

Development programs are collapsing; political systems are continually being threatened by the extragovernmental agencies, that is, by the military and vigilantes. Social systems have been taxed to their limits, resulting in a breakdown in civility and an increase in crime, carnage, and civil unrest. There is more despair than hope on the continent. All of these occurrences have created a media cadre whose targets are either the elected or the de facto governments. The private media have, on occasion, at the risk of losing their freedoms, taken on the governing agencies. Investigative journalism is as much a tool for development as it is a tool for exposing the excesses of governments and the shortcomings of their policies. The private media, whose cooperation in development have been taken for granted, now focus on calling into question the legitimacy of the governing agencies.

Consequently, Africa's media play the dissenting role and occasionally pay a hefty price for it. Liberia's Samuel Doe issued Decree 88A which banned criticism of government, and two newspapers, the *Daily Observer* and the *Sun Times,* were shut down because of their potential to depart from Doe's agenda. There have been similar instances of government crackdown on media staffers.

Item: Equatorial Guinea's only major private newspaper, *La Verdad,* was banned in September 1993, following charges that it had published information embarrassing to and subversive of the country's popularly elected government.

Item: In Ghana, reporters on private daily newspapers and newsmagazines often walk a tightrope in deference to the country's popularly elected government.

Item: The Kenyan government undercut the desire of communicators to restructure and strengthen the media in attempts to make them active in discussing national issues.

Item: Liberia's armed forces and the insurgents under the control of Charles Taylor have dampened the expression of ideas and the exercise of basic human rights.

Item: In Malawi, the media have been tamed by the long authoritarian rule of the former Kamuzu Banda government.

Item: In Nigeria, on-and-off publication censorships have been enforced, particularly against *Newswatch,* a newsmagazine whose editors were huddled into jail for allegedly publishing material that insinuated a plan by the country's military to rule unconstitutionally for at least five years.

Item: In both Rwanda and Burundi, civil war and economic chaos have made mere communication a life-threatening activity. Communicators, then, are hard-pressed to fulfill even their basic news-gathering functions.

Item: Zaire under Mobutu Sese Seko has been a fiefdom for authoritarianism and blatant fiscal abuse.

These examples typify the frequently threatened freedoms of Africa's mass communicators. In essence, anarchy, into which a number of sub-Saharan African countries have been thrust, has undermined media freedom. Such media environments pose major challenges to the media staffers in the region and shape the region's evolving media philosophy.

Given the limitations of both the philosophies of endorsement and of dissent in stemming the tide of economic collapse in much of the continent, what is the prognosis? It is unlikely that the continent will arrest the decline if business is conducted as usual. Ghana has been a model about-face for the continent largely because of its creative, dedicated leadership. Its natural resources are still at levels prior to that of pre-Rawlings days. Yet, its gross domestic product has grown at about 5 percent a year during the past decade and inflation has dropped from a high of 142 percent to under 15 percent; and it had a $43 million surplus in 1993. Should sub-Saharan Africa's media strive to uphold their philosophy of dissent or to achieve a balance between dissent and support? If the former, then the relationship would be purely adversarial; if the latter, then it would tend toward the ideal of developmental journalism. This part-promoter, part-critic philosophy of the U.S. press was advocated by Pool (1977). It is relevant to the African media context. To the extent that Africa's media philosophies are influenced by the humpty-dumpty of the region's politics, the media will fail to demonstrate creative strengths to lead and to play a dissenting, uncooperative role as occasion demands.

CONCLUSIONS

This chapter has provided an overview of the economic and political challenges in Africa and has described four major philosophical approaches to defining the region's media role: the offensive, the endorsement, the dissent, and the relevance. While it stands to reason that an offensive media philosophy of preindependent sub-Saharan Africa is threatened and that the necessity for nurturing such a philosophy seems unwarranted, it is unlikely that the continent's media will grow in ways that will enable them to function at top performance without some form of government recognition for their unique role.

The endorsement role makes the media subservient to the powers that be, leaving little room for media independence. An unfettered media system is ideally positioned to contribute to the region's development agendas. Therefore, a concluding point here is that, to the extent that media activities are constrained by governments' policies and actions, their role in meeting the mammoth challenges of the continent will be truncated.

The philosophy of dissent, if taken to an extreme, may result in a disruption of the accomplishment of development agendas, more so when such dissension is fomented by groups catering to narrow economic or political interests. What, therefore, should the balance among these three contending philosophies be? No prescriptions are presented here. Nonetheless, the approaches detailed in this chapter present pointers for continuing discussions of these issues.

REFERENCES

Abbott, G. C. (1993). *Debt relief and sustainable development in sub-Saharan Africa.* Hants, England: Edward Elgar.
Abdolfathi, F. (1971). The American image of Africa: An exploratory discussion. *Pan-Africanist, 3,* 37–38.
Ake, C. (1991). Rethinking African democracy. *Journal of Democracy, 2,* 32–44.
Altschull, J. H. (1984). *Agents of power: The role of the news media in human affairs.* New York: Longman.

Ansah, P., Fall, C., Kouleu, B. C., & Mwaura, P. (1981). *Rural journalism in Africa.* Paris: UNESCO.

Ayittey, G. B. N. (1992). *Africa betrayed.* New York: St. Martin's.

Babiker, M. A. (1985). *Press and politics in the Sudan.* London: Biddles Ltd.

Brice, K. (1992). Muzzling the press. *Africa Report, 37,* 49–51.

Chavangi, N. A. (1992). Household based tree planting activities for fuelwood supply in Kenya: The role of the Kenya woodfuel development program. In D. R. F. Taylor & F. Mackenzie (Eds.), *Development from within* (pp. 148–169). London: Routledge.

Claassen, G. (1989). Lead story heterogeneity in three PWV area newspapers: An exploratory study. *Ecquid Novi, 10,* 115–127.

Da Costa, A. L. (1980). New criteria for the selection of news in African countries. In A. L. da Costa, Y. Aboubakr, P. Chopra, & F. R. Matta, *News values and principles of cross-cultural communication,* no. 85 (pp. 7–15). Paris: UNESCO.

Dahlgren, P. (1982). The Third World on TV news: Western ways of seeing the "other." In W. C. Adams (Ed.), *Coverage of international news* (pp. 45–65). Norwood, NJ: Ablex.

Davidson, B. (1992). *The black man's burden: Africa and the curse of the nation-state.* New York: Times Books.

Diamond, L. (1993). International and domestic factors in Africa's trend toward democracy. In F. Eribo, O. Oyediran, M. Wubneh, & L. Zonn (Eds.), *Window on Africa: Democratization and media exposure* (pp. 1–27). Greenville, NC: Center for International Programs Publication No. 1, East Carolina University.

Dumont, R. (1979). Remuneration levels and corruption in French-speaking Africa. In M. Ekpo (Ed.), *Bureaucratic corruption in sub-Saharan Africa: Toward a search for cases and consequences* (pp. 401–410). Washington, DC: University Press of America.

Fair, J. E. (1993). War, famine, and poverty: Race in the construction of Africa's media image. In F. Eribo, O. Oyediran, M. Wubneh, & L. Zonn (Eds.), *Window on Africa: Democratization and media exposure* (pp. 125–139). Greenville, NC: Center for International Programs Publication No. 1, East Carolina University.

Faringer, G. L. (1991). *Press freedom in Africa.* New York: Praeger.

Fitzgerald, M. A. (1989). The news hole: Reporting Africa. *Africa Report, 34,* 59–62.

Gordon, A. A., & Gordon, D. L. (1992). Introduction. In A. A. Gordon & D. L. Gordon (Eds.), *Understanding contemporary Africa* (pp. 1–5). Boulder, CO: Lynne Rienner.

Greenberg, E. S. (1980). *The American political system: A radical approach* (2nd ed.). Cambridge, MA: Winthrop.

Greenstone, D. (1979). Corruption and self-interest in Kampala and Nairobi: A comment on local political politics in East Africa. In M. Ekpo (Ed.), *Bureaucratic corruption in sub-Saharan Africa: Toward a search for cases and consequences* (pp. 261–274). Washington, DC: University Press of America.

Hachten, W. A. (1987). *The world news prism: Changing media, clashing ideologies.* Ames, Iowa: Iowa State University Press.

Hachten, W. A. (1993). *The growth of media in the Third World: African failures, Asian successes.* Ames, Iowa: Iowa State University Press.

Heath, C. W. (1992). Structural changes in Kenya's broadcasting system: A manifestation of presidential authoritarianism. *Gazette, 37,* 37–51.

Ibelema, M., & Onwudiwe, E. (1994). "Today" in Africa. *Issue: A Journal of Opinion,* *22,* 12–14.

Jackson, G. S. (1993). *Breaking story: The South African press.* Boulder, CO: Westview.

Jose, B. (1975). Press freedom in Africa. *African Affairs, 74* (July), 255–262.

Land, M. (1992). Ivoirien television, willing vector of cultural imperialism. *The Howard Journal of Communications, 4,* 10–27.

Levine, V. (1975). *Political corruption: The Ghana case.* Stanford, CA: Stanford University.

Maja-Pearce, A. (1992). The press in East Africa: Kenya, Uganda, Tanzania. *Index on Censorship* (July), 50–73.

Misser, F. (1993). Zaire's missing millions: Where did all the money go? *African Business* (February), pp. 18–19.

Moemeka, A. A. (1981). *Local radio: Community education for development.* Zaria, Nigeria: Ahmadu Bello University Press.

Moemeka, A. A. (1994, October). *Media, rural communities and sustainable development: Access, participation and utilization.* Paper presented at the ninth biennial meeting of the African Council for Communication Education, Accra, Ghana.

Mosia, L., Riddle, C., & Zaffiro, J. (1994). From revolutionary to regime radio: Three decades of nationalist broadcasting in Southern Africa. *Africa Media Review, 8,* 1–24.

Mudimbe, V. Y. (1988). *The invention of Africa.* Bloomington: IN: Indiana University Press.

Nafziger, W. W. (1993). *The debt crisis in Africa.* Baltimore, MD: The Johns Hopkins University Press.

Nnaemeka, T. I. (1990). Cultural influences, modern changes, and the sociology of modern African political communication. *Journal of Black Studies, 20,* 306–323.

Ogundimu, F. (1994). Images of Africa on U.S. television: Do you have problems with that? *Issue: A Journal of Opinion, 22,* 7–11.

Omu, F. I. A. (1968). The dilemma of press freedom in colonial Africa: The West African example. *Journal of African History, 9,* 279–298.

Paletz, D. L., Reichert, P., & McIntyre, B. (1971). How the media support local governmental authority. *Public Opinion Quarterly, 35,* 80–92.

Pool, I. (1977). Newsmen and statesmen: Adversaries or cronies? In L. L. Sellers & W. L. Rivers (Eds.), *Mass media issues: Articles & commentaries* (pp. 191–202). Englewood Cliffs, NJ: Prentice-Hall.

Pratt, C. B. (1980). The reportage and images of Africa in six U.S. news and opinion magazines: A comparative study. *Gazette, 26,* 31–45.

Pratt, C. B. (1994). Public relations, industrial peace, and economic development. In A. A. Moemeka (Ed.), *Communicating for development: A new pan-disciplinary perspective* (pp. 167–187). Albany, New York: State University of New York Press.

Sesay, A. (1987). Some possible futures of great power intervention in Africa. In O. Aluko (Ed.), *Africa and the great powers in the 1980s* (pp. 255–288). Lanham, MD: University Press of America.

Staniland, M. (1991). *American intellectuals and African nationalists, 1955–1970.* New Haven, CT: Yale University Press.

Stevenson, R. L. (1993). Communication and development: Lessons from and for Africa. In F. Eribo, O. Oyediran, M. Wubneh, & L. Zonn (Eds.), *Window on Africa:*

Democratization and media exposure (pp. 97–124). Greenville, NC: Center for International Programs Publication No. 1, East Carolina University.

Stokke, O. (1971). The mass media in Africa and Africa in international mass media— An introduction. In O. Stokke (Ed.), *Reporting Africa* (pp. 9–25). Uppsala: Scandinavian Institute of African Studies.

Strieker, G. (1986). Interviewed on "Assignment Africa." In "Inside Story, Special Edition," produced by David Royale.

Tuchman, G. (1978a). *Making news: A study in the construction of reality.* New York: Free Press.

Tuchman, G. (1978b). Professionalism as an agent of legitimization. *Journal of Communication, 28,* 106–113.

Tunstall, J. (1971). *Journalists at work.* London: Constable.

Ungar, S. J. (1989). *Africa: The people and politics of an emerging continent.* New York: Simon & Schuster.

Weaver, D. H., Buddenbaum, J. M., & Fair, J. E. (1985). Press freedom, media, and coming development, 1950–1979: A study of 134 nations. *Journal of Communication, 35,* 104–117.

Weaver, D. H., & Wilhoit, G. C. (1983). Foreign news coverage in two U.S. wire services: An update. *Journal of Communication, 33,* 132–148.

Wilcox, D. L. (1975). *Mass media in black Africa: Philosophy and control.* New York: Praeger.

The World Bank. (1993). *World development report 1993—Investing in health.* New York: Oxford University Press.

The World Resources Institute. (1994). *World resources 1994–95.* New York: Oxford University Press.

Zaffiro, J. J. (1988). Regional pressure and the erosion of media freedom in an African democracy: The case of Botswana. *Journal of Communication, 38,* 108–120.

Zinyama, L. M. (1992). Local farmer organizations and rural development in Zimbabwe. In D. R. F. Taylor & F. Mackenzie (Eds.), *Development from within* (pp. 33–57). London: Routledge.

2 Mass Media Development and Government Relations

The intolerance of alternative viewpoints on the part of many educated
African leaders is the root of the continent's problems.
—George B. N. Ayittey in *Africa Betrayed* (1992)

Constitutional protections for media staffers in Africa are taken for granted.
While the region's various constitutions guarantee journalists' freedoms, the
realities are far different: journalists may well assume that no such guarantees
are indeed available. Even international conventions regarding the mass media
are not practical realities for African governments.

The nonbinding Article 19 of the 1948 United Nations Universal Declaration
of Human Rights and its restatement in Article 19 of the 1966 International
Covenant on Civil and Political Rights enunciate everyone's right "to seek,
receive and impart information and ideas." While a number of African governments acknowledge publicly the merits of such prescriptions, they have demonstrated more than a passing interest in their countries' mass media. Even
though their constitutions prima facie protect the expression of ideas, such expressions have little fervor in the harsh realities of media–government relations,
as indicated in Merrill's (1988) finding that African countries have an inclination
toward press control.

Africa's media are used to legitimize government policies and actions. Ruijter
(1989) characterizes government–media relations in Africa as: (1) manipulative,
in that official communiques from government sources constitute the bulk of
news on the continent; (2) collaborative, resulting in an interdependency between the state and the media; (3) supportive of the legal and moral underpin-
nings of the state; and (4) preventive, in that the media face stumbling blocks

in their attempts to play the watchdog role and to uphold the social norms of the state machinery.

Journalists' objections to governmental encroachment on their activities have resulted in smaller media budgets, in longer jail sentences, and in higher levels of public humiliation. Even though popular governance is touted as an African reality, most African governments are authoritarian; they perpetuate the limited interests of the political elite. This was demonstrated by Nigeria's military government, which passed Decree No. 4 on March 29, 1984, to make its actions immune to legal challenges on the heels of mounting opposition to that government. As Ogbondah (1994) observes, "Decree No. 4 was the harshest and most repressive press law enacted under any military regime, in the sense that it provided for the trial of alleged offenders by a military tribunal . . ." (pp. 104– 105).

Another example is provided by Zambia, which, from independence in 1964 through 1972, encouraged multiparty politics. The 1972 Constitution recognized only one party, which stymied the development of the country's mass media. After 1972, politics in this landlocked, one-party state was dominated by the United National Independence Party (UNIP). In the 1980s, major undercurrents of change and grass roots movements were fomented, resulting in a further clampdown on both the opposition forces and the media. In December 1990, the country's constitution was amended to allow for the establishment of other political parties. Yet, the nation's principal media—the Zambia News Agency, the *Sunday Times of Zambia, The Times of Zambia,* the *Zambia Daily Mail,* and the Zambia National Broadcasting Corporation—continue to criticize UNIP policies. Nonetheless, the onset of political pluralism did not result in renewed journalistic activity reflective of newly found freedoms. The UNIP-controlled government has exercised its control of the press by shuffling journalists from one position to another. The government also reassigned three journalists— Komani Kachinga of the *Times of Zambia,* Cyrus Sikazwe of the *Daily Mail,* and Laxon Kaemba of the Zambia Publishing Company—without substantive justification.

A further illustration of strained government–media relations is provided by the South African press. Since the official proclamation of apartheid in 1948, the South African press has been influenced by four factors: the political and economic exclusion of Blacks, the government's sanctions against the media, the ideological control on the media, and the ideology of the state. These four factors, in South Africa, coalesced in a largely authoritarian state, prior to the era of the Nelson Mandela government. The South African government shut down black newspapers such as *The Sowetan, World, Weekend World, Post,* and *Sunday Post,* and, in 1986, abducted and detained Zwelakhe Sisulu, the black editor of the *New Nation.*

An illustration of South Africa's authoritarian tradition is the July 21, 1985, announcement of a state of emergency, renewed for the third time in June 1988. The South African government's rationale was that to restore order, particularly in the black community, and to reduce nationwide violence required that restrictions be placed on both the domestic and international media that were covering the nation's economic difficulties and social unrest. The government made it illegal for the press to quote any banned organization, for example, the multiracial United Democratic Front.

Another dimension of South Africa's media control was the proposed registration of journalists. Since 1950, there have been calls by the government to register journalists and news agencies. Those calls came to a head in the 1982 Steyn Commission II recommendation for a register that would exclude journalists convicted of breaking a statutory code of conduct, and in a June 1988 recommendation that some news agencies be registered (Tomaselli & Louw, 1989). The government had also attempted to create an official roster of journalists, by which it would have gathered information such as the names, addresses, and journalists' clients. De Beer (1989) does not subscribe to the Western argument that restrictions on the press under the State of Emergency Regulations is tantamount to authoritarianism. He argues that such a possibility, in South Africa, is debatable and suggests that a postapartheid South Africa will embrace the developmental and social responsibility systems.

However, one would argue that, in the perceptions of South Africa's black majority, the illegitimacy of the pre-Mandela government calls into question the honorable intentions of the bureaucratic controls to which Blacks in general and the black alternative press in particular had been subjected. Such questioning becomes accentuated in light of the parliamentary composition which, under apartheid laws, was skewed to the disadvantage of the majority black population. The reasoning had always been that the electoral process of a non-broad-based, nonpopularly elected government is just as bereft of legitimate authority as is the legislation that emanates from it. Phelan (1987) provides an additional perspective on this point:

Although the laws regulating the press are theoretically color-blind, their administration is most certainly not. Even before the state of emergency, when no one could keep up with the more than eight thousand general detentions . . . the number of detentions and arrests among black journalists, relative to all other journalists, was markedly greater. (p. 65)

The unpredictable interpretations and enactments of South Africa's various laws and policies that affected government–press relations blunted the will of most black journalists and made their working conditions hazardous. Because the black journalist, in the minds of the English and the Afrikaner, "became identified with agitation, not only for racial equality, but also for the communist cause" (Phelan, 1987, p. 69), she or he was forced to work in racially mixed groups which then began editing their own publications. This media development resulted in the demise of the independent black press in South Africa.

Such development is compromised by the government's overreaction to the seeming challenges to its stronghold on the country.

Nigeria's *Newswatch* illustrates this phenomenon as a critical element in Africa's government–press relations. The magazine, which circulates 150,000 copies weekly in Africa, Europe, and North America "changed the form of print journalism in Nigeria [and] introduced bold, investigative formats to news reporting in Nigeria" (Agbese, 1989, p. 331). Consequently, the Nigerian government had reason to ban publication of the magazine for six months, beginning April 6, 1987.

In much of the former British Africa, free-expression doctrines vis-à-vis the press were rooted in those of Britain. However, such historical affinity was challenged when it dawned on the 1985–1993 military government of Nigeria's Ibrahim Babangida that the country's private media may be having a field day in exposing government excesses. In fact, on July 22, 1993, his government issued a decree that banned four publications: the *National Concord,* the *Punch,* the *Daily Sketch,* and the *Nigerian Observer.* Earlier, *Newswatch* had become a symbol of the challenge to governments' disregard for financial and social accountability. Such events have implications for the region's continuing uneasy relations between its media and governments.

The rest of this chapter addresses two issues: (1) reasons for the blurring of differences between the news content of private and state-owned media; (2) the implications of such blurring for both the development role and for government–media relations.

The finding that a number of Africa's private news media tend to have editorial content similar to that of the government media (Pratt, 1991) may be explained by four major factors.

The first is the unifying function of the press. Because African governments have emphasized continually the overriding importance of integrating people's loyalties into one national symbol (e.g., Arikpo, 1967, p. 165), it is possible that such governmental concerns manifest themselves as pressures on journalists to conform to set norms. Consequently, such journalists may indicate more homogeneous than heterogeneous perceptions of their national roles.

The second factor is the effect of "cultural synchronization" (Hamelink, 1983), specifically the homogenizing effects of national cultural synchronization. Hamelink observed that in the absence of a single national culture in the Third World, the small, urban, foreign-oriented elites have a decisive influence on the cultural environment of the rest of the population. Because the urban elites are agents of foreign cultural influence, their domestic actions have a synchronic mode by which

decisions regarding the cultural environment in a given country are made in accordance with the interests and needs of a powerful central nation and imposed with subtle but devastating effectiveness without regard for the adaptive necessities of the dependent nation. (Hamelink, 1983, p. 22)

Thus, because media houses in Africa are managed by journalists whose news-value criteria are occasionally influenced by foreign news values primarily through the agenda-setting influence of the transnational news services, such journalists are likely to demonstrate perceptions that tend toward homogeneity. Beyond that, governmental intervention in the form of military dictatorships and in the funding of newspaper operations influenced African newspaper editors' attitudes toward media issues (Roser & Brown, 1986). The reasons suggested for such influence included the possibility that the editors had a strong sense of nationalism that carried more weight than their journalistic values and that dependence of their newspapers on government policies may have led to more acceptance of governmental restrictions and controls in news transmissions.

The third is the occurrence of "reference group behavior," a magnet element that leads to in-groupness and conformity among journalists and a steady expectation of continued employment (Breed, 1955). The influence of "reference group behavior" also brings to the fore its homogenizing effects on the journalists' ethics and on their perceptions of editorial role in national development. Sobowale (1978/1979) reported, for example, that

Nigerian journalists still very much respect the opinions of their reference groups. The perception of people whose opinions they value considerably influences what they think about the jobs they do and the decision to go on doing it. (p. 189)

Consequently, if Africa's editorial staffs, in comparison with those on, say, U.S. newspapers, are not "inner-directed high professional" journalists, but are "other-directed" (Schwartz, 1978), do they, therefore, conduct themselves within the strict confines of the limited interests of the urban elites or of their newspaper proprietors? The limited growth in the industrial sector has worsened the availability of newsprint and other printing materials, purchased in hard currencies, to the newspaper industry. It has increased the cost of newspaper distribution. And it has reduced newspaper advertising revenues. It is not surprising, then, that journalists may emphasize a careerist attribute—job security—rather than a professional attribute: independent thought and action, based on the ideals of professionalism.

A final major factor is rooted in both the African personality and in the African religion. The African personality emphasizes "wholesome human relations at all cost," altruism, "community fellow-feeling," and a live-and-let-live philosophy (Sofola, 1973). The influences of these characteristics are so far-reaching in the continent that they minimize the effects of ethnic-group rivalries and conflicts on the African personality. Also, African traditional religions, which are more popular than imported religions, have a powerful hold on Africans and enforce standards acceptable to them (Amadi, 1982). Because the practice of African religions requires that morals extend to all areas of the lives of individuals and of society and community welfare, such religions have an overall homogenizing influence on the African (Mbiti, 1975, pp. 180–181).

It is to the implications of these four factors for the development role of the media and for developments in government–media relations that we now turn.

IMPLICATIONS OF GOVERNMENT–PRESS RELATIONS

Several implications of the relations between African governments and media are noteworthy. The first is governments' homogenizing influence on Africa's media—particularly those in countries where popularly elected governments are not the norm. Ugboajah's (1980) study of the editorial positions on four development issues among four private and four government newspaper in Nigeria showed that of the 25 editorials evaluated, eight were antigovernment, eight were pro-government and nine were neutral. These results showed that only one former state government newspaper—the *New Nigerian*—carried antigovernment editorials. An implication of this finding is that government ownership does not necessarily presage the undermining of the media in serving as viable institutions.

However, a content analysis of the news and editorial content of two Nigerian daily newspapers, the *Daily Times* and the *New Nigerian*, found a softening of the editorial tone of the newspapers after they were acquired by the federal military government (Ibe, 1985). The author attributed it to the sensitivity of the editors to the federal government's agenda.

It is this tendency of Africa's media, regardless of ownership, to behave in synchrony that has, since the mid-1980s, fueled debates about the need for privately controlled media, particularly in broadcasting. The Christian Council of Ghana, in a 1990 memorandum to the government, recommended that the country's media be privatized and that governments' involvement in the media be terminated. This, the council believed, would make the country's media's role more significant in development.

In May 1970, Radio Syd of The Gambia became the first private radio station to go on the air in Africa. Mali, Nigeria, Uganda, and Zambia, to name a few, have granted licenses to private organizations or groups to operate radio stations; all four countries are considering similar licenses for television. The Nigerian plan, directed by the National Broadcasting Commission, resulted in six private television stations and one radio station on the air, and in the approval of a dozen cable-satellite retransmission operators to set up shop.

Uganda has granted at least two and Mali at least six radio licenses to individuals; today, there is a smattering of private broadcasting stations across Africa. While this seeming privatization may augur well for the future of independent broadcasting, two reasons suggest that that may not be so. First, the regulations under which such private stations are set up are so limiting that they raise major questions about Africa's resolve toward full-blown privatization. Radio Syd of The Gambia, for example, is required to coordinate its programming with state-owned Radio Gambia in reporting national events. In Mali, the state has always wielded de facto authority over radio through decrees which established conditions for the application for licenses and for the installation and operation of private radio stations and audiovisual services.

Article 9 of Nigeria's National Broadcasting Commission Decree 1992, for example, states that the commission must be satisfied that an applicant for a private license

can give an understanding that the licensed station shall be used to promote national interest, unity and cohesion and that it shall not be used to offend the religious sensibilities or promote ethnicity, sectionalism, hatred and disaffection among the peoples of Nigeria.

Such broadcasting regulations are as stringent as those for state-owned operations, casting doubt on the level of realistic autonomy such operations have.

Second, African governments have at their disposal alternative forms of media control. The total control of the importation of newsprint and broadcasting equipment, for example, makes all media dependent on the whims of government economic policies. Further, private broadcasting stations cannot be protected from heavy-handed, overbearing governments, which could issue directives of a general nature to the broadcasting stations, which are, then, required to comply.

Additionally, governments' media policies have overtly constrained the press's activities. In the Sudan, all the three daily newspapers are subjected to extremes of press censorship imposed by the military since 1989. In Mali, the National Committee for Equal Access to State Media ensures that media coverage reflects the economic, social, and cultural diversities in the country. The High Council of Communication decides on conditions for operating radio and television broadcasting and on the granting and withdrawal of licenses.

In Nigeria, the appointment in May 1987 of Lieutenant Colonel Victor Lawrence Ogbomo, by the military governor of Plateau state, as the acting general manager of the Plateau Publishing Company (a state government–owned newspaper house and publisher of the *Nigerian Standard*) was interpreted as a direct government control of a media house, its operations, and its editorial autonomy.

Between December 1988 and March 1990, the government of Kenya restructured its broadcasting system as part of a strategy to better manage public opinion and to enhance the authoritarian policies of the country's president, Daniel arap Moi (Heath, 1992). That strategy was inimical to the editorial independence and function of the state-run media because, among other things, it further homogenized their roles, which further limited their contributions to national development.

The second implication is the blurring of the boundaries between the editorial content of government and private print media. For one thing, ownership of newspapers is not a particularly strong factor in the role of newspapers in development, which calls into question the rationale for the continuing case for private ownership of Africa's media as a solution to the limitations of the region's media in exercising independent, effective, and persuasive influence on development.

For another, the prevalence of the use of government sources for news by the press in general suggests that private newspapers are more likely than government newspapers to be cautious in expressing editorial opinions that may attract the ire of the powers that be. Perhaps because of such caution, the private newspapers are, therefore, more likely than the government newspapers to speculate about national issues. This means that speculation is more likely to occur among private newspapers, primarily because they tend to verify their news sources more rigorously than do government newspapers, thus lending credence to the argument for the privatization of the media.

Further, the uneasy relations that have developed between Africa's media and government have discouraged the former from making clear distinctions between news and views. The time-honored maxim that "news is sacred and comment is free" has occasionally been ignored. Journalism goes beyond the mere reporting of what a person does or says; for a number of Africa's private newspapers, in-depth reporting and explaining constitute the overriding philosophy, which is based on the belief that it is better to present all the available facts and data to the reader in a comprehensive manner and leave her or him to form whatever opinions are necessary.

This possibility gains credence for two reasons. The first is the notion expressed by Jose (1975) that African newspapers that were once anticolonist (that is, against the colonial government) could no longer afford to be so because the urgent tasks of nation-building required that they tone down their antigovernment rhetoric.

The second is the "conformity-deviation problem" of newspapers (Breed, 1955), by which Africa's media staffers may readily conform to government media policies and their volatile enforcement. Such policies are subsequently revised by successive governments, which continually redefine local and national interests.

Thus, assigning "government," "nongovernment," or "private" labels to media staffers, at best a suggestive effort, leaves little room for the nurturing of professional norms that are truly one or the other. African governments' continuing pronouncements that an unfettered media system is a worthwhile ingredient for national development and of media professionalism are just that: pronouncements. The governments' encroachment mechanisms on the media are as ingenuous as they are far-reaching, resulting in media–government relations that continually undermine the autonomy of the former for the benefit of the latter.

REFERENCES

Agbese, P. O. (1989). State, media and the imperatives of repression: An analysis of the ban on *Newswatch*. *International Third World Studies Journal and Review, 1*, 325–334.

Amadi, E. (1982). *Ethics in Nigerian culture.* Ibadan, Nigeria: Heinemann.

Arikpo, O. (1967). *The development of Nigeria.* Baltimore, MD: Penguin.

Ayittey, G. B. N. (1992). *Africa betrayed.* New York: St. Martin's Press.

Breed, W. (1955). Social control in the newsroom: A functional analysis. *Social Forces, 33* (May), 326–335.

De Beer, A. S. (1989). The press in a post-apartheid South Africa: A functional analysis. *Ecquid Novi, 10,* 141–164.

Hamelink, C. J. (1983). *Cultural autonomy in global communications.* New York: Longman.

Heath, C. W. (1992). Structural changes in Kenya's broadcasting system: A manifestation of presidential authoritarianism. *Gazette, 50,* 37–51.

Ibe, C. C. (1985). *Ownership control vs. editorial content: A study of the (Nigerian) Daily Times and the New Nigerian.* Unpublished master's thesis, Ohio University, Athens, OH.

Jose, B. (1975). Press freedom in Africa. *African Affairs, 74* (July), 255–262.

Mbiti, J. S. (1975). *Introduction to African religions.* New York: Praeger.

Merrill, J. C. (1988). Inclination of nations to control press and attitudes on professionalization. *Journalism Quarterly, 65* (4) (Winter), 839–844.

Ogbondah, C. W. (1994). *Military regimes and the press in Nigeria, 1966–1993.* Lanham, MD: University Press of America.

Phelan, J. M. (1987). *Apartheid media: Disinformation and dissent in South Africa.* Westport, CT: Lawrence Hill & Company.

Pratt, C. B. (1991). Editorials in national development: Perceptions of Nigerian journalists. *Political Communication and Persuasion: An International Journal, 8,* 221–232.

Roser, C., & Brown, L. (1986). African newspaper editors and the New World Information Order. *Journalism Quarterly, 63* (1) (Spring), 114–121.

Ruijter, J. M. (1989). State and media in Africa–A quarrelsome though faithful marriage. *Gazette, 44,* 57–69.

Schwartz, S. H. (1978). Inner-directed and other-directed values of professional journalists. *Journalism Quarterly, 55* (4) (Winter), 721–725, 754.

Sobowale, I. A. (1979). Characteristics and professional attitudes of Nigerian journalists (Doctoral dissertation, Syracuse University, 1978). *Dissertation Abstracts International, 40,* 15-A.

Sofola, J. A. (1973). *African culture and the African personality (What makes an African person African).* Ibadan, Nigeria: African Resources Publishers.

Stevenson, R. L. (1988). *Communication, development, and the Third World: The global politics of information.* New York: Longman.

Tomaselli, K. G., & Louw, P. E. (1989). Moves toward the registration of South Africa journalists: An overview from a critical point of view. *Ecquid Novi, 10,* 95–114.

Ugboajah, F. O. (1980). *Communication policies in Nigeria.* Paris: UNESCO.

3 Education and Training of Media Personnel

How does an African become a journalist? Prior to the 1960s, the answer was largely that she or he learned journalism in the marketplace, usually under circumstances that fostered the acquisition of strong writing skills and the demonstration of self-discipline. After the 1960s, the answer was largely that she or he enrolled in a liberal arts or social science program in a university or polytechnic. The pre-1960s offered on-the-job training; the post-1960s offered a vastly different educational experience.

In this chapter, education and training are not used interchangeably. Education, on the one hand, will be limited to the formal exposure journalists received in higher educational institutions such as universities to pursue their professional duties. Training, on the other, will be limited to the skills-oriented activities journalists engage in, either on the job or in polytechnics and various training institutes, to improve on-the-job performance. This distinction, prima facie, suggests a two-pronged approach to the training and education of African journalists: at the nonuniversity and university levels.

For several years, after much of Africa became independent, the education and training received by African journalists reflected their colonial histories; for example, those in former French West Africa and in former British West Africa adopted the orthodoxies of the educational and training systems of their former colonial governments. It simply made sense; it was economically expedient and logistically convenient for them to do so in light of the availability of colonial infrastructures, which had been firmly established. Revamping them at a time when other pressing national issues demanded priority attention seemed illogical. Even though changes have since been made in the education and training of such journalists, vestiges of colonial dependencies are still apparent.

The debates in the 1970s over the New World Information and Communication

Order created national concerns about the appropriateness of media fare and of the journalistic ideologies on which it is based. At issue was the perceived imperialism of the international media practices and their unwholesome influences on the Third World media. Several recommendations of the international community were adopted by Third World governments. One was to offer better training facilities in their home countries for journalists. Understandably, not all developing countries can provide the full-blown training and education that journalists need to cope with the challenges of their new nation-states. Nonetheless, we can discern two training models, which, for convenience and meaningfulness, could be described as the colonial and the emerging models of training and education.

THE COLONIAL MODEL

The mass media systems established in the colonies were patterned on the national character and colonial policies of the mother countries (Kucera, 1968). The colonial training model required, therefore, that African journalists be exposed to the semblance of the type of training that was available to colonists in their home countries. This required that they serve as apprentices on the foreign-owned newspapers, from which they learned the basics of journalism and of reporting. This pattern was pervasive in much of Africa, even shortly after a number of its countries attained independence. But this pattern had historical precedents that went far beyond Africa. Even in the colonists' home countries, journalism was seen more as a craft than as a profession. In the United States, where the oldest journalism school was founded September 1, 1908, at the University of Missouri, there have been debates on whether journalism is a profession (Dennis & Merrill, 1984).

In much of Europe, journalism education had traditionally been kept out of the ivory towers of higher educational institutions, which used what had been labeled the "Fleet Street" method. Journalists were given rigorous hands-on training and encouraged to mature professionally on the job.

The colonial model, in essence, was industry-driven, robbing journalists of the level of respect attributed to, say, physicians, lawyers, social workers, and accountants. As Merrill (Dennis & Merrill, 1984) argues, journalism does not require "... formal minimum entrance requirements. ... No journalist is expected (or required) to abide by any code of ethics. No journalist is certified or licensed—at least in the United States" (p. 152). Journalists are not licensed in Africa, either.

These hallmarks of nonprofessionalism of journalism have, in large part, shaped the training and educational offerings for developing journalistic expertise. Africa's newspapers that were owned by foreign businesses ran their African operations with local staffs, but sent some of them to the newsrooms of their home countries for workshops and seminars in journalism. For example, *The Standard* (Kenya) and the *Zimbabwe Times,* both owned by the London-based London and Rhodesia (Lonrho) Publishing Company, sent a number of

Africans to the newsrooms of its foreign affiliates for training. Similarly, Cecil King's Daily Mirror Group of London and the Roy Thomson newspaper companies, which owned newspapers in several African countries, provided their African staffs with overseas training. South Africa's Argus Group, which owned Africa's largest newspaper chain and also published five of Zimbabwe's major newspapers (the *Post,* the *Herald,* the *Sunday Mail,* the *Chronicle,* the *Sunday News*), engaged in similar practices. By this method, the first crop of African journalists was exposed to Western-style journalism. Such nationalists as Nnamdi Azikiwe (Nigeria) and Kwame Nkrumah (Ghana) had been exposed to U.S. journalism during their college days there.

Radio and television stations, the "broadcasting corporations" as they are commonly known in much of Africa, also offer in-service training for broadcast journalists. Such in-service training also transcended the postindependent era, during which development themes began to be woven into training modules.

THE DEVELOPMENT MODEL

The second training model evolved at the dawn of independence, during which a move was made toward providing formal, structured education to journalists. This training model was undertaken in two areas: in polytechnics and journalism institutes, and in universities. The overarching goal was national development.

In polytechnics, technical colleges, and journalism institutes, the emphasis has been on a mix of training, hands-on experience, and education from both liberal arts and social science perspectives. Usually, working journalists and public information officers are given release time to enroll in a number of courses in the basics of news reporting and writing, investigative research methods, media law, and interviewing techniques. On completing such courses, successful enrollees earn diplomas. Some of these courses are government-sponsored; others are industry-sponsored; still others are organized by governments in collaboration with one or more international agencies such as the Pan-African News Agency, the International Press Institute, the Friedrich Ebert Foundation, the Thomson Foundation, Germany's Deutsche Welle, and the Reston (Virginia)-based Center for Foreign Journalists. The Poynter Institute for Media Studies in St. Petersburg, Florida, nurtured the development of South Africa's Institute for the Advancement of Journalism by providing expertise in curriculum development, developing training materials, and making available a rotating training staff. The goal is to expose journalists to news-gathering and reporting principles that are not only rooted in African value systems, but that examine those systems from comparative standpoints. There is, however, some evidence that, several years after independence, a dire need for journalists with specialized training in investigative journalism and development issues threatens the goals of development communications (Scotton, 1986; Mwaffisi, 1991).

In Senegal, the Dakar-based Centre d'Etudes des Sciences et Techniques de

L'Information, was established about a decade after the country's independence from France. The founding of the center was made possible with grants from 10 nations, including France. It offers curricula attractive to students from French Equatorial and West Africa.

In Cameroon, three major institutions, two at universities (in Yaoundé and Buéa) and one in Yaoundé (Ecole Supérieure Internationale de Journalisme de Yaoundé), offer development-oriented education to journalists. The latter program emphasizes development through communications. Similar programs abound on the continent: Institut des Sciences et Techniques de L'Information (Zaire), the journalism or mass communication institutes in Ghana, Kenya, Tanzania, and Nigeria (the Nigerian Institute of Journalism and the Times Institute of Journalism).

A Nairobi-based, nongovernmental organization, the African Council for Communication Education (ACCE), established in 1976, draws its membership from 25 African countries and from North America. Its functions:

1. To assess the training needs of communication training institutions in Africa;
2. To assist in curriculum design and development for journalism education;
3. To facilitate the exchange of resources among training institutions in Africa;
4. To develop research programs for various communications projects;
5. To promote awareness, among African governments, of the role of the media in national development; and
6. To advocate the accreditation or certification of journalism training centers in Africa.

To accomplish these goals, the ACCE holds training workshops and seminars and conferences. The theme of its ninth biennial conference, held in mid-October 1994 in Accra, Ghana, was "The Media and 'Sustainable' Development."

A major postindependent development of journalism training in Africa are the university-level courses, which include liberal arts and social science courses as part of their offerings. Their curricula were developed on the understanding that the journalist is much more than a communicator; she or he is an agent for social change, a calling that requires a comprehensive understanding of the total environment in which journalism is used. The training modules adopted were influenced by those in a number of U.S. higher-educational institutions.

Among the first such programs are those offered by the University of Potchefstroom (South Africa) and the Jackson College of Journalism at the University of Nigeria, Nsukka. The University of Lagos (Nigeria) Institute (now Department) of Mass Communication and the Department of Mass Communication at Bayero University, Kano, Nigeria, were established in 1967 and 1980, respectively, and, like the Jackson College program, offer majors in journalism and broadcasting. Today, several of Nigeria's universities and polytechnics offer a smorgasbord of workshops, courses, and curricula in communication and journalism. In 1988, ACCE published *A Directory of Communication Training Institutions in Africa,* which excluded training programs in South Africa. It indicates that training in mass communication is a growth area in educational offerings in Africa. The Faculte des Sciences de la Sante: Unite Audio Visaulle in Benin, Centre de Formation Professionnelle de L'Information in Burkina Faso, the National Film and Television Institute in Ghana, the National Mass Communication Training Centre in the Sudan, the School of Journalism at the University of Nairobi, Kenya—the list is extensive. The demand for such programs is strong; the supply is struggling to match it. Since the 1960s, there have been developments in both the number of such institutions and in the sophistication of their courses.

ISSUES IN JOURNALISM TRAINING

Perhaps the most vexing issue in the training of African journalists, aside from the inadequacy of training facilities, is ideology. Golding notes (1977) that it is inappropriate for Third World journalists to be exposed largely to the theoretical orthodoxy that is primarily alien to the environments in which they practice. Yet, 10 years later, Murphy and Scotton (1987) observe that "It is the stress on practical training and technical/professional performance that has made American journalism education widely acceptable in Africa and much of the Third World" (p. 30). African governments continue to send their top journalists to workshops and training institutes in, say, the United States (Third World journalists, 1984). Perhaps the culprit in the ideological exposure of African journalists is the dominant journalistic training of the instructional staff, a majority of whom had been and continue to be trained in foreign schools of journalism. Such foreign training is understandable in light of the absence of well-developed, well-staffed graduate programs on the continent. Efforts by the University of Lagos, Nigeria, to offer a doctoral program in mass communication, beginning in the 1986–1987 academic year, have fallen on hard times. The program has not been supported by extensive, up-to-date library holdings, by high faculty morale, and by adequate scholarly and secretarial support for both faculty and graduate students. As Chimutengwende (1984) observes, "Government also slights communication training, allocating inadequate resources to this task and failing to develop consistent policies toward mass media education" (p. 367). Foreign training for journalism educators in Africa will continue to be a reality, raising the question of their preparedness to respond to the specific needs of the continent. Mojekwu (1987) suggests that such educators be retrained "to bring about a reorientation in their perceptions of events and the environment so that the knowledge that is transmitted to trainees will derive from, and be relevant to, our needs" (p. 82).

In the former Soviet Union, for example, journalists were required to take a smattering of courses in Soviet communist ideology and press philosophy. The concerns of African governments are reflective of the rationale for journalistic indoctrination to which the former Soviet journalist was subjected. That rationale held that, if journalists understood, defined, and reported the news within the framework of the country's political system, it would be unnecessary to censor the press in much the same manner if such journalists had not had any training in media–government ideologies. If those ideologies were relevant to the development needs of Africa, perhaps that would not be an issue. However, the adoption of training models that have not been sensitive to environmental needs have resulted in a call by Nwosu (1987) for a training philosophy that promotes national ideals that include balanced development, patriotism, cultural integrity, and self-reliance. Jimada (1987) describes these as the Afro-centric perspective to training and education.

African educators have essentially free rein in determining curricular content, and journalists have been known to adopt free-press ideals. In reality, the demonstration of such ideals has pitted the journalist against the government. The underlying message is that learned educational values cannot be honed risk-free in much of Africa. The clash between journalistic and governmental ideologies resulted in strained government–press relations, as detailed in the two preceding chapters.

A companion issue is that, even though Africa's population is largely rural, the journalistic ideology is more aligned with urban values than with rural aspirations. Ogundimu (1990) explains this shortcoming as emanating from the training curricula: "Aside from occasional workshops on rural journalism, very few of [the] schools pay attention to the problem. The exception seems to be in French-speaking Africa, where many of the technical training schools also offer courses on some aspect of rural journalism" (p. 89).

Herein lie continuing questions on the ideological relevance of the pedagogy of Africa's training institutes and the hands-on experiences of their graduates. Even though one-half dozen journalism institutions were established in Africa by the 1960s, when a number of them became independent, the admonition offered them by Hachten (1968) at that time is as valid now as it was then: "the best place to train beginning journalists is in Africa, where they will work. Also, it is highly desirable that Africans train Africans." The message is clear: The training of journalists should be based on an ideology that is demonstrably relevant to and consistent with their national interests.

REFERENCES

Chimutengwende, C. C. (1984). The role of communications training and technology in African development. In G. Gerbner & M. Siefert (Eds.), *World communications: A handbook* (pp. 360–370). New York: Longman.

Dennis, E. E., & Merrill, J. C. (1984). *Basic issues in mass communication.* New York: Macmillan.

Golding, P. (1977). Media professionalism in the Third World: The transfer of an ideology. In J. Curran, M. Gurevitch, & J. Woollacott (Eds.), *Mass communication and society* (pp. 301–304). London: Edward Arnold.

Hachten, W. A. (1968). The training of African journalists. *Gazette, 14,* 101–110.

Jimada, U. (1987). Towards a philosophy of communication training. In F. O. Ugboajah, I. Nwosu, & A. T. Adaba (Eds.), *Communication training and practice in Nigeria*, Africa Media Monograph Series No. 3 (pp. 59–65). Nairobi, Kenya: African Council on Communication Education.

Kucera, G. Z. (1968). *Broadcasting in Africa: A study of Belgian, British and French colonial policies*. Unpublished doctoral dissertation, Michigan State University, East Lansing.

Mogekwu, M. (1987). Training the Nigerian journalist for the Nigerian audience. In F. O. Ugboajah, I. Nwosu, & A. T. Adaba (Eds.), *Communication training and practice in Nigeria*, Africa Media Monograph Series No. 3 (pp. 77–84). Nairobi, Kenya: African Council on Communication Education.

Murphy, S. M., & Scotton, J. F. (1987). Dependency and journalism education in Africa: Are there alternative models? *Africa Media Review, 1,* 11–35.

Mwaffisi, S. (1991). Development journalism: How prepared are Tanzanian journalists? *Africa Media Review, 5,* 85–93.

Nwosu, I. E. (1987). Operational guidelines for communication training and research in an African context. In J. Domatob, A. Jika, & I. Nwosu (Eds.), *Mass media and the African society*, Africa Media Monograph Series No. 4 (pp. 367–388). Nairobi, Kenya: African Council on Communication Education.

Ogundimu, F. (1990). They don't teach survival skills: Journalism education in Africa. *Gannett Center Journal* (Fall), 81–91.

Scotton, J. F. (1986). Kenyan students are guided into investigative journalism. *Journalism Educator, 41,* 20–22.

Third World journalists to study in U.S. (1984, February 11). *Editor & Publisher,* p. 27.

4   New Technologies, Their Implications, and Special Issues

[S]ound, responsible and coherent management [is] necessary to enable every administration to develop its telecommunication services. (p. 425)
—Meeting of the Plan Committee for Africa, Yaoundé, Cameroon, March 18–25, 1987

A Ghanaian family in Sunyani watches Cable News Network for world news fed via broadcast satellites from the United States and elsewhere. African government officials sign a contract with the Rockville, Maryland-based Orion Satellite Corporation to provide communication services in their country. Families in rural Botswana revel in their newfound communications link—the cellular phone. A researcher at the National University of Abidjan, Côte d'Ivoire, communicates with other researchers worldwide through the Internet. A newspaper reporter writes and swaps stories on her computer, and sends final drafts electronically to the printers. And a high school teacher on the outskirts of Gaborone tapes a television program fed via earth stations in neighboring Zimbabwe for later use in his social studies class. These are just a few examples of the communication revolution that is taking hold of much of urban Africa. In other words, communication technologies are beginning to change the pace, contexts, and strategies of the region's efforts.

The purpose of this chapter is threefold. First, it discusses infrastructural issues related to the growing use of such technologies for development, particularly in sub-Saharan Africa. Second, it outlines considerations and three propositions for their effective use. Third, in light of the mammoth difficulties the continent confronts in its search for sustained development, it suggests a strategic issues-management approach for the effective use of new communication technologies for planning and development.

GLOBAL COMMUNICATION TECHNOLOGIES: SPECIAL ISSUES

Pool (1983) states that electronic devices create an unprecedented flux in machines that think, that make great libraries accessible to users' own premises, and that allow discussion among peoples a half-world apart. Such technologies have other advantages such as the potential for democratizing and decentralizing communication systems, for diversifying information sources, and for broadening the range of choices and information reach (Boafo, 1991b). In sub-Saharan Africa, the increasing use of new communication technologies for socioeconomic development has significant implications for (1) the public interest, (2) the infrastructural support systems, and (3) the effectiveness of such technologies in promoting development.

An additional issue raised in this chapter is the extent to which such technologies have any discernible favorable effects on the communications infrastructure of the region. On this issue, Frederick (1993) believes that the fundamental structure of communication remains unchanged:

Despite the advent of new communication technologies, the problems of communication between and among peoples and nations remain unchanged. The basic structure and function of communication remains the same: Just as before, people today want to inform, they want to be informed, and they want to communicate. The revolution in communication has not changed this. (pp. 41–42)

The anticipated changes that technology will bring, argues Frederick (1993), are yet to become a reality:

Everyone talks about the information society. Yet there is evidence that global communication has led more to divergence and division than to unity.... [I]mprovements in modern communications technologies may have led inevitably to greater social isolation and alienation. (pp. 267–268)

One major concern here is that audiences for whom communication is critical are not being adequately served by the available communications technologies (Frederick, 1993). If this were so, then the contributions of communication technologies to development, particularly in the Third World, may be more cosmetic than substantive. And herein lie special issues in the use of communication technologies for development in Africa.

NEW COMMUNICATION TECHNOLOGIES FOR AFRICA'S DEVELOPMENT

Asia's media systems, particularly those of the "Four Tigers" (Hong Kong, Taiwan, Singapore, and South Korea), boast stunning developments that augur well for the political development and stability of their free-market capitalistic societies. However, Africa's media development has been plagued by wars and economic and social problems (Hachten, 1993). Understandably, the success of the "Four Tigers" can be attributed to their homogeneity in language and to their political stability, characteristics that African countries tend not to have in large measure.

The historical difficulties in attaining sustained growth in Africa have directed the attention of development specialists to a variety of answers, including the use of new communication technologies. For example, during a meeting in Dakar, Senegal, in 1962, the International Telecommunication Union (ITU) Regional Plan Committee for Africa established the Pan-African Telecommunications Network (PANAFTEL), a telecommunications organization of 50 African nations. Two years later, the Washington, D.C.–based International Telecommunications Satellite Organization (INTELSAT), a cooperative of owners and users, was established. This worldwide telecommunications organization of more than 170 countries and territories has improved significantly the business climate of and communication transmission in much of Africa.

However, since its founding, the 32 sub-Saharan African signatories to the organization have raised questions about costs of services and relevance of programs. The African countries recognized that INTELSAT has been organized for the express advantage of the developed countries. Thus, to reduce the shortcomings of relying on INTELSAT alone, it has become important to strengthen the Africa-based telecommunications organization, PANAFTEL, and its affiliated agencies such as the African Postal and Telecommunication Union and the Pan-African Telecommunications Union (PATU).

PANAFTEL's founding has given birth to subregional telecommunication networks in Africa: (1) Regional African Satellite Communication System (RASCOM); (2) the Southern Africa Development Coordination Conference Telecommunications Network (SADCC); and (3) four PANAFTEL subregional networks, which are PANAFTEL-North (for North Africa), and PANAFTEL-West, PANAFTEL-Central, and PANAFTEL-South (for sub-Saharan Africa). Each of the latter four subregional networks has its own telephone exchange system.

In 1987, the Organization of African Unity, in collaboration with the ITU and PATU, launched a feasibility study on the use of communication technologies for development. The resulting report, approved in 1991, reaffirmed RASCOM as an agency for collaborative national development through coordinated telecommunications systems. To date, RASCOM has made modest contributions to the satellite capabilities and coordination of a number of African nations. Even though its impact on the telecommunications infrastructure of the region is yet to be measured, studies have not been conducted to ascertain its direct benefits for Africans.

The SADCC has been active in a variety of development projects, particularly throughout the subequatorial region. Nonetheless, it faces the historical problems of Africa's development agencies: inadequate finances, limited administrative support, miniscule program coordination among countries, logistical limitations, and shortage of technical personnel.

Another global satellite organization, the 76-member, London-based International Maritime Satellite Organization (INMARSAT), is expanding its services in Africa to include the use of laptop computer–size pay phones that allow the transmission of voice and data from faraway rural areas to INMARSAT ground stations for further network distribution. There is the obvious problem of equipment cost, which is beyond the reach of the average African. These technological challenges are all the more taxing in light of the documented limited success in the use of the mass media for Third World development (e.g., Hornik, 1988; Stevenson, 1988).

Among African governments, there has been a marked increase in the use of computers to leapfrog and close the gap between the North and the South (Lewis & Samoff, 1992) and as "the magical solution to Africa's development crisis" (Berman, 1992, p. 214). Frederick (1993) identifies two societal advantages of this latest development strategy. First, in the social service sector, computers, as communications media, assist in everything from health care delivery to educational administration. Second, in the economy, they facilitate more efficient production and marketing systems that counteract rural-to-urban migration and improve overall living standards. But the outcomes of their use for socioeconomic development are not as realistic as they initially appear. Berman (1992) notes that their use "is likely to reinforce existing distributions of power and wealth, create reified images of society based upon quantitative data of dubious value and accuracy, and accentuate the authoritarian relationship between the state and an increasingly marginalized populace" (p. 227). On a broader scale, Boafo (1991a) observes:

The application of communication technology systems to black Africa's development problems has been generally palliative, inadequately planned, and lacking in input or participation from the bulk of the population. Communication technology, resources, and processes have not been accorded the seriousness that they deserve in the development process in black Africa. (p. 110)

The unbridled introduction of new technologies into the developing countries (Mehra, 1988) "necessitates proper understanding of the underlying principles that guide the conduct of communication professionals" (Okigbo, 1989, p. 136) in their use of new communication technologies. Because Western-type technologies are not indigenous to the African environment, they have the potential to disrupt traditional lifestyles and to alter the time-honored relationships of audiences with traditional media channels. Such social changes could endanger the very foundation of "alternative development," which emphasizes increased direct audience participation in development planning and implementation. Because of the unique characteristics of traditional media forms for communicating development-oriented messages, Africa's development can be more realistically attained if the emphasis is on the practical use of such media, not on the mere transfer of Western technologies. Fadeyibi (1984) argues that the mass media have failed to promote development because emphasis has been placed more on the physiotechnical rather than on audience factors. Thus, the "availability of Western mass-media channels is not development per se; it is their use or abuse, much more than their presence, that makes the difference between development and stagnation" (Fadeyibi, 1984, p. 59).

The mass media can be helpful in fulfilling development goals. Given proper conditions, the use of communication technologies such as the telephone is helpful in attaining national development (e.g., Hudson, 1987, 1982; Parker, 1987). The program-based use of such technologies in bringing about strong, buoyant economies in the industrialized world has been presented as evidence of their potential in bringing about similar outcomes in the Third World, based on the modernization paradigm enunciated by Lerner (1958). This paradigm, which applies the linear approach to development, holds, in essence, that what is good for the developed nations is also good for the developing nations.

Indeed, Africa's social changes, when engendered by the use of communication technologies can, in some contexts, foster audience participation in the development process. When, for example, such technologies are used as media for organizing group discussions of development themes or for interfacing development themes with storytellers' performances, then such media can have development benefits.

The Independent Commission for World Wide Telecommunications Development (the Maitland Commission) issued a report, *The Missing Link,* in January 1985. Some recommendations of that report support the Lerner (1958) paradigm of development. For example, one of the commission's criteria for measuring the appropriateness of telecommunications technologies is the efficiency with which they connect geographically distant points (for example, rural to urban centers), primarily because rural dwellers want to talk only with people in the cities (Hudson, 1984, 1986; and Parker, 1982, 1984, 1987). Shields and Samarajiva (1990) criticize the assumption "that all useful information is thought to be located in the city and that the only useful communication links are those connecting rural areas to the metropolis" (p. 210).

The rest of this chapter focuses on two issues. First, it discusses the social and ethical implications of the use of communication technologies for Africa's development. It does so by raising issues on the use of technologies for development, noting particularly those issues related to a planned policy intervention. Second, it summarizes, as propositions, the implications of the use of communication technologies for development and concludes by suggesting that future research test such propositions empirically.

PRACTICAL CONSIDERATIONS IN THE USE OF TECHNOLOGIES FOR DEVELOPMENT

Governmental and nongovernmental organizations, as actors in the dominant coalition for development in sub-Saharan Africa, introduce technologies that have social and ethical implications for development. Sometimes such implications emanate as outcomes, not as the mere use of such technologies but as those of the communicators' professional values.

During much of this century, telecommunications revolutionized the media environment of the developed world. They brought a homogenization of media content and the development of media values, further perpetuated by political, social, and economic systems. One effect of that homogenization is in the concept of news. Although imported modern technologies facilitate speedy news dissemination, they are not sensitive to their differential impacts on audiences. Universal news values are established and fomented through the dominance of global wire services (e.g., Associated Press and Agence France-Press) and global satellite organizations (e.g., INTELSAT and INMARSAT). For Africa, such news-value homogenization is fostered in a limited sense by the Pan African News Agency and the Pan African Telecommunications Union.

The adoption of technology in developing countries is characterized by the developed countries' precedents and by the policy makers urge to keep up with usage practices in the developed countries (Ha, 1995). Because technological devices were developed in response to the value systems of the industrialized market economies of the developed world, programming has been influenced in large measure by the value systems of the manufacturing countries and their transferred technologies, and by the corporate values of the multinational corporations (MNCs). Formal and informal media education, which enables the audience to apply critical judgments to its use of media content, is both crucial and indispensable in fostering national development (Domatob, 1991). This means that the social impact of such technologies on the developing countries in general should be tempered by an extensive media education, whose continued absence may threaten the very foundation of the social values of recipient nations.

From the perspective of social organizations, Africa's journalism education and training, by which development strategies are formulated, are modeled largely on Western epistemological principles (Domatob, 1987; Golding, 1979; Krimsky, 1990; Murphy & Scotton, 1987; Nwosu, 1987; Ogundimu, 1990). The consistency of such professional values with those in the West has raised companion questions about the relevance of current journalism education to the African social value system in general and about the seemingly inherent imperialism of such education (Nwosu, 1987; Golding, 1979; Bourgault, 1987, 1995).

All practices in much of sub-Saharan Africa point to programming values that are still rooted in those of the hardware-manufacturing countries.

To help the development analyst identify the social impact of technology on the family, Halloran (1986) poses two questions: (1) Will new methods of communication lead the family to increased privacy and to reinforced isolation and anonymity? (2) Will media technology lead to more media autonomy or will it reinforce media dependence on capital? Halloran (1986) notes that the answers would depend on the differential opportunities for media use and on the consequences of media use on different groups and classes.

A major implication of the use of imported technologies is relevance, specifically their utilitarian value. Do imported advanced technologies bring about the greatest good for the greatest number of Africans? Are the masses the major beneficiaries of such technology transfer? As Todd (1985) notes, "technology transfer still holds considerable promise provided it is used with far more cultural and technological insight and sensitivity than were applied in the past" (p. 20). However, "contrary to many expectations, the volume and structure of technology transfer from metropolitan to satellite countries in recent decades has not contributed to the independence of the latter, but instead has often increased the dependence" (Hamelink, 1983, p. 17).

Ejiofor (1976) admits that MNCs in Africa bring useful, superior technology to the continent; however, such technologies infuse a feeling of inferiority in Africans who tend to be victims of the "imported-stuff-is-better" syndrome. Beyond that, the benefits of MNC-transferred technology to the developing nations accrue largely to three groups: the transnational corporations, which deliver the products; the transnational banks, which finance the purchase of the products; and a "new class" of officials connected with the ruling government (Hamelink, 1983). In essence, then, these technologies cater to the well-being of a few. One implication of this outcome is that the media are under constant threat from their governments and, therefore, could not critically examine the development policies of their countries. A recent example is found in Angola, where an independent journalist, Ricardo de Mello, was assassinated in January 1995 for his criticisms of government policies. The current military junta in Nigeria has all but annihilated the resolve of the country's independent media in exposing mismanagement and corruption in government agencies.

There have been serious concerns about using communication technologies ineffectively (e.g., Frederick, 1993) for Africa's development, about protecting the region's indigenous practices, and about fostering social goals. One implication of this outcome is that the media, in responding to occasionally restraining agendas, tend to accept government controls on their activities and fail to critically examine development policies. However, the ministries of information, social and economic development, and private media organizations use formal and informal research methods infrequently to ascertain the precise nature of the public interest. Even so, the results have only a peripheral relevance, if at all, to the management of the development process. The point is that the application of social-scientific methods to an understanding of a broad range of public issues has been given short shrift on the continent; yet such methods are important in determining the relevance of media technologies to development. Robertson (1985) emphasizes this point:

Too often, statism rules; the most interesting and ostensibly important areas of enquiry are surrounded by protective privilege and bureaucratic wadding. It is not "the people" or "the nation" which are being protected from inquisitive students; it is the private parts of officialdom and its associated classes. (p. 285)

To position governments' agendas, a number of African governments withhold information from, or strategically share information with, the media and their audiences. Inarguably, even though this phenomenon is not unique to Africa, its continentwide effect has been far-reaching, as Robertson (1985) states:

the amount of accessible reported data is far outweighed by the mass of unreported but potentially useful data in private hoards. The wastage is dreadful, and the greatly diminished utility of collected data redounds again on our cumulative ability to prove our worth to the people who were the objects of our enquiries. (pp. 287–288)

But more than that, the value of technologies to the African society is circumscribed by a paucity of empirical and qualitative evidence on the extent to which such technologies can be incorporated into existing social norms. The default option has been to place full blame on either the MNCs (and their associated agencies) or on external agencies—the sources of much of Africa's technologies. Yet, responsibility for articulating and enforcing policies on the ethical, symmetrical use of technologies rests largely on African governments and their peoples. African policy makers seem either insensitive to programmatic considerations of technology use or transfer, or are oblivious about the optimum social and political conditions that make their use meaningful nationally.

An ethical use of such technologies must also be predicated on extensive studies that indicate, in precise terms, the benefits and problems of their use. It is not enough to assume that because such modern technologies have revolutionized Western industrial societies, their effects in Africa will very well be the same. (The failure of the dominant paradigm of development suggests difficulties in making valid, cross-national assumptions.) In fact, if modern communication technologies had been used in an attempt to improve the well-being of Africans, then their social and economic impacts are yet to be felt. Three facts signify this failure. First, poverty on the continent is growing faster than that in any other world region. Between 1970 and 1985, for example, the number of Africans living in poverty increased by 75 percent to about one-half of the continent's population. Second, food export capability of the continent dropped sharply in the 1980s. Third, during the past decade, economies in most of the region showed little growth, which resulted in economic and political decline that continues today (Stevenson, 1993). Further, Davidson (1992) argues that, because of events in the 1980s, many African countries' economies are today actually worse than they were during the colonial era.

In light of the slow pace of Africa's sustained development, it is important that, in applying utilitarian considerations, specific benefits of new technologies be identified and tapped. As Hudson (1987) notes,

it is necessary to adopt strategies that will both reduce risks and increase rewards. Risk reduction can take many forms. It may include better efforts to communicate what is known about the contribution of [technologies] to development to planners and policy makers in developing country governments and funding institutions. (pp. 32–33)

Further, as outlined in a preceding paragraph, policy making should address the relevance of imported technologies in Africa. For example, with the abundance of labor in the region, how important is the introduction of capital-intensive technologies to its development? Can such policy making strike a balance between capital-intensive technologies and labor-intensive environments? Do African nations have the ability to finance, operate, manage, and maintain capital-intensive technologies? In essence, the choice and use of technology in Africa should tilt in favor of a type of technology that is a mix between the simple and the advanced technology. Perhaps in agreement with Adams (1984), such technology should be intermediate, which, because it falls between traditional and ultramodern technologies, is usually more efficient economically than either of the other alternatives and is simpler and less capital-intensive than Western technologies.

Mehra (1988), however, disagrees with the use of intermediate technology, stating that technology need not be evaluated by level, but primarily by whether it is likely to help achieve the socioeconomic goals of the developing nations into which they are introduced. Parker (1987) also observes that, despite growing evidence in favor of using appropriate, low-cost technologies for development, the worldwide institutional barriers to implementation remain formidable.

Therefore, it is even more important in Africa than elsewhere that technologies that are used be linked to extensive training programs for the abundant work force, who should be encouraged to view such technologies not as threats to their jobs but as partners in improving productivity to levels that would not otherwise be possible. This is particularly crucial in Africa, where the use of technology should be increasingly perceived for its benefits and challenges than for its problems.

Finally, indigenous communication values need not be threatened by imported technologies. Nor should the structure of traditional media be transformed to accommodate modern technologies. Dissanayake (1977) poses two related questions: "Is it ethically and aesthetically right to tamper with them [traditional media]? Is it possible to effect a union between traditional media and electronic media?'' (p. 123).

African countries have attempted to incorporate selectively foreign media values into their communication environments. Several African scholars have also called for an incorporation of the local culture into radio and television programs in order to address the effects of cultural imperialism (Ugboajah, 1985a). Ugboajah (1985b) specifically calls for a cultural engineering, that is, the '' 'delinking' or 'self-reliance,' the creation of a balance in the information systems so as to engineer flexible adaptation, national integration and national information autonomy'' (pp. 180–181). And Dissanayake (1977) was prompted to suggest that ''the most judicious course of action would be to make no fundamental changes in the content and structure of traditional media but rather use their forms for the transmission of modern messages'' (p. 124).

Tradition-based dissemination strategies have major advantages to the African. Technologies that are suitable for use with local mores, without altering the latter, can in the long run be perceived as credible channels for development messages and can, therefore, enable media institutions to contribute ethically to the continuing development of their societies.

Moreover, technology can facilitate unity and understanding among Africans. For example, Lardner (1993) proposes the development of a Pan-African broadcasting network run by Africans and the establishment of an African media database. The latter will be an interactive computer program that will hold data on the penetration rate of technologies such as television, cable television, and videocassettes in Africa.

THREE PROPOSITIONS

Developments in the use of communication technologies have not kept pace with other segments of communications development. In Africa, even though the reach of technologies, for example, microcomputers and cellular phones, is becoming widespread in urban areas, there has not been a concomitant growth in policies and resource development to make their use streamlined for the region's sustained development. Do communication technologies, for example, result in additional constraints on the press? Do they imply that a single entity will have a monopoly over the use of such technologies or that such an entity will breed others within undesirable social standings? Pool (1983) attempts to come to grips with the debates over progress versus infrastructure in the U.S. context. Pool (1983) writes:

While the printing press was without doubt the foundation of modern democracy, the response to the flood of publishing that it brought forth has been censorship as often as press freedom. In some times and places the even more capacious new media will open wider the floodgates for discourse, but in other times and places, in fear of that flood, attempts will be made to shut the gates. (p. 251)

In discussing the implications of the use of communication technologies for development, this chapter adopts positive and normative perspectives. The former perspective means that it addresses development within the context of what development agents *do;* the latter within the context of what development agents *should do.* This chapter, therefore, sheds light on the pervasiveness of the importance of ethical considerations in the use of communication technologies for development. The implications of this discourse for the development specialist can be reduced to three major propositions:

1. Effective communication technologies–based development projects will be those that demonstrate the relevance of indigenous resources in the development of sub-Saharan Africa.

2. Effective communication technologies–based development projects will be those that demonstrate simultaneously the utilitarian value of technologies in national development.

3. Effective communication technologies–based development projects that blend with indigenous resources and apply utilitarian considerations will be more likely to result in expected developmental outcomes than are those that do not demonstrate such a characteristic or consideration.

It is suggested that these propositions be tested empirically through extensive field research. The presence of communication technologies per se does not translate into development. The obverse reasoning is that their absence does not necessarily create insurmountable barriers to development. The key, then, is the extent to which African governments are committed to ensuring that infrastructures of development are used precisely to accomplish stated goals, without engendering situations in which such infrastructures will pose barriers to development.

From this chapter, one thing is apparent: The inadequate development of the capabilities of much of Africa's telecommunication technologies translates into constrained development, a situation on which Riverson (1993) offers a three-point recommendation. First, that a telecommunications agency, which he named the Pan-African Telecommunication Academy, plan and support the development of telecommunications systems for Africa. Second, that financial support be available to establish earth stations and terrestrial facilities. Finally, that African governments should essentially have a hands-off policy in the administration of such telecommunications facilities. While these recommendations seem logical, Africa's mass communications environment, of which telecommunications are a sector, has been particularly vulnerable to governmental interference and control. The implications of these outcomes for the continuing use of new communication technologies suggest that African governments will fail to derive the full potential of such technologies if the latter are subjected to current governmental controls faced by the mass media in general. If that were so, then the new communication technologies will be just another fanciful, high-priced gadget in Africa's communications-for-development arsenal.

A STRATEGIC ISSUES–MANAGEMENT APPROACH

This section outlines considerations for managing the transfer and use of communication technologies for strategic development. The transfer is managed by both private and government organizations. One shortcoming of the transfer mechanism of such technologies is a much-overlooked dimension: management processes for the use of communication technologies. During a meeting of the Plan Committee for Africa in Cameroon in March 1987, a roundtable discussion titled "Telecommunication management and development prospect for the telecommunication industry in Africa" noted that the management of telecommunication hampered its development as a whole (Meeting of the Plan, 1987).

Soon after attaining political independence, many African countries created five- or ten-year development plans. Additionally, a number of African governments have adopted or responded favorably to continentwide plans: Africa's Priority Program for Economic Recovery, 1986–1990; the United Nations Program of Action for African Economic Recovery and Development, 1986–1990; the March 1988 Khartoum Declaration of the Khartoum Conference on the Human Dimension of Africa's Economic Recovery and Development. More recently, the May 1994 conference of the UN Economic Commission for Africa in Addis Ababa, Ethiopia, formulated strategies for developing Africa's human capacities. These plans have at least three major weaknesses that make a strategic issues-management approach toward the use of technologies appealing to development specialists.

First, the plans are instruments of political and economic leverage; they are sales pitches for resource allocation and disposition. A relatively affluent or an economically inconsequential region could become the focus of a plan because of the region's political expediency. Second, such plans do not attract strong national commitments. Finally, their operations are essentially short-term; they run their course without systematic, timely interventions.

The use of technologies is a major development element on the continent. How can such development agencies manage a technology-based development process that overrides the limitations of current plans? Part of the answer lies in the management process of the development agencies. Therefore, development agencies in the region need to refocus their attention on strategic planning for development that places issues management where it appropriately belongs: in the core of agency plans.

Issues management developed in the West as a strategic public response to the complexities of private-sector impact on national economies; it has evolved into a paradigm of participatory style of management (Renfro, 1993). That response has been extended to the public sector because (1) it is "the people's business"; (2) it is subject to the same forces of change as the private sector;

and (3) it is similar to the private sector in its service offerings (Renfro, 1993).

The adoption of issues management requires that an organization or a political system look not only at issues that confront society's introduction of technologies during the next 12 to 36 months, as Ewing (1987) suggests in his issues-management model. More than that, it requires a strategic vision that looks three to 20 years ahead (Ansoff, 1980) or, as Renfro (1993) describes it, that looks at the "Structure of the Future." The taxonomy of the issue of concern for a development agency has four overlapping "levels of the future" and suggested time frames: surface indicators, up to one year; structural/institutional change, one to seven years; values/lifestyles, five to 20 years; and philosophies of mankind, 10 to 100 years. In each of these four areas, the development agent will examine the social, technological, economic, and legislative/regulatory implications of the use of new communication technologies for attaining purposeful changes in society.

Possibly, the near absence of such futuristic management processes, even *before* new technologies are in place, robs the continent of some of its resolve for attaining sustainable development. Because an issues-management approach is aligned with bottom-up participatory development, it can enable the development process to be more sensitive to sociopolitical considerations, to be more integrated into the larger matrices of public policies and strategic plans, and to be more sensitive to public needs.

Issues management, applied to the effective use of technologies in Africa, will include five practical steps: scanning, monitoring, tracking, analyzing, and developing strategies (e.g., Ewing, 1987).

Scanning requires an evaluation of the sociocultural environment and societal needs to determine the appropriateness of technologies as well as how and in what contexts they should be used. This scanning process involves extensive field work, which, in Africa, can be a daunting experience. The paucity of technology for the systematic monitoring of the environment and the collection of data, the absence of systematic data depository or information sources, and the absence of political and social infrastructures for environmental scanning lead to uncertainties in the environment scanning behaviors of researchers in Africa (Adegbite, 1986; Fubara, 1986; Mrema, 1987; Sawyerr, 1993).

Environmental scanning, consistent with the basic-needs approach to development, will require evaluating the potentials of technologies in "meeting specific needs of particular poverty groups; fulfilling such basic needs of people as health care, nutrition, sanitation, and shelter; . . . and self-determination, self-reliance, and cultural autonomy" (Melkote, 1991, p. 176). As outlined in a preceding paragraph, bureaucratic and interviewee self-imposed controls over the availability of government records and interviewees to researchers make such scanning for the use of technologies a monumental task.

Environmental monitoring for effective introduction of technologies entails keeping an eye on shifts in public attitudes and circumstances, as well as on regulatory or legislative agencies. Because both scanning and monitoring are dependent on access to interviewees, to members of focus groups, or to government officials, gauging changes among the people or in national policies has become increasingly difficult.

Tracking involves identifying the parameters of the social effects of technologies. The data derived from the preceding three phases are then analyzed for their relevance to the introduction of technologies. The point here is not to assume that modern gadgetry is usually more effective in information distribution and in the adoption of new practices.

Moemeka's (1981) survey found that residents in Obamkpa, a village in Nigeria's Delta state, preferred traditional media to modern media for exposure to three development projects because the use of traditional media tended not to require the same literacy skills that were required for the use of, say, newspapers or magazines. More important, the residents were familiar with the traditional media, which also reinforced existing interrelationships within communities.

The final step in the issues-management process is developing strategies based on the three earlier steps and reporting the strategies to management. Such reports should outline in an executive summary format and in detail the pros and cons of using such strategies for technology transfer. Because of the unusual deference toward authority figures in Africa's bureaucratic structures and governments' encroachment on field staffs, such reports tend not to present findings forthrightly critical of official establishments.

If the political leaders fail to demonstrate management skills and criticize wantonly the commercialization of new communication technologies, then the benefits for Africans of those technologies will be diminished. In essence, then, it is the management of the use of the new technologies that has posed more challenges than their paucity on the continent.

CONCLUSION

The problems of communication technologies in Africa lie more in managing their use than in focusing on their availability. Policy makers have to debunk the notion that having every form of new communication technology will result in the modernization of their countries. The traditional top-down paradigm by which the state determines societal needs should give way to a pragmatic, issues-management approach, which emphasizes long-term planning and the practical utility of the technologies in benefiting the public at large. For example, telephones, which foster interpersonal communication, will be given higher priority than computers, which require a lot of training and the importation and maintenance of software and hardware. Both the public and private sectors could determine priorities for investing in and using technologies. Ohajah (1995) bemoans the current state of even basic technologies in Africa:

[it] has the world's lowest number of phone lines, the highest costs for international calls, and the lowest call-completion rates. It has the fewest number of host computers for Internet and the lowest levels of actual and planned investment in communications technology. (p. 16A)

An issues-management approach will also enable the state to adopt communication technologies that are based on societal needs and on the indigenous culture. It is only after these have been done that the contributions of media technologies can be fully realized. A judicious use of the delivery and message capacity of communication technologies will give African nations the essential infrastructure and management processes to conduct business among themselves and with the rest of the world.

REFERENCES

Adams, W. (1984). Intermediate technology and development. In M. J. Betz, P. Mc-Gowan, & R. T. Wigland (Eds.), *Appropriate technology: Choice and development.* (pp. 15–29). Durham, NC: Duke Press Policy Studies.
Adegbite, O. (1986). Planning in Nigerian business. *Long Range Planning, 19,* 98–103.
Ansoff, H. I. (1980). Strategic issue management. *Strategic Management Journal, 1,* 131–148.
Berman, B. J. (1992). The state, computers, and African development: The information non-revolution. In S. G. Lewis & J. Samoff (Eds.), *Microcomputers in African development: Critical perspectives* (pp. 213–229). Boulder, CO: Westview.
Boafo, S. T. K. (1991a). Communication technology and dependent development in sub-Saharan Africa. In G. Sussman & J. A. Lent (Eds.), *Transnational communications: Wiring the Third World* (pp. 103–124). Newbury Park, CA: Sage.
———. (1991b). Video-cassette recorders in Ghana: Impact on press freedom in sub-Saharan Africa. In C. Sparks (Ed.), *New communication technologies: A challenge for press freedom,* no. 106 (pp. 55–68). Paris: UNESCO.
Bourgault, L. M. (1987, November). *Training African media personnel: Some psycho-cultural considerations.* Paper presented at the annual meeting of the African Studies Association, Denver, CO.
———. 1995. Mass media in sub-Saharan Africa. Bloomington: Indiana University Press.
Davidson, B. (1992). *The black man's burden: Africa and the curse of the nation-state.* New York: Times Books.
Dissanayake, W. (1977). New wine in old bottles: Can folk media convey modern messages? *Journal of Communication, 27* (2), 122–124.
Domatob, J. K. (1987). Communication training for self-reliance in Black Africa: Challenges and strategies. *Gazette, 40,* 167–182.
———. (1991). Serious problems face media education in sub-Saharan Africa. *Media Development, 27* (1), 31–34.
Ejiofor, P. N. O. (1976). Multinational corporations as agents of imperialism. In B. O. Onibonoje, K. Omotoso, & O. A. Lawal (Eds.), *The indigenes for national development* (pp. 13–24). Ibadan, Nigeria: Onibonoje Publishers.
Ewing, R. P. (1987). *Managing the new bottom line: Issues management for senior executives.* Homewood, IL: Dow Jones-Irwin.
Fadeyibi, O. A. (1984). Mass non-communication in developing nations: An overview based on mass communications research prior to the mid-seventies. In S. Thomas (Ed.), *Studies in mass communication and technology,* vol. 1 (pp. 54–60). Norwood, NJ: Ablex.

Frederick, H. H. (1993). *Global communication & international relations.* Belmont, CA: Wadsworth.

Fubara, B. A. (1986). Corporate planning in Nigeria. *Long Range Planning, 19,* 125–132.

Golding, P. (1979). Media professionalism in the Third World: The transfer of an ideology. In J. Curran, M. Gurevitch, & J. Woollacott (Eds.), *Mass communication and society* (pp. 291–308). Beverly Hills, CA: Sage.

Ha, L. (1995). *Concerns about advertising practices in a developing country: An examination of China's new advertising regulations.* Working paper.

Hachten, W. A. (1993). *The growth of media in the Third World: African failures, Asian successes.* Ames, Iowa: Iowa State University Press.

Halloran, J. D. (1986). The social implications of technological innovations in communication. In M. Traber (Ed.), *The myth of the information revolution: Social and ethical implications of communication technology* (pp. 46–63). London: Sage.

Hamelink, C. J. (1988). *The technology gamble. Informatics and public policy: A study of technology choice.* Norwood, NJ: Ablex.

———. (1983). *Cultural autonomy in global communications.* New York: Longman.

Hornik, R. C. (1988). *Development communication: Information, agriculture, and nutrition in the Third World.* New York: Longman.

Hudson, H. E. (1982). Toward a model for predicting development benefits from telecommunication investment. In M. Jussawalla & D. M. Lamberton (Eds.), *Communication economics and development* (pp. 159–189). New York: Pergamon.

———. (1984). *When telephones reach the village: The role of telecommunications in rural development.* Geneva: International Telecommunication Union.

———. (1986). Access to information resources: The developmental context of the space WARC. In D. A. Demac (Ed.), *Tracing new orbits: Cooperation and competition in global satellite development* (pp. 209–221) New York: Columbia University.

———. (1987, October). Telecommunications and the developing countries. *IEEE Communications Magazine, 25* (10), 28–33.

Krimsky, G. A. (1990). Third World press. *Gannett Center Journal, 4* (4), 61–71.

Lardner, T. (1993). *In convergence—press democracy and technology in Africa.* Working Paper. New York: The Freedom Forum Media Studies Center at Columbia University.

Lerner, D. (1958). *The passing of traditional society: Modernizing the Middle East.* Glencoe, IL: Free Press.

Lewis, S. G., & Samoff, J. (1992). Introduction. In S. G. Lewis & J. Samoff (Eds.), *Microcomputers in African development: Critical perspectives* (pp. 1–24). Boulder, CO: Westview.

Meeting of the Plan Committee for Africa. (1987). *Telecommunication Journal, 54* (7), 417–425.

Mehra, A. (1988). Harnessing new communication technologies for development in Asia. *Media Asia, 15* (2), 63–67.

Melkote, S. R. (1991). *Communication for development in the Third World: Theory and practice.* New Delhi: Sage.

Moemeka, A. A. (1981). *Local radio: Community education for development.* Zaria, Nigeria: Ahmadu Bello University Press.

Mrema, E. L. (1987). Strategic planning in Tanzania. *Long Range Planning, 20,* 105–110.

Murphy, S. M., & Scotton, J. F. (1987). Dependency and journalism education in Africa: Are there alternative models? *Africa Media Review, 1,* 11–35.

Nwosu, I. E. (1987). Operational guidelines for communication training and research in an African context. In J. Domatob, A. Jika, & I. Nwosu (Eds.), *Mass media and the African society,* Africa media monograph series No. 4 (pp. 367–388). Nairobi, Kenya: African Council on Communication Education.

Ogundimu, F. (1990). They don't teach survival skills: Journalism education in Africa. *Gannett Center Journal, 4* (4), 81–91.

Ohajah, E. (1995, April 14). Africa is being cut out of the net. *Star* (Minneapolis) *Tribune,* p. 16A.

Okigbo, C. (1989). Communication ethics and social change: A Nigerian perspective. In T. W. Cooper, C. G. Christians, F. F. Plude, & R. A. White (Eds.), *Communication ethics and global change* (pp. 124–136). White Plains, NY: Longman.

Parker, E. B. (1982). Communications satellites for rural development. In J. R. Schement, F. Gutierrez, & M. A. Sirbu, Jr. (Eds.), *Telecommunications policy handbook* (pp. 3–10). New York: Praeger.

———. (1984). Appropriate telecommunications for economic development. *Telecommunications Policy* (September), 173–180.

———. (1987). Micro earth station satellite networks and economic development. *Telematics and Informatics, 4* (2), 109–112.

Pool, I. S. (1983). *Technologies of freedom.* Cambridge, MA. Belknap.

Renfro, W. L. (1993). *Issues management in strategic planning.* Westport, CT: Quorum Books.

Riverson, L. K. (1993). *Telecommunications development: The case of Africa.* Lanham, MD: University Press of America.

Robertson, A. F. (1985). Doing research in Africa. *African Affairs, 84* (335), 279–290.

Sawyerr, O. O. (1993). Environmental uncertainty and environmental scanning activities of Nigerian manufacturing executives: A comparative analysis. *Strategic Management Journal, 14,* 287–299.

Shields, P., & Samarajiva, R. (1990). Telecommunication, rural development and the Maitland report. *Gazette, 46,* 197–217.

Stevenson, R. L. (1988). *Communication, development, and the Third World: The global politics of information.* New York: Longman.

———. (1993). Communication and development: Lessons from and for Africa. In F. Eribo, O. Oyediran, M. Wubneh, & L. Zonn (Eds.), *Window on Africa: Democratization and media exposure* (pp. 97–124). Greenville, NC: Center for International Programs Publication No. 1, East Carolina University.

Todd, R. D. (1985). Technology education: An international perspective. In *Technology education: A perspective on implementation* (pp. 19–24). International Technology Education Association, Reston, VA.

Ugboajah, F. O. (Ed.). (1985a). *Mass communication, culture and society in West Africa.* New York: Hans Zell.

Ugboajah, F. O. (1985b). De-linking the Western professional model: Introduction to part III. In F. O. Ugboajah (Ed.), *Mass communication, culture and society in West Africa* (pp. 179–186). New York: Hans Zell.

II NORTH AFRICA

_____ Kuldip R. Rampal

5 Setting and Philosophical Contexts

ALGERIA

Located in the center of North Africa, Algeria is a Muslim country with a population estimated in 1994 at just under 28 million. According to U.S. government estimates, the country had a per capita income of $4,300 in 1992 and a literacy rate of approximately 60 percent.

Long under the control of a military dictatorship, the Algerian press appeared to be on the verge of benefiting from an open political climate as the country held its first multiparty national elections in late 1991. Two rounds of elections to a 430-seat National Assembly were scheduled for December 26, 1991, and January 16, 1992. In a surprising turn of events, however, Algeria reverted to its authoritarian ways when the second round of elections was canceled following a strong lead established by the opposition Islamic Salvation Front (FIS) in the first round. As the FIS, a fundamentalist Islamic party, was poised to win the elections, a six-man High Security Council canceled the second round and nullified the results to the first. A state of emergency was declared for 12 months on February 9, 1992, by the military-backed High State Council and extended indefinitely on February 9, 1993. As a result, a measure of freedom that the Algerian press had enjoyed since 1989 became tenuous once again. The Algerian press philosophy can be best understood by briefly tracing the political developments that have been instrumental in shaping it since the country's independence.

Annexed by France in 1842, Algeria became an independent country on July 3, 1962, following an eight-year war of liberation led by the National Liberation Front (Front de Liberation Nationale—FLN). Banks (1991, p. 16) says that ever since its founding in 1954, the FLN has been dedicated to socialism, nonalignment, and Pan-Arabism. The founder of the FLN, Ahmed Ben Bella, became the country's first president with the adoption of a constitution in 1963, which established the FLN as the sole political party. Under Bella's leadership, the foundation was laid for a single-party socialist state.

The single-party socialist system resulted in a highly controlled press during much of the country's postindependence history. In a move to eliminate the European-owned press, which was seen as a vehicle for foreign propaganda and a vestige of the colonial past, the Bella regime nationalized it in 1963 and established complete control of the press by 1964. This step was also consistent with the government's socialist policy of nationalizing foreign economic interests in Algeria. Independent-minded domestic press was also brought under government control through a policy that all newspaper editors be appointed by the FLN to ensure ideological conformity. According to Kurian (1982, p. 1064), the function of the press was defined as "transmitting and explaining official policies and educating citizens through the judicious selection of informational and ideological material."

Bella was deposed in a military coup in June 1965 and his successor, Col. Houari Boumedienne, promised to continue socialist policies. Mass media were placed under the control of the Ministry of Information and Culture. Kurian (1982, p. 1064) describes the objectives of the press under a 1968 ordinance as follows:

[J]ournalists were admonished to perform their work in a spirit of militant fervor and to report on the achievements of the new socialist order. To affirm the principle of collegiality, directors and editors of newspapers were replaced by anonymous editorial boards staffed by party die-hards. During this period, some newspapers were suspended and others merged; the resulting structure remained unchanged throughout the Boumedienne years.

Algeria's single-party socialist political system was consolidated through a new constitution adopted in 1976, with the FLN as its "vanguard force." The FLN control of the press continued following the death of Boumedienne in 1978, and through the successive regimes. In its annual survey of civil liberties and press freedoms around the world, the U.S.-based Freedom House noted in 1981 that in Algeria "media are governmental means for active indoctrination; no opposition voice is allowed, and foreign publications are closely watched" (Gastil, 1981, p. 320). Before the 1989 constitutional reforms, press freedom was allowed within the framework of socialist policies. Article 55 of the constitution said that "freedom of expression and assembly are guaranteed, but they may not be used to undermine the bases of the socialist revolution."

A 1982 legislation, called the Information Code, consolidated total government and party control over the media, and made the Information Ministry the editor of all publications and broadcasting operations. The government also exerted its influence to silence critical newspapers published by Algerian opposition groups in France. During 1986–1988, the French government cooperated with the Algerian government in suppressing three such newspapers published by a pro-democracy Algerian opposition group based in France. During most of the 1980s, Algerian mass media were regarded as being in the service of the state, charged with affirming socialist policies, recording achievements of the new order, and mobilizing the energies of the citizens on behalf of national goals (*Europa World Yearbook,* 1992, p. 320; Nelson, 1986, p. 268).

The media situation worsened in 1988 when protests broke out among Islamic fundamentalists and students against the entrenched political controls and deteriorating economic conditions. According to official sources, 159 people were killed in confrontations with government forces. The country's media were prohibited from reporting freely on the riots. Television and radio were later accused by journalists of having engaged in a campaign of disinformation and distortion and of having supported the repression. Foreign journalists were also prevented from covering the riots. According to Article 19's World Report, "film crews had video cassettes confiscated and were routinely prevented from sending footage via satellite. Many correspondents were refused visas to enter Algeria and some . . . were expelled on arrival" (1991, p. 349).

Constitutional/Media Reforms

In response to the unrest, President Bendjedid Chadli, in office since 1979, proposed constitutional amendments that would reduce the conservative influence of the FLN, allowing non-FLN candidates to participate in elections and making the prime minister answerable to the National People's Assembly rather than to the president (*Europa Yearbook,* 1992, p. 320).

In February 1989, a new constitution signifying the end of the one-party socialist state was approved in a national referendum. It eliminated all mention of socialism and permitted the formation of political associations outside the FLN. The new constitution guaranteed the fundamental rights "of man and of the citizen" as opposed to the earlier reference as rights of "the people." It also guaranteed "the freedom of conscience and opinion, freedom of intellectual, artistic and scientific creation, and freedom of expression and assembly" (*Europa Yearbook,* 1992, p. 328).

The political reforms resulted in a degree of press freedom also. Following the 1988 riots, many Algerian journalists left the official Union of Journalists, Writers and Interpreters. They released a document which revealed the scale of censorship imposed on the media over many years as well as the self-censorship that was practiced. The document disclosed a blacklist of journalists prevented from writing or traveling in Algeria or abroad. Journalists also protested over the excessive powers of the government-appointed editors (Article 19, 1991, p. 351).

Following such protests, the government submitted a new Information Code to the National Assembly. Journalists were not consulted, however, in the drafting of the new code. Approved in mid-1989, the new code formally ended the state monopoly of the press, although it left the principal newspapers under the control of the FLN. Journalists criticized this code by saying that it "does not guarantee freedom, independence and pluralism of the press" (Article 19, 1991, p. 351).

The government responded with a more stringent code in March 1990, which mandated imprisonment for any journalist who "offends by word, sound, images, drawings or any other means" Islam or any other religion. The revised code also stipulated that unless official exemption was obtained, "periodicals of general information created after promulgation of the present law are to be edited in the Arabic language" (Banks, 1991, p. 17). It is an offense under the code, punishable by up to 10 years' imprisonment, to publish or distribute information which could harm state security or national unity. The code does not guarantee the protection of journalists' sources (Article 19, 1991, p. 351).

When considered within the historical perspective and the 1989 constitutional reforms, however, the Algerian press acquired more freedoms than it had ever enjoyed since independence. First, the state monopoly of the media for many years was ended in 1989, allowing many political parties to produce their own publications. Second, constitutional guarantees of freedom of expression and freedom of conscience and opinion allowed the press to operate with a greater degree of freedom than ever before, notwithstanding the journalists' demands for "freedom, independence and pluralism of the press," as indicated above.

As a result of the constitutional reforms, 25 political organizations and many more independent civic associations were formed. Many opposition leaders returned from exile. In August 1990, a general amnesty permitted the release of thousands of political prisoners (*Europa Yearbook*, 1992, p. 320). Among the new political groups was FIS, which campaigned for the institution of an Islamic state and the implementation of Islamic law. As indicated earlier, the Algerian government canceled the second round of elections scheduled for January 16, 1992, after the fundamentalists won the first round.

The Islamic fundamentalists have been waging a guerrilla war against the military-backed authorities since the cancellation of the elections. As of mid-1994, approximately 4,000 people, including a number of journalists, had been killed and, despite the introduction of tough new security measures, the violence continued to escalate. The militants were killing foreign visitors, judges, policemen, government officials, journalists, intellectuals, and even foreign workers in their effort to destabilize the government. The authorities had refused to hold talks with the fundamentalists, accusing them of being "terrorists." As a result of this political turmoil, the gains made in press freedom since the ending of state monopoly of the press in 1989 had become meaningless.

LIBYA

Located on the north-central coast of Africa, Libya is fourth in size among the countries on this continent. Libya's population was estimated to be just over

5 million in 1994, with a literacy rate of 64 percent. Largely because of the substantial oil revenues of the country, Libyans had a per capita income of $6,600 in 1993, according to U.S. government estimates.

The Libyan press was nationalized in 1972 and continues to be under the firm control of the government of Col. Muammar al-Qadhafi. The country's only daily newspaper and other media have been used to mobilize and organize the entire population for state purposes. The major national goals established by Qadhafi are the implementation of a self-styled "democratic" system and pursuit of Pan-Arabism. Qadhafi realized after the military coup in 1969 that government control of the privately owned press was not sufficient to achieve these goals. Besides, he claimed that such media were incompatible with the "true" democratic state he envisioned, in which there would be no political parties and people would rule directly. In Qadhafi's view, privately owned media could not be counted upon to reflect public opinion because they would follow the dictates of their owners, a problem that would be eliminated with public ownership of media.

The ownership pattern of mass media in Qadhafi's Libya, therefore, is very similar to those in Marxist-Leninist states. But the similarity ends there because Qadhafi has rejected both communism and Western-style democracy in favor of his own brand of democracy, espoused in his three-volume *Green Book,* which explains his views on political philosophy, political systems, and economics. Qadhafi also addresses the issues of ownership and role of the press in this book. A brief historical perspective of political developments in Libya is necessary to understand the Libyan press philosophy.

Libya was under Turkish control from the mid-sixteenth century to the beginning of the twentieth century. It was conquered by Italy in 1911–1912 and ruled as an Italian colony until its occupation by British and French troops in 1942, who subsequently administered the country. Libya gained independence on December 24, 1951, when a constitutional monarchy was installed, with Mohammad Idris Al-Senussi as the king. Under King Idris, the country maintained a pro-Western stance and was recognized as belonging to the conservative traditionalist bloc in the Arab League (Metz, 1989, p. 38).

Although all political parties were banned under the monarchy and there were no party newspapers (Banks, 1991, p. 402), the press reflected a variety of political leanings. Newspapers and periodicals published views ranging from conservative, religious, and anticommunist to leftist and radical. They were all kept under control, however, by strict press laws and the threat of suspension of publication licenses (First, 1974, p. 122). Newspapers were also dependent on government subsidies. By the late 1960s, there were nine daily newspapers— five in Arabic, three in English, and one in Italian. Two of the Arabic-language newspapers were published by the government, with the remaining seven newspapers classified as "independent" (Merrill, et al., 1975, p. 301). In addition, 11 weekly and biweekly newspapers, and nine magazines were published. Cultural influences brought by the Western colonial nations and the pro-Western stance of the monarchy were instrumental in creating a demand for books and magazines from the West, which were readily available during the rule of King Idris.

In spite of the stringent press laws, Libyan media had some degree of freedom during the rule of King Idris, in view of the fact that independent newspapers were allowed to be published and press organs could be privately owned. Under Qadhafi, however, both the ownership and operational patterns of media were radically changed.

Military Coup, Qadhafi's Political Ideology, and the Press

On September 1, 1969, while King Idris was in Turkey for medical treatment, a group of military officers seized control of the government in a bloodless coup and established a revolutionary regime under a military-controlled Revolutionary Command Council (RCC). The RCC initially remained anonymous but was soon revealed as a group of young officers, with Qadhafi, aged 27, as the leader. King Idris accepted exile in Egypt, where he died in May 1983.

Under Qadhafi, Libya overnight turned from a conservative, pro-Western monarchy to a radical, leftist state. The RCC announced that the major goals of the revolution were the adoption of socialism, restructuring of the society on the basis of Islamic principles, and unity of Arab states to support the Palestinian cause against Israel. Qadhafi's socialism was to integrate Islamic principles with social, political, and economic reforms. He categorically rejected communism— in large part because it was atheistic—and Western-style capitalism. He also proclaimed neutrality between the superpowers, resulting in the ouster of American and British military bases in 1970. Expatriate Western communities were forced to leave the country the same year. In June 1971, an official party, the Arab Socialist Union (ASU), was organized, while an earlier royal ban on opposition political parties continued (Harris, 1986, pp. 43–61). The RCC established its own newspaper, *Al-Thawra* (The Revolution), to help explain its ideas to the public.

ASU's intent was to raise the political consciousness of Libyans in line with Qadhafi's socialistic ideology. In May 1970, the RCC began what were called "Revolutionary Intellectuals Seminars" in an effort to co-opt intellectuals to the cause of the revolution. Harris (1986, p. 17) says that public discussions between Qadhafi and various groups of intellectuals alienated the intellectuals as Qadhafi refuted all ideas but his own. He also quickly muzzled the private press with tough censorship laws. In addition, press subsidies were sharply reduced to both private and government newspapers. The economic base of the press was further weakened when Qadhafi announced in early 1970 that government advertising could appear only in *Al-Thawra.*

Even though the press had been censored heavily since the coup, Qadhafi and the RCC recognized early in 1972 that censorship was insufficient to bring all thought into conformity with the goals of the Revolution. The RCC moved to eliminate all newspapers with the exception of its official organ. It suspended the publication of the 10 daily newspapers early in 1972 and later, the same year, their licenses were revoked. Little remained of the Libyan press as a result of these actions. Even the ASU's official organ, *Al-Thawra,* was shut down for a variety of reasons: it was badly written; its editorials were unsound; the intellectuals did not write for it. The remaining publications came under tight government supervision (First, 1974, pp. 122–123, 133). *Al-Fajr al-Jadid* (The New Dawn), which was founded in 1969, replaced *Al-Thawra* in 1972 as the official mouthpiece of the government. This continues to be the only daily newspaper in Libya (*Europa Yearbook,* 1992, p. 1748).

The Cultural Revolution and the Third Universal Theory

Disillusioned that the Libyan society was not being reshaped as quickly as he had envisioned, Qadhafi launched a "cultural revolution" in April 1973. Its aims were laid down in a five-point program: "People's committees" would be set up to carry out the revolution; the "politically sick" would be purged; the revolutionary masses would be armed; a campaign would begin against bureaucracy and administrative abuses; and imported publications which propagated communism, atheism, or capitalism would be burned. The people's committees set about the task of supervising all aspects of social and economic life, criticizing and dismissing officials and business executives who failed to show the revolutionary fervor, and destroying offensive books and magazines (Fisher, 1991, p. 682).

The cultural revolution manifested the beginnings of Qadhafi's political philosophy that was to emerge in clearer form in the next few years. The political philosophy, in turn, would set the tone of the Libyan press for years to come.

In the early 1970s, Qadhafi began to synthesize and expand his ideas of Arab unity, independence, economic egalitarianism, and cultural authenticity into what he called the "Third Universal Theory." He presented this theory in May 1973 as "an alternative to capitalist materialism and communist atheism" (Fisher, 1991, p. 682). Metz (1989, p. 209) says that this theory rejected the class exploitation of capitalism and the class warfare of communism on the belief that political systems based on both ideologies were dominated by a small elite. The Third Universal Theory sought to eliminate class differences. It embodies the Islamic principle of consultation, by which community or even national affairs would be conducted through mutual consultation in which the views of all citizens were exchanged. This principle was manifested later in Libya in the creation of people's committees and popular congresses.

By mid-1973, more than 2,000 people's committees were operating in Libya. Qadhafi urged them to challenge traditional authority and to take over and run government organs themselves. People's committees were established in such widely divergent organizations as universities, private business firms, government bureaucracies, and the broadcast media (Metz, 1989, p. 47).

The Green Book and the Press

Qadhafi relinquished his governmental duties in April 1974 to devote full time to ideological concerns and mass organization. His political and economic theories, including a codification of the Third Universal Theory, appeared in what has now become his famous work, *The Green Book.* Divided into three parts, this book details "The Solution of the Problem of Democracy," published in 1976; "The Solution of the Economic Problem," (1978); and, "The Social Basis of the Third Universal Theory" (1979).

The first part of *The Green Book* presents Qadhafi's view of the press and its relationship to "people's democracy" in a comprehensive manner. In keeping with his socialistic philosophy, Qadhafi says that the press fundamentally is a means of expression for the society and, therefore, cannot be a vehicle for individual or corporate opinion. Elaborating that view, Qadhafi says that any newspaper owned by an individual is his own and expresses only his point of view. Any claim that a newspaper represents public opinion is groundless because it actually expresses the viewpoints of the individual owner. By the same token, any publication issued by a group or organization is a means of expression for that particular group or organization. It represents its own point of view and not the viewpoint of public opinion. Logically and democratically, therefore, says Qadhafi, the press cannot be owned by either individuals, groups, or organizations (Qadhafi, 1976).

Qadhafi goes on to lay the parameters of a "democratic" press. Such a press is issued by a popular committee based on Islamic principles and comprising all the various categories of society. "In this case only, and not otherwise, will the press or any information medium be an expression of the whole society and a bearer of the viewpoint of its categories, and thereby the press or information medium will indeed be democratic." To Qadhafi, a newspaper issued by a popular committee representing various interests would be devoid of the "selfish interests" of a capitalist newspaper, and ideological and atheist constraints of a communist newspaper.

MOROCCO AND WESTERN SAHARA

The Kingdom of Morocco, as the country is known, is located in the northwest corner of Africa. Its population in 1994 was estimated at approximately 28.5 million, including 214,000 people living in the territory of Western Sahara, claimed and controlled by Morocco. It is a developing country with a literacy rate of 51 percent and a per capita income of $2,500 in 1993, according to U.S. government estimates.

Morocco's centralized, multiparty system of government, with strong powers vested in the king, allows the press to operate at about the middle of "controlled"–"free press" continuum, with frequent shifts toward the "controlled" end. A brief description of the country's political structure is necessary to put the press situation in a proper perspective.

Morocco is a constitutional monarchy, with a hereditary king as head of state. Legislative power is vested in the unicameral Chamber of Representatives, with 333 members who are elected for six years. Of the total membership, 222 are directly elected on the basis of universal adult suffrage. The remaining 111 are elected by indirect vote through an electoral college representing the town councils, the regional assemblies, the chambers of commerce, industry and agriculture, and trade unions. The king, as sovereign head of state, appoints the prime minister and other ministers, has the right to dissolve Parliament and approves legislation. Traditionally, about 15 political parties have actively participated in national elections.

In the first general election held after the 1972 constitution, supporters of King Hassan's policies won a majority of seats in the Chamber. A number of other seats were won by pro-monarchist Independents. In the second general election, held in September 1984, the center-right parties supporting the king and the monarchy again dominated the Chamber of Representatives, but a socialist party, USFP, did make strong gains with 36 seats. The USFP's gains were attributed to protests earlier in 1984 by people concerned about rumors of imminent increases in food prices and education fees. The next legislative elections, due in 1990, were held in June 1993 and were hailed by opposition parties as the most equitable since independence, with USFP winning 56 seats. Of the 222 directly contested seats, opposition parties, calling themselves Bloc Democratique, won 99 seats. The indirect election of the remaining 111 members of the Chamber of Representatives was less favorable to the opposition parties.

In addition to the relatively open political system, Morocco's constitution provides for "[f]reedom of movement, opinion and speech and the right of assembly." These freedoms, however, are tempered by the fact that the constitution establishes the preeminence of the monarchy and leaves wide-ranging discretionary powers for the king, such as the right to dissolve the Chamber of Representatives "by decree" (*Europa Yearbook,* 1991, p. 1855). There are a number of prohibited topics including criticism of the king, the monarchical political system, Islam, and state policy on Western Sahara, a disputed territory under Moroccan control. According to Article 23 of the constitution, the person of the king is "inviolable and sacred." Article 28 says that the king's speeches to Parliament and to the nation cannot be judged or debated. The constitution provides for an independent judiciary. Judges, however, are appointed on the recommendation of a body known as the Supreme Council of the Judiciary which is presided over by the king.

A government-enacted press code has regulated the country's press since 1958. Its major provisions are as follows: (1) Monarchical power must not be criticized; (2) No newspaper or periodical may begin publication without first informing the judicial authorities; (3) Two copies of each issue of a publication must be sent to the prosecutor's office and the information service of the Ministry of the Interior prior to distribution; and (4) There are severe penalties for publication of news held to be false, or for articles considered offensive to the king and the royal family (*Code de la Presse au Moroc,* 1992).

Newspapers are private or party, and quite diverse. Government guidance of the press is common, and backed up with confiscation of particular issues and the closing of publications. Broadcasting is both publicly and privately owned, but it is under strong government control. In recent years, it has been opened to political parties for campaign statements. In the territory of Western Sahara, which Morocco claims and controls, the media are extensions of the Moroccan media and reflect their philosophy.

THE SUDAN

The largest country in Africa, the Sudan's population in 1994 was estimated at 29.4 million. Unlike North African Arab countries, the Sudan has a highly heterogeneous population. Approximately 70 percent of the population is Arab-Islamic and occupies the northern two-thirds of the country, while the predominantly black south is both Christian and animist. The Sudan's 597 tribes speak more than 400 languages. Arabic, the official language of the country, is spoken by 51 percent of the population. English has been designated the "principal" language in the Southern region. The World Bank estimated that the population had a literacy rate of 27 percent in 1990. The U.S. government estimated that per capita income for the Sudan in 1994 was $700.

Although the Sudan has had a turbulent political history since its independence in 1956, with several military coups until the latest in 1989, the country enjoyed a good measure of press freedom during the civilian parliamentary rule from May 1986 until June 1989. Following the multiparty general election in April 1986, the press flourished within the framework of constitutional freedoms. There were at least 40 privately owned newspapers and periodicals, often engaging in criticism of governmental policies. As in earlier coups, the press lost its freedom once again on June 30, 1989, when Brig. Gen. Omar Hassan Ahmad al-Bashir overthrew the civilian government. In announcements following the coup, the new leadership declared the suspension of the constitution, the dissolution of Parliament and all political institutions, and the banning of all newspapers except the army newspaper (Bechtold, 1990, p. 584; *Keesing's Record of World Events,* June 1989, p. 36728). The military regime has since published two government dailies also. Broadcasting has been state controlled since independence.

Apart from the brief periods of democratic governments in the Sudan, the country has lived under authoritarian regimes for most of the years since independence. Calls for a multiparty political system continue to be crushed, as indicated by the arrest of Sayed Ahmed al-Hussein, the deputy general secretary of the banned opposition Democratic Unionist Party (DUP), on November 17,

1993. Al-Hussein had persistently campaigned for a peaceful solution to the civil war in southern Sudan and for a multiparty system.

The persisting media philosophy, therefore, has been in keeping with the predominantly authoritarian political rule in the country since its independence in 1956. Civilian and military governments alternated in quick succession until 1969. In May 1969 power was seized by a group of officers led by Col. Jaafar Mohammed Numayri. All existing political institutions and organizations were abolished. A "Democratic Republic of the Sudan" was proclaimed, with supreme authority in the hands of the Revolutionary Command Council (RCC).

Before the 1969 coup, private ownership of the press was allowed, but it was strictly controlled under the military regime of Gen. Ibrahim Abboud. The character of the Sudanese press that is seen to this day was shaped during the 16-year military regime of Colonel Numayri that lasted from 1969 to 1985. Claiming that the privately owned Sudanese press was propagating foreign ideologies and distorting government statements, the Numayri regime issued a decree in August 1970 to nationalize the press and news agencies. Before nationalization, five domestic news agencies were operating in the country.

Explaining the press philosophy under Numayri, Nasser (1982, p. 188) said that the Sudanese government, as those of several other Arab states, had assigned a "mobilization" role to the mass media. The political regime, he said, gave guidance to mass media on government goals and on news presentation and interpretation. The press was structured and centralized in support of socialist programs and "the newspapers faithfully reflect the party line of the regime or the ideas of the ruling elites." Arguing that newspapers had given "arbitrary" interpretations of the goals of the revolution, Numayri wanted to run the nationalized press "in harmony with the general political plan of the Sudanese Socialist Union." To make sure that journalists would support the government's media philosophy, they could not be employed unless they had formal journalism training, talent, and membership in the Sudanese Socialist Union (Wilcox, 1982, p. 220). The Sudanese government's view of the press is that the information media play an important role in the national, political, economic, and social revolution and, therefore, should be used actively to clarify and accomplish its goals.

TUNISIA

Located at the northernmost tip of Africa, Tunisia is an Islamic country. The U.S. government estimated that the country's population of 8.7 million persons had a per capita income in 1993 of $4,000. According to UNESCO data, the country had a 65.3 percent literacy rate in 1990. Since independence, Tunisia has been a nonaligned nation, maintaining good relations with Arab countries, the West, and what was known as the Eastern bloc.

After experiencing more than three decades of strong governmental controls, the Tunisian press saw a considerable improvement in the political climate of the country, beginning in 1987, to enable it to function quite openly. Soon after becoming president in November 1987, General Zine El-Abidine Ben Ali promised a new era of democracy, freedom of the press, trade unions, and political parties in Tunisia. A number of constitutional reforms were adopted by 1988, leading to the pardoning of thousands of political prisoners and restoration of civil rights. These reforms have enabled the press to exercise its constitutional right of press freedom, although within the framework of a relatively strong press code established by the government. The factors that have influenced the country's media philosophy are traced here briefly.

The Tunisian press philosophy has been shaped by a political system that has had a strong party system, but operated essentially under one-man rule since independence. The private, party, and government press has been under government pressure, which began in the early days of the independence movement. Under the leadership of Habib Bourguiba of the Neo-Destour Party, who spearheaded the independence drive, journalism was viewed as an important vehicle to promote the independence cause. *L'Action Tunisienne,* a newspaper he founded in 1932, served in that role, and in years just prior to independence in 1956 the newspaper *Mission* became Bourguiba's ideological mouthpiece.

Following Tunisia's independence, Bourguiba served as the country's president for over three decades and exerted a strong influence on the political system. Having been a journalist himself during the independence movement, he saw the press as an important instrument to accomplish his political objectives. His Neo-Destour Party, therefore, continued to publish newspapers. A constitution adopted by the party in 1959 granted considerable civil rights, including freedom of the press, but it allowed the president and government to limit them without recourse to the courts and the National Assembly. The constitution also gave the president the right to rule by decree during legislative adjournments.

The Neo-Destour Party was renamed the Destourian Socialist Party (Parti Socialiste Destourien—PSD) in 1964, with a moderately left-wing tendency. The political system under Bourguiba, until he was deposed in 1987, was one of personalized authoritarianism, with the PSD acting as a ruling organ of government. Bourguiba was able to neutralize challenges to his political authority while the PSD dominated elections by a campaign of harassing opposing political parties (Defense & Diplomacy, 1989). Even after the one-party system was ended in 1981, the PSD devised a system whereby only licensed parties could contest elections, and those parties had to receive at least 5 percent of the vote before they could hold a National Assembly seat. As a result, the PSD thwarted political challenge and built a one-party state.

As a result of the authoritarian political system, the media during most of the Bourguiba years were subject to pervasive party influence and increasingly repressive government influence (Banks, 1991, p. 684). Ever since Tunisia's independence, the PSD has been involved in publishing party organs, *L'Action* in French and *Al-Amal* in Arabic. There was not much of opposition press in the country between 1956 and 1987.

Bourguiba was deposed on November 7, 1987, by his prime minister, Gen. Zine al-Abidine Ben Ali. Soon after taking power, Ben Ali, who was sworn in as president, promised a new era of democracy, freedom of the press, trade unions, and political parties. One of Ben Ali's first acts as president was to permit the publication of opposition newspapers that had been suspended under Bourguiba.

The ruling party's name was changed in early 1988 to Democratic Constitutional Assembly (Rassemblement Constitutionnel Democratique—RCD) to reflect the new administration's commitment to democratic reform. In July 1988, Ben Ali repeated his commitment to freedom of expression. A legislation concerning the press was amended to allow newspapers the opportunity to prove the truth of allegedly defamatory articles, except articles about the president and members of the government, to escape conviction for libel. Seizure and suspension of newspapers, allowed under the 1975 press code, was to be controlled by the judiciary, and no longer by the Ministry of the Interior, under the revised Article 73 (*Code de la Presse,* 1988). By November 1988, two opposition papers were being published regularly without governmental interference, and press freedom had been guaranteed in a national pact between the government and leading political and trade organizations.

In late 1989, Ben Ali publicly opposed the concept of a religious political party, and the government subsequently refused an application by a fundamentalist Islamic political party, Hizb al-Nahda, for legal recognition. This resulted in clashes between police and students at several universities, which the government attributed to Islamic fundamentalists. Al-Nahda and three recognized opposition parties rejected a subsequent offer by Ben Ali to discuss electoral reforms and refused to participate in municipal elections in June 1990 on the grounds that they were neither free nor fair. The government retaliated by suspending the al-Nahda newspaper, *al-Fajr,* following the publication of an article by the movement's exiled leader, which strongly criticized the Tunisian government (*Europa Yearbook,* 1991, p. 2614). In early 1990, the Communist Workers' Party, another unrecognized group, was allowed to publish its weekly newspaper, *al-Badil,* but it was also suspended within a year for government criticism (*Tunisia and Human Rights,* 1992).

Clearly, under President Ben Ali opposition parties and their press organs have been allowed, resulting in the emergence of a diverse press even though the government keeps a close watch over the opposition press. That is a major improvement in the country's press situation from the Bourguiba years, when the opposition and its press were heavily suppressed and the government used media as instruments of political indoctrination. Press under Ben Ali is relatively free, but his ruling RCD newspapers continue to play a very influential role in the country, and broadcasting remains an instrument of promoting the government's viewpoint. The national news agency is government owned and the Tunisian press code protects the president and other government functionaries from criticism.

In spite of the advantageous position of the government-run media, Tunisia, as Morocco, has a more diverse and free press than seen in most Arab and African countries. These two countries can certainly claim to have a more vigorous press as compared with the press of Algeria, Libya, and the Sudan.

REFERENCES

Article 19. (1991). World Report. *Information, freedom and censorship* London: Library Association Publishing.

Banks, A. (1991). *Political handbook of the world.* Binghamton, NY: CSA Publications.

Bechtold, P. K. (1990). More turbulence in Sudan: A new politics this time? *The Middle East Journal, 44* (4).

Code de la Presse. (1988). Republique Tunisienne. Tunis: Ministere de l'Information.

Code de la Presse au Maroc. (1992). Rabat: Ministry of Information.

Defense & Diplomacy. (1989). *Special Report: The Republic of Tunisia.*

The Europa World Yearbook. (1991). London: Europa Publications.

The Europa World Yearbook. (1992). London: Europa Publications.

First, R. (1974). *Libya: The elusive revolution.* New York: Africana Publishing Co.

Fisher, W. B. (1991). Libya. In *The Middle East and North Africa 1992.* London: Europa Publications.

Gastil, R. D. (1981). *Freedom in the world: Political rights and civil liberties.* Westport, CT: Greenwood Press.

Harris, L. C. (1986). *Libya: Qadhafi's revolution and the modern state.* Boulder, CO: Westview Press.

Keesing's record of world events. (June 1989). The Sudan, vol. 35, no. 6. New York: Longman.

Kurian, G. (1982). *World press encyclopedia.* New York: Facts on File.

Merrill, J. C., Bryan, C. R. & Alisky, M. (1975). Libya. In *The foreign press.* Baton Rouge, LA: Louisiana State University Press.

Metz, H. C. (1989). *Libya: A country study.* Washington, DC: U.S. Government Printing Office.

Nasser, M. K. (1982). The Middle East press: Tool of politics. In J. L. Curry and J. R. Dassin (Eds.), *Press control around the world.* New York: Praeger Publishers.

Nelson, H. D. (1986). *Algeria: A country study.* Washington, DC: U.S. Government Printing Office.

Qadhafi, M. al. (1976). *The green book, part I: The solution of the problem of democracy.* London: Martin Brian and O'Keeffe.

Tunisia and human rights. (1992). Tunis: Tunisian External Communication Agency.

Wilcox, D. L. (1982). Black African states. In J. L. Curry & J. R. Dassin (Eds.), *Press control around the world.* New York: Praeger.

The World Factbook. (1994). Washington, DC: The Central Intelligence Agency.

6 Mass Media Development and Government Relations

ALGERIA

During Algeria's war of independence from France, the pro-independence press had developed an aggressive spirit even though the French authorities banned the publication and distribution of all such publications. The French-owned publications supporting continued French rule of Algeria were not affected by this ban. The pro-independence National Liberation Front (FLN) moved its official organ, *El Moudjahid,* to Tunisia in 1956, which was smuggled into Algeria and widely circulated. Other pro-independence publications, published underground or abroad, also reached the Algerian population (Kurian, 1982, p. 1063).

Immediately after independence in 1962, the country's press continued to show vigor by its candid coverage of domestic issues, although the government exercised control through intimidation and periodical threats of nationalization. Even though such threats resulted in an increasingly pro-government press on major issues, the Bella regime was not tolerant of any criticism of party and state policies. It particularly targeted French-owned publications as hostile to the independence of Algeria.

For much of the postindependence history of Algeria, elections at both local and national levels were managed by the Bella regime's National Liberation Front (FLN), which allowed little opposition to the system. The governmental style was patterned after that of the Marxist states, with the FLN Congress as the highest party organ, which convened every five years and to which a central committee was responsible. The FLN monopoly over the political system continued until 1989, when opposition parties were allowed to be formed.

In June 1990, Algerians took part in the first free elections since independence for municipal and provincial governments. To the surprise of many observers, an Islamic fundamentalist political party, Islamic Salvation Front (Front Islamique du Salut—FIS), obtained 53 percent of the popular vote and a majority of the 15,000 seats being contested. The ruling FLN came second.

In April 1991, President Chadli announced that Algeria's first multiparty national election would take place on June 27. A new electoral bill submitted to the National People's Assembly increased the number of seats in the assembly from 295 to 542. Mortimer (1992, p. 113) says that the bill was designed to create a disproportionate number of districts in the sparsely populated southern regions, the only part of the country in which the FLN had prevailed in the local elections of June 1990. Since the assembly was controlled completely by the FLN, the bill passed easily.

The FIS vehemently denounced this maneuver. In May 1991, the FIS organized an indefinite general strike and held large demonstrations, demanding the resignation of President Chadli and abrogation of the new electoral law. Violent confrontations in June between Islamic fundamentalists and the security forces resulted in the deaths of about 50 demonstrators and members of the riot police (*Europa World Yearbook,* 1992, p. 320). In response, President Chadli declared a state of emergency and postponed the general election scheduled for June 27.

A new prime minister, Sid Ahmed Ghozali, pledged to organize "free and clean" elections sometime in 1991. Despite Ghozali's pledge, the climate of agitation persisted. As further clashes occurred, Islamic firebrand Ali Belhadj urged his followers to stock weapons for the defense of Islamic values. In late June, the army surrounded the FIS headquarters and arrested party leaders and some 750 other party activists (Mortimer, 1992, p 113).

Ghozali pushed for a revision of the electoral law and after much debate the National Assembly defined 430 constituencies. A multiparty, two-round general election was scheduled to take place on December 26, 1991, and January 16, 1992. In the 231 seats contested in the first round, the FIS won a decisive victory with 188 seats. The Socialist Forces Front won 25 seats and the ruling FLN only 15 seats (*The Statesman's Yearbook,* 1992–93, p. 77).

Just as it appeared that the FIS would easily win a parliamentary majority following the second round, the army moved in. President Chadli was forced to resign on January 11 and his functions were assumed by the five-member High State Council, composed of army generals (*The Economist,* January 18, 1992, p. 34). Claiming that national security and public order would be threatened if the Islamic fundamentalists gained power, the generals canceled the second round of elections.

Riots and shootings broke out in early February in several cities, including the capital Algiers, in support of the FIS. On February 9, the government imposed a state of emergency and in early March the FIS was dissolved by a court order. The Algerian democratic experiment thus came to an end (*The Economist,* February 15, 1992, p. 37). With the imposition of martial law, what little gains the press had made in its freedom were suspended. Strict rules were imposed on the press under an antiterrorism law issued in September 1992 that barred the press from publishing statements from underground groups that could be deemed subversive. In early 1993, the military regime imposed censorship on press reports on security matters, presumably anything that discussed the activities of the Muslim extremists. The censorship announcement followed the suspension a day earlier of the independent daily *El Watan,* for "prematurely" writing about the killing of five policemen, apparently by Muslim extremists. A government spokesman said that information concerning all aspects of security would be subject to an "embargo" and could be published only after being cleared by the government (*The Straits Times,* January 7, 1993).

The martial law, which was to have lasted for only a year, was extended indefinitely on February 9, 1993. There is little prospect, therefore, of any relaxation of government control of the press until the political situation is resolved. The status of press–government relations prior to the imposition of martial law is discussed below.

Press–Government Relations

Before the 1989 political reforms, Algerian press manifested the characteristics of a government-controlled press. It was didactic in tone and was encouraged to address the urgent goals of national integration and modernization (Faringer, 1991, p. 22). Newspapers, therefore, mostly played up officially approved material with little or no analysis or comment. Nasser (1982, p. 188) noted that the Algerian press, along with the press of Libya and the Sudan, was assigned a "mobilization" role, with the government giving the press guidance on national goals and on news presentation and interpretation. Journalists were in effect state functionaries who had the responsibility of engaging the public in the construction of socialism through the judicious selection of informational and ideological material. Consequently, the media did not dissent from the socialist system or national policy goals. Frank discussions of economic and social problems could be found, nevertheless, as well as criticisms of bureaucratic inefficiency and ineptitute (Nelson, 1986, p. 269).

The press performance improved after the 1989 constitutional reforms and manifested much vigor until martial law was imposed in early 1992. As Article 19 (World Report, 1991, p. 352) reported:

The new atmosphere of debate and criticism of government policies by the public, and journalists in particular, has encouraged editors and directors of newspapers to be less acquiescent on official directives. Many have started publishing investigative reports about the political and social situation in the country, official corruption and abuse of power, and opened their columns to the public or their own journalists to freely express their opinions.

The new journalism, however, did not escape harassment. For example, on January 31, 1989, the editor and two reporters of *Al-Joumhouria* were arrested and charged with libel after they reported the existence of large-scale corruption involving influential people close to the Chadli Benjedid family. After protests organized by a journalists' union, they were released. In August 1989, the editor in chief of the FLN-owned weekly *Revolution Africaine* was dismissed after he wrote an article criticizing the influence of Muslim groups on members of the FLN (Article 19, 1991, p. 352). Although foreign publications were allowed into the country, they did not escape harassment. The Paris weekly, *Jeune Afrique,* was frequently banned for its pro-Moroccan stand on the disputed territory of Western Sahara. Individual issues of other foreign publications were also confiscated at times, if their treatment of Algerian matters was found to be questionable by the government.

LIBYA

The Libyan leader, Col. Muammar al-Qadhafi, asserted in the first part of his *The Green Book* (1976) that since democracies of the West and elsewhere were ridden by special rather than popular interests, their press systems were correspondingly not free. So, to Qadhafi, the "problem" of press freedom in the West was directly linked to the "problem" of democracy. Press freedom would be possible only when a truly democratic system was implemented, he said.

Qadhafi set about to do just that in 1977, the year after he completed "The Solution of the Problem of Democracy." In March of that year, a new form of direct democracy, the Jamahiriya (state of the masses), was promulgated and the official name of the country was changed to Socialist People's Libyan Arab Jamahiriya. Under this system, every adult is supposed to be able to share in policy making through the Basic People's Congresses of which there are some 2,000 throughout Libya. These congresses appoint Popular Committees to execute policy. Provincial and urban affairs are handled by Popular Committees responsible to Municipality People's Congresses, of which there are 13. Officials of these congresses and committees form at national level the General People's Congress (GPC), which has replaced the Arab Socialist Union, Qadhafi's original political party (Harris, 1986, pp. 63–81; *The Stateman's Yearbook,* 1992–93, pp. 892–893).

The GPC, which meets for about a week early each year, is the highest policy-making body in the country. The GPC, however, has delegated most of its important authority to its general secretary and the General Secretariat and to the General People's Committee. The Revolutionary Command Council, which under Qadhafi's leadership had seized power in a bloodless coup on September 1, 1969, was abolished in 1977 and its five surviving members became the General Secretariat, with Qadhafi as the Leader of the Revolution. Members of the General People's Committee, the equivalents of ministers under other forms of government, head the 21 government secretariats that execute policy at national level. The Secretariat of Information, Culture and Revolutionary Guidance is in charge of the press (Metz, 1989, pp. 178–195; Fisher, 1991, p. 703).

The "revolutionary" guidance of the media was typified by the media's treatment of the country's police force in 1983. The official Libyan press targeted the police as lacking revolutionary zeal. The press demanded greater direct responsibility for the masses in protecting the people's security. Articles recalled that the police were descended from the mobile forces of the Idris regime, headed by "fascist, bourgeois officers" who had suppressed all manifestations of discontent with the royalist system. Police officials were accused of engaging in licentious behavior, of drinking liquor, and of carrying on illegal businesses. They were charged with being "feudalistic in their behavior, of being ill-educated because many lacked a high school diploma, and often unfit for duty because of advancing age" (Metz, 1989, p. 285). The official press also carried a large number of stories in the mid-1980s on cases of smuggling, illegal deposit of money abroad, bribery, and misappropriation of funds by public officials (Metz, 1989, p. 286). In another media campaign, Qadhafi successfully used the official press to push for the adoption of several proposals rejected by the GPC in 1984. The proposals included compulsory universal military training, a measure aimed at inducting females into the service in greater numbers, and reduction in the number of municipalities to the number of military districts, apparently in an effort to reduce local autonomy (Harris, 1986, p. 67).

In an interview with Italian journalist Oriana Fallaci in 1979, Qadhafi demonstrated the extent to which he believes himself as a conduit for divine truth, claiming that *"The Green Book* is the guide to the emancipation of man. *The Green Book* is the gospel. The new gospel. The gospel of the new era, the era of the masses. In your gospels it's written: 'In the beginning there was the word.' *The Green Book* is the word. One of its words can destroy the world. Or save it. The Third World only needs my *Green Book*. My word." (Harris, 1986, p. 50).

Political analysts claim that Qadhafi has used the so-called "democratic" system and the "revolutionary" press to consolidate his dictatorial authority. Metz (1989, p. 190) says that Qadhafi's practical political decision making has contradicted his political theories. For ideological reasons, he genuinely wanted the masses to evolve into a self-governing polity. For pragmatic reasons, however, he vetoed popular policies with which he disagreed, using the rationale that he was protecting the people from "opportunists" and "counter-revolutionaries." Harris (1986, p. 58) has also noted that Qadhafi's belief that he personally knows the "truth" has made it very difficult to encourage popular participation in the government. Harris says that although political authority theoretically rests with the masses, political activism is illegal except in support of government policies. The U.S. State Department Human Rights Report for 1985 concluded that there were several thousand political prisoners in Libya. Televised accounts of trials of Libyan dissidents occasionally revealed the telltale marks of injury on the hands and faces of defendants (Harris, 1986, p. 69). Roumani (1983, p. 166) says that Qadhafi's ideology, although based on the Islamic principles, is closer to Marxist ideals.

In its annual surveys of civil liberties around the world, the U.S.-based Freedom House has classified Libya as a "military dictatorship" under the control of one person since the 1969 coup. The Freedom House says that although there is no political party in Libya, the effort to mobilize and organize the entire population for state purposes follows the socialist one-party model. Libyan media are government-controlled means of active indoctrination (Gastil, 1991).

Metz (1989, pp. 189–190) says that on November 3, 1986, *Az Zahf al Akhdar* (The Green March), the mouthpiece of the revolutionary committees, carried a long article, probably written by Qadhafi, which, surprisingly, argued the urgent need to form a new political party. In an astonishing assertion, the article indicated that such a new political party would replace the people's congresses. According to the article, the people's congresses should be "crushed" because of the "exploitation, stealing, monopoly, haughtiness, domination, favoritism, tribalism, reactionism and corruption" among the masses, which they represented. The statement was apparently motivated by recognition of the need to purge the GPC and the people's congresses of elements that voiced opposition to some of Qadhafi's policies. However, no new party had been formed as of the time of this writing.

Press–Government Relations

Reporting in the media is largely confined to the activities of officials and state bodies. Foreign journalists are seldom allowed to enter Libya other than when doing so serves some government purpose. For example, journalists were flown in from all over the world in early February 1992 to witness what they understood would be the court examination of two Libyans named by Britain and the United States as responsible for blowing up the Pan Am airliner over Lockerbie, Scotland, in December 1988. The journalists heard instead a prepared statement from the judge that the West had failed to hand over vital evidence and, therefore, sufficient information did not exist to build a case against the two men. Both Britain and the United States rejected the Libyan claim and emphasized that Libya was given sufficient evidence to establish the guilt of the two men (*The Economist,* February 22, 1992, p. 43).

On rare occasions when foreign reporters are allowed into the country, their movements are strictly circumscribed. Libyan reporters are often hired more out of their fervor for the "revolution" than for their journalistic training or skills and routinely rely on government handouts for news. News story ideas and ideas for media "campaigns," such as the ones mentioned earlier, frequently originate at the Secretariat of Information, Culture and Revolutionary Guidance.

Even though all publishing is done by government bodies, publishers are still very careful in remaining within the press philosophy prescribed by Qadhafi in *The Green Book.* Qadhafi's view that individuals or group publications should represent their views, as opposed to speaking on behalf of the public at large, is followed scrupulously. Underwood (1982, p. 1083) says that trade union publications, for example, deal only with issues of concern to their members, such as working or living conditions. "They never comment on national or international events and, of course, never criticize any government rules or decisions." The same publishing philosophy is observed by publications for other interest groups.

Underwood says that a number of other official guidelines, which amount to "censorship rules," have shaped the press since 1980. They stipulate that (a) only literature of the 1969 revolution is to be published; (b) priority is to be given to the political thought of the revolution; (c) young writers who truly express the ideology of the revolution are to be encouraged; (d) no private writing or expression of personal feeling is to be published unless it agrees with the revolution's thought; (e) nothing from earlier Libyan writers is to be published that does not serve the revolution's interest; (f) symbolic or nonfactual writing, or any light work of written art is not to be published; (g) writers are not to be paid for their intellectual work, in order to discover which are true revolutionaries and which are writing only for money; (h) a committee selected by the country's writers' union must evaluate any literary or artistic work before it can be published.

Opposition Media

Exiled Libyan opposition has been active in media campaigns against the Qadhafi regime for several years. The National Front for the Salvation of Libya (NFSL) is the best known of the various opposition groups. Founded in 1981, it is led by Muhammad Yusuf al-Maqaryaf, an economist who left the Libyan government while serving as ambassador to India in 1980. The NFSL publishes a number of magazines and newsletters including the glossy *Al-Inqadh* (Salvation). Antigovernment radio stations have broadcast to Libya at various times, notably Sawt ash-Sha'b al-Libi (Voice of the Libyan People), which is supported by the NFSL and has broadcast from the Sudan, Iraq, and most recently Chad. The NFSL was based in the Sudan until the fall of the Numayri regime in 1985, after which its operations were dispersed (Anderson, 1986, p. 232). The NFSL, which rejects military and dictatorial rule, is pushing for a democratic government with constitutional guarantees, free elections, free press, and separation of powers among the executive, legislative, and judicial branches (Metz, 1989, p. 203).

MOROCCO AND WESTERN SAHARA

From 1912 to 1956, Morocco was divided into a French protectorate and a Spanish protectorate, with the seaport of Tangier becoming an international zone. Under pressure by Moroccan nationalists, the French and Spanish relinquished their protectorates and the country became independent in 1956. The international status of Tangier was abolished the same year.

Morocco also claims and administers the territory of Western Sahara, which has been a cause for ongoing confrontation between Morocco and the pro-independence Polisario Front. Known earlier as the Spanish Sahara, Spain partitioned the territory between Morocco and neighboring Mauritania in April 1976, with Morocco acquiring the northern two-thirds. Under pressure from Polisario guerrillas, Mauritania abandoned all claims to its portion in August 1979. Morocco moved to occupy that sector shortly thereafter and has since asserted administrative control over the entire Western Sahara. In February 1976, the Polisario Front formally proclaimed a government in exile of the Sahrawi Arab Democratic Republic (SDAR). This government in exile was seated as a member of the Organization for African Unity in 1984.

To end the guerrilla war that has pitted Morocco against the Polisario Front since 1975, all parties to the conflict have agreed since 1981 to the need for a referendum on the territory's future but disagreements on the procedures have not resulted in one. Morocco's King Hassan II finally agreed to a U.N.-sponsored plan for a referendum that was to have taken place in February 1992. The parties, however, disagreed once again on who should vote in the referendum and the planned February vote was canceled (*The Economist,* January 4, 1992, p. 32).

Since Western Sahara continues to be under Morocco's control, this chapter will combine a review of the mass media in both Morocco and Western Sahara. It should be noted here, however, that what little media are available in Western Sahara are extensions of the Moroccan media.

Although the nationalist Moroccan press faced severe censorship restrictions prior to the country's independence, such publications continued to appear to push the independence cause. More notable in that category were *Al Alam* of the Istiqlal Party, which provided most of the nation's leadership before independence, and *Al Ray al-Amm* of the Democratic Independence Party. Both newspapers were heavily censored and often suspended before being suppressed in 1952 in the wake of pro-independence riots in Casablanca. The French-language press under the French protectorate, however, was not subject to such a strong treatment by the authorities. The more prominent of such publications were *Le Petit Marocain, La Vigie Marocaine, Le Courrier du Maroc,* and *Echo du Moroc.*

The tradition of party affiliation of newspapers, established by the nationalists in preindependence years, has continued in the postindependence period and remains strong today. With the split of the Istiqlal Party into factions in 1959, for example, politically sponsored newspapers proliferated. Kurian (1982, p. 641) says that the conservative, loyalist Popular Movement and the Party of Independent Liberals were each represented by three journals. The Moroccan Communist Party published three newspapers until the party was banned in 1959. Government began to publish newspapers also. The Ministry of Information, in cooperation with the royalist Front for the Defense of Constitutional Institutions, published two dailies and two weeklies.

Press Code

To curb what were seen as the excesses of the press, especially newspapers with nonmonarchist leanings or those of the Communist Party, the government enacted a press code in November 1958. The code, modified in 1960 and 1973, continues to be the main instrument for press regulation in the country. Borrowing some of its language from the constitution, the code says that all Moroccan newspapers are obliged to publish the king's speeches in full or in part without making any comment or criticism. Under the code, anyone who attacks, by any means, including writing and speech, the person of the king is subject to imprisonment from five to twenty years and/or a fine ranging from 100,000 to one million dirhams (U.S. $1 = 9.20 dirhams in early 1994).

Article 5 of the code says that no newspaper or periodical may begin publication without first informing the judicial authorities. Article 8 says that two copies of each issue must be sent to the prosecutor's office and the information service of the Ministry of the Interior prior to distribution. The Minister of the Interior may order the seizure of any newspaper or periodical which may pose a threat to public order, according to Article 77 of the code. This Article also allows the prime minister to prohibit a publication if it "has threatened the institutional, political or religious basis of the Kingdom."

The amendments of 1973 introduced additional provisions authorizing severe penalties for publication of news held to be false, or for articles considered offensive to the king and the royal family. Under Article 41, the penalties include five to twenty years of hard labor and a fine of between 100,000 and one million dirhams (*Code de la Presse au Maroc,* 1992).

Press–Government Relations

Kurian (1982, p. 643) noted that within the bounds of the press laws, the Moroccan press enjoyed a substantial degree of press freedom "to criticize the powers that be, with the sole exception of the King." He added, however, that the press's ongoing struggle to debate national issues in the open and the government's efforts to contain the vehemence of such debate had produced a virtual tug-of-war between the two.

By 1980 the national press included 10 daily newspapers of widely differing political orientations. The outspoken nature of some publications led to frequent government crackdowns. For example, *al-Mouharir,* a publication of the Socialist Union of Popular Forces (USFP), was suspended in the wake of the June 1981 riots in Casablanca. The newspaper was accused of aiding the party in its "antigovernment" activities. Known as the voice of the radical opposition, this paper was frequently critical of the government's economic and foreign policies (Kurian, 1982, p. 642).

Also in June 1981, the government suspended *al-Bayane,* an organ of the Party of Progress and Socialism (PPS) for allegedly reporting the June 1981 riots in an inflammatory manner. Formed in 1968 to replace the banned Moroccan Communist Party, the PPS obtained legal status in 1974 and had severely criticized economic liberalization moves in the country. Publication of *al-Bayane* resumed in mid-July 1981. A number of its issues were confiscated in early 1984 because of its reporting of further Casablanca disturbances. The newspaper was suspended again from October 1986 until January 1987 (Banks, 1991, p. 455).

In his assessment of press freedom and civil rights in Morocco in 1981, Gastil noted that the country's newspapers were quite diverse. He went on to say: "Recently there has been no formal censorship; there are other pressures, including the confiscation of particular issues. . . . In the past the use of torture has been quite common and may continue; the rule of law also has been weakened by the frequent use of prolonged detention without trial" (1981, p. 378). In 1992, Gastil's annual report on political rights and civil liberties, which takes into account freedom of speech and the press, found Morocco "partly free." This press situation can be attributed to the fact that in the Moroccan political system, monarchical authoritarianism coexists with manifest pluralism made possible by a multiparty Chamber of Representatives.

Actions against newspapers continued in the 1980s, with the government seizing an issue of *Anoual* in March 1987, apparently in response to its coverage of prison conditions. The government took a similar action against *al-Bayane* in January 1981, because of its stories on problems in the educational system and recent demonstrations at Fez University. Banks (1991, p. 455) says that the USFP's *al-Ithihad al-Ichtiraki* was also informed that it would be censored because of its coverage of the student disturbances. This paper and *al-Bayane,* two of the key Arabic-language opposition newspapers, were censored for a brief period in 1988.

Article 19 (World Report, 1991, p. 383) reported that attacks on the press and harassment of journalists had been a growing trend in Morocco. For example, *al-Massar,* an opposition weekly newspaper and organ of a radical wing of the USFP, was issued a court order in December 1988 to cease publication until its editor-owner, Ahmed Benjelloun, paid libel damages of $18,450 to a local public official. The case arose out of a letter published by the paper, which was signed by 12 people and accused the official of stealing land belonging to them. Benjelloun was also sentenced to two months' suspended term and a fine of $123.

Benjelloun found himself in a court battle again within months, when he carried an article in his new paper, *al-Tariq,* criticizing a court judgment regarding a dispute between an employee and the public administration. The court had ruled in favor of the public administration, a decision Benjelloun reported as "unjust" and "cynical." He was accused of defamation of the judicial system and was sentenced to four months in jail and a fine of $615 in June 1990.

In 1989, Mohamed Idrissi Kaitouni, publisher of the Istiqlal party newspaper *l'Opinion,* printed a joint statement by two human rights groups alleging that the authorities were responsible for the deaths of four Moroccans in detention. Kaitouni was tried and sentenced to two years in jail and fined $246 for publishing "false news likely to disturb public order." Article 19 reported that since Kaitouni had won widespread public support during the trial, he was pardoned by King Hassan II three days later.

Government actions, however, continued against other publications. A weekly, *Asrar,* was brought to court on October 10, 1989, for "defamation against a pro-government party." Another weekly, *al-Ousbue As-Sahafi,* was prosecuted on October 17, 1989, for "defamation of justice." Its publisher, Mustapha Alaoui, was sentenced to three months in jail and fined $615 on May 19, 1990. On October 15, 1990, publisher Mohamed Labrini and editor Abdelkader Himer of the daily newspaper *al-Ittihad al-Ichtoraki* were tried on charges of defaming the courts and tribunals. Their alleged offending article described the poor conditions and corruption under which courts and tribunals in Casablanca function, causing long delays in examination and judgment of cases. About 120 lawyers defended the journalists, who insisted they had no intention of defaming the judiciary and that their article was published in the public interest (Article 19, 1991, p. 383).

One of the biggest setbacks for the Moroccan press in the 1980s was the closure of two reputable magazines following government pressures. *Lamalif,* which had established its credibility as a serious public affairs magazine since 1968, was closed by the owners, Zakiya Daoud and her husband Mohamed Loghlam, after the magazine refused to toe the government line. The Ministry of the Interior was said to have been displeased with a series of articles describing the poverty-stricken state of large sectors of Moroccan society. The editor, Zakiya Daoud, was advised by the government to stop such negative writing or cease publication. The publishers refused to go along with the government's wishes and closed the magazine in June 1988. According to Article 19 (1991, p. 384), the king himself had demanded that the magazine be closed.

The other magazine that ceased publication was a French-language, independent monthly from Casablanca called *Kalima,* which was known for discussing sociocultural issues considered taboo in the country. The authorities seized the March 1989 issue because it contained articles on the Moroccan press and Moroccan writers' statements supporting the British writer Salman Rushdie. After the seizure of this issue, the owner decided to close down *Kalima* for reasons of "repetitive seizure causing a great financial loss."

Quality of Journalism

Because most of the newspapers and periodicals are affiliated with political parties, they are primarily engaged in political writing along ideological lines.

This journalistic approach is also the consequence of much of the media's heavy reliance on the government and/or political parties for financial support. Article 19 (1991, p. 383) notes that many publications are of a "poor quality." Owners hesitate to invest money to improve their papers and increase readership because of the absence of legal guarantees to protect against the financial risk, since the authorities can intervene at any time, without reason, to order suspension or closure.

In view of the constitutional right of "freedom of opinion and speech" and political diversity of Morocco, there is a considerable variety of opinion in the Moroccan press. Journalists often reflect aggressiveness in news coverage, although news writing is heavily opinionated. Western-style "watchdog" or "investigative" journalism is inhibited, however, by the constant threat of state action against such writing. For example, a reporter of *al-Ittihad al-Ichtiraki* was arrested in 1988 while taking pictures of a hotel alleged to be a brothel. He was kept in police custody for two days. In another case, a reporter with the feminist weekly, *March 8,* was arrested in 1989 while she was recording interviews with people in the streets of Rabat. Although she was released after one day in custody, her recording equipment was confiscated.

There are other factors that make it difficult to practice vigorous journalism. The government often suppresses information on diplomatic and military developments affecting the Western Sahara conflict, the impact of AIDS, and other sensitive public issues. Journalists often find government officials secretive, uncooperative, and sometimes intimidating when approached for information on controversial public issues. Interviews with Moroccan journalists indicate that public officials have a negative attitude toward the press, which may be explained, to a degree, by the fact that journalists often are not professionally trained and tend to carry out their journalistic responsibilities from an ideological, rather than an objective, perspective.

THE SUDAN

The Sudan was governed as an Anglo-Egyptian condominium from 1898 until 1953, when it was allowed self-government. The country became fully independent on January 1, 1956, under a transitional constitution that provided for a democratic government. There was not much of native Sudanese press during most of the colonial years. The first such publication, *Hadarat al Sudan,* appeared in 1919 and was devoted to cultural and literary matters. The country's first daily newspaper, *al-Nil,* began publication in 1935, followed by a second daily four years later called *Sawt al-Sudan.* A 1930 press ordinance, which gave the authorities the right to license printing presses, kept the newspapers in check.

The press flourished during the two brief civilian governments after the Sudan's independence in 1956. The first democratic government was led by Prime Minister Ismail al-Azhari of the National Unionist Party until July 1956 and was followed by another under his Umma Party rival, Abdallah Khalil, until

November 1958. Kurian (1982, p. 1099) says that in 1956, the Sudan had 16 intensely partisan newspapers, including six dailies. The National Unionist Party was supported by two dailies and the Umma Party by one. By the end of the Khalil government in 1958, there were seven dailies, four semiweeklies, 15 weeklies, and 15 other publications.

Frustrations over political maneuverings and economic problems led Prime Minister Khalil to voluntarily transfer power to armed forces chief of staff, Gen. Ibrahim Abbud, until, as he put in his broadcast on the state-owned Radio Omdurman, "the mess could be straightened out" (Bechtold, 1990, p. 582). During the military rule under General Abbud, which lasted until October 1964, political parties were outlawed and all party newspapers were effectively suppressed. Bechtold says that although the Sudan acquired both political and economic stability during the approximately six years of the Abbud regime, except for a lingering rebellion in the south, civilian opposition to the military regime was increasing. Following an unarmed civilian uprising, the Abbud government resigned on October 21, 1964.

After a transitional period of six months, general elections were held in May 1965, in areas unaffected by the insurgency in the south, and parliamentary rule returned. The open political situation allowed the press to revive the spirit it manifested in the pre-Abbud period. Several new newspapers and periodicals were established. By 1968, there were 13 daily newspapers and 15 periodicals in the country. Except for four in English and one in Greek, all publications were in Arabic (Kurian, 1982, p. 1099).

Meanwhile, rebellion in the south had escalated into civil war, pitting much of the south against the north-dominated government in Khartoum. In addition, the economic situation was deteriorating. In May 1969, power was seized by a group of officers, led by Col. Jaafar Mohammed Numayri. All existing political institutions and organizations were abolished and a "Democratic Republic of the Sudan" was proclaimed under the supreme authority of a Revolutionary Command Council (RCC).

Press Nationalization

The Sudanese press entered its most restrictive period as a result of the 1969 military coup, a situation that lasted for 16 years. The RCC moved quickly to establish its control over the press. It nationalized the country's press and five operating news agencies in August 1970. Mahgoub Osman, who belonged to an opposition political party, told *The Democratic Journalist* (1987, p. 24) that the Numayri regime had nationalized the press because of "its rejection of any opinion opposed to its own." He also said that the Sudanese press was united in its opposition to that decree.

Following press nationalization in 1970, the Sudanese Press Corporation was set up by the government to direct operation of the country's print media. Kurian (1982, p. 1099) says that although the corporation was originally intended as a short-term arrangement to coordinate and integrate rather than directly control press operations, in the course of time it became a controlling authority. According to Wilcox (1982, p. 220), the corporation also registered and certified all journalists for employment. Certification of journalists, he noted, was "dependent upon an ideological framework considered appropriate to the goals of national and social development."

The corporation assigned the task of publishing most of the country's newspapers and periodicals to two publishing houses: El-Ayam and El-Sahafa (*The Europa World Yearbook*, 1984, p. 2451). In October 1971, a referendum confirmed General Numayri's nomination as president. The RCC was dissolved and the Sudanese Socialist Union (SSU) was recognized as the only political party. Under the one-party system, all publications except those of the government were suspended, resulting in a reduction of newspapers from 13 in 1968 to two belonging to the Sudanese Socialist Union. A few periodicals that remained were published by various ministries of the government and the armed forces (*Europa Yearbook*, 1984, p. 2451).

In his survey of political rights and civil liberties around the world, Gastil (1981, p. 400) noted that in the Sudan "the media have been used for active indoctrination." Osman (*The Democratic Journalist*, 1987, p. 24) says that the "period from 1970 to 1985 was the darkest in the history of the Sudanese press." He noted that during the 16 years of the Numayri regime, the press was used as "an instrument of the regime to justify its mispractices" rather than serving as an agent of social change. The technical aspects of the press did make improvements during this period, according to Osman.

Numayri, who had survived as many as 24 coup plots and actual attempts during his 16 years in power, was ousted in a coup on April 6, 1985, as he was returning from an official visit to the United States. Following a one-year transitional period under army control, a civilian government once again returned to power after a general election in April 1986, despite continued insurgency that precluded returns in 41 southern districts (Banks, 1991, p. 639). Sadiq al-Mahdi became prime minister in a coalition government of his Umma Party and the Democratic Unionist Party.

Civilian Rule and Press Freedom

Under the al-Mahdi government, which lasted until June 1989, the press experienced a period of new freedom and development. During this period, the Sudan had a relatively free press. Privately owned press was allowed to function once again and journalists reorganized themselves in an independent union. The official newspapers of the Numayri regime, *al Ayyam* and *as Sahafa,* were suspended for a few months in 1986 while the al-Mahdi government was in the process of returning these nationalized newspapers to the private sector. More than 40 newspapers and periodicals began publication, expressing political opinions ranging from communism to Islamic fundamentalism. An Article 19 censorship report (1990, p. 135) said that the press was often severely critical of the government. "Journalists on the independent *al-Ayyam,* the communist *al-Midan* and the English-language southern-oriented *Sudan Times* were particu-larly active in investigating government corruption and human rights abuses."

The censorship report also found that the Sudanese press gave little coverage to the famine brought about by the continuing civil war in the south. Fighting in the south escalated in 1986–1987, leading to reports that both the government and the rebel Sudan People's Liberation Army (SPLA) prevented commercial and relief food from reaching the towns affected by the civil war. By 1989, 300,000 people were said to have died of famine (p. 128).

Several reasons were cited by the censorship report for the press's lack of coverage of the famine. One was the example of the authorities' treatment of a Sudanese journalist, Mike Kilongson, who frequently provided material for the British Broadcasting Corporation from a southern regional capital. Kilongson was arrested on March 14, 1986, after he filed reports contradicting government pronouncements which insisted that there were no food shortages. Kilongson said that he was taken to a military torture camp and told that he should have reported an abundance of food in the Equatoria region. He was detained for two months (p. 129). The censorship report also claimed that mainstream newspapers in the capital Khartoum considered the war and famine embarrassing irritations. "For example, the arrival of the train from Aweil in Khartoum, carrying its starving passengers, was not reported in a single Arabic newspaper," the report said. The government also restricted news about the war and made it difficult for reporters to obtain travel permits to famine areas (p. 135). Such restrictions applied to the international press also (pp. 133–134).

Bechtold (1990, p. 583) says that the 50 months of the civilian rule that began with the al-Mahdi government were characterized by a series of coalition governments, political stagnation, economic decline, and a further deterioration of the security situation in the face of rebellion. Parliamentary democracy was terminated for a third time by the coup of June 30, 1989. Soon after the coup, Lt. Gen. Omar Hassan Ahmad al-Bashir, the head of the new military government, announced the formation of a military council with wide legislative and executive powers. Called the Revolutionary Command Council for National Salvation (RCC), it declared its primary aim to resolve the southern conflict. The constitution was suspended and a state of emergency was declared. All civilian newspapers, political parties, and nonreligious organizations were banned and their properties and assets confiscated (*Europa Yearbook,* 1992, p. 2545). With this coup, what had been called the "Second Spring" of the Sudanese press ended.

Press–Government Relations

The often independent and aggressive journalism of the al-Mahdi years has been effectively stopped under the al-Bashir regime. Sudanese journalists had established an independent trade union, called the Sudanese Journalists' Union, in 1987 to defend the rights of the press. Within this broad trade union there were a variety of factions supporting patriotic, democratic, and Islamic causes, among others. The trade union also promoted a code of conduct for journalists within the framework of press freedom and pushed for journalistic training and technical development of the press.

With the 1989 coup, however, the development of professionalism in journalism came to a halt as the government moved to mold journalists yet once again to suit its needs. Journalists working for the three government-owned newspapers have been carefully screened by the military authorities for loyalty to the government rather than competence and experience (Article 19, 1991, p. 392). In February 1990, the military government issued a decree which authorized the establishment of three press and publications houses under government control. These institutions have a monopoly on all press and other publications in the country.

The strong controls imposed on the press by the al-Bashir regime have not altogether eliminated the journalistic independence seen during the civilian government. Despite the ban on all but government-run newspapers, a number of leaflets and underground literature have been clandestinely produced and circulated. Article 19 (1991, p. 393) noted that one of the banned newspapers, Al-Midan, was being published regularly in 1991 on stencil and distributed secretly. Its editor was visited in prison by a member of the ruling military council and threatened with severe punishment if the publication did not stop. The banned Baath Party and the Communist Party have published newsletters in stencil form. Idris al-Banna, a member of the Umma Party, was brought to trial with nine others in December 1989 on a charge of "circulating antigovernment leaflets." Al-Banna was accused of writing a poem, while in prison, criticizing the new military government.

The government crackdown on such independent-minded journalists has increased. Article 19 (1991, p. 393) reports that many journalists have been arrested and detained without charge or trial since 1989. The most prominent example is that of Al-Fatih al-Mardi, executive editor of the now banned business journal Al-Saha al-Tigaria, who was arrested in June 1990 and charged with possession of a typewriter and two duplicating machines, along with "subversive" material on behalf of a political group called the National Alliance for the Salvation of the Country (NASC). NASC, representing various interest groups in the Sudan, had been formed in 1985 to campaign for the ouster of the Numayri regime and return to civilian rule (Banks, 1991, p. 643).

Subsequent to al-Mardi's arrest, two other journalists, including one employed by the UN Information Centre, who were found to have associated with al-Mardi were also arrested. In July 1990, all three were secretly tried before a military court on charges of "inciting hatred against the state and working by act or by word to undermine it." Such charges can carry the death penalty. Article 19 (1991, p. 394) says that for the first time since the junta came to power, lawyers for the accused were allowed to address the court directly, as opposed to the earlier practice of allowing defense lawyers to attend the trial as a "friend" of the defendants without the right to "talk" to the court. In August 1990, al-Mardi was sentenced to 14 years' imprisonment. The other two were acquitted.

The government-run media are also heavily censorsed. Information on the famine caused by the continuing civil war, incidents of AIDS in the country, and massacres carried out by militias and the government troops in the war has been routinely censored. In one massacre in Jabalain in December 1989, when an estimated 2,000 people were killed, information released by the government said that 200 people were killed (Article 19, 1991, p. 393).

The military government has also moved against the foreign press to curb what it perceives as negative publicity. Following government allegations in January 1990 that the BBC World Service had been biased against the Sudanese government, it arrested correspondents of the BBC, Reuters, and the *Financial Times*. The Reuters correspondent was later expelled from the country. The BBC correspondent, a Sudanese, was jailed for seven months and the *Financial Times* correspondent was detained for eight days and then released (*The Middle East Journal,* Summer 1990, p. 493).

TUNISIA

Like Algeria and Morocco, Tunisia was under French control for many years. Occupied by the French in 1881, Tunisia became a French protectorate in 1883 and remained so until 1955 when internal autonomy was granted following three years of guerrilla warfare against the French. On March 20, 1956, the protectorate status was terminated and Tunisia gained full independence.

During most of the protectorate years, pro-France newspapers dominated the press scene, with *La Depeche Tunisienne* as the leading newspaper. Until its closure in 1961 for financial reasons, *La Depeche* was the largest circulated newspaper in Tunisia. Kurian (1982, p. 1102) says that another French-language newspaper, *La Presse,* founded by a Tunisian named Henry Smadja in 1956, tried to take the place of *La Depeche* with its slightly pro-French outlook. With the nationalist sentiments running high in Tunisia, Smadja's French sympathies did not go very well with the authorities and ultimately he was fined and forced to leave the country in 1967. His newspaper was taken over by the government and lost much of its influence and readership.

Nationalist newspapers were introduced as pressure for political reforms began by the Destour (Constitution) Party during 1920–1934 (East, 1990, p. 516). The most influential of such newspapers was *La Voix du Tunisien,* the organ of the Destour Party. The party split in 1934 and was supplanted by the Neo-Destour Party, which became the spearhead of a drive for independence under the leadership of Habib Bourguiba. Bourguiba viewed journalism as an important vehicle to promote the independence cause. He had been writing for *La*

Voix du Tunisien until he founded his own newspaper, *L'Action Tunisienne,* in 1932. All nationalist newspapers were closed down by the French authorities in 1933, although *L'Action Tunisienne* was allowed to be published again in 1938. Kurian (1982, p. 1102) says that the newspaper *Mission* became Bourguiba's ideological mouthpiece between 1948 and 1952.

Following independence, Bourguiba's authority was consolidated in a series of political developments, which resulted in strong controls on the press for three decades. France granted full independence to Tunisia on March 20, 1956. Five days later, elections were held for a Constitutional Assembly, which met in April and appointed Bourguiba as prime minister under the monarchy of the Bey of Tunis. In July 1957, the assembly deposed the Bey, abolished the monarchy, and established a republic, with Bourguiba as president.

A new constitution was promulgated in June 1959 and the first National Assembly was elected in November that year. Until its revision in 1988, the constitution gave exceptionally broad powers to the president. According to a Defense & Diplomacy special report (1989), although the constitution granted considerable civil rights, including freedom of the press, it allowed the president and government to limit them without recourse to the courts and the National Assembly. The constitution also gave the president the right to rule by decree during legislative adjournments.

The Neo-Destour Party was renamed the Destourian Socialist Party (Parti Socialiste Destourien—PSD) in 1964, with a moderately left-wing tendency. Although a one-party system was not institutionalized, the PSD was the only legal party from the time the Communist Party (PCT) was banned in January 1963 until its return to legal status in 1981. Bourguiba's hold on power was confirmed by a PSD congress in 1974 when the constitution was altered to allow Bourguiba to become president for life (*Europa Yearbook,* 1991, p. 2612).

The political system under Bourguiba, until he was deposed in 1987, was one of personalized authoritarianism, with the PSD acting as a ruling organ of government. Bourguiba was able to neutralize challenges to his political authority while the PSD dominated elections by a campaign of harassing opposing political parties (Defense & Diplomacy, 1989). Even after the one-party system was ended in 1981, the PSD devised a system whereby only licensed parties could contest elections, and those parties had to receive at least 5 percent of the vote before they could hold a National Assembly seat. As a result, the PSD thwarted political challenge and built a one-party state. Members of the ruling party have held all seats in the National Assembly since it was established in 1959 (Defense & Diplomacy, 1989).

The highly regimented nature of the political system during the Bourguiba years has been acknowledged by the Ben Ali government. In a publication prepared by the Tunisian External Communication Agency, *"Tunisia and Human Rights,"* the section on political parties says: "The Constitution of the Republic of Tunisia clearly stipulates the right to form political parties. But until recently, this right was set about with such draconian conditions that they ended up by prohibiting the right being exercised'' (1992).

As a result of the authoritarian political system, the media during most of the Bourguiba years were subject to pervasive party influence and increasingly repressive government influence (Banks, 1991, p. 684). Ever since Tunisia's independence, the PSD has been involved in publishing party organs, *L'Action* in French and *Al-Amal* in Arabic. There was not much of opposition press in the country between 1956 and 1987. Kurian (1982, p. 1103) says that a pro-Communist monthly called *Tribune de Progres* was published from 1958 to 1962, but it was suppressed in 1962 along with the official Communist monthly, *Al Talia.* A few years later, *Jeune Afrique,* a magazine regarded highly for its incisive and critical analysis of events and situations in Tunisia and elsewhere in Africa, moved to Paris from its headquarters in Tunis. Founded in 1955 by a group of Tunisian intellectuals, the magazine had been suspended a number of times by the Tunisian authorities for its candid writing. An independent daily newspaper, *As-Sabah,* founded in 1951, has continued to be published in the country.

The status of the opposition press under the Bourguiba government can be explained in two phases. First, since Tunisia was a one-party state between 1963 and 1981, as explained earlier, the opposition press was not allowed to operate. It should be noted that in the late 1970s, Prime Minister Hedi Nouira had emphasized the need for ''opening up'' the PSD to accommodate different points of view, although he rejected opposition demands for a multiparty system (*Europa Yearbook,* 1991, p. 2612). As a result, a newspaper of the Democratic Socialist Movement, *Ar-Rai,* was allowed to be published on a weekly basis starting in 1977, although the party was not officially recognized until 1983. This newspaper, however, was under close scrutiny by the government.

Commenting on the quality of the Tunisian press, Kurian (1982, p. 1103) said that government control of the media was pervasive. ''The news media are dominated by information provided by government agencies. There is very little difference in content between the PSD-owned newspapers and the private ones.'' He also noted that on politically important subjects and issues of national policy, ''the basic approach tends to be the same in all newspapers.''

The second phase of the opposition press under Bourguiba began with the ending of the one-party system in July 1981. The suspension of the Communist Party (PCT) was lifted and Bourguiba announced that any political group which obtained 5 percent of the votes cast in the legislative elections in November would also be recognized as a party. Several opposition parties protested against these conditions. An alliance of the ruling PSD and the Tunisian Workers Union (UGTT) won an overwhelming victory in the election, with 94.6 percent of the votes. Opposition groups, including an illegal fundamentalist organization called the Islamic Tendency Movement (MTI), complained of election irregularities (*Europa Yearbook,* 1991, p. 2612). The government reacted with a renewed crackdown on the opposition press. Gastil (1981, p. 408) reported that opposition papers are "frequently banned or fined" in Tunisia.

Elections to the National Assembly in November 1986 were boycotted by the opposition parties because of the rejection of many of their candidate lists and administrative suspension of their publications (Banks, 1991, p. 682). It should be noted here that under the Tunisian Code of the Press, enacted by the government in 1975, the Ministry of the Interior was given the power to seize or suspend newspapers that posed a threat to public order (*Code de la Presse,* 1988, p. 31). The government also reacted vigorously in 1986 against the rise of Islamic fundamentalism. In August, the owner of a Muslim publishing house, Editions Bouslama, was sentenced to jail for 14 months for distributing "subversive literature" (*Europa Yearbook,* 1991, p. 2613).

President Bourguiba's behavior became increasingly erratic in 1987. In September, he made a number of key appointments, including naming the new director-general of the Tunisian Broadcasting Company and editor of the state-owned daily newspaper. The following month, however, he revoked all of these appointments. Bourguiba was deposed on November 7, 1987 by his prime minister, Gen. Zine al-Abidine Ben Ali, when a group of doctors declared that he was unfit to govern. Banks (1991, p. 681) says that the takeover was generally welcomed by Tunisians who had become increasingly disturbed by the Bourguiba government's repression of "the press, trade unions, legal opposition parties, and other sources of dissent, including the growing Islamic fundamentalist movement."

Soon after taking power, Ben Ali, who was sworn in as president, promised a new era of democracy, freedom of the press, trade unions, and political parties. One of Ben Ali's first acts as president was to permit the publication of opposition newspapers that had been suspended under Bourguiba. Ben Ali also abolished the notorious State Security Court and freed thousands of political detainees. In April 1988, the National Assembly approved his proposals to institute a multiparty system, although, in order to gain legal recognition, no party would have the right to pursue purely religious, racial, regional, or linguistic objectives. These stipulations were designed to serve as a barrier to the legalization of militant Islamic groups (Banks, 1991, p. 682).

The ruling party's name was changed in early 1988 to Democratic Constitutional Assembly (Rassemblement Constitutionnel Democratique—RCD) to reflect the new administration's commitment to democratic reform. In July 1988, the president-for-life provision in the constitution was repealed by the National Assembly. The president is now elected directly every five years, with a maximum of three terms.

Also in July 1988, Ben Ali repeated his commitment to freedom of expression. A legislation concerning the press was amended to allow newspapers the opportunity to prove the truth of allegedly defamatory articles, except articles about the president and members of the government, to escape conviction for libel. Seizure and suspension of newspapers, allowed under the 1975 press code, was to be controlled by the judiciary and no longer by the Ministry of the Interior under the revised Article 73 (*Code de la Presse,* 1988). By November 1988, two opposition papers were being regularly published without governmental interference, and press freedom had been guaranteed in a national pact between the government and leading political and trade organizations.

The popularity of the Ben Ali government and the reforms he had implemented was reflected in the presidential and National assembly elections held in April 1989. Running unopposed, President Ben Ali received the approval of 99 percent of those voting, while the RCD won all 141 seats in the National Assembly even though six opposition parties also ran (Defense & Diplomacy, 1989). A party that has been gaining strong support among Tunisia's fundamental Islamics, called Hizb al-Nahda or the Renewal Party, has established itself as the government's primary opposition. Its candidates contested the 1989 election as independents since the party was not officially recognized, ostensibly on the grounds that it remained religion-based. It won approximately 13 percent of the votes cast, but failed to win any seats "because the electoral system favored the ruling party" (*Europa Yearbook,* 1991, p. 2613).

In late 1989, Ben Ali publicly opposed the concept of a religious political party, and the government subsequently refused a further application by al-Nahda for legal recognition. This resulted in clashes between police and students at several universities, which the government attributed to Islamic fundamentalists. Al-Nahda and three recognized opposition parties rejected a subsequent offer by Ben Ali to discuss electoral reforms and refused to participate in municipal elections in June 1990 on the grounds that they were neither free nor fair. The government retaliated by suspending the al-Nahda newspaper, *al-Fajr,* following the publication of an article by the movement's exiled leader, which strongly criticized the Tunisian government (*Europa Yearbook,* 1991, p. 2614). In early 1990, the Communist Workers' Party, another unrecognized group, was allowed to publish its weekly newspaper, *al-Badil,* but it was also suspended within a year for government criticism (*Tunisia and Human Rights,* 1992).

Press–Government Relations

Newspapers and periodicals in Tunisia reflect a wide range of opinion. Tunisians also have a wide open access to international television via parabolic satellite dishes. Journalists and academics acknowledge that since Ben Ali became president and since the 1988 constitutional reforms, the Tunisian press has found a far more agreeable political climate in which to operate than had been the case during the Bourguiba years. In September 1992, President Ben Ali approved measures designed to promote pluralism in the press and access to government-controlled media. The official media, including the national news agency, have been allowed to provide coverage of the activities and viewpoints of legally recognized political parties and their representatives. In June 1989, the government established an advisory body called the Higher Council of the

Press for consultation on legislation and other matters affecting the press. This body is comprised of influential representatives of the public and the press. Other governmental measures designed to support the press include the introduction of subsidies for the regional press and improvement of training facilities for media personnel (Besbes interview, May 19, 1994).

What was characterized during the Bourguiba years as a "loyalist" press (Rugh, 1979) has shown considerable independence under the Ben Ali government. But the policy of careful surveillance of the press has continued under this government, although it "acts with more sensitivity to public opinion when it intervenes" (Article 19, 1991, p. 397).

Several examples illustrate this freedom–control dichotomy. In September 1989, the publisher of the ruling RCD's organ, *Renouveau,* was dismissed after the newspaper published an article questioning the political situation in the country and rumors of a change of prime minister. When the weekly *al-Fajr* published an article on June 20, 1990, criticizing the government for not serving the people, the authorities suspended the publication by claiming that the article might disturb public order. The weekly magazine *Realites* was seized after it carried an article in December 1988 denouncing the continuing pattern of human rights violations. An independent newspaper, *Les Annonces,* was seized in 1988 for publishing a cartoon depicting a journalist as President Ben Ali. Later that year, the weekly *al-Maoukif* was suspended for publishing a statement from the unrecognized opposition group, al-Nahda. During 1991 and 1992, the government intensified the censorship of items published by sympathizers of the outlawed al-Nahda fundamentalist movement, which has been linked to violent activities (*Europa Yearbook,* 1992, p. 2699).

Article 19 (1991, p. 397) says that the most informative weekly magazines, *Le Maghreb* and *Realites,* have often been censored, harassed, and occasionally closed down for lengthy periods. Some editors still tacitly recognize their limits and generally toe the government line. For example, the managing editor of the weekly *Essahafah* dismissed two journalists in January 1990 because they had protested publicly against his decision to censor their articles on the Tunisian media.

Additional means are available to the government to keep the press in line. Since newsprint is mostly imported and subsidized by the government, the threat of withdrawal of paper has been used as an effective deterrent against criticism, according to Article 19 (p. 397). Journalists are required to obtain a press card from the government in order to legally work for a news organization and a journalist must cease such work if he or she has been suspended.

REFERENCES

Anderson, L. S. (1986). Qadhafi and his opposition. *The Middle East Journal, 40* (2), 225–237.

Article 19. (1990). Censorship Report. *A report on famine and censorship, April 1980.* London: Article 19, The International Centre on Censorship.

Article 19. (1991). World Report. *Information, freedom and censorship.* London: Library Association Publishing.

Banks, A. (1991). *Political handbook of the world.* Binghamton, NY: CSA Publications.

Besbes, E. (May 19, 1994). Director, Agence Tunisienne de Communication Exterieure. Personal interview in Tunis.

Bechtold, P. K. (1990). More turbulence in Sudan: A new politics this time? *The Middle East Journal, 44* (4).

Code de la Presse. (1988). Republique Tunisienne. Tunis: Ministere de l'Information.

Code de la Presse au Maroc. (1992). Information supplied by the Embassy of Maroc in Indonesia.

Defense & Diplomacy. (1989). *Special Report: The Republic of Tunisia.*

The Democratic Journalist. (1987). The situation of the Sudanese press, no. 2.

East, Roger, et al. (1990). *World fact file.* New York: Facts on File, Inc.

The Economist. (January 4, 1992). Win one, lose one. Vol. 322, no. 7740.

The Economist. (January 18, 1992). The soldiers cut in. Vol. 322, no. 7742.

The Economist. (February 15, 1992). "Fear of fundies." Vol. 322, no. 7746.

The Economist (February 22, 1992). Alive and fairly well. Vol. 322, no. 7747.

The Europa World Yearbook. (1984). London: Europa Publications.

The Europa World Yearbook. (1991). London: Europa Publications.

The Europa World Yearbook. (1992). London: Europa Publications.

Faringer, G. L. (1991). *Press freedom in Africa.* New York: Praeger.

Fisher, W. B. (1991). Libya. In *The Middle East and North Africa 1992.* London: Europa Publications.

Gastil, R. D. (1981–1991). See annual reports titled, *Freedom in the world: Political rights and civil liberties.* Westport, CT: Greenwood Press.

Harris, L. C. (1986). *Libya: Qadhafi's revolution and the modern state.* Boulder, CO: Westview Press.

Kurian, G. (1982). *World press encyclopedia.* New York: Facts on File.

Metz, H. C. (1989). *Libya: A country study.* Washington, DC: U.S. Government Printing Office.

The Middle East Journal. (Summer 1990). Chronology, *44* (3).

Mortimer, R. (1992). Algeria. In *Encyclopedia Americana 1992 annual.* Danbury, CT: Grolier, Inc.

Nasser, M. K. (1982). The Middle East press: Tool of politics. In J. L. Curry & J. R. Dassin (Eds.), *Press control around the world.* New York: Praeger Publishers.

Nelson, H. D. (1986). *Algeria: A country study.* Washington, DC: The American University.

Qadhafi, Muammar al. (1976). *The green book, part I: The solution of the problem of democracy.* London: Martin Brian and O'Keeffe.

Roumani, J. (Spring 1983). From republic to Jamahiriya: Libya's search for political community. *The Middle East Journal, 37* (2).

Rugh, W. A. (1979). *The Arab press.* Syracuse, NY: Syracuse University Press.

The Statesman's Yearbook. (1992–1993). Brian Hunter (Ed.). London: The Macmillan Press.

The Straits Times. (January 7, 1993). Algeria to gag press as war on extremists hots up. Singapore.

Tunisia and human rights. (1992). Tunis: Tunisian External Communication Agency.

Underwood, P. (1982). Libya. In G. Kurian (Ed.), *World press encyclopedia.* New York: Facts on File.

Wilcox, D. L. (1982). Black African States. In J. L. Curry & J. R. Dassin (Eds.), *Press Control Around the World,* New York: Praeger.

7 Contemporary Mass Media and Media Education

ALGERIA

From 1989, when constitutional reforms allowed a good measure of press freedom, until the imposition of martial law in early 1992, the Algerian press saw a substantial growth. The government induced journalists working for state-owned media to help in the establishment of private publications by offering them the equivalent of two years' salary. By mid-1991, the number of daily, weekly, and monthly publications had risen to 110. Most of the new papers continued to be printed on government presses, however, which later enabled it to suspend their publication as martial law was imposed. The government also imposed many restrictions on media, especially the Islamic fundamentalist press, after martial law was declared in February 1992. A number of newspapers were banned for a short time later in the year under a new decree permitting such action in cases of publications deemed to be operating "against public interest" (Banks, 1993, p. 20).

Because of the worsening political situation, the Algerian mass media remained under strong government control as of mid-1994. In its latest crackdown on the press, the army-backed government announced on January 6, 1993, that news reports on "security matters" would be censored. The phrase "security matters" was being interpreted quite loosely in view of the fact that four days earlier the government had suspended the independent daily *El-Watan* for "prematurely" writing about the killing of five policemen, apparently by Muslim extremists. The paper's publisher, executive editor, and three reporters were detained. An antiterrorism law passed in September 1992 bars newspapers from publishing statements from underground groups that could be deemed subversive by the government. The law was generally believed to be directed primarily against the banned Islamic Salvation Front (*The Straits Times,* January 7, 1993, p. 13).

In view of the actions taken against the press since the martial law, there appeared little prospect in early 1994 that the press would regain freedom soon. The status of media just prior to the imposition of martial law and since then is discussed below.

Newspapers and Magazines

Many political parties began to publish their own publications following the 1989 constitutional reforms, which permitted the establishment of opposition political parties. According to figures provided by the Algerian information ministry, in early 1994 there were 17 daily, 25 weekly, three bimonthly, and five monthly newspapers in the country. Several of these newspapers are published by political parties. The following are the major daily newspapers in the country: *Ach-Cha'ab* (80,000), former FLN newspaper in Arabic; *El-Moudjahid* (392,000), former FLN organ in French and Arabic; *An-Nasr* (340,000), in Arabic; *Al-Jumhuriyah* (70,000), former FLN journal in Arabic; *Horizons* (300,000), an evening daily in French, and *Al-Massa* (100,000), an evening newspaper in Arabic. Banks (1993, p. 20) says that in May 1992, the government directed that new independent editors be appointed to those publications which had formerly been under FLN control.

MDA, a pro-democracy opposition political party founded in 1990, began to publish *Al-Badil* in Algiers that year in French and Arabic, with a combined circulation of 130,000. Two new independent dailies were launched in late 1990, *Le Soir de l'Algerie* (150,000) in French and *Al Khabar* (52,000) in Arabic. Other independent dailies include *El Watan* (130,000), in French; *Le Matin,* in French; and *Al Djazair al Joum,* in Arabic. According to 1993 UNESCO *Statistical Yearbook,* the circulation rate of daily newspapers per 1,000 population in 1990 was 51.

The major weekly publications are *Algerie Actualite* (255,000), a government publication in French; *Revolution Africaine* (50,000), former FLN journal in French with socialist leanings; and, *Al-Hadaf* (110,000), a sports publication in French. Circulation of nondaily newspapers in Algeria in 1990 was put at 56 copies per 1,000 inhabitants.

A total of 48 periodicals were being published in the country in Algeria in 1994. Major periodicals include *Al Acala,* religious fortnightly; *Alouan,* cultural review monthly in Arabic; *Ach-Cha'ab ath-Thakafi,* a cultural monthly in Arabic; *Ach-Chabab,* a youth-oriented bimonthly in French and Arabic; *Al-Djeza'ir,* a monthly political journal in French and Arabic; *Al-Djeza'iria,* a monthly in French and Arabic for women; *Al-Djeich,* a monthly Algerian army review in French and Arabic; *Journal Officiel de la Republique Algerienne Democratique et Populaire,* a national political journal in French and Arabic; *Al-Kitab,* a political bulletin in French and Arabic published every two months;

and *Nouvelles Economiques,* a monthly in business and economics in French and Arabic.

Other important periodicals are *Revolution et Travail,* a monthly trade union journal in Arabic and French; *Revue Algerienne du Travail,* a French-language quarterly on labor issues; *Revue d'Histoire et de Civilisation du Maghreb,* an irregular publication in French and Arabic on history and civilization; *Al-Thakafa,* a cultural review published every two months; *Algerie Medicale,* a medical journal published twice a year; and *Bibliographie de l'Algerie,* published twice a year, listing books, theses, pamphlets, and periodicals published in Algeria.

Several publications available before the martial law have come under pressure from the military government and their status remains unclear. They include *Al-Mounqid,* an Arabic-language bimonthly published by the Islamic fundamentalist party, the FIS. *Sout Ech Chaab,* a Communist Party publication; *l'Avenir Ettajamou and Asalu,* a publication of the secular party known as the RCD; and three other opposition publications, *Alger Republicain, Le Progres,* and *Libre Algerie.*

Like its neighbors, Morocco and Tunisia, Algeria has been a heavy importer of publications from abroad, although the political turmoil has adversely affected such imports. For example, Algeria imported newspapers and periodicals worth $15.6 million in 1989. In 1991, however, only $500,000 worth of such publications were allowed into the country (*Statistical Yearbook,* 1993).

Books

Policy on publication and imports of books was also relaxed with the 1989 constitutional reforms. The prohibition on importation and circulation of previously banned books was lifted. In 1989, the state printing house itself published a book by the National Committee Against Torture on police torture during the October 1988 riots.

Book publishing in Algeria is done by two major publishers: Entreprise Nationale du Livre (ENAL) and Office des Publications Universitaires. ENAL publishes books of all types, and is sole importer, exporter, and distributor of all printed material. It also holds state monopoly for commercial advertising. The other publisher is responsible for publishing university textbooks. In 1991, 494 books were published in Algeria, including 282 in Arabic, 170 in French, and two in other languages. Of the total number of titles published, 82 were on religion, with the remainder being in a variety of general, academic, and professional areas. Algeria exported $100,000 worth of books in 1991. The country has been a heavy importer of books. In 1989, it imported books worth $23.3 million. However, imports of books had declined to worth $11.1 million in 1991 (*Statistical Yearbook,* 1991 and 1993).

Radio and Television

Radio and television broadcasting is done by the government-controlled Broadcasting Service of the Algerian Republic (Idha'at al-Jumhuriyat al-Jaza'iriyah). Known earlier as Radiodiffusion Television Algerienne, the broadcasting service has two separate bodies in charge of radio and television broadcasting. Radio broadcasting is done by Entreprise Nationale de Radiodiffusion, which operates on 26 AM, one FM, and 13 shortwave frequencies.

There are four radio networks in the country, with three aimed at domestic audiences and the fourth providing an international service. Domestic services are available in Arabic, French, and Kabyle. The Arabic service, available 24 hours daily, is the most comprehensive in terms of its reach throughout the country. The French service is on the air for more than 18 hours a day. In addition, there is a daily, seven-hour Holy Quran Service for domestic audiences. External broadcasting, aimed at Europe, the Middle East, and Northwest Africa, is done in Arabic, English, and Spanish for a total of seven and a half hours daily.

Domestic radio programming is categorized as follows: news and information programs, 14.7 percent; educational programs, 4.3 percent; cultural programs, 9.7 percent; religious programs, 7.2 percent; entertainment programs, 57.6 percent; and unclassified programs, 6.5 percent. According to UNESCO, 6 million radio receivers were reported to be in use in 1991, with 234 receivers for every 1,000 inhabitants (*Statistical Yearbook*, 1993).

Television was introduced in Algeria in 1957. The government-controlled Entreprise Nationale de Television (ENTV) operates a television network completed in 1970. There are 18 transmitting stations, broadcasting home services in Arabic, French, and Kabyle (a dialect of the Berber people). In 1990, the government announced plans for a second national television service. The new station was scheduled to broadcast in Arabic, French, and English for 20 hours a day. Algeria is a member of the Tunis-based Arab States Broadcasting Union (ASBU) established in 1969. This organization coordinates television news and sports programming exchange among the member states via ARABSAT communication satellite.

According to UNESCO *Statistical Yearbook* (1993), 1.9 million television receivers were in use in the country in 1991, of which more than 300,000 were color receivers. The number of television receivers per 1,000 population was put at 74. About 12 percent of Algerian television households had VCRs in 1992. Television uses the PAL color system of broadcasting.

As a result of leasing INTELSAT transponders and setting up microwave relay links, Algerian television is now available in about 97 percent of the country. A total of 65 hours of programming was being broadcast on a weekly basis in 1992. The programming schedule was categorized as follows: entertainment, 64.3 percent; news and information, 12.6 percent; education, 13.1 percent; cultural programs, 3.9 percent; religion, 2 percent; and unclassified programs, 4.1 percent. Locally produced programs are in Arabic, while imported programs are broadcast mostly in French. More than half of all television programming in the country is imported, much of it from France (Algerian Ministry of Information, 1993).

Television is playing a significant role in national education programs. A pilot project in distance education via television, conducted under the sponsorship of UNESCO in 1969, set the stage for expanded use of television for educational programming in subsequent years. Head (1974, p. 33) indicated that the educational television schedule had been substantially expanded to include series on teacher training, mathematics, science, and the English language. Broadcasting's role in development planning continues to receive an important emphasis (Head, 1985, p. 34). According to the Ministry of Information, approximately 18 percent of the television schedule is devoted to formal and nonformal educational programming. Secondary school courses are taught as part of formal educational programming, whereas a variety of developmental campaigns are carried out as part of nonformal education via television (Algerian Ministry of Information, 1993). The government defrays about 70 percent of the broadcasting budget, with most of the rest coming from a markup on electric utility bills.

Cinema

UNESCO figures show that Algeria produced two full-length films in 1985, although none was reported for 1991, the latest year listed (*Statistical Yearbook,* 1993). According to earlier UNESCO data, Algeria had a steady level of production during the 1970s and early 1980s, averaging between three and four full-length features annually plus one or two coproductions with France and Italy. A number of documentaries are also produced, usually through government sponsorship. Algeria has been a heavy importer of films, with 140 commercial films imported in 1985. Of this number, 35.1 percent were imported from the United States, 20.7 percent from India, 9 percent from France, and the remainder from a number of other countries. A total of 249 cinema halls were reported for 1988, with annual attendance for that year put at 21 million (*Statistical Yearbook,* 1993). The political turmoil in the country since the martial law has affected the importation and distribution of films.

Media Education and Training

Mass communication education is provided at the Higher Institute of Information and Communication (ISIC) in Algiers. The institute is successor to Ecole Nationale Superieure de Journalisme (National Higher School of Journalism) established in the capital after the country's independence from France in 1962. Borrowing from the French tradition, the school offered journalism education at the graduate level. Students seeking admission into the program had to have a good undergraduate degree, preferably in social sciences, and pass a competitive entrance examination in general knowledge and writing skills. Education in the school tended to be heavy in theory, although students were placed as interns with area newspapers to obtain practical training.

ISIC has continued the school's policy of offering journalism education at the graduate level, although it has a much wider scope. It offers graduate degree programs in both print and audiovisual media. In the first year of the two-year degree program, students are taught mostly theoretical courses on Algerian politics, foreign relations, and social and economic system, and media courses on history, law, and management. In the second year, they branch out to specialize in either print or audiovisual media. A variety of skills courses are offered during this year, with students producing laboratory publications under faculty supervision. They can specialize to work for Arabic or French-language media in the country. The institute has well-equipped laboratories for hands-on training in radio, television, film, photography, and print media.

ISIC maintains a cooperative relationship with sister institutions in Morocco and Tunisia, among others in the Arab world, and with a number of media institutions in Europe, especially France. Many Algerian journalists and other media professionals have obtained their education and training in France over the years. Algerian journalists have also taken advantage of media workshops and refresher courses offered by the Tunis-based African Center for the Improvement of Journalists and Communicators. Between 1983 and 1992, 82 Algerian journalists participated in these short-term courses and training sessions (*CAPJC*, 1992, p. 36).

Other sources of media training are the University of Constantine, located 200 miles to the east of Algiers, where an audiovisual center stresses use of the media for teaching and literacy. It also offers training for people seeking careers in television and film production. Radio-Television Algerie has for years trained film and television technicians on an apprenticeship basis. Instructional staff includes people trained in France.

LIBYA

All mass media in Libya have been forced to toe the government line ever since the 1969 coup and are controlled by the state through the Secretariat for Information. Publishing is done under the auspices of either the official Jamahiriya News Agency (JANA), the official Press Service, government secretariats, or government-sponsored trade unions. The Qadhafi government has assigned a "mobilization" role to the mass media and gives them guidance on its goals and on news presentation and interpretation.

The media have been structured and centralized to support the aims of the "revolution" and they faithfully promote the ideas of the ruling elite. Reporting is largely confined to the activities of officials and state bodies. Dissidents and opposition movements have been systematically crushed in the country and there have been attempts on Qadhafi's part to combat Libyan dissidents abroad (Harris, 1986, p. 69). There is little prospect for press freedom in Libya as long as Qadhafi remains in power.

Newspapers and Magazines

The status of the print media is best reflected in a speech given by Qadhafi to the 13th General People's Congress in March 1988. Discussing press freedom, Qadhafi dismissed the notion that any newspaper could reflect public opinion, on the grounds that it would follow the dictates of its owner. He affirmed that any Libyan who wished to publish a newspaper or pamphlet would be free to do so, provided that he did not receive money from foreign sources to support the venture. He insisted, however, that it was meaningless for one person to publish a newspaper or issue a circular "in the state of the masses because all are taking part in power through the people's congresses." He continued: "What you want to say in the circular, you can say at the people's congress where it can become a resolution and part of the policy of Jamahiriya." Qadhafi added that people would be free to publish their opinions in the form of graffiti on walls, provided that they erased them and repainted the wall after the graffiti had been read (*Keesing's Record of World Events,* May 1988, p. 35918).

This philosophy indicates why there is no general interest newspaper other than the official mouthpiece of the government, *Al-Fajr al-Jadid* (The New Dawn). The government organ since 1972, this newspaper has been published by JANA since January 1978. It is published in the capital Tripoli in Arabic, with a daily circulation of 40,000. In addition, two special interest dailies are produced for the army and trade unions. The three dailies had a total circulation of 70,000 in 1990. The circulation rate per 1,000 people was put at 15, which dropped from the 1985 rate of 17 copies per 1,000 people. Only one weekly newspaper was being published in the country in 1988, with a total circulation of 15,000. The circulation rate per 1,000 inhabitants for nondaily newspapers was put at 4 for 1988. Consumption of newsprint in Libya peaked in 1985. Newsprint consumption fell from 528 kilograms per 1,000 inhabitants in 1985 to 184 kilograms per 1,000 inhabitants in 1989 (*Statistical Yearbook,* 1993).

In 1993, 21 periodicals were being published in Libya. Some of the more prominent of these publications are *Az-Zahf al-Akhdar,* the ideological journal of the revolutionary committees; *Al-Watan al-Arabi,* a publication devoted to promoting Pan-Arabism; *Al-Jamahiriya,* a political weekly of the revolutionary committees; *Al-Usbu as-Siyasi,* another political weekly; *Risalat al-Jihad,* a monthly in Arabic, English, and French to promote the Palestinian cause; and *Ad-Daawa al-Islamia,* a weekly cultural publication in Arabic, English, and French produced by the World Islamic Call Society. Other publications are aimed at a variety of interest groups. All publications are printed in government print shops and are distributed by the government (*Middle East and North Africa,* 1994, p. 673). Ever since the Cultural Revolution of 1973, importation of newspapers and periodicals has declined sharply, with no such imports indicated after 1985 when Libya imported $1.1 million worth of such publications (*Statistical Yearbook*, 1993).

Books

Libya has had an active book publishing industry, although the number of titles generated has declined. A total of 481 titles were published in 1980, a substantial increase over the 129 titles published in 1975. In 1988, however, the number declined to 121, according to the latest UNESCO figures available. More than one-half of these titles were in literature, political science, and natural sciences. Most of the remaining titles were in other academic subjects. Fiction and general interest reading did not attract much publishing interest. A total of 553 copies of these 121 titles were produced in 1988. In 1985, Libya translated in Arabic 21 books published abroad. Of the books translated, 12 were originally published in French, three in German, and two in English. Latest available data indicate that Libya imported books worth $21.3 million in 1985, a substantial jump from the 1980 figure of $5.2 million (*Statistical Yearbook*, 1991 and 1993). There were three publishing houses in the country in 1992, including one founded by Libya and Tunisia in 1973 called Ad-Dar al-Arabia Lilkitab. The other two, Al-Fatah University Press and General Company for Publishing, publish academic and educational books.

Radio and Television

The Great Socialist People's Libyan Arab Jamahiriya Broadcasting Corporation is in charge of radio and television broadcasting. As with the contents of the press, the broadcast programming is closely controlled by the Secretariat of Information, Culture and Revolutionary Guidance. McDaniel (1982, pp. 187–189) says that the Libyan broadcasting system has been a primary vehicle for political development along the revolutionary goals set by Qadhafi, including the holding of "Revolutionary Intellectuals' Seminars" on television. Broadcasting is noncommercial and financed by the government. The government has had the following objectives for broadcasting since 1970:

1. To embody the Arab Revolutionary objectives of freedom, socialism and unity, and to permeate such objectives in the minds of the people;
2. To stress the fact that Libya is an integral part of the Arab homeland;
3. To tie up the Arab struggle to liberate the occupied Arab territories with the cause of freedom and liberation in the Third World (Elgabri, 1974, p. 29).

Radio broadcasting is done by the Libyan Jamahiriya Broadcasting based in Tripoli. Domestic service transmissions are done via five high-power and thirteen low-power AM stations, and three FM stations, primarily in Arabic. Most of the programming originates at the Tripoli-based central station of the radio network, with Benghazi being another important broadcasting center. Programming begins at 5 A.M. and is available until midnight on most of the stations. There are nine daily news broadcasts starting at 6 A.M. A Holy Koran service is also available on radio every day for at least 14 hours. English- and French-language domestic programming is also broadcast daily. Each of these language programs is limited to two hours, including news bulletins. An estimated 1,060,000 radio receivers were in use in Libya in 1991, or 225 per 1,000 population, according to UNESCO figures.

A high-power shortwave transmitter located at Sabratah, near Tripoli, and a low-power shortwave transmitter in Benghazi are used for the external service. Almost 13 hours of daily external service programming is broadcast in Arabic, which includes several news broadcasts. Since September 1971, the external service has offered special daily broadcasts to the Arab world, in particular the Israeli-occupied territories of the West Bank and Gaza. In addition to Arabic, programs in several European languages are also broadcast (*World Radio TV Handbook,* 1993). Libyan external services are also broadcast from Malta as the Voice of the Mediterranean (VOM). Founded jointly by the Libyan and Maltese governments in 1988, the VOM operates a network broadcasting in English and Arabic.

Television programming is offered by the People's Revolution Broadcasting Television. There are 13 television transmitters in the country, broadcasting programming from the Tripoli central station for approximately six hours daily. Limited amounts of programming in English, Italian, and French are also available. In 1991, there were an estimated 467,000 television receivers, or 99 sets per 1,000 population (*Statistical Yearbook,* 1993). Transmission is done by using the PAL color standard. Libyans along the Mediterranean coast also have access to television signals from Italy and Malta. Programs from Egypt and Tunisia can also be received. Of all the North African countries, Libya has been least active in using broadcasting for promoting formal or nonformal education. One possible explanation for that is that the Qadhafi regime has placed national mobilization in support of his "revolutionary" political objectives so high on his agenda.

Libya has substantially improved its telecommunications systems since the early 1980s by leasing transponders from the International Telecommunications Satellite (INTELSAT) Organization. Libya is a member of the regional Arab Satellite (ARABSAT) Organization, which offers weekly exchanges of television programs to member states. Libya is also a member of the Tunis-based Arab States Broadcasting Union, the main broadcasters' association in the Middle East and North Africa, which coordinates transmission of news and sports programming among member states via a transponder leased from ARABSAT.

Cinema

Libya has not had much of a domestic movie industry, with no productions reported since 1975. In that year, two films were produced in the country. Libyans, however, have shown much interest in films from a number of other countries, although the Qadhafi regime appears to have restricted access to films from abroad in recent years. Last reported figures by UNESCO indicate that Libya imported 169 commercial films in 1979. The imports from specific countries for that year were broken down as follows: United States, 60.4 percent; Italy, 10.1 percent; Hong Kong, 5.9 percent; India, 5.3 percent; Japan, 4.1 percent; Britain, 3.0 percent; France, 2.4 percent; and films from other countries, 8.9 percent. There were 12.3 cinema seats per 1,000 population in the country in 1975, a figure that declined to 7.7 in 1980 (*Statistical Yearbook,* 1986; *Statistical Digest,* 1986).

Media Education and Training

The Libyan government has not shown the same level of commitment to mass communication education as have the governments of Algeria, Morocco, and Tunisia. That situation is partly explained by the fact that there has not been a huge demand for trained personnel for print media following media nationalization in 1972, which resulted in the reduction of newspapers from ten to one and the closure of many periodicals. In addition, Colonel Qadhafi wanted media writing left to those who were ideologically in tune with him, which meant that journalists increasingly came from the civil service staff. The Qadhafi government, however, moved systematically to expand the size and operations of the broadcast media to promote the revolutionary fervor of the regime, necessitating an increased need for trained broadcast personnel.

The University of Benghazi offers a degree program in communication studies, where students can specialize in either print or broadcast media. Broadcast education, however, is more in demand because of the substantially increased job opportunities in that field. The curriculum is heavy in the political indoctrination of students, focusing on Qadhafi's view of politics, democracy, and the "Arab nation," among other subjects. Skills training is provided in conjunction with the Libyan broadcasting system and other media. Before the souring of U.S.-Libyan relations during the Reagan presidency, many Libyan broadcast personnel received education and training at American institutions. In 1975, agreements were reached with the University of South Carolina and Ohio University to institute college degree programs for broadcasting staff members (McDaniel, 1982, p. 190). Broadcast technicians often participated in training sessions conducted by broadcast equipment manufacturers in Europe and Japan.

In recent years, Libyan media personnel have increasingly turned to training opportunities available within the Islamic world. These have included the Saudi Arabia–based Islamic States Broadcasting Services Organization, which provides training of personnel for member broadcasting systems, and the Tunis-based Arab States Broadcasting Union, which operates a training center from Damascus, Syria. A number of Libyan media personnel have participated in media workshops and refresher courses offered by the Tunis-based African Center for the Improvement of Journalists and Communicators (*CAPJC,* 1992, p. 36).

MOROCCO AND WESTERN SAHARA

The Moroccan press is unique in the North African context because of its diversity. The diversity becomes particularly significant because the press is subject to tight constraints imposed by the press code and a strong monarchy. Publications advocating a variety of political viewpoints abound. Privately owned broadcasting is allowed, a unique phenomenon in North Africa and among the Arab states at large. Moroccans are generally allowed free access to a wide variety of news, information, and entertainment from abroad through hundreds of imported publications and satellite television reception. Coverage of news at home, however, is substantially regulated by the government. A state-supported press association, the National Moroccan Press Union, has existed since 1963 to defend the interests of the press and journalists. However, it receives state subsidy for both its office premises and operations (Abdelmalek, 1992).

Newspapers and Magazines

The Moroccan press is affiliated with about 15 political parties. Each party has one or two publications promoting its political views and activities. Since 1987, the state has subsidized these publications along with the trade union press. The independent press, of which there is little, consists of monthly magazines with very low circulations and is mostly dependent on advertising revenue. A publishing license must be obtained from the government before a newspaper can begin publication. In addition, regulations also require that two copies of each issue must be sent to the Ministry of Justice, Ministry of Information, and to the National Library.

In 1994, 17 daily newspapers were being published in Morocco, nine of them in Casablanca and eight in the capital Rabat. The Casablanca dailies and their circulation ranges, estimated by the Ministry of Information, are as follows: *Al-Bayane* (30,000–40,000), organ of the Party of Progress and Socialism; *Al-Ittihad Al-Ichtiraki* (75,000–90,000), organ of the opposition Socialist Union of Popular Forces Party; *Assahra Al-Maghrebia* (31,000–45,000), pro-government newspaper, published by a member of the royal family; *Bayane Al-Yaoum* (20,000–35,000), a political party publication; *Liberation* (10,000–20,000), French-language organ of the opposition Socialist Union of Popular Forces Party; *Lamanana Del Sahara y Del Maghreb* (5,000–11,000), a society group newspaper; *Rissalat al-Oumma* (7,000–22,000), organ of the Constitutional Union Party, which is moderate in orientation and is said to have the royal support; and two French-language newspapers called *Le Matin du Sahara* (90,000–130,000), and *Maroc Soir* (27,000–35,000), both pro-government newspapers owned by the Maroc Soir Group belonging to a member of the royal family (*La Presse Marocaine,* 1994; *Middle East and North Africa,* 1994; Abdesslam interview, May 12, 1994).

The following newspapers are published daily in Rabat in Arabic, unless otherwise noted: *Al-Alam* (45,000–90,000), organ of the opposition Istiqlal Party; *Al-Anba'a* (5,000–22,000), published by the Ministry of Information; *Al-Maghrib* (5,000–25,000), French-language organ of the National Assembly of Independents Party, branded commonly as the "King's party"; *Al-Mithaq Al-Watani* (7,000–25,000), Arabic-language organ of the National Assembly of Independents; *Al-Haraka* (5,000–18,000), a political party newspaper; *Anoual* (10,000–25,000), organ of the opposition party called Organization for Democratic and Popular Action; *An-Nidal Ad-Dimoukrati* (5,000–15,000), organ of the National Democratic Party; and *L'Opinion* (40,000–65,000), French-language organ of the opposition Istiqlal Party (*La Presse Marocaine,* 1994). The nondaily newspaper press is very small in number in Morocco, with only five such newspapers reported for 1988 by UNESCO, the latest data available.

Total circulation of daily newspapers in 1990 was put at 320,000 by UNESCO, an increase of 30,000 from the 1988 total circulation of 290,000. Circulation of newspapers per 1,000 inhabitants was 13 for 1990, which was below the average of 17 for Africa as a whole. The circulation of nondaily newspapers was put at 35,000 for 1988, with one copy per 1,000 inhabitants (*Statistical Yearbook,* 1993).

A total of 126 periodicals were being published in Morocco as of 1993, including 87 in Arabic and 39 in French. The capital Rabat and Casablanca were the largest publishing centers, with 37 and 17 periodicals, respectively. Five periodicals were published from Fes, six from Tangier, and five from Meknes. The remainder were published from 11 other cities. The periodicity of the 126 publications was as follows: weekly, 38; twice weekly, 22; monthly, 14; quarterly, 1; twice yearly, 1; and irregular, 11. The focus and language of publication of the periodicals is as follows: general interest, 38 in Arabic and 11 in French; regional interest, 21 in Arabic; culture, 8 in Arabic and 3 in French; science, 2 in French; sports, 6 in Arabic and 3 in French; economic, 1 in Arabic and 4 in French; arts, 4 in Arabic and 2 in French; entertainment, 8 in Arabic and 4 in French; education, 2 in French; professional, 1 in Arabic and 3 in French; others, 5 in French (*La Presse Marocaine,* 1994).

As with newspapers, most of the periodicals are publications of political parties and their affiliates. Other public groups such as associations, professional chambers, unions, and governmental agencies also publish periodicals. Almost all periodicals have small circulations and are heavily dependent on subsidies. *Le Journal de Tanger,* published from Tangier in French, English, Spanish, and

Arabic, is the largest periodical with a circulation of 12,000. News periodicals not affiliated to political parties include the business weeklies *La Vie Economique* and *Le Courrier Economique, An-Nidal,* and *Les Echos Africains.* Most periodicals cater to a small but partisan readership and they are generally characterized by their editorial outspokenness, resulting frequently in government action.

In addition, Morocco imports a wide variety of European and Arabic newspapers and magazines, but there are legal controls on their circulation. A major source of news in Morocco is *Ash-Sharq al-Awsat* (The Middle East), which is edited in London and printed simultaneously there and in eight other centers, including Casablanca. This right-wing daily newspaper is owned by members of the Saudi royal family and faithfully follows the government line. The Moroccan Press Code prohibits the importation of newspapers and periodicals containing news and information contradicting the political and religious foundation of the Moroccan society. The volume of imports of such publications has been declining over the years. For example, the country imported $13.1 million worth of newspapers and periodicals in 1980, but such imports dropped to $5.9 million in 1985 and $3.9 million in 1991 (*Statistical Yearbook,* 1993).

Several foreign publications have faced government crackdowns in recent years. For example, the authorities banned an issue of the Paris-based monthly magazine *Jeune Afrique* in June 1989 without giving any explanation. The banned issue had contained an article on child labor in Morocco. The magazine's circulation in Morocco at the time was put at approximately 13,000 (Ansah, 1991, p. 30). Another magazine, *Jeune Afrique Plus,* was also banned in the same month because it contained an article on the Western Sahara conflict. A map in the article had shown Morocco and Western Sahara as two separate countries. Two other French publications, *Le Monde Diplomatique* and *Liberation,* have been banned in Morocco a number of times since the late 1980s.

The Polisario government-in-exile supplies news from Western Sahara through its information section in Algiers. From the Moroccan side, news is supplied by the Maghreb Arab Press, the national news agency, and other official sources. Polisario also publishes a paper in French, *Sahara Libre,* twice every month, and a monthly in Spanish, *20 de Mayo,* primarily for distribution abroad. No publications are produced in the Western Sahara itself (Drost, 1991, p. 559).

Books

Morocco's book publishing industry is quite small and the country is a heavy importer of books and related publications. In 1980, for example, the country's book exports were put at $200,000 and imports at $14.6 million. In 1985, exports doubled to $400,000 and imports declined to $11.7 million. In 1991, however, the country imported $22.7 million worth of such publications, while exports were valued at $800,000 (*Statistical Yearbook,* 1993). Book publishing in Morocco is done primarily by three private companies and a government publishing house. The three private companies, all based in Casablanca, are: Dar el-Kitab, which publishes titles in the areas of philosophy, history, Africana, and general and social science; Editions La Porte, which publishes educational books, guides, and books on law and economics; and Editions Maghrebines, which specializes in publishing general nonfiction works. The government publishing house, Imprimerie Officielle, is based in Rabat.

State Subsidies

Moroccan print media are heavily dependent on state subsidies. The subsidies come in the form of direct and indirect aid, as follows (Laroussi interview, May 11, 1994; Abdelmalek, 1992):

1. A 20 million dirhams annual subsidy by the king (The exchange rate in early 1994 was U.S. $1 = 9.11 DH).
2. 25 percent discount on purchase of newsprint, which amounted to a subsidy of 7.6 million dirhams in 1990, and no tax on newsprint purchases.
3. 500,000 dirhams annual subsidy toward the distribution of newspapers abroad.
4. 1,900,00 dirhams subsidy toward telephone and telex communications for journalistic purposes.
5. Free subscription to the national news agency, Maghreb Arab Press.
6. Free access to photographs of all national events.
7. Free postal delivery for newspapers within the country.
8. Free railway transportation within the country for 120 journalists, selected on the basis of strong professional credentials, and a discount of 20 percent for other journalists.
9. 50 percent discount to journalists for travel domestically and abroad on the national airline and on Moroccan bus services.
10. 50 percent discount on hotel accommodations for journalists.
11. Free rail transport for national press publications.
12. Free transport of newspapers by the national airline to Agadir, El Ayoun, and Dakhla with an average of five kilograms for every newspaper.
13. Free transport of national press publications on the Moroccan coach lines.

Radio and Television

Broadcasting is under the jurisdiction of the Ministry of Information. The government-controlled Radiodiffusion Television Marocaine (RTM) offers radio and television services. RTM's Moroccan Radio, which began broadcasting as Radio Maroc in 1928, controls both operations and programming. RTM's headquarters are located in Rabat, with regional radio stations in Tangier, Casablanca, Laayoune, Dakhla, Marrakech, Agadir, Fes, Oujda, and Tetouan.

Moroccan Radio's national services are provided in Arabic on AM frequency and in French on FM frequency. In addition, 11 local radio stations provide programming primarily in Arabic, with some Berber-language programming (Benchekroun interview, May 12, 1994; *World Radio TV Handbook,* 1993). Radio transmissions can be received by 95 percent of the population. The radio service depends entirely on government revenues for its budget and, unlike television, does not carry any advertising. Moroccan Radio also operates a foreign service radio network, broadcasting in Arabic for 19 hours a day, in French for 15.5 hours, in English for 90 minutes a day, and in Spanish for one hour daily. The domestic and overseas transmissions of Moroccan Radio amount to 110 hours daily (Abdelmalek, 1992).

Morocco also has had a private radio station since July 1980, Radio Mediterranee Internationale, popularly known as Medi-I, located in Tangier. Owned by Moroccan and French groups, it broadcasts 20 hours daily in Arabic and French on AM, FM, and shortwave frequencies. Entertainment programming takes up much of the programming schedule on this station, with several news broadcasts in Arabic and French. Abdelmalek (1992) says that the station has been a commercial success. The Voice of America (VOA) has operated a relay station in Tangier for a number of years. The VOA, in return, has allowed Morocco to use some of its high-powered transmission facilities for external broadcasting.

There were approximately 5.4 million radio receivers in Morocco in 1991, which amounted to 210 receivers per 1,000 inhabitants (*Statistical Yearbook,* 1993). The RTM had a total of 22 AM, 7 FM, and 7 shortwave stations in 1993 (*World Radio TV Handbook,* 1993). It also provides radio relay service to Gibraltar, Spain, and Western Sahara.

Programming on RTM radio stations is broken down as follows: entertainment, 50 percent; news and information, 19 percent; cultural programs, 19 percent; educational programs, 6 percent; and religious programs, 6 percent (Moroccan Ministry of Information, 1994). Network A, which broadcasts in Arabic 24 hours a day, has a news bulletin each hour on the hour. Network B is on 19 hours daily, with broadcasts in French, English, and Spanish. Network C, which is also on for 19 hours daily, broadcasts in Berber in Arabic, with much of the latter a relay of the Network A programming (*World Radio TV Handbook,* 1993). Readings and commentaries of Koranic texts are heard at least twice a day and are supplemented with discussions by prominent Islamic scholars on social and economic issues.

The television operations of RTM, which began in 1962, consist of a 6-hour daily service and 15-hour weekend and holiday service in Arabic and French. The station's transmissions, which reach 70.7 percent of the country, can be picked up by 84 percent of the population. With its headquarters in Rabat, the network has 26 stations and 35 additional low-power rebroadcast sites across the country. Morocco is also linked to two communication satellite services, INTELSAT and ARABSAT. Launched in 1985 at a cost of about $100 million, the ARABSAT communication satellite is designed to promote news and cultural program exchanges among member Islamic nations. The RTM television service is financially supported by the government as well as by advertising revenues. The government imposes a surcharge on Moroccans' electric bill to raise revenues for radio and television operations (*Radiodiffusion Television Marocaine,* 1994; Benzahra interview, May 12, 1994).

RTM's television programming is categorized as follows: entertainment, 52 percent; news and information, 18 percent; cultural programs, 17 percent; religious programs, 5.5 percent; educational programs, 4.5 percent; and advertising, 3 percent. Radio and television have been used for educational broadcasting since the early 1960s in conjunction with the Ministry of Education. Formal educational programming, offering courses in high school curricula, and programs aimed at social development are broadcast (Moroccan Ministry of Information, 1994).

A private television company, 2M International, was established in 1988 and commenced transmission in 1989. Owned jointly by Moroccan financial institutions and foreign concerns, this private, commercial service is the first of its kind in Africa and the Arab world. The programs are carried in French and Arabic, with a daily service of 15 hours. 2M International offers programming primarily on subscription basis, with daily two-hour broadcasts that can be received free of charge. The station has extended its reach to France also through a cable television service called Canal Inter (Abdelmalek, 1992). The station takes a more liberal approach in its programming as compared with the government-owned RTM channel. 2M carries both French- and Arabic-language programming. The Moroccan government also relays a Saudi government-sponsored television service operated from London, called the Middle East Broadcasting Company (MBC). The MBC channel carries both news and entertainment programming.

Moroccan television is heavily dependent on French, American, and Egyptian programs. Although 55 percent of the programs are domestic productions, Article 19 (1991, p. 385) says that local production is "poor." Moroccan artists and writers are underused and sometimes banned because of their political opinions. Nothing is broadcast on television without the consent of the Ministry of the Interior and the Ministry of Information.

Because of its geographical location, Morocco receives a number of television channels from Europe including those broadcast by satellite. Satellite channels that can be received included: TV 5 (a consortium of francophone stations); RAI Uno (Italy); Channels 2, 5, 6, and Canal Plus (France); World Net (U.S.); Swedish TV; RTP2 (Portugal); and TV2 (Spain). Morocco has inaugurated a private subscription channel offered by 2M International. Article 19 (1991, p. 385) says that although privately owned, 2M does not escape government control.

A state agency called S.A.P. is charged with coordinating the regulation, production and placement of television advertising within the framework of

national economic objectives (Abdelmalek, 1992). It produced 265 advertisements for television in 1988, with a revenue of 80 million dirhams for that year.
About 103 hours of advertising were placed through this agency in 1988. The
agency is a member of a professional advertising association in Africa known
as the African Union of Communication (Abdelmalek, 1992).

An estimated 1.9 million television receivers were in use in Morocco in 1991,
or 74 sets per 1,000 population (*Statistical Yearbook,* 1993). Three out of four
homes have at least one television set as of mid-1994. Morocco uses the French
SECAM color broadcasting system.

Western Sahara has a sparse and limited telecommunications system. Broadcasting is tied into Morocco's system by radio relay and two INTELSAT earth
stations linked to Rabat. In addition, two AM radio stations in the capital Laayoune and Dakhla provide local programs. The two television transmitters in
Western Sahara are linked to Moroccan RTM television via satellite and carry
its programming. In 1991, a total of 44,000 radio receivers and 5,000 television
receivers were in use in Western Sahara. These totals amounted to 183 radio
receivers and 21 television receivers per 1,000 population in that region (*Statistical Yearbook,* 1993). It should be noted that Polisario's radio station, Idha'at
al-Wataniyah (National Radio), broadcasts in Arabic and Spanish from a base
in Algeria.

Cinema

Very few African countries produce full-length feature films and Morocco is
not one of them. No such film was produced in the country between 1970 and
1989, according to the *Statistical Yearbook* (1991). A government-established
film company, Le Centre Cinematographique Marocain, has existed in the country since 1944 "to produce and distribute films and profit from them." The
company is not involved in the production of full-length feature films, however.
It maintains sophisticated film processing laboratories and oversees imports and
exports of films through about 50 film societies in the country. It also serves as
a film regulatory agency (Abdelmalek, 1992).

Morocco is a major importer of films, with 434 imported in 1988 and 347 in
1989. In 1989, 36.3 percent of the films came from the United States, 19.9
percent from France, 7.8 percent from Italy, 16.7 percent from India, 9.2 percent
from the United Kingdom, 0.6 percent from Federal Republic of Germany, and
9.5 percent from other countries. There were 253 cinemas in 1989, with a seating
capacity of 166,100. The cinema attendance for 1989 was put at 30.2 million
(*Statistical Yearbook,* 1993; Abdelmalek, 1992).

Media Education and Training

Mass communication education and training in Morocco is provided by the
Institut Superieur de Journalisme (ISJ) established by the government in 1977,

and comes under the jurisdiction of the Ministry of Information. Located in the capital Rabat, ISJ offers only a graduate degree program, with specialties in print and audiovisual media. Applicants must have an undergraduate degree or equivalent and pass a competitive examination in order to be admitted into the program. The entrance examination consists of written and oral tests. Students are tested on their facility with languages, including English, German, Spanish, and French, and on their general knowledge. Only about 10 percent of the applicants are accepted by the institute, which takes about 70 students each year. Approximately 50 percent of the students are females. About 50 students are from Morocco, with the remaining being from other North African countries and some from as far away as Indonesia and Bangladesh.

Only about 25 percent of the students come into the program straight from their undergraduate education. The remainder are from government agencies, usually employed in some communication specialist capacity, who take study leaves to complete the degree program. Since Morocco has both Arabic- and French-language media, IFJ offers curricula in both languages. Just over half of the students enrolled take the Arabic-language option, with the rest taking it in French. In the first of the two years of study, students take courses on Moroccan political institutions and economy, foreign policy and international relations, contemporary problems, communication law and history, media management, and introductory courses in print and audiovisual media. In the second year, they take theory courses such as sociology of information, media and national development, international law of information, advertising and public relations, and also pursue a specialized study in print or audiovisual media. IFJ encourages students to develop facility in other European languages, especially English, German, and Spanish. There were 22 faculty members at the institute in 1994, most holding doctorate degrees.

The institute has a modest library, offering a relatively small choice of books and current reference materials. Laboratories, however, are very well equipped. Macintosh computer and photo labs are used to teach skills courses to print majors, who produce an Arabic-language newspaper called *Lissan Al Irfan* three times a year plus a magazine of the same name under faculty supervision. Students taking the French-language option produce a newspaper called *IS Journal* once a year. The institute subscribes to the Maghreb Arabe Presse and Agence France Presse news agencies to enable students to work with wire copy. There are excellent facilities for production work for broadcasting majors, although they learn under simulated conditions in the absence of an institute-run radio or television station. There are also good production and editing facilities for students interested in studying film. In addition to the skills training, the institute emphasizes the importance of communication research. All students are required to write a research thesis on subjects pertaining to communication and information sciences. Students receive a diploma in higher studies in journalism upon the satisfactory completion of all of these requirements (Laamouri interview, May 11, 1994).

Very few of the graduates in print media go on to work as journalists. They prefer to take jobs with government departments or in public relations because of better pay. Another reason cited by some students interviewed at the institute was that there is little opportunity for them to practice objective journalism because Morocco's mostly political party press is so opinionated in its news coverage.

The IFJ is scheduled to expand its mission starting in 1995, when it will offer specialties in public relations, advertising, and telecommunications. The institute's name will also be changed to the Higher Institute of Information and Communication. Other training facilities in communication studies in Morocco include the National Institute of Telecommunication, the National School of Public Administration, and the School of Information Sciences. Many Moroccan media professionals have attended communication education and training programs in France. Within the Arab world, the Damascus-based training center of the Arab States Broadcasting Union is an important source of refresher training. Moroccan media professionals also attend workshops given at the African Center for Improvement of Journalists and Communicators in Tunis. During 1983 and 1992, 103 Moroccan media personnel participated in these workshops (*CAPJC*, 1992, p. 36).

THE SUDAN

As of early 1994, there was little hope that the Sudanese press would see any relaxation of the strong political controls in the near future. On May 15, 1990, Lieutenant General al-Bashir had said that a multiparty system was "unsuitable" for the Sudan. The government continued to push ahead for full imposition of the Islamic law to replace the one substantially based on the English common law with the judiciary functioning as a separate and independent body. The press is actively used to mobilize public support for carrying out that objective. The constitution and the national assembly remained abolished. Thus, prospects for press freedom in the Sudan looked very poor.

Newspapers and Magazines

The 1989 coup was a major setback for freedom of expression in the Sudan. Press censorship was imposed immediately following the coup. Since then, the al-Bashir regime has carried out its objective of bringing media under government control. It has banned all newspapers and magazines with the exception of the weekly military paper, *Al-Guwat al-Musalaha.* Two government-controlled dailies, *Al-Sudani al-Hadith* and *Al-Inqadh al-Watani,* were launched in August and September 1989, respectively (*The Middle East Journal,* Winter 1990, p. 126). In May 1990, the Ministry of Culture and Information launched a new English-language weekly newspaper, *New Horizon.*

Before the coup, 22 daily newspapers were being published in the capital of Khartoum, 19 in Arabic and three in English. In addition, there were six nondaily newspapers. Among the dailies were *Al-Ithadi,* published by the Democratic Unionist Party; *Al-Hadaf,* the official organ of the Baath Party; *Al-Umma,* the organ of the Umma Party, the party of the deposed Prime Minister al-Mahdi; *Al-Midan,* organ of the Sudan Communist Party; *Ar-Rayah,* the official organ of the National Islamic Front; *Alwan* and *Sawt al-Gamahir;* dailies which also supported the National Islamic Front; and the English-language *Sudan News* and *Sudan Times (Europa Yearbook,* 1988, p. 2485). *The Sudan Times,* which was edited by a southerner and former minister, Bona Malwal, was the most popular English-language newspaper in the country. It was also regarded as having the best coverage of the civil war in southern Sudan and of human rights issues. Several independent newspapers were also banned. Another reputable newspaper, *al-Khartoum,* banned following the coup, was reported to have resumed publication from Cairo, Egypt, in April 1993 and is apparently being smuggled into the Sudan.

The al-Bashir regime continued to be in power as of early 1994, rejecting proposals for a return to a multiparty political system. Its control over the media remained strong. The number of newspapers was still limited to two dailies, *Al-Inqadh al-Watani* and *Al-Sudani al-Hadith,* and two weeklies, *Al-Guwwat al-Musallaha* and *New Horizon.* No reliable circulation figures for these newspapers were available at the time of this writing from UNESCO or other sources. In 1988, before the coup, the Sudan had a total daily newspaper circulation of 590,000 or about 25 copies per 1,000 population. Circulation for the 10 nondaily newspapers then was estimated to be 135,000, or 6 copies per 1,000 inhabitants. Total circulation for daily newspapers in 1990 was estimated to be 610,000, with 24 copies per 1,000 inhabitants. It is significant to note that the Sudan, which does not produce any newsprint of its own, sharply reduced its imports of newsprint from 8,500 metric tons in 1985 to 4,000 metric tons in 1991 (*Statistical Yearbook,* 1993).

The number of magazines has also fallen since the 1989 coup. All but two of the ten periodicals being published in 1988 were closed. Of the ten periodicals, nine were general interest publications and one was a political party journal. *Al-Eza'a,* a weekly focusing on cultural affairs, was the most successful publication with a circulation of 40,000. Others included one illustrated magazine; two devoted to politics, philosophy, religion, and culture; and five children and youth-oriented magazines. Total magazine circulation in 1988 was 136,000, which amounted to six copies per 1,000 population (*Statistical Yearbook,* 1993).

As with newspapers, magazine publishing has also been done by the government since the coup. The Ministry of Culture and Information produces several periodicals, with *Sudanow* being the best known. This English-language monthly is devoted to political, social, and economic subjects. Its circulation, 10,000 copies per issue before the 1989 coup, has dropped to about 5,000 copies since then. Another well-known magazine is *Al-Guwwat al-Musallaha,* a monthly for the armed forces, in addition to a weekly of the same name. This magazine has a circulation of 7,500 (*Africa South of the Sahara,* 1994, p. 865). Unlike Algeria, Morocco, and Tunisia, the Sudan is not an importer of foreign newspapers and periodicals. This situation can be attributed to the tight media controls imposed by the al-Bashir government. The UNESCO *Statistical Yearbook* last reported such imports in 1980, which were valued at $600,000. During the al-Mahdi civilian rule, the country did import newspapers and journals from a number of Arab countries (*The Democratic Journalist,* 1987, pp. 24–25).

Books

The status of the book publishing industry has not been very clear since the 1989 coup. Available data indicate that the Sudan produced 138 book titles in 1980 and imported books valued at $3.5 million that year (*Statistical Digest,* 1986; *Statistical Yearbook,* 1991). Because of lack of book publishing facilities in the Sudan, its Ministry of Education was said to be having a number of textbooks printed abroad as recently as 1987 (*The Democratic Journalist,* 1987, p. 24). Out of a total of seven publishers in the country, at least three were listed as book publishers in 1992. They are the Khartoum University Press, which publishes academic, general and educational books in Arabic and English; Al-Ayyam Press Co., publisher of fiction and nonfiction, arts, poetry, and reference books; and As-Sahafa Publishing and Printing House, which publishes fiction and government publications (*Europa Yearbook,* 1992, p. 2555).

Radio and Television

Broadcasting, a government monopoly since the country's independence, is managed by the state-owned National Radio and Television Corporation. Under its aegis, radio service is provided by the Sudan National Broadcasting Corporation (SNBC) and television service by the Sudan Television.

Radio service, which began in 1940, was available mostly in the north of the country as late as 1972 because all radio transmitters had been concentrated in the vicinity of the capital, Khartoum (Shummo, 1974, p. 47). In early 1980s, the three medium-wave and five shortwave transmitters in the country were still inadequate to provide service to the entire country (Kurian, 1982, p. 1100). Transmission facilities have been expanded since then, with provincial medium-wave transmitters now located in the south at Juba, in the east at Port Sudan, and in the west at Nyala. A total of 14 medium-wave and five shortwave transmitters were operating in the country in 1993 (*World Radio and TV Handbook,* 1993).

Radio Omdurman, the national radio station, broadcasts primarily in Arabic but also carries programs in English, French, and vernacular southern Sudan languages. A number of regional radio stations are also in operation. The total annual broadcasting hours for radio were 5,205 in 1989, with much of the programming classified as entertainment (30.5 percent) and news and informative programs (21 percent). Educational programs for rural development formed 7 percent of the broadcasting schedule. About 2 percent of the programming was related to the teaching of specific curricula. Religious and cultural programs were also important components of the broadcasting schedule (*Statistical Yearbook,* 1991). SNBC is financed by a combination of revenues from receiver license fees and advertising. In 1989, advertising took up 3.6 percent of the total broadcasting hours.

A military radio station called the National Unity Radio went on the air following the coup. It provides a daily four-hour service from 1 P.M. to 5 P.M. on shortwave from the city of Omdurman. As of early 1994, the Sudan had a limited external broadcasting service. A joint Sudanese-Egyptian station, which opened in 1982, broadcasts daily in Arabic. Head (1985, p. 321) said that a missionary group, known as the Sudan Interior Mission, was operating a radio complex called "External Love Winning Africa" in Monrovia, Liberia, on the west coast of Africa. The station, broadcasting in 10 Liberian languages as well as English, was providing informational and educational programming in addition to religious broadcasts. According to UNESCO data, there were 6.48 million radio receivers in the Sudan in 1991, or 250 receivers per 1,000 population.

Television service, which started in 1963, is provided by the commercial, government-controlled Sudan Television Service. The national network, with its main station in Omdurman, relays its service via regional stations in Gezira (central region) and Atbara (northern region). Color broadcasting uses the PAL system. With the installation of a microwave transmission network, television service has been available in at least 90 percent of the inhabited areas since 1983 (*Europa Yearbook,* 1992).

Since the 1989 military coup, the authorities have appointed military officers to key positions within the National Radio and Television Corporation. Television is now openly used as a medium for political propaganda and for encouraging support for government policies from the population (Article 19, 1991, p. 392).

The single television service, available seven hours daily, broadcasts mainly in Arabic but has a daily news bulletin and some programs in English. The station categorized its 2,360 hours of broadcasting time in 1989 as follows: entertainment, 42.7 percent; news bulletins and other informative programs, 28.5 percent; educational, cultural, religious, 8.5 percent each; advertisements, 3.4 percent. The entertainment programming was heavy in plays, with films, music, sports, and other entertainment programs lagging much behind. Educational programming was dominated by curriculum-related instructional programming, followed by programs for rural development (*Statistical Yearbook,* 1991). Head (1974, 1985) noted that as much as 40 percent of television programming in the Sudan is imported, most of it from the United States and Arab countries. This situation was attributed by the director-general of the Sudanese television to the substantially greater costs involved in producing local programs.

The Sudan is also taking advantage of the satellite technology. A nationwide satellite network has been established with 14 earth stations in the provinces to improve the country's telecommunications system. The earth stations are linked through the Sudan Satellite System (SUDOSAT) inaugurated in 1978. The system is used to provide a television signal across the vast territory of the country. The Sudan is also a member of the Tunis-based Arab States Broadcasting Union and Jeddah-based Islamic States Broadcasting Services Organization, which coordinate exchange of television programming among member states. The Sudan has external television satellite links with INTELSAT and ARABSAT.

According to UNESCO data, 2 million television receivers were in use in the Sudan in 1991, which amounted to 77 receivers for every 1,000 inhabitants. This figure compares very favorably with Africa's average of 37 receivers per 1,000 inhabitants in 1991, but is lower than the average of 103 for Arab states (*Statistical Yearbook,* 1993).

Cinema

The Sudan's film industry is underdeveloped, with only four feature-length films completed between 1980 and 1989. One film was produced in the country in 1991. Until the 1989 coup, the Sudan was a heavy importer of films. In 1988, it imported 135 films, of which 19.3 percent came from India and the remaining 80.7 percent from other unspecified countries. Imports declined to 104 films in 1989, the year of the coup. Of the 104 films, 34.6 percent came from India and the remainder from "other countries." (*Statistical Yearbook,* 1993). Although traditionally most films have come from India, the Sudan has also regularly imported films from the United States, France, Britain, Italy, Germany, and Hong Kong, among other countries. No movie import figures are available since the 1989 coup.

Latest figures available from UNESCO indicate that there were 56 cinema halls in the Sudan in 1983, with a total seating capacity of 97,200 or 4.8 seats for every 1,000 inhabitants. The annual attendance for that year was 300,000. In addition, there were 30 mobile cinema units, which attracted an attendance of 1,000,000 that year (*Statistical Yearbook,* 1990).

Media Education and Training

As in Libya, elimination of privately owned press as a result of media nationalization has provided little incentive to push journalism education in the Sudan, although the government has provided a variety of opportunities for the training of broadcast personnel. For many years, broadcast education in the Sudan was limited to technical training provided by vocational and trade schools. Print media training was obtained through apprenticeship with newspapers. As a result, Egypt was a favorite destination for the Sudanese students seeking mass communication degrees. Now Omdurman University in the Sudan offers an undergraduate degree program in print and audiovisual media. The curriculum, however, concentrates mostly on theory, with little opportunity for skills training and program production. Egypt continues to attract many Sudanese students. In recent years, a number of them have also enrolled in communication education institutes in Algeria, Morocco, and Tunisia.

Broadcast personnel have traditionally received technical training from equipment suppliers and training in program production through foreign-government-sponsored programs in the Sudan, especially those of Germany, United States, and Britain. Many broadcast personnel have been trained in these and other Western countries, including Australia. Other sources of training include the African Center for the Improvement of Journalists and Communicators in Tunisia, the Arab States Broadcasting Union, and the Islamic States Broadcasting Services Organization.

TUNISIA

The Tunisian press has shown an increasing tendency to shed the "loyalist" role it performed during the Bourguiba years. The 1988 political reforms made by President Ben Ali's government have allowed the development of a diverse press. But the government-enacted press code continues to inhibit press freedom in spite of the revisions made to ease regulation of the press. There continue to be strong defamation laws and a variety of other restrictions.

Press Freedom and Press Code

The Tunisian press is guaranteed freedom under Article 8 of the constitution, which says: "Freedom of opinion, expression, press, publication and assembly are guaranteed within the conditions defined by the law." The constitution says that these freedoms can be limited in the interest of "protecting the rights of others, the public order, national defense and social and economic development" (Constitution de la Republique Tunisienne, June 1, 1959).

An 80-article press code further outlines the conditions under which the press can operate. The press code, originally promulgated under the Bourguiba government in 1975, was revised in 1988. Under the code, the Ministry of the Interior controls the system of registration of newspapers and periodicals. The code states that two copies of all materials printed or reprinted in Tunisia for distribution to the public must be submitted to the Ministry of Information in addition to several other government departments. Copies of foreign publications must be submitted to the Ministry of Information and Ministry of the Interior prior to their distribution.

Another section of the press code provides for a mandatory right to reply by public authorities and private persons to inaccurate reports in newspapers and periodicals. The code says that the response must be published free of charge "at a prominent place and using the same type style that was used for the story in question'' (*Code de la Presse,* 1988, p. 17). Publishers who refuse to do so face a fine.

Special provisions in the press code and harsh sentences of up to five years' imprisonment and about $2,000 fine, explained in Articles 48 and 52, protect the president and all members of the government, including a citizen assigned to government service on a temporary basis, against abuse and slander. Article 54 says that any expression which abuses and injures a person is punishable by a jail sentence of up to three months and a fine of up to approximately $1,200. Punishment is also provided for publications insulting a group on racial or religious grounds or for inciting hatred toward citizens. In addition to these punishments, publications can be seized or suspended for these crimes or for threatening the public order under Article 73 of the code.

The 1988 revisions to the press code have introduced some reforms also. News can be published without any prepublication conditions. Seizure now involves only the issue that is condemned for such action rather than altogether closing down the publication. Suspending a newspaper or a periodical is no longer the responsibility of the Ministry of the Interior but of the courts. Truth has been allowed as a defense in libel suits, although this defense still does not apply in libel suits involving the head of state and members of the government. The revised press code obliges newspapers to reveal the sources of funding and it limits the number of newspapers owned by an individual to two publications of the same periodicity (*Code de la Presse,* 1988).

The code was revised in August 1993 following campaigns led by Tunisian journalists, human rights groups, and opposition parties against government censorship and control of the media, including the arrest and detention of journalists and the banning of newspapers. The press code still contains many restrictive provisions including broad powers to punish the ''dissemination of false information,'' the possession of publications which might disturb public order, and criticism of the president. Publication of information that incites hatred between races, religions, and public groups is punishable by from two months' to three years' imprisonment and a fine of $1,000 to $2,000. Slander continues to be a criminal offense and is punishable with imprisonment and fine. The code also provides for a government-controlled licensing system for new publications (*Revue Tunisienne de Communication,* July/December 1993, pp. 157–161). In June 1989, the government created the High Council on Communication to provide advice on any new laws and regulations affecting the media. Its members were chosen from various political persuasions and intellectual groups.

Newspapers and Magazines

Like Algeria and Morocco, several Tunisian newspapers and periodicals are affiliated with political parties. Seven daily newspapers were being published in Tunisia in 1993, four in Arabic and three in French. They are as follows: *Al Horriya,* in Arabic, and *Le Renouveau,* in French, both organs of the ruling

Democratic Constitutional Rally (RCD) party; *La Presse,* government organ in French; *As-Sabah* and *Ash-Shourouk,* privately owned, in Arabic; *Le Temps,* privately owned, in French; and a new Arabic-language newspaper, *As-Sahafa.*

In 1993 there were 25 weekly publications in Tunisia, including several newspapers affiliated with political parties. Weekly newspapers include: *Al Tariq Al Jadid,* organ of the Tunisian Communist Party now known as the Renovation Movement; *Al Mostakbal, L'Avenir,* and *Ar-Rai,* organs of the Democratic Socialist Movement; *Al Wahada,* organ of the Popular Unity Party; *Al-Mawqaf,* organ of the Progressive Socialist Assembly; *Al-Biladi,* organ of the Democratic Constitutional Rally; *Al-Fajr,* published by Hizb an-Nahdah, an Islamic fundamentalist group; and *Al Watan,* organ of the Unionist Democratic Union. *Tunisia News,* an independent English-language weekly newspaper, was established in late 1992.

The government provides a variety of aid and subsidies to the press. Each party-affiliated newspaper receives a government grant of $80,000 annually. All politically oriented publications are entitled to government-subsidized newsprint. In addition, Tunisian journalists are entitled to free travel on national railways and a 50 percent reduction of fare on public buses and on air tickets. Moreover, as a result of a presidential decision, a special project was launched in January 1992 to help journalists acquire their own homes (Besbes interview, May 19, 1994; *Tunisia and Human Rights,* 1992).

Total circulation of daily newspapers in 1990 was estimated to be 300,000 copies, which amounted to an estimated 37 copies per 1,000 inhabitants. Newspaper circulation has declined since 1980, when 43 copies per 1,000 people were being circulated, according to UNESCO estimates. This figure compares favorably with Africa's average of 17 newspapers per 1,000 people in 1990 but is less than the Arab states' average of 38 copies. Weekly newspapers had an estimated total circulation of 244,000 in 1988, according to the latest available figures from UNESCO sources. That figure translated into an estimated 32 copies per 1,000 inhabitants. In 1991, 11,092 metric tons of newsprint was being consumed in Tunisia as compared with 9,900 metric tons in 1985. All newsprint is imported (*Statistical Yearbook,* 1993).

According to data supplied by the Tunisian government, 137 periodicals were being published in the country in 1991 in addition to the eight nondaily, party newspapers listed above. Of the total of 150 dailies and periodicals published in the country, 95 are in Arabic, 48 in French, six in Arabic and French, and one in Italian (*Tunisia: Basic Data,* 1993). There has been a sharp rise in the number of periodicals following the political reforms introduced by the Ben Ali government. In 1986, the year before Ben Ali became president, a total of 10 periodicals were being published in Tunisia (*Statistical Yearbook,* 1991).

Many of the periodicals, as newspapers, are affiliated with political parties. Most have circulations between 5,000 to 10,000. The major periodicals with circulations of 50,000 or more are: *Al-Akhbar,* a weekly newsmagazine; *Al-Anouar at-Tounissia* and *Ash-Shuruk,* general interest weeklies; *Irfane,* a youth-oriented monthly; *Jeunesse Magazine,* a general interest monthly in Arabic and French; and *Al-Moussawar,* a general interest weekly. Other well-circulated magazines are *Tunis Hebdo* (40,000), a sports and general interest weekly; *Dialogue* (30,000), a cultural and political weekly; and *Realities* (25,000) and *Le Temps* (42,000), weekly newsmagazines (*Middle East and North Africa,* 1994, pp. 851–852).

According to government figures, 500 imported newspapers and periodicals were being distributed in the country in 1991. Indeed, a wide variety of publications from Europe, especially France, North America, and the Middle East can be purchased at newsstands in Tunisia. UNESCO data indicate that Tunisia imported newspapers and periodicals valued at $4.6 million in 1991, a substantial increase over the 1985 figure of $3.7 million. In 1991, Tunisia's exports of newspapers and periodicals were valued at $1.1 million (*Statistical Yearbook,* 1993).

Foreign publications go through a careful government scrutiny before they can be distributed. *Jeune Afrique,* a French-language political weekly started by Tunisian intellectuals and then moved to Paris to escape the controls under the Bourguiba years, has occasionally come under pressure from the Ben Ali government. The magazine, which was altogether banned in Tunisia between July 1984 and January 1985, saw its circulation restricted from 24,000 to 6,000 in late 1988 (Ansah, 1991, p. 30). In November 1989, the authorities confiscated an issue of the monthly *Jeune Afrique Economie* because of an article that criticized the country's economic situation. An issue of the French newspaper *Le Monde* was banned from distribution in June 1990 because of an article about the Tunisian people's apathy toward that month's local elections (Article 19, 1991, p. 398).

Books

Tunisia has a sizable book industry. Latest available UNESCO data indicate that 293 titles were published in Tunisia in 1988, with a total of 879,000 copies. School textbooks and government publications are not included in this data. Of the 293 books, 137 were in literature, with social sciences, arts, history/geography, religion, and applied sciences being other key areas of publication. According to figures supplied by the Tunisian External Communication Agency, 883 books were published in the country in 1993 (*Tunisia: Basic Data,* 1993).

A number of well-known books were banned during the Bourguiba years on the grounds that they harmed public morals, public order, or defamed government officials. Most of these books were unbanned after Ben Ali became president in 1987. His government, however, is known to have banned at least three books during 1989 and 1990, including one called *Crimes of Corruption in the State of Law* (Article 19, 1991, p. 399).

There were 150 publishing and printing companies in the country in 1993, including the Government Publishing House. At least 13 of them were involved in book publishing (*Tunisia: Basic Data,* 1993). Tunisia is also a heavy importer of books. In 1991, books valued at $9.1 million were imported, while book exports amounted to $1.9 million. In 1985, $4.8 million worth of books were imported against $1.6 million in exports (*Statistical Yearbook,* 1993).

Radio and Television

Nationwide radio and television services are operated by the government-owned Radiodiffusion Television Tunisienne (RTT). RTT has enjoyed monopoly status since its inception in 1966. All areas of the country can receive radio broadcasts and 95 percent can pick up the national television station.

Tunisian radio, which began service in 1936, consists of a national service, an international service, and two regional services, Radio-Sfax and Radio-Monastir. The national service, broadcast on FM, AM, and shortwave frequencies, offers news, information, and cultural and entertainment programming. The international service, known as Radio Tunis Channel Internationale (RTCI), broadcasts in French for 15 hours daily, with one hour of programming each in English, Italian, and German. In addition to Europe, its service is also directed to Middle East and the Arabian Gulf countries.

Radio-Sfax, created in 1961 with a regional focus, offers 20 hours of service each day. The station established a television program production department in 1990, which contributes programs to the national television channel. Another radio station with a regional/local appeal is Radio-Monastir, which went on the air in 1977. It broadcasts 18 hours each day. This station does some television production also. Three additional local stations are Radio Kef, established in November 1991 to serve the northwest of the country; Radio Gafsa, established in November 1991 to serve the southwest of the country; and Radio Tataouine, established in November 1993 to serve the southeast of the country. These three local stations broadcast each 10 hours daily on FM frequencies. These stations produce some television programming also for the national channel (Herguem interview, May 19, 1994).

These services were being relayed via a total of seven AM and eight FM stations, and seven shortwave frequencies in 1994. According to UNESCO data, there were an estimated 1.64 million radio receivers in use in Tunisia in 1991, or 199 per 1,000 population. This compared well with the African average of 170 radio receivers per 1,000, but was less than the Arab states' average of 251 (*Statistical Yearbook,* 1993).

Although still government controlled, radio is not as strong a government mouthpiece as it used to be during the Bourguiba years. With the 1988 political reforms, President Ben Ali made a commitment to allow legalized political parties better access to government-controlled media. Head (1974, p. 31) said that broadcasting, which had played an important role in the independence struggle, continued to have important political functions after independence. President Bourguiba addressed the nation every week on the radio and there was at least one ideological program called "Presidential Directives" (Kurian, 1982, p. 1104).

News and informational programming makes up a significant component of the overall programming schedule, with several news bulletins each day. Viewpoints of the opposition political parties on public issues are also heard on the radio (Essid, 1992). Tunisia has been a pioneer among North African nations in using radio and television in distance learning programs. The broadcast media were first used in 1969 to promote adult literacy, a practice which has continued. Broadcasting has also been used for promoting a variety of nonformal educational campaigns, such as family planning, since the early 1960s. Because of the cultural ties developed with France during the colonial days, radio programs from France continue to be popular in Tunisia, as in other North African countries with similar histories.

Television broadcasting, which was inaugurated in Tunisia on May 31, 1966, reached practically all of the country by 1972. Television relay stations have been built throughout the country, with a total of 19 in operation as of early 1994. Although a wide variety of European and other channels are available with the use of parabolic dish antennas, Tunisia itself broadcasts on two channels. The national channel, called TV 7, transmits programs in Arabic for 12 hours during weekdays and for 15 hours on the weekends. A second channel was introduced on June 12, 1983. Called Tunis 2, it broadcasts news, cultural, and entertainment programming in the Tunis area from 8:30 P.M. to midnight in French and Arabic. About 65 percent of the programming carried on the Tunisian television channels is produced locally. The rest of the programming is imported from a number of Arab countries, especially from Egypt, Syria, and Lebanon. Tunisia also imports some programming from North Africa and Europe. The national channel, TV 7, also began sending its transmissions internationally through satellite on November 7, 1992. Its signals can be received in North Africa, Europe, and the Middle East.

In addition to the two Tunisian channels, France Deux, a channel relayed from France, has been available since June 1989. This channel was earlier called Antenne 2. The Italian channel RAI-Uno has also been available since the 1960 Olympic Games held in Italy, when the Italian government provided reception equipment to the Tunisian government to enable Tunisians to watch the games. These two channels are relayed through the facilities of RTT, allowing Tunisians a choice of over-the-air television channels. Another channel, known as the Maghreb Channel, was established on March 20, 1990 to broadcast programs from the countries of the Maghreb. The Union of Arab Maghreb, proclaimed in February 1989 in a treaty signed in Morocco, comprises Algeria, Libya, Mauritania, Morocco, and Tunisia. Since reception of satellite television programming is legal in Tunisia, the wealthier are buying satellite dishes in increasing numbers. Buyers of satellite dishes are required under the law to notify the Ministry of Communication. Dozens of stations from Europe and other countries can be received with the use of such equipment.

Citing accomplishments of the RTT, its director-general said that carrying the national channel via satellite to other countries has been a major achievement. Decentralization of radio and procurement of some television programming through regional production centers were also noted as key accomplishments. Viewer surveys had helped in the improvement of television programming, he said. A new channel for young adults was scheduled to go on the air in late 1994. It will broadcast primarily in Arabic, with some programming in French (Herguem interview, May 19, 1994).

Pay television has been available in Tunisia since November 1992 through Channel Canal Horizon located in Tunis. It receives programming from France and retransmits on a pay basis in Tunisia at a charge of $22 per month. This commercial-free channel carries films, sports, and music. Its signal is available free of charge for two hours daily.

UNESCO data indicate that there were an estimated 650,000 television receivers in the country in 1991, or 79 for every 1,000 population. This compared favorably with the African average of 37 sets for 1,000 population that year but was considerably less than the Arab states' average of 103 receivers (*Statistical Yearbook*, 1993). Color broadcasting is done by using the SECAM system.

Budget for the state-owned radio and television stations is provided through state subsidies, advertisements, and a surcharge on all electricity bills. The two Tunisian television channels have been accepting advertising since 1988. Approximately 40 percent of the budget comes from the electricity surcharge and the remaining 60 percent from a combination of advertising revenues and state subsidies (Herguem interview, May 19, 1994).

Cinema

Tunisian government figures indicate that a total of 54 films were produced in the country up to 1993. According to the most recent UNESCO data, no full-length feature film was produced in Tunisia in 1991. Film production is largely state controlled, although 18 independent amateur film companies were also operating as of 1993 (*Tunisia: Basic Data*, 1992). Tunisian producers often look for coproducers from other countries because of financial and technical constraints. Article 19 (1991, p. 399) says that films are frequently censored for violence and sexual themes. "Very few cases of politically motivated censorship are known," it says.

Like other North African countries, Tunisia is a heavy importer of feature films. Latest available UNESCO data indicate that Tunisia imported 165 films in 1987, with 57 percent coming from the United States and 9.7 percent from France. Other countries represented were Italy, India, Britain, Germany, and Hong Kong. There were 81 cinema halls in the country in 1993, with a seating capacity of 18,600. The number of cinema seats per 1,000 population was put at 2.3 in 1987 (*Statistical Yearbook*, 1991).

Journalism Education and Training

Of the five North African countries studied in this section, Tunisia has the most comprehensive and well-developed facilities in mass communication education and training. The Tunis University's Institute of Press and Information Sciences (IPSI) has offered a four-year print and broadcast journalism degree program since 1967, although journalism training programs date back to 1956. IPSI's main goal is to bridge the gap between academic achievement and vocational needs by educating students to master the techniques required to work in a newspaper, magazine, or broadcast newsroom (Methnani interview, May 18, 1994).

Students wishing to study at IPSI apply to the Ministry of Education and Sciences for admission. The ministry selects applicants from among secondary school graduates, practicing journalists, and foreign students. Admission prerequisites include secondary school studies in art and literature, facility with French and English in addition to Arabic, and good oral and written skills. Approximately 5 percent of students are professional journalists. State aid is available to students seeking education in journalism and broadcasting.

The degree program consists of two cycles of two years each. Two-thirds of the curriculum of the first cycle is devoted to basic studies (languages, economics, law, information theory, history, and geography, etc.), while the remaining third is devoted to studies in journalism. Successful completion of the first cycle leads to the awarding of a Journalism Aptitude Certificate. Second-cycle studies are more specialized. Third-year students have to major in economics, political science, or culture studies, while fourth-year students specialize in either print or broadcast journalism. Fourth-year studies also include a two-month internship and the completion of a report on the internship. Students are also required to do research work and write a thesis on a media-related topic before graduation. At the end of the second cycle, students are awarded the degree Maitrise en Journalisme, which is considered equivalent to master's degree in the United States (Methnani interview, May 18, 1994).

Approximately 89 percent of the students graduate from the program. According to a faculty member at IPSI, the placement rate of graduates with print and broadcast industries is very high. A number of them are said to find teaching positions in high schools. Out of a total of 561 students enrolled in 1994, 51 were from foreign countries, mostly from Africa and the Middle East. Sixty-five percent of the students were females. A total of 747 students graduated from the institute from 1971 to 1992. The institute has a total of 40 full-time faculty members and approximately 35 part-time faculty (Osman interview, May 19, 1994).

IPSI also offers a one-year, postgraduate professional degree program in journalism called Diploma d'Etudes Superieures Specialisees (DESS). This program is open to graduates in journalism as well as other disciplines. The institute is in the process of introducing a doctoral degree program in communication and information sciences.

IPSI publishes a scholarly journal called *La Revue Tunisienne de Communication* twice a year, an annual report listing students' research papers, and reports on seminars and colloquia held at the institute. It also publishes textbooks and other books on media-related topics. The institute has excellent facilities, including a specialized mass media library, a language library, Macintosh computer labs, radio and television studios and production labs, a printing room, and satellite television.

IPSI has a cooperative relationship with mass communication education institutes in Morocco, Algeria, Egypt, Jordan, Senegal, and Cameroon. It is also affiliated with several French journalism institutes, including Centre de Formation et de Perfectionment des Journalists, Institute Française de Press, and Ecole Française des Attaches de Presse. Other affiliations are with universities in Canada, Belgium, Portugal, Spain, and Germany. During 1985–1986, IPSI engaged in a faculty exchange program with the University of Missouri School of Journalism in the United States. IPSI also works closely with UNESCO in planning its institutional activities (Methnani interview, May 18, 1994).

Center for the Improvement of Journalists and Communicators

In keeping with its official policy of pushing for the development of indigenous communication systems in developing countries, Tunisia has established an institution called Le Centre Africain de Perfectionnement des Journalistes et Communicateurs (CAPJC). Inaugurated in February 1983, the center aims at improving the skills of professional journalists and communicators through refresher courses, workshops, and specialized programs. It also provides training in the use of new technologies in the field of communications.

The CAPJC was established with aid from Friedrich Naumann Foundation of West Germany, following requests by the Tunisian Ministry of Information and the Tunisian Association of Journalists. The foundation, which had earlier helped in the development of IPSI, provided sufficient funding in the initial years for equipment and staff to get the training operations of the center under way. The administrative operations of the center are financed by the Tunisian government, which levies a special tax on press enterprises to facilitate continued training of journalists. The center operates under the jurisdiction of the State Secretary of Information. In recent years, the center has received funding from a variety of other international sources to finance its education and training activities. Among others, aid has come from UNESCO, the United States Information Agency, France, and the Arab States Broadcasting Union. These funds are used to cover travel, room, and registration expenses of workshop participants, and to pay stipends to experts giving the workshops (Najar interview, May 19, 1994).

The center has well-equipped print and broadcast laboratories. It also has a library and satellite telecommunications facilities to carry out its activities. Training sessions are conducted by academics and professionals from Tunisia and other countries. The center holds approximately 12 training sessions per year, with each session lasting from one to three weeks. Topics for 1994 included "Arabic Diction," "Page Makeup," "Economic Journalism," "Sports Journalism," and "Regional Radio and Television Reporting." The center also offers evening courses, which are completed in six months.

The CAPJC organized 156 activities from 1983 to 1992 and has trained 3,004 professional journalists and communicators. Of these, 2,316 were Tunisians and 688 were from 60 different countries, including 239 from Africa south of the Sahara (*CAPJC*, 1992). The center does not give any diploma, although a document indicating attendance in a training program is given. Topics for the center's activities are determined through surveys of media professionals.

REFERENCES

Abdelmalek, L. (1992). Press information received from the ambassador of Morocco in Indonesia. Dated November 26, 1992.

Abdesslam, A. M. (May 12, 1994). Journalist at the Maghreb Arabe Presse News Agency. Personal interview in Rabat.

Africa south of the Sahara. (1994). London: Europa Publications.

Algerian Ministry of Information. (1993). Information supplied by the ministry.

Ansah, P. A. V. (1991). The press, pluralism and freedom in Africa. *Media Development, 38* (4).

Article 19. (1991). World Report. *Information, freedom and censorship.* London: Library Association Publishing.

Banks, A. (1993). *Political handbook of the world.* Binghamton, NY: CSA Publications.

Benchekroun, H. (May 12, 1994). Broadcast journalist at Moroccan Radio. Personal interview in Rabat.

Benzahra, Y. (May 12, 1994). Chief of International Cooperation Service of RTM. Personal interview in Rabat.

Besbes, E. (May 19, 1994). Director, Agence Tunisienne de Communication Exterieure. Personal interview in Tunis.

CAPJC. (1992). Report of the Centre Africain de Perfectionnement des Journalistes et Communicateteurs, 1983–1992. Tunis: Secretariat D'Etat a L'Information.

Code de la Presse. (1988). Republique Tunisienne. Tunis: Ministere de L'Information.

Constitution de la Republique Tunisienne. (1959). In *Code de la Presse,* Republique Tunisienne. Tunis: Ministere de l'Information.

The Democratic Journalist. (1987). The situation of the Sudanese press, no. 2.

Drost, H. (1991). *The world's news media.* Essex, U.K.: Longman Current Affairs.

Elgabri, A. Z. (1974). The Maghreb. In *Broadcasting in Africa.* S. W. Head (Ed.), Philadelphia: Temple University Press.

Essid, R. (1992). Information received from the Tunisian press attaché in Jakarta, Indonesia.

The Europa World Yearbook. (1988). London: Europa Publications.

The Europa World Yearbook. (1992). London: Europa Publications.

Harris, L. C. (1986). *Libya: Qadhafi's revolution and the modern state.* Boulder, CO: Westview Press.

Head, S. W. (1974). *Broadcasting in Africa.* Philadelphia: Temple University Press.

Head, S. W. (1985). *World broadcasting systems: A comparative analysis.* Belmont, CA: Wadsworth Publishing Co.

Herguem, A. (May 19, 1994). Director-General, Radiodiffusion Television Tunisienne. Personal interview in Tunis.

Keesing's Record of World Events. (May 1988). Libya, vol. 34, no. 5. New York: Longman.

Kurian, G. (1982). *World press encyclopedia.* New York: Facts on File.

La presse marocaine. (1994). Rabat: Ministry of Information.

Laamouri, M. (May 11, 1994). Director, Institut Superieur de Journalisme, Morocco. Personal interview in Rabat.

Laroussi, C. (May 11, 1994). Director of Communication, Ministry of Information. Personal interview in Rabat.

McDaniel, D. O. (1982). Libya. In D. A. Boyd, *Broadcasting in the Arab world.* Philadelphia: Temple University Press.

Methnani, R. (May 18, 1994). Dean, Institute of Press and Information Sciences, Tunisia. Personal interview in Tunis.

Middle East and North Africa. (1994). London: Europa Publications.

The Middle East Journal. (Winter 1990). Chronology, *44* (1).

Moroccan Ministry of Information. (1994). Media information supplied by the ministry.

Najar, R. (May 19, 1994). Director, Centre Africain de Perfectionnement des Journalistes et Communicateurs, Tunis. Personal interview in Tunis.

Osman, D. B. (May 19, 1994). Faculty member at the Institute of Press and Information Sciences, Tunisia. Personal interview in Tunis.

Radiodiffusion television marocaine. (1994). Rabat: Ministry of Information.

Revue Tunisienne de communication. (July/December 1993). Actualite Juridique: Amendment du Code de la Presse, no. 24.

Shummo, A. M. (1974). The Sudan. In *Broadcasting in Africa.* S. W. Head (Ed.), Philadelphia: Temple University Press.

Statistical Digest. (1986). UNESCO. Paris: UNESCO.

Statistical Yearbook. (1986). UNESCO. Paris: UNESCO.

Statistical Yearbook. (1990). UNESCO. Paris: UNESCO.

Statistical Yearbook. (1991). UNESCO. Paris: UNESCO.

Statistical Yearbook. (1993). UNESCO. Paris: UNESCO.

The Straits Times. (January 7, 1993). Algeria to gag press as war on extremists hots up. Singapore.

Tunisia: Basic data. (1993). Tunis: Ministry of Culture and Information.

Tunisia and human rights. (1992). Tunis: Agence Tunisienne de Communication Exterieure.

World radio TV handbook. (1993). New York: Billboard Publications, Inc.

8 Interregional/ International Exchanges, New Technologies, and Special Problems

Because of their common Arab heritage, Algeria, Libya, Morocco, the Sudan, and Tunisia participate in a variety of media exchanges among themselves and with the rest of the Arab and Islamic world. In addition, these North African countries have cooperative agreements with a number of international media organizations. The most common interregional and international media exchanges are discussed in the section that follows. After this section, we will discuss the five North African countries' news agencies and their exchange relationships, the status of new technologies and telecommunications, and special problems and challenges.

ASBU INTERREGIONAL/INTERNATIONAL EXCHANGES

Perhaps the single most important organization designed to strengthen cooperation among broadcasting organizations in the Arab states is the Arab States Broadcasting Union (ASBU). Established in 1969 with its headquarters in Tunis, the ASBU comprises the radio and television broadcasting organizations in the 21 Arab states. It coordinates daily news exchange and weekly exchanges of television programs from member countries via the Arab communication satellite (ARABSAT). Its main objectives are as follows:

1. To consolidate the spirit of the Arab brotherhood;
2. To acquaint the peoples of the world with the authenticity of the Arab Nation, its capabilities, its aspirations, and its causes;
3. To help create a New World Communication Order that guarantees to all national cultures the right to emerge, to develop, and to establish a constructive dialogue between them;

4. To reinforce broadcasting technology in the Arab world and coordinate its issues;

5. To establish schedules of the frequencies required by the member states and coordinate them in conformity with the international norms and technical standards;

6. To coordinate the efforts of member institutions as far as utilizing satellites is concerned, especially the use of the ARABSAT;

7. To represent the member institutions, defend their interests when negotiating the rights of transmitting major events, and provide them with all necessary facilities in this field (*Union de Radiodiffusion des Etats Arabes,* 1994).

In order to promote news and program exchanges between its members, the ASBU has leased a transponder on ARABSAT to be used around the clock by its members. Launched in 1985, the satellite is operated by the multinational ARABSAT organization based in Riyadh, Saudi Arabia, with which the ASBU cooperates on finding ways for the most effective use of the Arab satellite by the ASBU members. The Arab satellite is intended for the exclusive use of member Arab broadcasters, who are linked together through the ASBU.

In the field of programming, the ASBU exchanges radio programs by mail, and daily news exchanges and weekly exchanges of sports and other television programs via ARABSAT. It also coordinates the transmission of Arab and international sports events for ASBU members as well as other political or cultural events. The process of news exchange is an interesting one. There are two daily half-hour news exchanges, one in midmorning and the other in late afternoon, via Channel 23 on the ARABSAT. One hour before transmission begins, news directors from all over the Arab world participate in a telephone news conference coordinated at the Tunis center in conjunction with ASBU's Arab Center for News and Program Exchanges in Algiers. Since a member country is limited to a maximum of six minutes of news items, up to five countries are chosen in the news conference to transmit news. Viewers with satellite receivers can watch the news directly from ARABSAT. The news is also carried through the domestic newscasts of member countries. Although the ASBU policy is to "exchange" news, that is, to rotate news transmission among member countries, Saudi Arabia and Egypt are generally more active because of the level of news they generate. Among the North African countries, the Sudan and Mauritania are the least active in the news exchange program (Kara interview, May 18, 1994).

Sports exchanges, carried on a weekly basis on Mondays, are also planned through a telephone conference. Programs are limited to a maximum of 75 minutes. Both regional and international sports events, in which teams from Arab states participate, are carried in the programming exchange. On behalf of its members, the ASBU also negotiates coverage rights for major sports events such as the Olympic Games, the World Cup, and the African Games, and provides facilities for their coverage.

As part of its other ongoing activities, the ASBU sponsors seminars, symposia, and workshops on topics related to broadcasting, which are conducted by experts from international broadcasting organizations, telecommunications industry representatives, and speakers from the ASBU member countries. Some of the topics covered in recent years are: (a) Digital transmission techniques and developments; (b) status of HDTV, including criteria for the choice of an HDTV production standard; (c) high-power sound broadcasting transmitters, including digital modulation for high-power AM transmitters and evolution of the design of TV and FM broadcasting; (d) development and implementation considerations in broadcast teletext and data broadcasting; (e) emerging technologies in radio and television, including transition from analog to digital environment in TV, new video tape recording formats, and digital audio for radio. The most recent symposium, held in October 1993 in Tunis, was entitled "Satellite Communication and Broadcasting." It focused on the issues of tariffs and deregulation, digital video compression, and the future of satellite broadcasting. The symposium was attended by 125 broadcasting representatives from North Africa and the Middle East. The ASBU publishes the proceedings of the seminars and symposia for circulation and its research archives (Adwan interview, May 18, 1994).

The permanent bodies of the ASBU include the Arab Center for Radio and Television Audience Research, based in Baghdad, Iraq; and the Arab Training Center for Radio and Television, located in Damascus, Syria. The latter carries out specialized technical and news training courses throughout the year for the benefit of the staff of the ASBU member broadcasting organizations.

The ASBU has a wide-ranging, cooperative, working relationship with a number of international broadcasting organizations. They include the European Broadcasting Union, based in Geneva, Switzerland; the Asia-Pacific Broadcasting Union, Kuala Lumpur, Malaysia; the National Broadcasters Association, Ottawa, Canada; the Caribbean Broadcasting Union, Barbados; the Organization of Ibero-American Television (OTI), Mexico City; the Union of National Radio and Television Organizations of Africa (URTNA), Dakar, Senegal; and the International Association of Broadcasters, Montevideo, Uruguay.

An official of the ASBU explained that its relationship with these organizations extends to three broad areas: (a) coordination of studies of matters of mutual interest and actively seeking solution of international questions affecting broadcasting; (b) coordination of efforts to gain an effective voice in international forums on matters that affect broadcasting; and (c) programming exchange. For example, the ASBU is active in participating in the triennial conferences of the International Association of Broadcasters. In the last conference, held in Mexico in 1992, several issues of continuing interest to the ASBU were discussed, including technical standards for HDTV and digital audio, acquisition of sports rights, training of broadcast personnel, and North-South cooperation in international broadcasting.

In the area of programming, the ASBU coordinates three daily news exchanges with European Broadcasting Union's Eurovision via its satellite links.

Sports, cultural programs, and other types of material are also exchanged, although there is more traffic from Eurovision and North American broadcasting organizations to ASBU member countries. Program exchange relationships exist with a number of other international broadcasting organizations. The ASBU also maintains a close professional relationship with a number of specialized UN organizations, especially the UNESCO and the International Telecommunications Union (Suleiman interview, May 18, 1994).

The ASBU has sponsored an Arab radio and television festival every two years since 1981, in collaboration with Radiodiffusion Television Tunisienne. Broadcasting organizations participate with various programs to compete for awards. The ASBU also organizes the Arab Song Festival on a yearly basis to promote Arab songs in broadcasting programs.

Commenting on the challenges facing the ASBU, its programming coordinator said that the news policy in the entire Arab world, including North Africa, needs to open up so that the ASBU can facilitate a free flow of information. As it is, only news stories compatible with an individual government's political stance stood a chance of being aired. Programming exchange is not taking place on an equitable basis among member countries, she said, partly because of lack of modern equipment on the part of some member countries. Lack of well-trained broadcast personnel in several member countries continues to be a problem in spite of the training programs implemented by member countries and the ASBU. More training courses are needed in each of the television organizations. Finally, in her opinion, the ASBU member states rely too much on Western news organizations for news. She said that as much as possible news about Arab countries and the world at large should be covered by Arab broadcasters themselves to provide the Arab perspective on issues.

INTERREGIONAL/INTERNATIONAL EXCHANGES BY COUNTRIES

The North African countries have a variety of regional and international operating agreements. They include the following:

Maghrebvision Television Network

There has been a degree of success among the Maghreb countries (Algeria, Libya, Morocco, Mauritania, and Tunisia) in establishing regional media cooperation. Morocco's efforts to establish a North African regional news agency, called the Maghreb Arab Press, back in 1959 failed because of political differences among the countries. Discussions began in 1966 to establish a regional television organization, Maghrebvision, for joint production and broadcasting of television programming. They led to the creation of Maghrebvision by Morocco, Tunisia, and Algeria in 1970, linking the capitals of the three countries by microwave. But differences in political and economic policies of the member countries stalled the development of a true Maghreb network, limiting the venture to carrying primarily cultural fare on an exchange basis. The programming generated little audience interest.

During his presidency of the Arab Maghreb Union in 1990, Tunisian President Ben Ali pushed for the rejuvenation of Maghrebvision and a Maghreb channel began broadcasting on March 20, 1990. Although the creation of the Maghreb channel elevated regional cooperating in television broadcasting to more than just exchange of programming among member countries' TV stations, the nature of the programming broadcast on this channel did not change appreciably. To remedy that situation, the channel began to provide a greater coverage of the Maghreb starting January 1993. As of mid-1994, however, the channel had not established itself as a serious and credible source of news and public affairs programming about the Maghreb (El Youssoufi interview, May 12, 1994).

Islamic States Broadcasting Organization (ISBO)

Founded in 1959 in Saudi Arabia, the ISBO's objectives include propagation of Islamic teaching, protection of Islamic heritage, promotion of Islamic solidarity, and furthering cooperative relations with regional and international information and cultural organizations. These objectives are accomplished through production of radio and television programs, exchange of programs between broadcasting corporations of member states, teaching Arabic language by audiovisual means, and training of broadcast personnel of member states. Algeria, Morocco, and Tunisia are not as active in exchanging programming through the ISBO as the Sudan and Libya because of the relatively tolerant approach to religion of the former three. As a result, the three countries exchange primarily cultural and some religious programming through the ISBO.

Union Radio Television Nationale Africaine (URTNA)

Founded in 1962, this Union of National Radio and Television Organizations of Africa has 47 full members, including the North African countries, and seven associate members. The major aims of URTNA, based in Dakar, Senegal, are as follows:

1. To promote, maintain and develop cooperation among the members;
2. To support in every domain the interests of radio and television organizations which have accepted its statutes and to establish relations with other such organizations;
3. To promote and coordinate the study of all matters relating to radio and television and to ensure the exchange of information on all questions of general interest;
4. To use its best endeavors to ensure that all its members honor the provisions of international and intra-African agreements in all matters relating to radio and television;

5. To coordinate and collaborate closely with member organizations in the coverage of national and international events (*World Radio TV Handbook,* 1993, p. 46).

The work of URTNA is published in the *URTNA Review,* produced biannually in English and French; and in studies and reports. As of mid-1994, Morocco was not active with this organization because of differences over the Western Sahara issue.

The International Council of French-Language Broadcasting (CIREF)

Algeria, Morocco, and Tunisia are members of this Brussels-based organization, which coordinates exchange of programming among French-speaking countries. It also sponsors training programs for broadcast personnel and provides assistance in program production. Broadcasting personnel from the three North African countries often receive training at the organization headquarters.

The Broadcasting Organization of the Nonaligned Countries

The North African countries belong to this Belgrade-based organization, which facilitates exchange of broadcast programming among nonaligned countries. The North African countries, especially Tunisia, have also supported the Non-Aligned News Agencies Pool, also based in Belgrade, which provides exchange of news agency material among member countries. Because of political problems in Yugoslavia, both of these organizations have not been active in recent years. The material exchanged through them was said to be heavily tainted by the views of governments of member states.

Federation of Arab Journalists

Journalists' associations in North African countries are members of this federation founded in 1964. Based in Baghdad, Iraq, this organization represents some 20,000 journalists from 17 member countries. Among the objectives of the federation is lobbying on behalf of member associations on issues affecting journalists, especially in press–government relations.

International Audiovisual University

Broadcasting organizations of Algeria, Morocco, and Tunisia are affiliated with this Paris-based university. Broadcast personnel from these countries often receive technical and program production training at the university. The university puts a special emphasis on using broadcasting for educational and socioeconomic development.

European Broadcasting Union (EBU)

The North African countries have an active working relationship with this Geneva-based organization. Founded in 1950, the EBU objectives include news and program exchanges in television and radio, and promotion of cooperation with broadcasting organizations of the entire world. The North African countries engage in a daily exchange of news with the EBU. In addition, they receive a variety of sports and cultural programming from the EBU. There is a greater traffic of television programming through this exchange relationship (Benzahra interview, May 12, 1994; Herguem interview, May 19, 1994).

REGIONAL COOPERATION THROUGH PRESS AGENCIES

Although the Moroccan plans for the establishment of a regional North African news agency did not materialize, as indicated earlier, the individual news agencies of the Maghreb nations do cooperate by exchanging their services. The organization and operations of the news agencies of the five North African countries are discussed below.

Algeria

The state-owned Algerie Presse Service (APS), based in Algiers, has been the exclusive national news agency since 1962. It provides news service in Arabic, French, and English. APS was established in 1961 by Algerian journalists in exile in Tunisia during the Algerian war as a section of the information department of the National Liberation Front (FLN), to help spread the Algerian view of the war. The FLN continued to retain control over the agency following Algeria's independence in 1962, when the APS moved to Algiers. President Ben Bella had more than just a news-gathering function in mind for the APS. In a speech in 1963, he said: "It is clear that this agency cannot be simply an organism for the diffusion of facts, but it must be above all political and ideological, in the service of the nation and of all the vital forces of the country. To accomplish this mission, the APS must collaborate closely with the party, the government and all national organizations" (Rugh, 1979, p. 142).

Until the 1989 constitutional reforms, the APS, as all other media in the country, considered itself in the service of the state. The agency's news coverage and feature editorial material affirmed socialist policies and recorded achievements of the FLN under socialism. That practice by and large remained intact even after the 1989 constitutional reforms, which permitted the formation of political parties outside the FLN and allowed freedom of expression. Absence of any significant change in the editorial policy of the APS was attributed to its continued control by the FLN government, which had not renounced socialism, and to the APS's government-appointed editors, who had been chosen on the basis of their ideological conformity to the FLN policies. In the relatively open period for the press from February 1989 until early January 1992, many Algerian journalists questioned the professional integrity of editors and it appeared that the press was ready to move into a new era of professionalism. The imposition of military rule in January 1992 once again brought the press, including the APS, under the tight control of the government.

The APS has 46 domestic and 13 overseas bureaus. It is also the sole importer and distributor of news from international wire services, a policy that enables it to regulate the flow of foreign news into the country. Such a policy, according to several journalists interviewed by the author in Morocco and Tunisia, allows the news agencies to edit news in conformity with their government's domestic and foreign policies. Special APS services include features, photos and economic news bulletins, and an audio service. Wire services from the United States, Britain, France, Spain, Germany, Italy, Russia, China, and the former Eastern bloc nations have news bureaus in Algeria. The APS exchanges its news service with the services provided by news agencies in other Maghreb countries, including Libya, Morocco, and Tunisia (Algerian Press Attache, June 1, 1994).

Libya

The Libyan News Agency (LNA), with its headquarters in Tripoli, was founded in 1965 as the national news agency in association with the Ministry of Information. Following the 1969 coup, the agency's name was changed to Jamahiriyah News Agency (JANA) and it was placed under the Secretariat of Information, Culture and Revolutionary Guidance. It has been primarily a tool for political mobilization since then. JANA is a major source of national news and all of the international news. With bureaus throughout Libya and seven in foreign countries as of 1992, it distributes news and features in Arabic and English. JANA subscribes to the major international news agencies and is the sole authorized distributor of foreign news in Libya. It frequently gives its own slant and interpretation to international news before distribution. In addition to serving the government-run media in the country, JANA makes its service available to foreign subscribers.

JANA has taken a special interest in using copy from the Belgrade-based Non-Aligned News Agencies Pool, in keeping with Qadhafi's aim of Libya playing a key role among the nonaligned Third World countries. The activist stance taken by JANA in promoting the revolutionary goals of Colonel Qadhafi has not made it attractive to news agencies and media editors in the moderate North African countries like Algeria, Morocco, and Tunisia. Nonetheless, their news agencies, and that of the Sudan, do exchange their services with JANA (Abdesslam interview, May 12, 1994).

Morocco and Western Sahara

The national news agency is Maghreb Arabe Presse (MAP), which was founded in 1959. It operated as a private company until 1974, when it was placed under government control under the jurisdiction of the Ministry of Information. Located in a modern, multistory building in the capital Rabat, MAP is equipped with the latest technology to receive, transmit, and process information. It has 23 domestic and 17 international bureaus. Its foreign bureaus are in Washington D.C., New York, Moscow, London, Paris, Bonn, Brussels, Rome, Geneva, Mexico City, Madrid, Algiers, Tunis, Cairo, Jeddah, Beirut, and Dakar.

MAP describes its objectives in the news areas as follows: (1) to seek both in Morocco and abroad material that constitutes a complete and objective news; (2) to make available to subscribers both in Morocco and abroad MAP news; (3) to disseminate, on behalf of public authorities, news that they would like to publish; (4) to promote, both in Morocco and abroad, the policies and objectives of the Kingdom of Morocco. By its charter, the agency is required to provide a comprehensive coverage of national and regional events (*Maghreb Arabe Presse News Agency,* 1994).

In an interview, a MAP journalist further elaborated on the agency's objectives. He said that although the agency is committed to being objective, MAP views some issues as extremely sensitive, implying that objectivity may not be the paramount concern in their treatment. One such issue is the disputed territory of Western Sahara, which Morocco claims as an integral part of the country. The press is also not allowed to criticize the king. Treatment of such matters is under strict editorial control. (Abdesslam interview, May 12, 1994).

Providing further insights into the treatment of MAP copy, he said that its coverage of controversial issues is at times ignored by Morocco's party-affiliated press, which prefers to have its own correspondents cover such issues. He also said that opposition party press is quite vigorous, but the king is always off limits to all Moroccan media, and, like other media in the country, MAP is not allowed to criticize any religion because Morocco tends to take a more secular view of society even though it is a Muslim state.

MAP has a staff of 226 full-time journalists and editors, and a number of stringers. Most of the agency's journalistic staff are graduates of the Higher Institute of Journalism in Rabat. The agency has a national telegraphic network of 8,000 kilometers and international telegraphic network of 115,000 kilometers. The news agency is also connected by satellite with Washington D.C., New York, Mexico City, and Jakarta. The satellite network totals 22,000 kilometers.

MAP's working languages are Arabic, French, English, and Spanish. It provides its national service in Arabic and French, and international service in English and Spanish. The national service, which transmits an average of 450,000 words each day, is available free of charge to all media in Morocco. Unlike Western news agencies, MAP does not provide a photo service, leaving it for individual media to plan photographs for their news-editorial content. In addition to providing news about Morocco, MAP's international service covers news from Arab states and Africa. The international service is provided through bilateral exchange accords with agencies in Latin America, the Arab world and Africa.

MAP subscribes to the Arabic-language services of Reuters and Agence France Presse, and French-language service of the Associated Press. It also serves as a carrier to international news agencies, providing Moroccan media subscription to these agencies at subsidized costs. Moroccan media, however, are allowed to take a direct subscription to international agencies by paying full costs. Editors at MAP edit any material from the foreign wire service copy that does not conform to the country's press policy. For example, MAP invariably rewrites Reuters' reference to Yasser Arafat as "PLO Chief" to "President of the PLO." MAP also does not allow criticism of any Arab government in its own copy or that received from foreign press agencies (Abdesslam interview, May 12, 1994).

MAP's Arabic and French news services are provided to some 222 subscribers including newspapers, television and radio stations, government agencies, and embassies. MAP exchanges its news service with those of its counterparts in the Maghreb. The government provides MAP's annual budget and views the news agency's free service to the media as a form of subsidy for them. Outside Morocco, some 50 Moroccan embassies in Africa, Latin America, Asia, Europe, and the Middle East receive MAP news services in four different languages, Arabic, French, English, and Spanish. News agencies from the United States, Britain, France, Spain, Italy, Austria, Russia, and China have bureaus in Morocco (Oumnia interview, May 12, 1994).

Commenting on the quality of MAP, a staff member said that in comparison to Western news agencies, MAP is slow in providing news coverage. Reasons cited were lack of efficient staff, bureaucratic obstacles, and limited number of correspondents. He added, however, that the agency offered a better service compared with that of most Arab news agencies. According to MAP's chief of international service, UNESCO has commended the impartiality and credibility of the agency's coverage of government and opposition viewpoints (Oumnia interview, May 12, 1994).

The Sudan

The government-controlled Sudanese News Agency (SUNA) was founded in 1946 as the Sudan Press Agency. It has gone through name changes twice, first in 1960 when it became the Sudan News Agency and then in 1971 when it was given its current name upon the nationalization of the country's media by Col. Jaafar Mohammed Numayri.

SUNA is the oldest national news agency in the Arab world. It operated independently during the civilian governments of the 1950s and 1960s. Upon its nationalization, it was brought under the control of the Ministry of Culture and Information. In a reorganization move, Numayri abolished the ministry in November 1981 and brought SUNA under his direct supervision. The news agency was assigned the task of gathering and disseminating domestic and world news "within the framework of the State's general policy regarding the values and genuine traditions of the Sudanese people'' (Nelson, 1982, p. 232). SUNA regained its editorial independence during the three-year parliamentary government of al-Mahdi in the 1980s although it continued to be publicly owned. Under the al-Bashir regime, the agency has once again been brought under government control and has lost editorial independence.

A news agency that had operated before the 1969 coup was revived by the Sudanese journalists after the ouster of Numayri in 1985. Known as the Sudanese Press Agency, its objective was to provide news in a credible manner in view of the tarnished reputation of SUNA under Numayri's control. The Sudanese Press Agency provided a credible alternative service during the al-Mahdi years, but, as with SUNA, it has also been brought under government control since the 1989 coup. SUNA continues to be the primary news agency supplying news to both print and broadcast media.

As in Algeria, Libya, and Tunisia, media in the Sudan cannot subscribe to international news agencies directly. International wire service copy must go through SUNA so that the material can be edited before being passed on to the press, radio, and television. The government-employed SUNA editors thus have a considerable power to shape the presentation of foreign news (*The Democratic Journalist,* 1987, p. 25). The Maghreb news agencies exchange their services with that of SUNA on a subscription basis. In 1993, five foreign news agencies had their bureaus in the Sudan. They were the Agence France-Presse, Middle East News Agency, New China News Agency, the Iraqi News Agency, and the Syrian News Agency. News agencies in the Maghreb countries subscribe to SUNA, although it does not have an exchange relationship with the news agencies of the Maghreb countries.

Tunisia

Domestic and international news is provided by the government-controlled Tunis Afrique Presse (TAP). Established in 1961, TAP is called a public corporation, although the government owns 94 percent interest with the remainder held by the privately owned press and the agency employees. TAP's budget is provided by the government, which also appoints the chairman of the agency's governing board.

The operational policy of TAP has been established by the government. A TAP journalist said that although the agency provides some coverage of the opposition party activity in Tunisia, ''we mostly cover government activity.'' He acknowledged that the agency takes a pro-government stance in its coverage, without becoming a propaganda organ. News regarding presidential activities is written at the presidential palace and sent to the agency (Zaouchi interview, May 17, 1994).

TAP provides its domestic service in Arabic and French, with some news in English since November 1993. It also provides a photo service pertaining to domestic events. The agency has eight national bureaus and four international bureaus in Washington, D.C., Paris, Cairo, and Algiers. It also maintains stringers in Berlin, Brussels, Rome, Stockholm, Tokyo, Rabat, and Belgrade. As of mid-1994, the agency had a staff of 174 journalists and a number of stringers. The domestic service provides an average of 100 news stories daily. In addition to its daily service, TAP provides weekly review of salient news developments.

TAP has a limited international news service, focusing primarily on African and Palestinian affairs. The focus on the latter was explained in view of the location of the headquarters of the Palestine Liberation Organization in Tunis. The international service provides an average of 150 dispatches daily in Arabic and French. The agency, however, relies on Western news agencies for much of its foreign news. In addition to its daily service, TAP also provides weekly and monthly bulletins.

TAP's other services include a daily bulletin, called the Arab Maghreb Union Pool, for the Maghreb countries' news agencies. It also transmits by radio, a news bulletin to Arab countries and Africa with an average of 25 dispatches a day in Arabic. Another bulletin is edited in French for transmission to Europe and the African continent. A number of African countries are said to use the TAP service (*Agence Tunis Afrique Presse,* 1992, pp. 64–66).

TAP's domestic service is taken by all media in Tunisia, government ministries, and provincial governments. The agency's Economic and Financial News Service is received by most banks in the country. The domestic news service is offered to media on a subscription basis, with rates ranging from $300 to $500 per month. TAP's news services are received by the news agencies of all Maghreb countries, Egypt's Middle East News Agency, Agence France Press, and Italy's ANSA news agency. The AFP subscribes to TAP on a paid basis, while all other agencies receive TAP service on a news exchange basis. The international service of TAP, called TAP-EX, is sent via satellite to Tunisian embassies (Zaouchi interview, May 17, 1994).

International news agency subscription to Tunisian media is provided through TAP, which takes AFP, Reuters, AP, Itar-TASS, Xinhua, and ANSA and makes them available to Tunisian media at subsidized costs. This arrangement also gives TAP editorial control of the copy sent by the international wire agencies. AFP and Reuters are more popular among the Tunisian media than any of the other international news agencies. A number of foreign news agencies maintain bureaus in Tunis. They include Reuters, UPI, AFP, Agencia EFE from Spain, ANSA and Inter Press Service from Italy, ITAR-TASS and RIA-Novosti from Russia, New China News Agency, and Yugoslavia's Tanjug (Zaouchi interview, May 17, 1994).

NEW TECHNOLOGIES AND TELECOMMUNICATIONS

With the launching of France's TDF-1 and TDF-2, and the Luxembourg-based ASTRA direct broadcast satellites in the late 1980s, a variety of European television stations can be picked up in North Africa through parabolic-antenna satellite receiver systems. Governments in Algeria, Morocco, and Tunisia have taken a tolerant attitude toward the reception of such signals by their people, although concerns have been expressed about potential harm to national cultures and identities from the often permissive Western programming. Fundamental Islamic groups in the region have taken a particularly negative view of Western entertainment programming because of their belief that it is eroding traditional Islamic values. Such concerns have translated into satellite dish vandalism in Algeria, where the fundamentalists have been especially active in opposing strong inroads made by Western social and cultural values (Adhoum, 1992, p. 15).

Nevertheless, the installation of satellite dishes continues to grow. Available figures show that in 1989, there were 2,000 parabolic dishes in private use in Tunisia, with an estimated satellite television audience of 100,000. The number of such dishes in Tunisia alone was expected to grow to 350,000 by 1995 (Adhoum, 1992, p. 16). A visitor to urban areas in Algeria, Morocco, and Tunisia will find hundreds of such dishes on rooftops and balconies. Reception of satellite programming in Libya and the Sudan is restricted to commercial areas.

A selected list of the direct broadcast satellite channels available as of May 1994 in Algeria, Morocco, and Tunisia by country of origin is given below (Tunisian External Communication Agency, 1994):

France:	TF-1, M6, France Deux, Canal Plus, EuroNews
Belgium:	TV5
Germany:	DSF, RTL, RTL Plus, Sat-1, 3 Sat, Teleclub, Pro 7
Italy:	RAI 1, RAI 2
Portugal:	RTP
Spain:	TVE, TVE 2, Galavision
Sweden:	Nordic Channel
Turkey:	Majic Box, Aurasya, Star, TRT-INT
U.K.:	MTV, Super Channel, EuroSport, BBC, MBC, Children's Channel
U.S.A.:	CNN, Worldnet, NBC Superchannel

In addition, a number of radio stations from European countries are also available via satellite in the North African countries.

At least two of the North African countries have taken their own television programming beyond their borders. On November 7, 1992, Tunisia began to carry its national channel, Channel 7, via the European EUTELSAT satellite. This channel can be received via satellite dishes or cable in all of Europe, parts of the Middle East, and Mediterranean countries, including Algeria, Morocco, and Libya. The director of the Tunisian External Communication Agency said that the aim of these broadcasts is to establish a bridge between Tunisia and neighboring countries, whether they are in the Maghreb, the Middle East, or

Europe. Another purpose is to keep the Tunisian nationals living abroad in contact with developments back home (Besbes interview, May 19, 1994).

On March 3, 1993, Morocco also introduced its government-run national channel, RTM, and RTM's radio service to Europe, the Middle East, and Mediterranean countries via the EUTELSAT satellite. Explaining the objectives of the satellite services, an RTM statement said that in view of the explosion of satellite broadcasting around the world, it was incumbent upon a "modern, democratic, outward-looking, and tolerant Morocco" to reach out to international listeners and viewers. Television programming consisting of information, education, and entertainment is transmitted for 12 hours daily and 14 hours on holidays and weekends. Programs are broadcast in Arabic and French. RTM also transmits six daily news programs in Arabic, French, and Spanish (*La RTM a L'Heure du Satellite*, 1994).

Both Morocco and Tunisia have good telecommunications facilities by African standards. Latest available figures indicate that there were 362,000 telephones in Morocco in 1988, or 1.6 telephones per 100 inhabitants (*Statistical Yearbook*, 1992). Direct automatic international dialing is available in urban areas. Morocco's government-owned telecommunications system is composed of wire lines, cable, and radio relay links. Principal centers are Casablanca and Rabat, with secondary centers in Fes, Marrakech, Oujda, Tangier, and Tetouan. Morocco is linked with INTELSAT via two earth stations and with ARABSAT through one earth station. It also has radio relay links with Gibraltar and Spain, and coaxial cable and microwave links to Algeria, Syria, Jordan, Egypt, Libya, and Tunisia. The telecommunications system of Western Sahara is tied into Morocco's system by radio relay, microwave, and Morocco's two INTELSAT earth stations. There were 2,000 telephones in the Western Sahara region in 1989.

Telecommunications in Tunisia are under the control of the Ministry of Transport and Communications. According to government figures, there were approximately 400,000 telephones in the country as of 1992. In per capita terms, that figure translated into 4.6 telephones per 100 inhabitants as of late 1992, as compared with 2.9 in 1986 and 1.7 in 1980. All urban areas offer automatic, direct-dial national and international telephone service. The mobile telephone network's capacity had been expanded from 1,000 to 2,000 subscribers as of 1992 and a plan was being implemented to establish base stations throughout the country. A major program to expand telephone service to 1,000 rural areas has been under way since 1988. A national data transmission network has been set up in Tunisia, allowing companies and government agencies access to national and international data banks. Two satellite earth stations link Tunisia to INTELSAT and ARABSAT. The country also maintains radio relay and coaxial cable links with Algeria and Libya (*Telecommunications in Tunisia*, 1994).

Algeria has well-developed domestic and international telecommunications services. It was one of the first countries to use satellites for domestic communications. By 1985, 17 ground stations were being used to provide domestic telephone and telex services, although the quality of such services was far better in the north than in the south. The completion of 19 ground satellite stations in the south by 1990 has expanded telecommunication services throughout the country. The government, which controls the telecommunications system, has continued to modernize the infrastructure by establishing digital exchanges. There were 959,000 telephones in the country as of 1988, which amounted to four telephones per 100 inhabitants (*Statistical Yearbook,* 1992). Major urban centers are well served by automatic, direct-dial domestic and international telephone services. Telex services are also available throughout the country. Algeria also maintains radio relay links with Italy, France, Spain, Morocco, and Tunisia, and coaxial cable links with Morocco and Tunisia. Its international satellite links are provided through two INTELSAT earth stations, one ARABSAT station, and one Intersputnik station (Algerian Ministry of Information, 1993).

The Libyan government launched a major telecommunications infrastructure development program in the late 1970s, which has resulted in a modern system based on radio relay, coaxial cable, and 14 domestic satellite stations. In 1991, there were 370,000 telephones in the country, or 9.25 units per 100 people (*The World Factbook,* 1992). Automatic, direct-dial telephone service is available in urban centers. International telecommunications links are facilitated by two INTELSAT earth stations and one ARABSAT station.

The Sudan has a large, well-equipped telecommunications system by African standards, but barely adequate and poorly maintained by modern standards. The system uses microwave, cable, radio communications, and a domestic satellite system to link the country. The Sudan Satellite System (SUDOSAT) had a network of 14 earth stations as of 1991. Available figures indicate that there were 78,000 telephones in the country in 1985, or 0.4 per 100 inhabitants (*Statistical Yearbook,* 1992). International links were provided through one INTELSAT and one ARABSAT earth station.

SPECIAL PROBLEMS AND CHALLENGES

While there are a variety of unique problems facing the press in each of the North African countries studied in this section, the most compelling common problem is that of political controls on the press in all five countries. By the standards of the Arab world, the Moroccan press has a considerable variety and freedom, but the press code provides for strong controls at the same time. The Interior Ministry can seize any publication that it perceives to endanger social stability. Criticism of Islam, the monarchical system, the king, or Morocco's claim to sovereignty over Western Sahara is not permitted. Criticism of the president is prohibited under the Tunisian press code, which, among other things, also restricts publication of "false information," or information which might disturb public order. In Algeria, even before the military took control of the country in January 1992 and imposed tight controls on the press, it was a criminal offense under the 1990 Information Code to publish or distribute information which could harm "national unity" or state security. Violations of these provisions could lead to imprisonment for up to 10 years. In Libya, in spite of Colonel Qadhafi's self-styled "democratic" system, all media are owned and operated by the government. The situation is the same in the Sudan, where privately owned media have been banned following the 1989 coup. Another common problem, at least in Algeria, Morocco, and Tunisia, is how to cope with the cultural threat posed by Western television programming now widely available in these countries through direct broadcast satellite television from Europe. As indicated earlier, this has become a serious issue to Islamic fundamentalists in Algeria.

Media in each of the five North African countries are facing other problems. The worst situation at the time of this writing in mid-1994 was in Algeria, where 4,000 people had been killed in political violence since January 1992, when the military canceled parliamentary elections that the fundamentalist Islamic Salvation Front was almost certain to win. The militants were waging an insurgency that had included the assassination of scores of political figures, journalists, and intellectuals (*The Straits Times,* July 12, 1994, p. 3). The London-based media watchdog group Article 19 reported that at least 16 journalists and writers were killed in Algeria in 1993 by violent Islamic groups who justify the killings in the name of religion as "sentences and not crimes" (*Article 19 Bulletin,* January/February, 1994, p. 3).

The "sentences" on the journalists, writers, and intellectuals were imposed because they had opposed the activities of the Islamic radical movement. Victims included the writer Tahar Djaout, Professor Mohamed Boucebsi, and television journalist Smail Yefsah. Many other journalists and intellectuals had escaped attempts on their lives, including Omar Belhouchet, editor in chief of *al-Watan.* Journalists had received death threats by letter and telephone, and their families had been harassed. Many were using pseudonyms or resorting to self-censorship in order to survive. Some had left the country or quit the profession; others altered their working patterns or went into hiding (ibid).

The media's role in Libya has become quite uncertain in view of the inconsistency Colonel Qadhafi has shown in recent years in the implementation of his "revolutionary democracy of the masses." As he routinely denounces and pursues dissidents seeking genuine political openness in the country, he has not spared his own "people's congresses," with newspaper articles calling them "reactionary and corrupt." On the one hand, he speaks of "direct democracy" in which people would rule without government mediation, yet, on the other hand, he has vetoed a number of popular policies using the rationale that he was protecting people from "counter-revolutionaries." The government-owned press launches a series of attacks against the military, the police, and other institutions and then takes a conciliatory tone toward the same entities in subsequent articles (Metz, 1989, p. 190). The media appear to be operating at the whim of Colonel Qadhafi.

Morocco's predominantly party-affiliated press promotes party news regardless of its newsworthiness. There is little tradition of objective reporting, a practice that dates back to the colonial days. Until recently, journalists have been members of the party for which they write. But as professionally educated and trained journalists join the industry, they bemoan the working conditions. They say news story ideas and angles are handed down to them by the editors, whether or not the topic or the angle is professionally acceptable to them. They are allowed little freedom in coming up with story topics or in structuring their stories. Both the government and party press function in the image of their sponsors, so there is little objectivity in news writing even though journalists often want to be objective. Well-educated Moroccan readers, therefore, routinely turn to international publications for reliable information about their own country.

In view of their average newspaper salary of approximately $275 per month, journalists are often compelled to take second jobs, resulting in potential conflict-of-interest problems. A variety of government perks for journalists, such as junkets and subsidized travel in covering news stories, further compromise their objectivity. Sensationalism is another ethical problem identified by journalists. Party press often plays up stories for political reasons rather than for their news value. The Moroccan National Press Syndicate, a professional organization, is striving to address these issues. Several students at the journalism institute in Rabat said that they are educated and trained to work for specialized press, but there is little opportunity to do so because the Moroccan press is heavily politically oriented.

Several problems were cited in the broadcasting area also. People are hired as news directors and journalists at RTM because of their political loyalties even though they may not have any professional media background or journalism education. This leads to a lack of professionalism in news and public affairs programming. Even experienced journalists are limited in doing their jobs properly. "There is lack of footage and good reporting because oftentimes the stations do not provide transportation to journalists to go and cover the event," said one RTM journalist. Another journalist said that there are restrictions on what reporters working for the government media can cover. "Controversial issues like strikes are often not covered," she said. Access to information remains a severe problem. The RTM's financial constraints also make it difficult for the station to produce quality programming. Attempts to make the RTM an autonomous organization have failed.

The privately owned television station, 2M, has increasingly hired professionally trained journalists and offers better working conditions, so its news programs are found to be considerably better from both technical and journalistic standpoints. This station is found to be more candid in discussing issues of wider public interest and, unlike RTM, does not have any taboos (RTM English Service Staff interview, May 12, 1994).

In the Sudan, the al-Bashir military regime continues to crack down on dissidents seeking political and personal freedoms. Sayed Ahmed al-Hussein, the deputy general secretary of the banned opposition Democratic Unionist Party, was arrested in November 1993. He has persistently campaigned for return to a multiparty political system and press freedoms (*Article 19 Bulletin,* January/ February, 1994, p. 6). Journalists and academics have also faced frequent and arbitrary arrests. Although the media are government owned, they continue to be subjected to heavy censorship. Close links have developed between the military junta and the Islamic fundamentalists since the 1989 coup. The government continues to push for the implementation of the Islamic sharia law, which would eliminate any possibility of the press regaining its freedom. The military regime continues to be highly sensitive about coverage given to the Sudan by the international press. Government displeasure over specific news reports has resulted in the detention and expulsion of foreign correspondents.

In Tunisia, as a result of President Ben Ali's moves to relax political and media controls, a diverse press has emerged and it has regained some of the credibility it had lost before 1987. However, as in Morocco, the Tunisian press is mostly either pro-government or affiliated with political parties, reflecting their respective viewpoints. Like Morocco, there is little tradition of independent, objective journalism in Tunisia. The Tunisian press code does not make it easier for such a press to emerge, as it prohibits any criticism of the president and establishes a number of other restrictions.

In September 1992, President Ben Ali announced guidelines designed to improve the quality of news coverage in the government-owned media. Major provisions of the new guidelines are as follows: (1) the news agency TAP and national radio and television can cover the activities of the main opposition parties; (2) official media can cover the views of the main legally recognized parties on national and international issues "as long as these opinions are not incompatible with the higher interests of the nation, and do not harm Tunisia's relations with other countries"; (3) representatives of the main political parties are allowed to participate in current affairs programs on national radio and television (*The Tunisian Mass Media,* 1994). In spite of these new freedoms allowed the government media, news coverage continues to favor the government and its policies. Educated Tunisians, therefore, turn to external media for impartial coverage of domestic events.

Noting the challenges facing Tunisian broadcasting, the director-general of RTT said that both the technical and aesthetic quality of locally produced television programs could show further improvement. He said that RTT has to win the fight of quality, otherwise it would continue to lose audiences to satellite television. He noted that competing successfully with other Arab channels, such as the Saudi-owned Middle East Broadcasting Channel (MBC) from London, was also a big challenge. MBC has become an important alternative news source in North Africa. More training programs are needed for engineers and technical personnel at the RTT to adapt to new technologies in broadcasting, he said (Herguem interview, May 19, 1994).

Another area of challenge came from Mustapha Masmoudi, the former information minister of Tunisia whom UNESCO's director-general had called "the father of the New World Information Order (NWIO)." Back in 1977, Masmoudi had used this term to launch a movement that called for a more equitable flow of information between developed and developing countries. Under the NWIO movement, he wanted communication to be regarded as a "social goal and a cultural product, and not as a material commodity" (Sussman, Spring 1982, pp. 7–8).

Masmoudi now serves as chairman of the Mass Media Institute in Tunis, which provides a variety of consultancy services pertaining to media industries. Asked if the NWIO movement had yielded any positive results, Masmoudi said that the most tangible positive result had come in the form of the International Program for the Development of Communication, designed to help developing countries build their communication infrastructures. In addition, he said everyone in the media now is more mindful of the North-South dialogue, and CNN has made it possible for people around the world to take their point of view to America. Developing countries have been more keen to develop their own programming resources rather than to continue to rely on Western suppliers, he said. For example, the ARABSAT has been a major venture toward developing the Arab countries' reliance on themselves for news and other programming.

Masmoudi said that the new challenge for developing countries vis-à-vis the West was to secure their interests in terms of space allocation for communication satellites, which are being used for both direct broadcast satellite television and for establishing the proposed information superhighway. He said President Clinton was right in believing that "the highway of information" will be the engine behind the construction of a new world following the fall of communism in Eastern Europe and the Soviet Union. "This new slogan deserves to be supported to the extent that the 'highway' can work in both directions, across the frontiers which separate the North and the South," Masmoudi said. (Masmoudi, January 1994, p. 5).

REFERENCES

Abdesslam, A. M. (May 12, 1994). Journalist at the Maghreb Arabe Presse News Agency in Morocco. Personal interview in Rabat.

Adhoum, M. (1992). Tunisia's response to the advent of European direct broadcast satellite television. Paper presented at the AEJMC Convention in Montreal, Canada.

Adwan, N. (May 18, 1994). Director of Research, Arab States Broadcasting Union, Tunisia. Personal interview in Tunis.

Agence Tunis Afrique Presse. (1992). Tunis: Tunis Afrique Presse.

Algerian Ministry of Information. (1993). Information supplied by the ministry.

Algerian Press Attache. (June 1, 1994). Embassy of Algeria, Washington, DC. Telephone interview.

Article 19 Bulletin. (January/February 1994). London: Article 19.

Benzahra, Y. (May 12, 1994). Chief of International Cooperation Service, RTM. Personal interview in Rabat.

Besbes, E. (May 19, 1994). Director, Agence Tunisienne de Communication Exterieure. Personal interview in Tunis.

The Democratic Journalist. (1987). The situation of the Sudanese press, no. 2.

El Youssoufi, N. (May 12, 1994). Journalist with Radiodiffusion Television Marocaine, Morocco. Personal interview in Rabat.

Herguem, A. (May 19, 1994). Director-General, Radiodiffusion Television Tunisienne. Personal interview in Tunis.

Kara, J. (May 18, 1994). News and Sports Coordinator, Arab States Broadcasting Union, Tunisia. Personal interview in Tunis.

La RTM a l'heure du satellite. (1994). Typed document provided by the Ministry of Information, Rabat, Morocco.

Maghreb Arabe Presse News Agency. (May 12, 1994). Typed document provided by MAP.

Masmoudi, M. (May 18, 1994). Chairman, Mass Media Instute, Tunis. Personal interview in Tunis.

———. (January 1994). The highway of information. Paper presented at the East-West Center, Honolulu, Hawaii.

Metz, H. C. (1989). *Libya: A country study.* Washington, DC: U.S. Government Printing Office.

Nelson, H. (1982). *Sudan: A country study.* Washington, DC: The American University.

Oumnia, O. (May 12, 1994). Chief of International Service, Maghreb Arabe Presse, Morocco. Personal interview in Rabat.

RTM English Service Staff. (May 12, 1994). Personal interview with staff members Hamid Benchekroun, Abdellah Tassaft, Naziha El Youssoufi, Zouhour Himmich, and Badia Benaddi in Rabat, Morocco.

Rugh, W. A. (1979). *The Arab press.* Syracuse, NY: Syracuse University Press.

Statistical Yearbook. (1992). UNESCO. Paris: UNESCO.

The Straits Times. (July 12, 1994). Algerian gunmen dressed as police kill foreigners. Singapore.

Suleiman, A. R. (May 18, 1994). Technical Director, Arab States Broadcasting Union, Tunisia. Personal interview in Tunis.

Sussman, L. (Spring 1982). The New World Information Order and freedom of the press. Hitesman Lecture Series. Baton Rouge: Louisiana State University.

Telecommunications in Tunisia. (1994). Typed information provided by the Tunisian External Communication Agency.

Tunsian External Communication Agency. (1994). Information supplied by staff member Fathi Azouz.

The Tunisian mass media. (1994). Typed information provided by the Tunisian External Communication Agency.

Union de Radiodiffusion des Etats Arabes. (1994). Tunis: Union de Radiodiffusion des Etats Arabes.

World radio TV handbook. (1993). New York: Billboard Publications, Inc.

The world factbook. (1992). Washington. D.C.: Superintendent of Documents.

Zaouchi, H. (May 17, 1994). TAP Journalist. Personal interview in Tunis.

III   THE CARIBBEAN REGION

_____ Vibert C. Cambridge

9 Setting and Philosophical Contexts

INTRODUCTION

Several terms have been associated with the islands and the mainland territories whose shores are washed by the Caribbean Sea. These terms include West Indies, Antilles, Overseas Departments, Commonwealth Caribbean, Caribbean Community (CARICOM), and more recently, the Organization of Caribbean States. Some of these terms are slowly falling into disuse as the region formulates strategies for political and economic cooperation. The Organization of Caribbean States is the most recent formulation and refers to an emerging economic and trading block similar to the North America Free Trade Area. The organization became operational in June 1994.

The term "West Indies" refers to the former British colonial territories. The term "Antilles" is used to identify current and former Dutch territories. The term "Overseas Department" is used to refer specifically to France's mainland possession and the islands still dependent on France.

The term "Commonwealth Caribbean" describes the independent nation states of the former British West Indies. The term "CARICOM" (the abbreviation for "Caribbean Community") and "Commonwealth Caribbean" are of the postindependence era, which began with Jamaica's independence in 1962. The ideas behind the postindependence developments in economic and political cooperation were articulated in a report submitted to the Caribbean Common Market Council of Ministers in 1980:

The roots of the Caribbean Community are not buried in doctrines of integration economics. CARICOM is not just the product of regional economic planning. Responsive as it is to the economic and political realities of the post-war world, Caribbean regionalism is the outgrowth of more than 300 years of West Indian kinship—the vagaries of the socio-economic political history of a transplanted people from which is evolving a Caribbean identity. Without that element of West Indian identity a Community of the Caribbean would be mere markings on parchment—a Community without a soul, without vision of a shared destiny, without the will to persist and survive. (A Group of Caribbean Experts, 1981, p. 1)

Although initially conceived as a grouping of former British colonies, CARI-COM is now more inclusive; it embraces territories with French, Dutch, and Spanish colonial traditions. The non-English-speaking territories have "observer" status in this regional economic, political, and cultural organization.

This section of the book discusses the mass media practices in the former British colonial possessions—Antigua and Barbuda, The Commonwealth of the Bahamas, Barbados, Belize, Dominica, Grenada, Guyana, Jamaica, Montserrat, St. Christopher and Nevis, St. Lucia, St. Vincent and the Grenadines, and Trinidad and Tobago. I utilize arguments offered by Clive Thomas to justify this focus.

In his important work, *The Poor and the Powerless: Economic Policy and Change in the Caribbean,* Clive Thomas (1985) identifies several factors that complicate the construction of a framework for examining the region washed by the Caribbean Sea. He uses the terms "fragmentation and balkanization" to describe the complications. Specifically, he refers to differences in the: (a) geographic size and population size, (b) racial and ethnic composition of the societies—an outcome of African slavery, Asian (East Indian and Chinese), and European (Portuguese) indentureship and European settlers, (c) languages, (d) political and economic organization (independent states and dependencies), and (e) regional consciousness. These issues, he argues, conspire to create frameworks that are exclusive. Attempts at developing an integrated framework have the potential of producing "gazetteer" research—"forfeiting any in-depth analysis." He, therefore, decides on accepting CARICOM as the framework to examine the impact of economic policy on the "poor and powerless" in the Caribbean since World War II (Thomas, 1985).

Despite its many weaknesses . . . CARICOM's attempt at regional integration comes closest to providing a framework for this shared regional consciousness within the Caribbean. All the major classes, groups, and strata in these territories have moulded into their social consciousness a particular view of the Caribbean, which they take into account in pursuing their interests and which directly influences their political behavior. In no other significant grouping of territories in the region (except possibly Central America which I believe should not be treated together with the Caribbean for the purposes at hand) is this community of interest as far advanced. (Thomas, 1985, p. 5)

Since the beginning of Caribbean political independence in 1962, three ideas have dominated Caribbean political organization. These are the democratic, the integrationist, and the socialist ideas. Serving as a superordinate reality has been the presence of charismatic leaders and the concomitant practices of patronage. The proximity of these territories to major global political, cultural, and economic centers and highly mobile populations has also conspired to influence the organization and practices of Caribbean states. These dynamics have included the "connecting" of Jamaican Garveyite "Back-to-Africa" with the Negritude and Negrissimo ideas from the Francophone Caribbean and Cuba. In the sphere of economics—Puerto Rico's "export-oriented" development model and the revolutionary socialist practices of Cuba have also been influential. These are some of the interactions that have given particular textures to the ideas of democracy, integration, and socialism in the Caribbean. It is this complex environment that has influenced the organization and the product of the mass media in the Caribbean Community.

This chapter will provide an overview of the key political, economic, and cultural indicators required for a systematic study of the mass media in the Caribbean. Included in that examination will be a survey of physical and cultural geography.

PHYSICAL AND CULTURAL GEOGRAPHY OF THE CARIBBEAN COMMUNITY

The territories that make up this region vary in area and population size. Guyana, for example, is 83,000 square miles with a population of less than 800,000, and has the lowest population density. Montserrat is the smallest in size—39.6 square miles with a population of 12,000. Jamaica covers 4,232 square miles and has the largest population—2,540,000. Barbados's total area is 166 square miles. In 1989, Barbados's population was reported to be 252,700, thus giving it the population density of 1522 persons per square mile—the highest in the region. There is a pattern of urban population concentration. However, in the mainland territories—Belize and Guyana—there are significant population centers in hinterland areas.

The geographic location of the Caribbean has made it a central location in international communication and trade. The Caribbean was a central location during the slave trade—an important destination in the Triangular Trade. The region has also been strategic vis-à-vis the Panama Canal. The Caribbean states are also clustered around the equator, placing them in the footprints of the majority of the North American communication satellites.

Antigua and Barbuda

Antigua and Barbuda is part of the Leeward Island group located in the Eastern Caribbean. It is situated about 260 miles southeast of Puerto Rico and some 37.5 miles north of the French overseas department Guadeloupe. In 1989 the population was estimated at 86,000. The primarily Christian population is almost entirely of African descent. The predominant denomination is the Church of

England. In 1990, 44 percent of the population was under the age of 15. The per capita income in 1985 was approximately U.S. $2, 124 per anum. The adult literacy rate was reported to be 88 percent in 1990 (Jamaican Institute of Political Education, 1990, p. 13).

Antigua and Barbuda obtained its political independence from Great Britain on November 1, 1981, and has been governed by the Antigua Labour Party since that time. Vere C. Bird served as prime minister from 1981 until his resignation from active politics in 1994. The current prime minister is the Hon. Lester Bird, a son of Vere C. Bird. Politically, the state is a parliamentary democracy within the British Commonwealth. This means that Queen Elizabeth II is the head of state and represented in the islands by a governor general.

Vere C. Bird is one of those strong, charismatic leaders who have dominated postindependence politics in the Commonwealth Caribbean. Members of the Bird family dominate the political, economic, and media life in Antigua and Barbuda. The principal opposition party is the United National Democratic Party. In the years since independence, the government of Antigua and Barbuda has been accused of oppressing its opposition and has been associated with several international scandals, ranging from arms trading with South Africa during Apartheid and drug-money laundering.

The media environment can be described as mixed. This means that there are state-operated and privately operated media. The print media are, for the most part, privately owned. In 1990 three partisan weekly newspapers dominated the country. *The Nation,* a 16-page tabloid established in 1982, is published by the Public Information Department of the Government of Antigua and Barbuda. The leader of the opposition, Tim Hector, is the assistant editor of *Outlet,* which was founded in 1975. The third weekly is *The Worker's Voice.* This newspaper, which was founded in 1943, is the official organ of the Antigua Trades and Labour Union and the Antigua Labor Party.

The electronic media are primarily government-owned and operated. The state-owned Antigua Broadcasting Service (ABS) operates radio and television services. ABS Radio was established in 1956 while ABS Television was established in 1963. There are two private operations. Radio ZDK was founded in 1970 and is owned by the Bird family. C.TV Entertainment System introduced cable television to Antigua and Barbuda in 1983. The Operations Manager of C.TV Entertainment System is also a member of the Bird family—Mr. Purcell Bird.

This pattern (state ownership, not family monopoly) is common throughout the CARICOM region and reflects a part of the British colonial legacy. The electronic media were considered a scarce resource to be controlled by the state. Rediffusion, the earliest commercial broadcaster in the Commonwealth Caribbean, was permitted to operate within very specific parameters, including the requirement to broadcast BBC programs.

The Commonwealth of the Bahamas

The Commonwealth of the Bahamas is a 700-mile-long archipelago located in the Atlantic Ocean, southeast of Florida. In 1989 the population was estimated at 247,000. Eighty-five percent were of African descent. The population is predominantly Christian: 29 percent Baptist, 23 percent Church of England, and 23 percent Roman Catholic. In 1990, 38 percent of the population was under the age of 14. The per capita income in 1985 was approximately U.S. $9,100 per anum. The adult literacy rate was reported to be 93 percent in 1990 (Jamaican Institute, 1990, p. 17).

The Progressive Liberal Party led The Commonwealth of the Bahamas to political independence from Great Britain on July 10, 1973. It governed the state until 1990 when it was defeated at the general elections by the Free National Movement. The postindependence years were dominated by Sir Lynden Pindling, the leader of the Progressive Liberal Party and the first prime minister. He too can be associated with the strong and charismatic leader tradition.

The state is a parliamentary democracy within the British Commonwealth. This means that Queen Elizabeth II is the head of state, represented by a governor general. During the later years of the PLP government, its leadership, including the prime minister, was accused of active participation in the illegal cocaine trafficking between South America and the United States. The nation's liberal financial regulations have made it an attractive site for off-shore banking and other financial transactions. This has also made it a prime location for money laundering. These conditions—tainted political leadership and evidence of financial criminality—occasioned a switch in national mood and led to the defeat of Sir Lynden Pindling and his PLP government in 1990.

The media environment in The Commonwealth of the Bahamas can also be described as mixed. Like Antigua and Barbuda, there are state-operated and privately operated media. The print media are primarily privately owned. The oldest newspaper in the Commonwealth of the Bahamas is the *Nassau Guardian.* This morning daily newspaper was founded in 1844. There are two more dailies and two weeklies. The afternoon daily, *The Tribune,* was established in 1903. The third daily, *Freeport News,* was founded in 1961. The *Official Gazette* and the *Bahamas Journal* are weekly publications. The *Official Gazette* is the only government-owned paper.

The electronic media are primarily government owned and operated. The state-owned Broadcasting Corporation of the Bahamas operates four radio stations and one television station. ZNS-1, the national radio service, was introduced in 1936. The three other stations (ZNS-11, ZNS-FM, and ZNS-111) are special services. ZNS-11 is a religious and educationally oriented station serving New Providence and the islands in Central Bahamas. ZNS-FM is a 24-hour contemporary music and news service also serving New Providence and the Central Bahamas islands. ZNS-111 is a 24-hour service serving the northern region—"Grand Bahama, Abaco, Bimini, Central Bahamas, and Florida's east coast" (Jamaican Institute, 1990, p. 19).

Barbados

This 166-square-mile nation-state is the site of the oldest parliament in the Americas. Barbados is farthest east in the CARICOM region. It is about 500 hundred miles southeast of Puerto Rico. Its closest neighbors are St. Lucia, Grenada, and Trinidad and Tobago (Jamaican Institute, 1990, p. 19). In 1989 the population was estimated at 256,800 with almost 30 percent under the age of 14. Eighty percent were of African descent. The population is predominantly Christian. Seventy percent are members of the Church of England. The per capita income in 1985 was approximately U.S. $5,000 per anum. The adult literacy rate was reported to be 96 percent in 1990 (Jamaican Institute, 1990, p. 19).

The Democratic Labour Party, led by Mr. Errol Barrow, piloted Barbados to political independence on November 30, 1966. Despite being the birthplace of two of the region's most charismatic leaders—Grantley Adams and Errol Barrow—political practices have not been dominated by any single personality for very long periods. The two-party system has been very efficient in this parliamentary democracy. The two dominant political parties, Errol Barrow's Democratic Labor Party and Sir Grantley Adams's Barbados Labour Party, have shared the political leadership of Barbados. Both parties have their origins in Barbados's labor movement, which shares a common heritage with the Caribbean labor movement. The origins of this heritage are to be found in the 1930s when Caribbean working people began to agitate for better economic rights as well as political independence. They also started the movement for Caribbean integration.

Both of these Barbadian political parties have been actively involved in the Caribbean integration process. Sir Grantley Adams was the first prime minister of the now defunct West Indian Federation. Errol Barrow has been recognized as one of the founders of the Caribbean Community. These initiatives have made Barbados the site for several significant financial and media institutions—the Caribbean Development Bank (CDB), the Caribbean Broadcasting Union (CBU), The Caribbean News Agency (CANA), and the Caribbean Publishers and Broadcasters Association (CPBA).

Barbados is also seen as the epitome of the conservative tradition in the region. The governments of Barbados are not known for taking any radical social or political positions in the postindependence era. This perception was sharpened when the then prime minister, Tom Adams, supported the U.S. invasion of Grenada. Tom Adams was the son of Grantley Adams.

The media environment in Barbados can also be described as mixed. There are state-operated and privately operated media. In 1990 there were nine newspapers—two dailies, three weekend tabloids, two Sunday publications, and two monthly tabloids. Only one, the *Official Gazette*, was state operated. The Advocate Company Ltd. and the Nation Publishing Company own and operate the majority of the newspapers. The Advocate Company, established in 1895, publishes the *Barbados Advocate* (one of the region's prestige papers), *Sunday Advocate*, and the *Weekend Investigator*. The Nation Publishing Company has been publishing the *Daily Nation, Weekend Nation,* and the *Sunday Sun* since 1973. The National Publishing Company also prints two important regional publications—the weekly *Caribbean Week* for Caribbean Communications Inc. and the *Caribbean Contact* for the Caribbean Conference of Churches. These publications enjoy significant regional circulation.

The electronic media are primarily government owned and operated. Radio services are provided by the state-owned Caribbean Broadcasting Corporation and by Barbados Rediffusion Service Ltd., a private company. The state-owned system operates two services—CBC Radio 900 and Liberty FM 900. CBC Radio was established in 1963 and Liberty FM in 1973. Both services are operated "semicommercially" (Jamaican Institute, 1990, p. 21). Barbados Rediffusion Service Ltd. is associated with the introduction and development of commercial radio broadcasting in the Commonwealth Caribbean (Central Rediffusion Services, 1956). Barbados Rediffusion Service Ltd., established in 1935, operates two radio services—the Barbados Rediffusion (one of the few remaining wired radio services in the world) and the Voice of Barbados, which was established in 1981.

The Caribbean Broadcasting Corporation operates two television services—CBC-TV and Subscription Television. CBC-TV, established in 1964, is the national over-the-air service. As the name implies, Subscription Television, established in 1987, is a subscription television service offering four channels of programming: two 24-hour channels, one 12-hour channel, and a pay-per-view channel (Jamaican Institute, 1990, p. 22).

Belize

This Central American state, formerly known as British Honduras, obtained its political independence from Great Britain on September 21, 1981. The 8,867-square-mile nation-state is located on the eastern coast of Central America. In the north and the west Belize is bordered by Mexico. Also bordering Belize in the west is Guatemala. Guatemala is also Belize's southern neighbor. In 1989 the estimated population was 179,400. The population is 52 percent African descent, 22 percent Mestizos, 15 percent Mayan, 6 percent Carib, and 5 percent Asian Indians.

In addition to English, the official language which is spoken by the majority of the population, Spanish is spoken by 32 percent of the population. The dominant religion is Christianity: 62 percent is Roman Catholic, 13 percent Methodist, 14 percent Anglican (Church of England), and 4 percent Mennonite. There are small communities of Bahais, Hindus, and Muslims. In 1990 more than half of the population (55.1 percent) was 14 years old or younger. Fifty-eight percent of the population is under the age of 19. Adult literacy is reported to be 93 percent. In 1990 the per capita income was approximately U.S. $1,275 per annum.[1]

Two political parties have dominated the political landscape. These are the People's United Party led by George Cadle Price and the United Democratic Party lead by Manuel Esquivel. These two parties have rotated national leadership with regularity. In June 1993, the United Democratic Party replaced the People's United Party, which had been in office for the previous four years (1989–1993). Without a doubt, George Price has been the dominant political personality in Belizean society. He led Belize to political independence and maintained Belizean territorial integrity in the postindependence years. Because of the frequency of rotations in political leadership, many of the manifestations of the extremes of Caribbean charismatic leaders are not evident here. This does not mean that the politics of patronage is not practiced in Belize. Each administration endeavors to position its supporters in key agencies, such as the Belizean Broadcasting Services.

Despite its location in Central America, Belize has very close cultural and political ties with the English-speaking nation-states in the Caribbean Sea. The Garifuna (Black Carib) presence in Belize is traceable to transported Africans from St. Vincent in the early nineteenth century.

The media environment in Belize can also be described as mixed with state-operated and privately operated companies. The political press has a strong presence in Belize. The dominant political parties—the People's United Party and the United Democratic Party—publish weekly tabloids. The People's United Party founded *The Belize Times* in 1956 while the United Democratic Party established *The Pulse* in 1988. In addition to these two weekly tabloids, there were two other independent weekly tabloid publications–*Amandala* and *The Reporter*. The latter is a described as a "Sunday weekly." The monthly magazine *Belize Today* and the monthly newsletter *Belize on the Move* are published by the Government Information Service. The Roman Catholic Diocese of Belize City and Belmopan publishes *The Christian Herald,* a monthly tabloid. The Society for the Promotion of Education and Research has published the monthly tabloid *The Christian Herald* since 1980.

Until the mid 1980s, broadcasting in Belize was primarily a semicommercial radio service operated by the government-owned Broadcasting Corporation of Belize. Belize Radio One and Friends FM are operated by the Broadcasting Corporation of Belize. Now, as a result of pirate television and access to the new communication technologies, there are privately owned and operated radio and television services. Love FM, established in 1992, is privately owned and operated. GBTV is operated by Great Belize Productions Ltd., a private company. Belizeans can also receive radio and television broadcasts from neighboring Central American countries.

Dominica

This 298-square-mile island is the farthest north in the Windward Islands. Its immediate neighbors in the north and the south are the French islands of Guadeloupe and Martinique, respectively. In 1984, the population was 82,500.[2] The population density was reported at approximately 300 persons per square mile. The population is primarily of African descent with a small Carib community. Roman Catholicism is the major denomination in this essentially Christian society. In 1990 adult literacy was 80 percent (Jamaican Institute, 1990, p. 29).

Dominica obtained its political independence from Great Britain in November 1978. It is a parliamentary democracy within the Commonwealth. The Democratic Freedom Party of Prime Minister Mary Eugenia Charles has been in office since 1980 when that party defeated the Dominica Labour Party. In 1981 there were two attempted coups. Dominica has close political ties with the United States and was one of the few Caribbean states that were actively involved in the U.S. invasion of Grenada.

Dominican politics has also been dominated by strong, charismatic leadership. In this case, the dominant personality has been a woman. Mary Eugenia Charles has been the first, and so far, the only female prime minister in the English-speaking Caribbean. Her strong affiliation with the United States has, at times, incurred the derision of other regional leaders.

The media environment in Dominica can be described as being highly partisan–dominated by the government, political parties, and community activists. In 1990 there were no daily newspapers; however, there were three weekly and four monthly papers. One of the weekly newspapers, *The New Chronicle*, was independent while the other two weekly newspapers—the *GIS Weekly News Bulletin* and the *Dominican Official Gazette*, were published by the government. The monthly press is dominated by political parties. The Dominican Freedom Party publishes the *Freedom Voice*, the Dominican Labour Party publishes *The Labourite*, the Ministry of Agriculture publishes *VWA DIABLOTIN*, and the Eastern Caribbean Institute for Democracy publishes *The Eastern Caribbean Connection.*

The electronic media environment is mixed. The two radio stations are operated by the government and a religious organization. DBS Radio, established in 1971, is operated by the Dominican Broadcasting Corporation. The Gospel Broadcasting Corporation of Chicago established the Voice of Life in 1976. Television was introduced in 1983 by Marpin TV, a privately owned and operated company.

Grenada

Grenada is farthest south of the Windward Islands. This 133-square-mile nation-state had an estimated population of 87,000 in 1989. The population density was 654 persons per square mile. Eighty-four percent of the population is of

African descent, 11 percent is of mixed ancestry, and the remaining five percent is of Arawak and East Indian ancestry. The society is essentially Christian. Sixty-four percent of the population is Roman Catholic and 22 percent is Anglican. Like the majority of the Caribbean, a substantial percentage of the population is under 15 years of age. Adult literacy was reported to be 95 percent in 1990 and the per capita income was U.S. $1,286.75 in 1990 (Jamaican Institute, 1990, p. 31).

Grenada, the "smallest independent country in the Western hemisphere" has been the site of dramatic political events in the Caribbean postindependence era. It obtained political independence from Great Britain on May 1, 1974. This was after a series of "delinking" processes that began in 1958 when the state joined the West Indian Federation. This regional organization broke up, due to a complex of reasons that included national pride, distribution of power, and race. It has been suggested that British Guiana, now Guyana, refused to join the federation because the Guyanese Indian political community feared domination by the region's substantial African population.

After the breakup of the West Indian Federation, Grenada obtained internal self-government and associated statehood in 1967. The "associated state" status was a standard element in Great Britain's decolonizing strategy in the Caribbean. Under this arrangement, the state was in total control of domestic policy while the British government controlled foreign policy. On February 7, 1974, Grenada obtained its full independence from Great Britain to become "the smallest independent country in the Western hemisphere" (Jamaican Institute, 1990, p. 31)

The political personality who dominated this era was Eric Gairy. His ascent to political power and his maintenance of that power illuminate an important dynamic of the African psyche in Caribbean politics. In Caribbean communities where there is a high degree of West African retentions, the "politics of magic" is evident. In many traditional West African communities power and influence is acquired and maintained on the basis of the individual's perceived powers of accessing information from the ancestors and maintaining contact with the invisible spirit world that inhabits all life spaces. Thus, the elders, the griot, and the obeah man wield considerable power and influence. Going with this power are other communal mechanisms, such as the "koutou" of the Ashanti. The "koutou" is a caucus of elders. This deliberative mechanism serves as a constraint to those inevitable opportunities that encourage the abuse of power. There is, however, a tendency among politicians in contemporary global Africa (continental Africa and its diaspora) to position their "magical powers" but ignore consultation and the nurturing of the communal traditions that constrain abuses of power.

Eric Gairy's return to Grenada from the oil refining industry in Curacao in the late 1950s was imbued with magic.[3] Local legend states that some period before his return, a noted Grenadian obeah woman announced that she had conclusive proof that a man named Eric Gairy would return to the island to lead the people out of their poverty and provide them with a better life. Her test was to throw a white sheet into the sea. If the sheet sank, Eric Gairy was not the spirits' choice. If the sheet floated, Eric Gairy was the spirits' choice. The sheet floated as a result of the substantial amount of starch put on the sheet by Eric Gairy and his strategists.[4]

Gairy's political leadership has been described as bizarre. He became a participant in the international Unidentified Flying Objects (UFOs) discourse. As the economic conditions of the island declined, Gairy increasingly used political violence to maintain his power. His force, the Mongoose Squad, had several similarities with Haiti's Ton Ton Macoute. It was this environment of corruption and autocracy that led to the overthrow of the Gairy government by the New Jewel Movement in March 1979, and the creation of the People's Revolutionary Government.

The People's Revolutionary Government (PRG) articulated a political and economic agenda that was socialist in orientation. Grenada established close ties with Castro's Cuba, the USSR and the Non-Aligned Movement. Grenada joined Jamaica and Guyana as a socialist bloc in the Commonwealth Caribbean. That shift alarmed the more conservative Caribbean states and the United States. The coup that took place in October 1993 resulted in the execution of Maurice Bishop and created the conditions for the invasion of Grenada by United States and Caribbean forces. Since the coup there has been continuing economic decline and a period of unstable political coalitions among the three dominant political parties (National Democratic Congress, Grenada United Party, and the New Jewel Movement). The current prime minister is Mr. Nicholas Braithwaithe, leader of the National Democratic Congress.

The Grenadian media environment is mixed. There are state- and privately operated mass media. The government publishes the weekly *Government Gazette*. Private companies publish four weekly publications—*Grenada Informer, Indies Times, The Grenada Voice,* and *The Grenada Newsletter*. The national radio station, Radio Grenada, is owned and operated by the government of Grenada. Television was introduced by the Discovery Foundation of the United States in 1986. In addition to these domestic resources, Grenada is in the footprint of all of the major U.S. satellites and receives the spillover broadcast signals from Trinidad and Tobago and neighboring states.

The Cooperative Republic of Guyana

Guyana is the largest member of the Caribbean community. This nation-state, located on the northeast shoulder of South America, is 83,000 square miles. Its South American neighbors are Suriname on the east, Brazil on the southwest, and Venezuela on the west. These boundaries were established during the British colonial period and have been challenged on many occasions.

Guyana's population in 1990 was reported at 779,000 with a population density of less than 10 persons per square mile. The population of the multiracial society is distributed according to the patterns of the colonial experience. In

1990 the indigenous population (Akawai, Arecuna, Arawak, Carib, Macusi, Patomonia, Warrau, Wapishana) represented 4 percent of the population and was concentrated in the hinterland. About 34 percent of the population is of African ancestry. They are located in rural and urban areas. Guyanese of African descent who reside in rural areas tend to live in those villages purchased by freed slaves immediately after the abolition of slavery. African slavery was abolished in 1834 in the Caribbean. However, there was a four-year period of apprenticeship which lasted until 1838 when all slaves were emancipated.

East Indian indentured labor was introduced to British Guiana in 1834, in anticipation of the movement of African Guyanese from the plantation economies of rural Guyana to the urban commercial centers. The movement of Indian indentured labor continued until the 1920s.[5] Indian Guyanese now account for 51 percent of the population. Their residential concentrations also conform to the dynamic of the politics and economics that brought them to Guyana. In 1994 the majority of Indian Guyanese resided in the rural agricultural belt that extends along the Atlantic coastline. Over the years, the Indian Guyanese population has also become occupationally diverse, with a strong urban presence. Guyanese and European and Chinese ancestries are also the product of this history. They account for approximately 2 percent of the population. The dominant Euro-Guyanese population is of Portuguese ancestry. Portuguese, East Indians, Chinese, and African populations were also part of the postemancipation labor migration. The Portuguese and Chinese participated more in the comprador activities—organizing and operating small businesses in both the rural and urban areas. These populations are concentrated in the urban centers.

The diversity of Guyanese society is also evident in its religious landscape. Fifty-seven percent of the population is Christian, while 33 percent is Hindu and 9 percent Moslem. In 1990 the per capita income was U.S. $651.55 per annum, one of the lowest in the Caribbean. The adult literacy rate was 90 percent. Over 36 percent of the population was 14 years or younger in 1990 (Jamaican Institute, 1990, p. 32).

Two personalities have dominated Guyanese political life since the end of World War II—Dr. Cheddi Jagan and Forbes Burnham. These two leaders have influenced the tone and direction of Guyanese politics since the late 1940s. Jagan and Burnham are associated with the creation of the People's Political Party (PPP), which led British Guiana to internal self-government in 1953. The perceived communist orientation of that party led to the suspension of the internal self-government constitution and the dismissal of the first government elected through universal adult suffrage in 1953—90 days after the elections. Politics in Guyana since 1953 has been characterized by "apanjat"—the politics of race.

In 1964 the African Guyanese–dominated People's National Congress (PNC) obtained political power. That party, headed by Forbes Burnham and supported by the United States and the British, led British Guiana to political independence on May 26, 1966. The nation became a republic on February 23, 1970. The PNC maintained political power until it was defeated by the PPP in 1993.

In his book *The West on Trial,* Cheddi Jagan (1972) described the colonial media environment as one that used all its resources and power to promote the interests of the Planter class that dominated British Guianese politics in the preindependence era. This practice of using the nation's media resources to support the existing power structure was continued by the PNC. For over 20 years (1964–1987), the media in Guyana were primarily state owned and operated. Some private newspapers existed, but they were in the main the political press. Since 1987, with support from the Washington, D.C.-based National Endowment for Democracy, there has been the emergence of a "free press." That organization facilitated the establishment of the *Stabreok News* in 1987. In addition to the *Stabreok News,* seven other newspapers are regularly published. The government-owned Guyana National Newspapers Ltd. publishes the *Guyana Chronicle,* a daily tabloid. The political press includes the *Mirror* (a PPP publication), the *New Nation* (a PNC publication), *Dayclean* (a publication of the Working Peoples' Alliance), *Open Word* (also associated with the Working Peoples' Alliance), and the *Democrat* (associated with the conservative politician Paul N. Tennassee). The *Catholic Standard* is "the official newspaper of the Diocese of Georgetown" (Jamaican Institute, 1990, pp. 32–33).

The dominant electronic medium in Guyana has tended to be radio. Radio broadcasting has remained state owned and operated for almost 25 years. The Guyana Broadcasting Corporation owns and operates two radio services—Radio Rorima and the Voice of Guyana. These two services cover almost 75 percent of the country. Like the Barbados, Jamaica, and Trinidad and Tobago Television, radio broadcasting was introduced to Guyana by the U.K.-based media company, Rediffusion, in the mid-1940s. In Guyana, the vehicle was Radio Demerara. The government of Guyana acquired that service in the mid-1970s and joined it with the state-owned Guyana Broadcasting Service (GBS) to create the Guyana Broadcasting Corporation (GBC).[6]

Television development in Guyana has been erratic. Television in Guyana is essentially "pirate television." In 1993 the author identified over 15 television operators, the majority of whom were involved in some degree of television piracy from the United States. The state-owned Guyana Television Broadcasting Co. Ltd. is under-capitalized and has a limited broadcast range.

Jamaica

Jamaica is the third largest island-state in the Commonwealth Caribbean. It is 4,244 square miles and had an estimated population of 2.54 million in 1989. The population density is approximately 600 persons per square mile.

People of African ancestry predominate in Jamaican society. According to the *Caribbean Media Directory,* 76 percent of the population is of African descent and 15 percent Afro-European. The remaining 9 percent is Afro-Chinese, Chinese, Afro-East Indian, East Indian, and Caucasian (Jamaican Institute, 1990, p. 35).

The nation is predominantly Christian—Anglican, Baptist, Roman Catholic, Methodist, and the Church of God. In addition, the Christian-based Rastafarian tradition exerts significant influence in the sphere of Jamaican spirituality and consciousness. In 1989 almost 37 percent of the population was 14 years old and under. Over 52 percent of the population is 15–59 years old. Eighty-two percent of the adult population is defined as literate. Compulsory free education is provided for all Jamaicans between 6 and 14 (Jamaican Institute, 1990, p. 35).

Jamaica is not only about charismatic leaders; it is also about a charismatic culture. Jamaica's political life and its popular culture have been a "brake and an accelerator" in Caribbean life, mostly an accelerator. The Jamaican worker riots of the 1930s determined the structure of Caribbean politics, initiating the establishment of worker-based political parties in the Caribbean. Out of this conflict came Alexander Bustamante and Norman Manley, two cousins, and the founders of the Jamaican Labour Party (JLP) and the People's National Party (PNP). These two political parties have shared political power in Jamaica over the past 60 years.

The Jamaican political process that started in the 1930s has been influential in every aspect of Caribbean politics. Jamaica participated in the region's quest for universal adult suffrage, political independence, and has been on both sides of the regional integration discourse. Sir Alexander Bustamante's JLP argued for Jamaica to leave the West Indian Federation. His point of view prevailed in the 1955 referendum on that issue. Jamaica's withdrawal brought the institution to an end. Michael Manley, the son of Norman Manley, has been one of the architects of the Caribbean Community.

On August 6, 1962, Jamaica became the first British colony in the British West Indies to obtain independence. The Jamaican Labour Party was in power at the time but was replaced by the PNP in 1972. Over the past 32 years, political power has alternated between the JLP and the PNP.

In 1974 the People's National Party declared that its electoral victory in 1972 gave it the mandate to establish a "democratic socialist" society. This was translated into a commitment to "partial nationalization, increased welfare expenditure, agricultural reform, and in foreign affairs, 'Third Worldism' and close alliance with Cuba." "Allegations of CIA destabilization" and declining economic conditions led to the defeat of the PNP in 1980. The JLP returned to power in 1980 with an aggressive, market-oriented policy.[7] In 1989 the JLP was replaced by PNP. The People's National Party is currently led by Mr. P. J. Patterson who appears to have adopted a less ideological and a more pragmatic approach to national development, apparently bringing to an end the politics of extremes that has dominated Jamaican society in the postindependence era.

In addition to Jamaica's political reverberations, Jamaican spirituality and creative expressions have influenced Jamaican and Caribbean consciousness. The Rastafarian, the University of the West Indies, Jamaican performing arts, especially its popular music (reggae) have been of substantial influence in the Caribbean and the wider Americas.[8]

The political and cultural environment has influenced the media environment, which can be described as mixed. The print media in Jamaica are established, diversified, and primarily privately owned. The Gleaner Company Ltd., publisher of *The Daily Gleaner* since 1834, is the biggest publisher. In addition to being the region's oldest regularly published newspaper, *The Daily Gleaner* is its most influential. The *Jamaica Weekly Gleaner* is an important record for the Jamaican and Caribbean diaspora in the United Kingdom and North America. The Gleaner Company is recognized as one of the "media giants" in the Commonwealth Caribbean. In addition to *The Daily Gleaner* and the *Jamaica Weekly Gleaner,* the Gleaner Company has nine other regular publications. *Flair, Sports Special,* and the *Financial Gleaner* are weekly inserts in *The Daily Gleaner.* The *Sunday Magazine* is inserted in the *Sunday Gleaner.* Other Gleaner publications include the "afternoon daily tabloid" *The Star* and the weeklies *Week-end Star* and *Children's Own.*

The Gleaner Company's domination of the newspaper industry has been challenged since the early 1980s by a variety of publications with national and community orientations. The Jamaican Record Ltd., established in 1988, has been a visible competitor. In 1990 this company published the "morning daily broadsheet," *The Jamaica Record* and several weekly publications, including *Jamaica Times, The Enquirer,* and the *Western Record*—a weekly tabloid "giving special news coverage to western Jamaica." Regional and community newspapers began appearing in 1980 with the establishment of the *Western Mirror.* Other such publications include *The Siren,* the *Twin City Sun,* and *Boulevard News. The Siren,* established in 1990, "publishes general news covering Montego Bay and its environs." The *Twin City Sun,* founded in June 1985, is described as a "community newspaper in the parish of St. Catherine for Portmore, Spanish Town and its environs." The *Boulevard News,* founded in 1986, is "the community newspaper with a national outlook," covering mainly a number of districts in the Corporate Area of Kingston and St. Andrew (Jamaican Institute, 1990, pp. 36–40).

Changes in the political and economic philosophy of Jamaica not only encouraged the proliferation of print media, they influenced the electronic media. Until the mid-1980s, broadcasting was dominated by the state-owned and publicly owned institutions. The dominant systems were the cooperatively owned Radio Jamaica Ltd. (RJR) and state-owned and semicommercially operated Jamaican Broadcasting Corporation (JBC). Radio Jamaica Ltd. (RJR) was incorporated by the U.K. entity, Rediffusion, in 1947 and began commercial broadcasting in 1950. In 1972 the system was "cooperativized." Under this arrangement, "mass representative organizations" owned 50.1 percent of RJR, with the government owning 25.1 percent and employees of RJR owning the remaining 24.8 percent. In 1990, RJR operated three national services: RJR, RJR Supreme Sound, and FAME FM.

The Jamaican Broadcasting Corporation was established in 1959 and operates two radio services—JBC Radio One and JBC Radio Two. Signals from JBC One cover the entire island and spill over to the Turks and Caicos and the Cayman Islands. In addition, Jamaica Information Service, the government information service, operates JIS Radio, which broadcasts educational and public affairs programming at daily allocated times on the RJR and JBC services.

Privately owned radio broadcasting services have emerged in Jamaica beginning in the late 1980s. The Grove Broadcasting Company Ltd. initiated this trend in February 1988 when it established IRIE FM, a station operating from Ocho Rios, that emphasizes reggae music and covers about 60 percent of Jamaica. IRIE FM was followed by Radio Klas-FM in August 1989 and Radio Waves FM in October, 1989. The respective operators of these systems are Island Broadcasting Services Ltd. and Western Broadcasting Services Ltd. Radio KLAS is national in scope while Radio Waves covers western Jamaica.

Television was introduced in 1963 by the Jamaican Broadcasting Corporation. The state monopolized television broadcasting until 1992 when a license was issued to CVM Television to operate a ''low powered service.'' The state-run service JBC TV is national in reach. Programming is provided by a variety of state entities in addition to JBC TV itself. These include JBC/CBF and JIS TV. JBC/CBF, the Cultural Broadcasting Facility is:

an arm of the Jamaican Broadcasting Corporation. . . . Devoted to producing Jamaican programmes of a cultural nature in the widest sense; for example: heritage, youth, environment, music, dance, drama, literature and fine arts are in the range of its production. Established mainly to help provide balance between Jamaican and foreign TV programmes; uses C.P.T.C [Creative Production and Training Centre] staff and facilities for its productions; hopes to develop its efficiency to producing quality programmes for sale in the overseas markets. (Jamaican Institute, 1990, p. 42)

JIS-TV broadcasts government information programs at specific times daily on JBC Television.

Several news agencies are active in the Jamaican media environment. These include the government news agency (JAMPRESS), the regional Caribbean News Agency (CANA), and three international services—Inter Press Service (IPS), Associated Press (AP), and United Press International (UPI). Several important regional media training institutions are also present in Jamaica. These include the Radio Education Unit and Caribbean Institute for Mass Communication (CARIMAC) of the University of the West Indies, and the Creative Production and Training Centre (CPTC). These institutions, along with the Center for Communication Studies at the University of Guyana, will be examined in a later chapter.

Montserrat

Montserrat is one of the few remaining British colonies in the Caribbean. This 39.6-square-mile island is located in the northeast of the Leeward island chain.

In 1990 the population was estimated at 12,500. The majority of the population is of African descent. Persons of Irish descent make up the rest of the population. The population density is approximately 315 persons per square mile.

The island's colonial status began in 1632 when the first British settlers arrived. Although there has been the clamor for independence, British rule was consolidated in 1990 when the constitution was changed to give the governor "extra powers to control financial services." This was due to scandals associated with off-shore banking on the island. Montserrat became a member of the CARICOM Community on May 1, 1974.

Politics here has also been dominated by a charismatic personality, John Osborne, and an entrenched two-party system. John Osborne's party, the Progressive Democratic Party (PDP), has dominated the political scene since 1973. The other party, the People's Liberation Movement (PLM), held power during the period 1983–1987.

Montserrat can be described as an international media site. In addition to publicly and privately owned mass media, Radio Antilles, a powerful pan-Caribbean radio station, broadcasts from the island. Radio Antilles, which broadcasts in English and French, serves as a relay station for the BBC, the Voice of America, and Radio Canada International (Jamaican Institute, 1990, p. 45). Montserrat is also a major popular music production site. The recording studio of Alphonse Cassel (Arrow) is located here.[9]

Two weekly newspapers dominate the Montserrat print media. These are the weekly tabloids—*The Montserrat Times* and *The Montserrat Reporter*. The former, established in 1982, is an independent publication. The latter, established in 1985, is the "organ of the National Development Party" (Jamaican Institute, 1990, p. 44).

There are four broadcasting services in addition to Radio Antilles. The government-owned Radio Montserrat (ZJB) was established in 1957 and is operated along commercial lines. The second radio service, GEM Radio, was established in 1984 and is owned and operated by the Caribbean Communications Company, a private company headquartered in the United States. Television is privately owned and operated. The Antilles Television Corporation established Antilles Television (ATV) in 1973 and introduced Satellite TV, a cable service, in 1982.

St. Christopher (Kitts) and Nevis

This 68-square-mile nation-state became an independent federal state on September 19, 1983. The estimated population was 46,000 in 1985 with a population density of 676 persons per square mile. Ninety-five percent of the population is of African descent. The adult literacy rate is 90 percent and 49.6 percent of the population is 20 years old or younger. In 1990 the society was predominantly Christian with 76 percent of the population being Protestant. In 1985 the per capita income was U.S. $1,409.00 (Jamaican Institute, 1990, p. 49).

Until 1967, Anguilla was part of the "union" with St. Christopher and Nevis. It seceded in 1967 and returned to British Dependency in 1971. The Labour Party dominated the political scene for 30 years until 1980, when it was replaced by a coalition of the People's Action Movement (PAM) and the Nevis Reform Party (NRP). The prime minister is Dr. Kennedy Simmonds. The state joined the Caribbean Community on July 26, 1974.

The print media are privately owned. The two weekly tabloid newspapers can be described as partisan. *The Democrat,* founded in 1948, is published by the People's Action Movement while *The Labour Spokesman,* founded in 1957, is published by the St. Kitts and Nevis Trades and Labour Union.

The broadcast media can be described as mixed. The government owns and operates a radio and a television service. Similar services are provided by the private sector. The government operates ZIZ Radio and ZIZ TV. The radio service was introduced in 1961 and the television service in 1972. The privately owned radio station Voice of Nevis Radio (VON Radio) was established in 1988. Trinity Broadcasting of Nevis Ltd. operates TBN-TV—a religious television service.

St. Lucia

The 238-square-mile nation-state of St. Lucia is the birthplace of two Nobel Laureates—Sir Arthur Lewis and Derek Walcott. The estimated population in 1990 was 140,000. This population is predominantly of African descent. Almost 50 percent of the population (49.6%) was 20 years old or under in 1990. The adult literacy rate is 80 percent. Ninety percent of the population is Roman Catholic (Jamaican Institute, 1990, p. 51).

Although English is the official language, there is a strong presence of French Patois in St. Lucia. This is a function of almost two centuries of French colonial rule and the island's close proximity to other French- and Patois-speaking countries. St. Lucia's northern neighbor is the French department Martinique. It was not until 1814 that St. Lucia became a British colony. It is now an independent member of the Commonwealth and a member of the Caribbean Community. St. Lucia has a parliamentary democracy. John Compton has been the dominant political personality.

The St. Lucian media environment is mixed. The print media are dominated by privately owned weekly tabloid newspapers. Among these is *The Weekend Voice,* established in 1885 and identified as the "oldest publication in the Eastern Caribbean" (Jamaican Institute, 1990, p. 51). Other privately owned weeklies include *The Voice of St. Lucia,* also founded in 1885, *The Star,* founded in 1957, and *The Crusader. The Crusader* is identified as being "close to the Peoples Progressive Party." The Archbishop of Castries publishes the *Catholic Chronicle* fortnightly. The government's principal print venture is the Government Information Services's *St. Lucia Achievement,* "a quarterly tabloid, with news, information and features on government activities'' (Jamaican Institute, 1990, p. 51).

The government's presence in the electronic media is through Radio St. Lucia (RSL), established in 1971. The private commercial station, Radio Caribbean (1982) International, broadcasts in English and in French. The French programs are targeted to markets in Martinique and Guadeloupe. There is no government presence in St. Lucian television. Helen Television Service (HTS), established in 1983, provides television service for approximately 85 percent of the island. In addition to its domestic services, Helen Television Service has pioneered regional television program exchanges in the Caribbean. The other television operators in St. Lucia are DBS TV, established in 1985, and Cable and Wireless (W.I.) Ltd. Cablevision, established in 1987.

St. Vincent and the Grenadines

St. Vincent and the Grenadines attained independent statehood on October 27, 1979. This 150-square-mile nation-state is in the Windward group of the Caribbean islands. It has been described as "a nation of 32 islands and cays." The island is of volcanic origin and is mountainous. St. Vincent's population in 1990 was estimated at 115,000. The population density at that time was 766 persons per square mile. Eighty-five percent of that population is of African descent. Caucasians, East Indians, and Caribs make up the remaining 15 percent. The dominant religion is Christianity. Forty percent of the population is Church of England (Anglican), 30 percent is Methodist, 10 percent is Roman Catholic, and the various Christian faiths comprise 20 percent. Like the rest of CARI-COM, St. Vincent and the Grenadines has a young population. In 1990, 50 percent of the population was 16 years old or younger. The adult literacy rate is 95 percent and the per capita income in 1990 was U.S. $906.00 (Jamaican Institute, 1990, p. 53).

St. Vincent and the Grenadines is a parliamentary democracy. Like the majority of the Commonwealth Caribbean, it is a constitutional monarchy within the Commonwealth, with Queen Elizabeth as the head of state. The queen is represented by a governor-general. The island-state became a British possession in the eighteenth century and has participated in all of the significant experiments in Caribbean politics. Until 1959, it was a member of the Windward Islands Federation. Between 1958 and 1962, it was part of the West Indian Federation. In October 1969, as part of Britain's decolonization practices in the Caribbean, St. Vincent and the Grenadines became an "Associated State with internal autonomy." Full independence came a decade later on October 27, 1979. Before that, on May 1, 1974, St. Vincent and the Grenadines joined CARICOM.

As with many other nations in the Caribbean, politics in St. Vincent and the Grenadines has been dominated by two charismatic personalities—Milton Cato and James Mitchell. The dominant practice has been coalition government. This pattern has been evident since 1972, when the independent candidate, James

Mitchell, who held the "balance of power" in that election, joined with the People's Political Party (PPP) and became the premier. That coalition replaced the Cato-led St. Vincent Labour Party (SVLP), which had dominated earlier preindependence politics and eventually led the country into independence. The coalition collapsed in 1974, facilitating the return to power by Milton Cato through a coalition between his St. Vincent Labour Party and the People's Political Party. That government led the nation to independence in 1979.

In December 1979, the SVLP won the general elections convincingly and formed the government. The economic and taxation policies and the scandals associated with this government led to its defeat in July 1984. The July 1984 elections ushered in a government led by the National Democratic Party which was founded in 1975 by James Mitchell. This "centrist" party has consolidated its popularity with the electorate. In the 1984 election, the NDP won nine of the thirteen seats in the House of Assembly. In the May 1989 elections, the party won all 15 seats in an enlarged House of Assembly. St. Vincentian politics provides a focus on political continuity in the region. Milton Cato reflects one political paradigm—the rise of the political leader from the labor movement. In a way, James Mitchell is an inheritor of both traditions—the leader who comes up from the labor movement and the practitioner of the politics of coalition. He is also part of a new tradition—the politics of the marketplace—he was among the early adopters of marketplace politics in CARICOM.

The media environment is mixed, with the presence of politically affiliated, state-owned, and privately owned media outlets. The political press dominates the print media. The *Caribbean Media Directory* identified six weekly print publications in St. Vincent and the Grenadines. Four of them are published by political organizations. The St. Vincent Labour Party publishes *The Star,* the National Democratic Party publishes *The New Times,* the United People's Movement and the Movement of National Unity publish *Justice* and *Unity,* respectively. The commercial print publications are represented by *The Vincentian* and *The News. The Vincentian* is published by the Vincentian Publishing Co. Ltd., a private company. The Advocate Company Ltd., a Barbadian-based private company which is emerging as a regional media power, prints *The News.*

The ownership of the electronic media is divided between the government of St. Vincent and the private sector. Through the National Broadcasting Corporation, the government operates radio in St. Vincent and the Grenadines. Radio St. Vincent and the Grenadines, established in 1972, provides radio service while SVG TV, established in 1980 by the St. Vincent and Grenadines Broadcasting Corporation Ltd., provides television in St. Lucia as well.

Trinidad and Tobago

"Trinibagonians"—the people of Trinidad and Tobago—have celebrated their creoleness and, in the process, have encouraged that process in the region. Trinidad has been a central player in Caribbean politics, culture, and communication in the post–World War II era. The first prime minister of independent Trinidad and Tobago was Eric Williams. His political ideas and his intellectual output have influenced Caribbean state craft. After a successful academic career, including a Ph.D. from Oxford University and a faculty career at Howard University in the United States, Eric Williams returned to the Caribbean anticolonial struggle in the late 1940s. He founded the People's National Movement (PNM) in 1956. His seminal work, *Capitalism and Slavery,* originally published in 1944, provides us with an insight to his intellectual map. He isolated reasons for Caribbean dependency and offered strategies for responding to those colonial linkages that perpetuated that dependency. Among his central ideas was greater Caribbean political, economic, and cultural integration. He was skeptical of the viability of the microeconomies of the small island communities in the global economy. He promoted efforts to stimulate a regional consciousness that was anchored on the strength of the emerging creolization that was evident in multiethnic/racial Trinidad and Tobago and inevitable in the wider Caribbean.

In 1989 the estimated population of the 1,970-square-mile twin-island nation-state was 1.2 million, with 43 percent of African descent, 40 percent of East Indian descent, 14 percent of "mixed" ancestry, and 1 percent of European ancestry. The category "mixed" represents people with a combination of Chinese, Lebanese, Spanish, African, and other heritages. Over 32 percent of the population was 14 years old or younger. The population density was reported at 609 persons per square mile (Jamaican Institute, 1990, p. 54).

Racial and ethnic diversity is also evident in religion. Fifty-two percent of the population was reported to be Christian with 36 percent Roman Catholic and 16 percent Anglican. That calculation does not reflect the syncretic "Shouter Baptist" presence.[10] Twenty-three percent of the population was Hindu and 6 percent was Moslem. This diversity is also evident in language. Although the official language is English, Hindi, French, Spanish, and various Patois are practiced. Adult literacy in Trinidad and Tobago is reported at 95 percent. Education is compulsory for all Trinidadians between the ages of 5 and 15. The annual per capita income in 1985 was reported at U.S. $7,127 in 1987, making it among the highest in the region.

Trinidad and Tobago's geographic location places it very close to the strategic sea lanes that move petroleum from Venezuelan and Trinidadian oil fields to the United States and Europe. This strategic location was central to the Allies' execution of World War II. Under the Lend Lease program during World War II, the British government leased Chaguaramus to the United States to establish a naval base. The U.S. Naval base at Chaguaramus would become a lightning rod in the formulation of Trinidad and Tobago's postindependence foreign policy and was the site for the signing of the Treaty of Chaguaramus that launched CARICOM.[11]

Eric Williams and his People's National Movement dominated political life in Trinidad and Tobago from 1956 to 1986. The People's National Movement changed the shape of party politics in that nation-state. As Trinidad and Tobago's first chief minister and its first prime minister, Eric Williams led his nation to political independence in August 31, 1962 and made Trinidad and Tobago one of the founder members of CARICOM on August 1, 1973.

Like Guyana, politics in Trinidad and Tobago is complicated by the tensions that exist between people of African and East Indian descent in the Caribbean. Trinidadian politics has also been influenced by the boom and bust of oil economies. Eric Williams and his PNM were described as pro-Western in foreign affairs and othrodox in their approach to economic management, "seeking to establish effective partnerships between the state and foreign private enterprise."[12]

These tensions led to several disruptions, including the 1970 Black Power demonstrations and army mutiny. The shrewd politcal maneuvering of Eric Williams allowed him to turn his opposition on itself and use increased oil revenues, the result of windfall profits from higher world oil prices between 1973 and 1974, to consolidate himself and his party as preeminent in Trinidadian and Caribbean politics. In the process, Eric William became more autocratic and even megalomaniacal. He showed his impatience with fellow Caribbean leaders by refusing to attend CARICOM summit meetings for almost a decade. When he died in 1981, his power was virtually unassailable.

The period since Eric Williams's death has been one of fragmentation and recoalescence. His party, the Peoples' National Movement (PNM), won the national elections in November 1981. Coterminous with his death and the 1981 elections, a new trend emerged in Trinidadian politics—coalation efforts to remove the PNM from office. In 1984 a coalation led by the predominantly East Indian National Alliance (NA) and the predominantly African Organization for National Reconstruction (ONR) established the National Alliance for Reconstruction (NAR). This grouping, which brought together the races, won the December 1986 election, thus ending the PNM's domination of Trinidad and Tobago politics.

Most of the aforementioned tensions have continued in the post-PNM era. Police corruption and drug-related scandals rocked the society in 1987. By 1990 the government was held hostage by Iman Yasin Abu Bakr and members of the Jamaat al Musilmeen. The government had to manage an economy whose principal commodity—oil—was not enjoying high world prices. Coupled with the fragilities associated with "mono-crop" economies, there were also internal fights between the two racial groups that dominated the National Alliance for Reconstruction. The National Alliance for Reconstruction was defeated in the 1991 national general elections. The PNM under the leadership of Dr. Patrick Manning now forms the government.

The political, intellectual, and creative feistiness of Trinidadian and Tobagan society is evident in the media environment. There is a vibrant free press. The oldest daily newspaper is the *Trinidad Guardian,* established in 1917. Other dailies include the *Trinidad Daily Express, Evening News,* and *The Evening Sun.* The weekly newspapers include *Trinidad Daily Express, The Sunday*

Guardian, The Weekend Sun, Tobago News, The Weekend Heat, The Bomb, TNT Mirror, Sunday Punch, The Blast, Catholic News. The All-Trinidad Sugar and General Workers Trade Union publishes *Battlefront* fortnightly. The Trinidad Express Newspapers group is emerging as one of the major media conglomerates in the Caribbean. This group has media-related property or relations in Guyana, Barbados, and Jamaica. Its activities include broadcasting and information processing.

The electronic media in Trinidad and Tobago are owned by the state and by private companies. Since 1991, with the deregulation of the media, there has been an increase in local private ownership. Before, the private companies were primarily foreign. The private British company, Rediffusion PLC, operates Radio Trinidad, established in 1947, and the automated station, Radio 95FM. As has been previously indicated, Rediffusion PLC has been responsible for introducing commercial broadcasting in the British colonial Caribbean.[13] Rediffusion established stations in Guyana, Trinidad and Tobago, Barbados, and Jamaica. Through signal spillover and a regional programming strategy, this company has left an indelible imprint on Caribbean radio broadcasting aesthetics. Since the deregulation of the electronic media, the Caribbean Communications Network has become a visible participant in radio broadcasting through Prime Radio Ltd.

The state-owned National Broadcasting Service (NBS), established in 1957, continues to operate Radio 610. As a result of internal competition, NBS is now developing programming to satisfy the various niches in Trinidad and Tobago. State monoply of television in Trinidad and Tobago ended in 1991 when the Caribbean Communications Network introduced T.V. 6. At that time, television in Trinidad and Tobago was provided by Trinidad and Tobago Television Co. Ltd (TT-TV). The United States–based National Broadcasting Corporation was a partner in the establishment of Trinidad and Tobago Television (TT-TV) in 1962.

Trinidad and Tobago is one of the few locations in the Caribbean with active, independent production companies. Banyan Productions in Trinidad and Tobago has been one of the region's leading producers of cultural programming materials for Caribbean and international television programming.

Trinidad and Tobago appears to be one of the few Caribbean societies developing a coherent information and communication strategy for participation in the global communication economy. The establishment of the Copyright Organization of Trinidad and Tobago (COTT) has provided a mechanism to ensure that Trinidadian talent is rewarded. The National Telecommunications White Paper of 1990 anticipated the nation's strategies in developing telecommunications, broadcasting, and information capacity for the twenty-first century.

SUMMARY AND CONCLUSIONS

The territories discussed in this chapter are not the entire Caribbean region. However, these countries form an important subgroup because they share many similarities with the wider region. These similarities are based on the experiences associated with African slavery and its aftermath. This exploration focused on a very discreet subset of that experience—the former British West Indies, now known as the Commonwealth Caribbean or CARICOM. This exploration however, is conscious of the centripetal force—the tendency to integration—that is always evident in Caribbean reality. In 1994, contential and island nation states washed by the Caribbean Sea agreed to pursue an Association of Caribbean States.

This chapter has isolated some of the variables that have influenced the development and operations of mass media in the Caribbean. These include the colonial history, anticolonial struggles, the labor movement, the creation of national political parties and the challenges of postindependence politics in multiracial societies. Another variable is the dominating charismatic personality who, as "founder" of the nation, influences the psychoculture of the society, sometimes, through the "politics of magic." At their best, these "founder-leaders" have inspired, provided essential ideas, and facilitated the development of relevant institutions. At the other extreme, they have facilitated the "coarsening" of the Caribbean character—"the sort of beastly behavior one to another that renders personal abuse respectable and violence the norm."[14] The complex issues associated with race, ethnicity, religion, age, gender, literacy, and technology all influence the organization of mass communication in these societies of predominantly African ancestry.

NOTES

1. From Caribbean Community Secretariat publication, dated May 1987.

2. Ibid.

3. The Dutch Antillean island Aruba has been a major oil refining site for the past 60 years. During World War II this capacity was strategic. This industry was an important employment site for British West Indians. British West Indian labor has always followed employment opportunities in the hemisphere. Walter Rodney demonstrated, in *A History of the Guyanese Working People, 1881–1905* (Baltimore: The Johns Hopkins University Press, 1981), that British West Indian labor contributed to the establishment of the timber and gold mining industries in British Guiana. Up to the mid-1980s, St. Lucians were the dominant population group in Mahdia, an important community in Guyana's "golden triangle." Similar relationships are associated with the construction of the Panama Canal, the consolidation of United Fruit Company in Central America, and Cuba. The Caribbean oil refining industry provided similar opportunities, particularly during World War II and the early 1950s.

4. Based on story told to the author during a visit to Grenada in 1982.

5. See Walter Rodney, *A History of the Guyanese Working People, 1881–1905* (Baltimore: The Johns Hopkins University Press, 1981); and Mohammed Shahabudden, *From Plantocracy to Nationalization: A Profile in Sugar* (Georgetown, Guyana: University of Guyana, 1983) for detailed discussions.

6. For an early history of radio broadcasting in Guyana, see E. K. Thomas, *Begin-*

nings of Broadcasting in the West Indies 1920–1949. Ph.D. dissertation, University of Missouri, 1979.

7. All quotations from *The Europa World Yearbook* (1991), p. 370.

8. For further discussion on Jamaican popular music, read/listen to *The Story of Jamaican Music,* a four-CD compilation by Island Records Ltd., 1993.

9. Alphonse Cassel, better known as "Arrow," is a major Soca performer and producer. Paul McCartney and Stevie Wonder recorded their global hit "Ebony and Ivory" at this studio.

10. The "Shouter Baptist" represents a valuable connection with West African religiosity. It also provides a rich site for the exploration of African retentions and survivals in the African diaspora in the Caribbean. The "Shouter Baptist" reality is connected with other syncretisms such as Voodoo and Santeria in the Americas.

11. For a substantial exploration of the topic, see Eric Williams, *From Columbus to Castro: The History of the Caribbean 1492–1969* (London: Andre Deutsch, 1983).

12. From *The Europa World Yearbook* (1991), p. 555.

13. Erwin Thomas's dissertation, *Beginnings of Broadcasting in the West Indies 1920– 1949,* examines this process and isolates the tensions between the Radio Corporation of America and the British government on the establishment of commercial broadcasting in the West Indies. In *Columbus to Castro,* Eric Williams reports that the British government was so indebted to the United States as a result of World War II that it was in an asymmetrical negotiating position in matters of foreign policy and economics. Thomas concludes that the British government's decision to facilitate the creation of Rediffusion and award it a license to operate in the West Indies and other parts of the British Empire involved the assertion of independence by the British in the asymmetrial condition.

14. For further discussions on this theme, see Rex Nettleford, *Inward Stretch Outward Reach: A Voice from the Caribbean* (London: MacMillian Caribbean, 1993).

REFERENCES

Central Rediffusion Services. (1956). *Commercial broadcasting in the West Indies.* London: Butterworths Scientific Publications.

The Europa World Yearbook. (1991). London: Europa Publications.

A Group of Caribbean Experts. (1981). *The Caribbean Community in the 1980s.* Georgetown, Guyana: The Caribbean Community Secretariat.

Jagan, C. (1972). *The West on trial: The fight for Guyana's freedom.* German Democratic Republic: Seven Seas Press.

Jamaican Institute of Political Education and the Eastern Caribbean Institute for Democracy. (1990). *Caribbean Media Directory.* Kingston, Jamaica: Jamaican Institute of Political Education and the Eastern Caribbean Institute for Democracy.

Nettleford, R. (1993). *Inward stretch, outward reach: A voice from the Caribbean.* London: MacMillan Caribbean.

Rodney, W. (1981). *A history of the Guyanese working people, 1881–1905.* Baltimore: The Johns Hopkins University Press.

Shahabudden, M. (1983). *From plantocracy to nationalization: A profile of sugar.* Georgetown, Guyana: University of Guyana.

Thomas, C. (1985). *The poor and the powerless: Economic policy and change in the Caribbean.* New York: Monthly Review Press.

Thomas, E. (1978). Beginnings of broadcasting in the West Indies 1920–1949. Unpublished Ph.D. dissertation, University of Missouri-Columbia.

Williams, E. (1964). *Capitalism and slavery*. London: Andre Deutsch.

———. (1983). *From Columbus to Castro: The history of the Caribbean 1492–1969*. London: Andre Deutsch.

10 Mass Media Development and Government Relations

INTRODUCTION

This chapter examines the determinants and the characteristics of mass media and government relations in the Commonwealth Caribbean in the postindependence period (1962–1994). The chapter will identify common tendencies and isolate the common challenges facing the relationship between mass communication and government in the future. Specifically, the chapter will discuss some historical practices that have shaped the legal environments that determine and define mass media's relations with Commonwealth Caribbean governments. This discussion is based on the premise that Commonwealth Caribbean states have common practices and tendencies in their mass media and government relations. Therefore, some Caribbean Community (CARICOM) states will be highlighted as exemplars of the general tendency.

COMMON FACTORS

In his examination of media regulations in Guyana, Hugh Daley (1993) remarked, "[the] legal structure [that determines and influences the mass media in Guyana] is typical in many ways of other Commonwealth Caribbean developing countries." He identified three periods in the development of that "legal structure:" (a) the colonial (from the early fifteenth century to 1962), (b) the postcolonial (from 1962 to the early 1980s), and (c) the current period of re-commercialization (from the early 1980s to the present).

The colonial period in Guyana extended from Dutch settlement in the mid-fifteenth century, through British acquisition in 1804, to Guyana's political independence in 1966. The postcolonial period in Guyana extended from 1966 and ends in 1985 when Forbes Burnham died. Burnham's death in 1985 signaled that nation's ideological shift from a centrally planned socialist economy and the "caudillismo" style of government. By 1985, most Commonwealth Caribbean states had accepted the ideas of free market economics and transparent electoral politics. This acceptance was a prerequisite for participating in the opportunities promised by the Caribbean policies articulated by U.S. presidents from 1980 to 1992.

Between 1962 and 1980, Commonwealth Caribbean governments developed several strategies to encourage national development. All of these strategies recognized the need for wider regional cooperation. Collectively, these micro-states envisioned an efficient and effective structure that was competitive in the global economy and could provide their citizens with an improving quality of life. This vision required harmonizing relations among the member states. This has proven to be difficult, particularly during the 1970s through the mid-1980s. The politics of the socialist experiments in Jamaica, Grenada, and Guyana clashed with the politics of the market dependent states that were the numerical majority. One outcome was the U.S. invasion of Grenada in 1982. However, by the end of the postcolonial period in the mid-1980s, there was a high degree of ideological congruence among the member states of the Caribbean Community.

CARIBBEAN PRINT MEDIA AND GOVERNMENT RELATIONS

The Colonial Period

The first newspaper in the Caribbean was established in Barbados in 1730. Examining the slow diffusion of the medium in the Caribbean, John Lent (1990, p. 8) offered these explanations:

(1) a press was not needed to disseminate information on an island so small and inter-personal in nature, (2) the colonizers felt that the islanders, mostly slaves, were not important or intelligent enough to have use of the printed word, (3) the unstable nature of the islands did not allow for the establishment of permanent institutions, and (4) governments feared the impact of the presses and thus did not encourage their development.

Lent does show that when newspapers were established, it was with the active support of the colonial administration. Invariably, these newspapers served as the mouthpieces of the colonial administration and tended to be aligned with the planter class that controlled the legislative branches of West Indian colonial governments. This type of relationship provided a foothold for British media giants in the region, such as the Thompson Newspapers Group and the Redif-fusion Broadcasting Company during the colonial period.

An independent press was also present during the colonial period. Despite its tenuous economic condition, the independent press was vocal. Several devices were used to control the independent press. The Official Secrets Act was the principal instrument, prohibiting the publication of anything defined as an "official secret." The independent press became associated with the anticolonial struggle in the British West Indies. Sedition laws were promulgated to deal with the independent press. These draconian instruments allowed the searching of newspaper offices and the seizure of presses. Other legal mechanisms included the establishment of specific newspaper laws.

Outside the legal framework, colonial administrators and governors used the power of patronage to influence the independent press. Government printing contracts and the publication of government notices were the favored devices. Failure to obtain government contracts jeopardized the economic existence of the independent press.

By the end of the colonial period, a multipaper reality existed in the Commonwealth Caribbean. The participants in this environment "understood" that the mass media were not expected to undermine national security and to encourage a breakdown of law and order.[1] The mass media were subject to the laws that protected public morals. Censorship was practiced. Films and books considered seditious or that were thought to undermine public morals were banned (Jagan, 1972, p. 120). The government and the ruling class could and did use their economic resources to influence their performance. In the absence of specific legislation, newspaper publishers recognized the constraints imposed by the existing laws of libel and slander. These colonial practices were consolidated during the postcolonial period.

The Postcolonial Period: 1962–1985

Formal political independence promised the beginning of a new era in the Caribbean. Power was to reside in the state and national resources were to be used for the development of the newly independent nations. The political thrust was clear: the development of societies that would rectify the social deformations resulting from the colonial experience. Among these were high levels of unemployment and illiteracy, poor housing, inadequate public health facilities, and inadequate social services.[2] In December 1952, Elsa Hagland, an economist with the Food and Agricultural Organization of the United Nations, then on a consultancy in British Guiana, is reported to have stated, "she had rarely seen such terrible signs of malnutrition . . . and was 'shocked to her bones' " (Jagan, 1972, p. 80).

The postindependence period also coincided with the ascendancy of the "powerful media paradigm." This perspective held that the mass media could directly influence the course of a society's development. The published works of U.S. scholars, such as Daniel Lerner (1958) and Wilbur Schramm (1964) were very influential. As early as 1967, Commonwealth Caribbean governments had articulated policies that demonstrated commitment to the proposition that a nation's mass communication resources should be used to promote and support social, economic, and political development—the "development communication paradigm" (Roppa and Clarke, 1969). Despite local variations, this orientation influenced communication and information policy in the Commonwealth Caribbean during most of the postindependence period. Caribbean leaders sought to create "a new person," one who could throw off the shackles of colonialism and be a leader in the world. These ambitions were evident in the region's pro-development stand in the Commonwealth, the Non-Aligned Movement, and especially in the United Nations debates on the New World Economic Order and the New World Information and Communication Order of the late 1970s and early 1980s. The Caribbean Community articulated a commitment to self-reliance and South-South cooperation. These ambitions required the active participation of the mass media in these tasks. Newspapers were expected to support and promote national development ambitions. This expectation was articulated under the rubric of "developmental journalism." Denis McQuail (1994, p. 131) has described that orientation as emphasizing the following:

[T]he primacy of the national development task (economic, social, cultural and political); the pursuit of cultural and informational autonomy; support for democracy; and solidarity with other developing countries. Because of the priority given to these ends, limited resources available for media can legitimately be allocated by government, and journalistic freedom can also be restricted. The responsibilities of the media are emphasized above their rights and freedoms.

This was not always achieved. An independent press, critical of the abuses of power and privilege, had developed during the colonial period and continued during the postcolonial period. In the early days of the postcolonial period, this independence was seen by the new leadership as neocolonial and counterproductive.

Several strategies were used to control this spirit of independence. These included the purchase of popular national newspapers by the governments, the appointment of party supporters to leading editorial positions, and the use of economic power. These practices were not new; they were a replay of the tactics used during the colonial era. Legal methods were also used. The dominant strategy was the use of "surety" deposits. The independent press was required to deposit varying sums of money before they could begin or continue publication. Examples of this practice include: St. Kitts' Press and Publications Board Bill of 1971, Guyana's Publications and Newspapers Act of 1972, and Grenada's Newspaper (Amendment) Act of 1975. The surety bonds were supposed to be a contribution to a fund to ensure the payment of libel and slander awards that might be adjudicated against the newspaper. The surety bond practice was so widespread that the Caribbean Press and Broadcasting Association, an association of private media operators, recommended to its membership the purchase of $200,000 libel insurance.

Other legal methods of press control during the postcolonial era included licenses for the importation of newsprint and equipment, the withdrawal or refusal of work permits for nonnational reporters, the denial of government advertising to those newspapers perceived as antigovernment. The loss of government advertising was substantial, given the size of the state-controlled economies in the postcolonial era. Across the Caribbean, governments had become active in their national economies, operating airlines, agricultural industries, banks, mines, shipping systems, tourist facilities, insurance companies, oil refineries, and supermarkets. In cases where advertising was given, settlements of accounts were extremely tardy.[3] In addition to legal methods, intimidation, force, and murder were used to control the independent press.[4] Despite these mechanisms of control, the independent press was not muzzled. Support came in the form of gifts and international pressure.

The Press in the Period of Recommercialization

Beginning in the early 1980s, with declining economies, the conditions of international aid agreements and new consumer demands necessitated a lessening of government control of the mass media. The general tendency has been to allow a multiplicity of media outlets. This has resulted in the proliferation of new newspapers across the region. Some of the newspapers are community oriented. Others adopt the sensational tactics of U.S. supermarket tabloid journalism to attract large national, regional, and international audiences. There is, therefore, increased competition for advertising revenues.

The popularity of the Caribbean tabloid press has brought to the fore issues of public morality. Regulation is difficult in the current multichannel environment. In the current period of recommercialization, market forces are the major determinants of press performance. Most Caribbean governments were not prepared for the proliferation of print and other media outlets that started to emerge in the early 1980s. The existing laws have proven inadequate. This is especially evident in the electronic media.

BROADCASTING AND GOVERNMENT RELATIONS

The Colonial Era

By 1894, the Postmaster General in British Guiana had been given exclusive authority to regulate the electromagnetic spectrum through the Post and Telegraph Ordinance. This ordinance provided the guidelines for operating telegraphy in the late nineteenth century. It also was the regulatory framework during the early diffusion of wired distribution and wireless (radio) in the late 1920s through the introduction of commercial broadcasting after the end of World War II. The British Guiana law was an adaptation of the United Kingdom's Telegraph Act of 1869. Similar laws were introduced in other former British West Indian colonies. These laws not only concentrated regulatory power in the office of the governor, they also facilitated the development of state-owned radio broadcasting. Although private individuals introduced radio in the Caribbean, it was the British government's support of the Rediffusion Broadcasting Company and the establishment of the Windward Island Broadcasting Company that created mass radio in the region.

The case of Trinidad and Tobago provides an adequate framework to examine the relations between the broadcasting media and Caribbean governments over the past five decades. Trinidad and Tobago also provides an indication of the future of those relations.[5] Formal over-the-air broadcasting began in 1947 by the Rediffusion Group. In 1941 the Rediffusion Group "acquired the assets" of the Trinidad Radio Distribution Company (TRDC) that had been operating a "wired distribution service" since 1935 (Beckles, 1991).

TRDC "re-transmitted programs received mainly from the BBC, to loudspeakers in homes and business places in and around Port of Spain via land lines."[6] By the beginning of the 1950s, the Rediffusion Group had established over-the-air stations in British Guiana, Barbados, and Jamaica, and in the process had created the first commercial broadcasting network in the Caribbean. Programming was influenced by the licenses issued by the local governors. These licenses required the broadcaster to relay or re-transmit a series of BBC programs. The U.S. Armed Forces Radio, which had significant "visibility" in the British West Indies during World War II, was another influence on programming. Armed Forces Radio introduced a variety of new program genres that began a dependency on U.S. programming sources (Cambridge, 1989).

By the end of the colonial period two tendencies were evident. The first was the expansion of commercial radio broadcasting and the introduction of television. In the case of Trinidad and Tobago, external companies, such as the Rediffusion Group and the Thompson Group of Great Britain, were involved in the extension of the radio services. The aim was to provide a broadcasting orientation that was more in tune with the culture and ambitions of the emerging independent state. Trinidad and Tobago television was introduced by a consortium that included Rediffusion, Thompson Television, and the Columbia Broadcasting System (Beckles, 1991, p. 2). The second tendency was the creation of state-owned radio and television services. Both types of companies were dependent on local advertising.

The Postcolonial Era

The tendency toward state ownership and operation was accelerated during the early postcolonial era. In Jamaica, the Rediffusion property RJR was cooperatived by the mid-1970s. Under this initiative, the Trade Union Movement, RJR workers, and the government of Jamaica became the principal shareholders. The government retained 25.1 percent of the shares. In Guyana, the Rediffusion property Radio Demerara was sold to the government in the late 1970s. By 1976 in Trinidad and Tobago, the government had control of radio and television services. The legal instruments that regulated broadcasting were essentially the same as during the previous colonial era.

However, what determined broadcasting and government relations was not laws and regulations, but national policy and the institutions established to achieve it.[7] Trinidad and Tobago's Third Five Year Plan (1969–1973) provides a clear example of the orientation of national policies that informed Caribbean broadcasting relations during the early postcolonial era. Beckles indicated that the major features of the Trinidad and Tobago plan were:

—the curtailment of foreign involvement in the media;

—direct governmental involvement in radio and television;

—expansion and intensification of government information services;

—government-controlled media enterprises to operate on a commercial basis;

—control of advertising content of all mass media;

—no political criteria for appointment to staff or publicly owned or controlled broadcasting stations (Beckles, 1991, p. 3).

Caribbean governments used licenses and political appointments to ensure compliance by the national broadcasting services. For example, between 1958 and February 1989, the Jamaica Broadcasting Corporation had changed general managers 14 times (Cambridge, 1989, pp. 340–341).

The rapid diffusion of VCRs and satellite dishes in the Caribbean during the mid-1980s undermined the dominant position that Caribbean governments had held in broadcasting. The new technologies facilitated the development of alternative, albeit pirate, television services. By the early 1980s, television had achieved significant penetration and was becoming the preferred evening medium for substantial sectors of the Caribbean audience. The alternative television services have raised issues of international piracy, the undermining of public morals, and cultural imperialism. The existing legislation was inherited from the colonial era and has proven to be inadequate (White, 1982). Aggrey Brown (1987), who has tracked programming trends, reported in 1986 that Caribbean television continued to "show an increase in the percentage of imported content over local content, moving from an average of 77 percent imported content in 1976 to an average of 87 percent in 1986."

These new trends, which were in response to the demand for something other than the pedantic and didactic offerings from national systems oriented to "development communication," also revealed the ineffectiveness of existing regulatory systems. This situation has permitted the continuation of control by patronage. It has been argued that beneficiaries of the loosening of regulations have tended to be supporters of the government in power at the time of the deregulation.

In summary, broadcasting and government relations in the postindependence era in the Caribbean have been conditioned by the ascendancy of television, the rapid diffusion of new communication technologies (VCRs and satellite dishes) that have permitted the development of alternative outlets, and the realization of the inadequacies of the existing regulatory structure. Some responses have taken place, such as the revision of copyright laws, the preparation of white papers on the future of the mass communication sector, and declarations of the intention to introduce Freedom of Information laws. It is clear that Caribbean governments have no intention to remove themselves completely from the broadcasting arena. This has been justified on the grounds that broadcasting should be a universal service and that there is no guarantee that the free market will ensure this. Government services are also being positioned as necessary to combat cultural domination (Demas, 1986, and Nettleford, 1993).

The Period of Recommercialization

It is probably too early to make conclusive observations on the nature of the relations between broadcast services and governments in the new era of recommercialized broadcasting. It is clear, however, that broadcasting will be influenced by a variety of other factors, including: (a) the expectations of an audience that shares many North American values and expectations, (b) the globalization of broadcasting, which will continue to undermine the efforts of domestic and regional broadcasters, and (c) the development of regional communication groupings that may develop the capacity to dominate mass communication in the Caribbean.

NOTES

1. Violence and resistance have been constant elements in Caribbean history. The practices of settlement and conquest are the earliest examples. The practices of piracy and pillage is another strand in this tradition. Other strands include slaver rebellions and other acts of resistance. By the 1930s, strikes and disturbances erupted across the British West Indies. Cheddi Jagan (1972) provides some details of this in *The West on Trial,* p. 61: "Social discontent had erupted in widespread strikes and disturbances in Trinidad in 1934; in St. Kitts in 1935; in British Guiana in 1935 and 1936; in Barbados, Trinidad and Jamaica in 1938 and 1939." These disturbances not only challenged the status quo but laid the foundation for the start of Caribbean political parties and the call for political independence. For more details see Williams (1964).

2. As early as 1939, the Moyne Commission, established by the British government, had described similar conditions across the British West Indian colonies.

3. By 1976, the Government of Guyana controlled over 80 percent of the Guyanese economy. Although not to the same level, the government of Trinidad and Tobago owned and operated the valuable oil refining industry. This ownership and control was part of the nationalizing practices adopted by Caribbean governments at the beginning of the postcolonial period.

4. John Lent (1990) has suggested, in his *Mass Communication in the Caribbean,*

p. 87, that the 1979 murder of a "Jesuit priest who supplied photographs to the *Standard* was an effort by the PNC government to control that newspaper.

5. The Express Company, a regional conglomerate, with important print, radio, and television holdings, is headquartered in Trinidad and Tobago. That company has links with the mass media in Guyana, Grenada, Barbados, and Jamaica. Mr. Ken Gordon, the CEO, served as a government minister during the NAR administration. That company has entered into strategic partnerships with international media companies such as the Cisneros Group in Venezuela. That unity is scheduled to introduce Direct Broadcast Satellite television to the region by 1996.

6. For details on radio distribution by that type of technology see Erwin Thomas's *Beginnings of broadcasting in the West Indies 1920–1949* (1978), also Gerald Smeyak's *The History and Development of Broadcasting in Guyana, South America* (1973).

7. Among the regional institutions developed was the Caribbean Broadcasting Union (CBU).

REFERENCES

Beckles, E. A. (1991). Broadcasting in Trinidad and Tobago. Paper presented to CAR-ICOM Technical Workshop on Communication Policies for the 1990s held in Kingston, Jamaica.

Brown, A. (1987). TV programming trends in the Anglophone Caribbean: The 1980s. A study for UNESCO's regional Office, Kingston, Jamaica.

Cambridge, V. C. (1989). *Mass media entertainment and human resources development: Radio serials in Jamaica from 1962.* Unpublished Ph.D. dissertation, Ohio University.

Daley, Hugh. (1993). The legal foundations of mass media regulations in Guyana: A Commonwealth Caribbean case study. ERIC Document: ED 208427.

Demas, W. (1986). Caribbean media imperatives: Future direction and policy. An address to the Seminar on Caribbean Media Imperatives, organized by the Press Association of Jamaica, Kingston, Jamaica, November 27–29.

Jagan, C. (1972). *The West on trial: The fight for Guyana's freedom.* German Democratic Republic: Seven Seas Press.

Lent, J. (1990). *Mass communication in the Caribbean.* Ames, Iowa: Iowa State University Press.

Lerner, D. (1958). *The passing of traditional society: Modernizing the Middle East.* Glencoe, IL: Free Press.

McQuail, D. (1994). *Mass communication theory: An introduction.* 3rd ed. London: Sage Publications.

Nettleford, R. (1993). *Inward stretch, outward reach: A voice from the Caribbean.* London: MacMillan Caribbean.

Roppa, G., & Clarke, N. (1969). The Commonwealth Caribbean: Regional co-operation in news and broadcasting exchange, report of a survey mission, November–December 1968. A report submitted to UNESCO.

Schramm, W. (1964). *Mass media and national development.* Stanford, CA: University Press.

Smeyak, G. P. (1973). *The history and development of broadcasting in Guyana, South America.* Master's thesis, The Ohio State University.

Thomas, E. K. (1978). *Beginnings of broadcasting in the West Indies 1920–1949*. Unpublished Ph.D. dissertation, University of Missouri-Columbia.

White, C. T. (1982). The Government of Belize and Transborder Video Satellite Service: Developing an appropriate regulatory structure. A report submitted to UNESCO.

Williams, E. E. (1964). *Capitalism and slavery*. London: Andre Deutsch.

11 Education, Training, and Caribbean Mass Communication

INTRODUCTION

Media education and training have always been a concern in the Caribbean.[1] During the colonial period the problem was obviated through the recruitment of expatriate practitioners and from a limited pool of fair-skinned nationals. Toward the end of the colonial period, there were efforts to increase the numbers of local practitioners through a variety of overseas training programs. Print journalists were sent to England to attend training programs organized by the Thompson Company. The BBC was the primary education and training location for Caribbean broadcasters.

With independence, the demand for locally educated and trained media personnel increased. The prevailing sentiment suggested that locally educated and trained media practitioners would become more conscious of the challenges facing the region and, as a result, be more effective. The costs associated with sending personnel overseas were also a constraint. Among the responses to this challenge was the establishment of a series of regional institutions and the development of a series of bilateral arrangements with international agencies to provide media education and training. Formal education programs were introduced at the Caribbean Institute of Mass Communication (CARIMAC) established at the University of the West Indies in 1974, the School of Communication Studies at the University of Guyana established in 1975, and the Creative Production and Training Center (CPTC) established in the early 1980s in Jamaica. Other formal education and training programs were offered by the School of Continuing Education of the University of the West Indies in collaboration with community colleges and professional associations in Barbados, St. Lucia, and Trinidad and Tobago starting in 1975.

Regional organizations such as the Caribbean Broadcasting Union (CBU), the Caribbean Conference of Churches (CCC), and the Caribbean Publishing and Broadcasting Association (CPBA) also became involved in the provision of media education and training services. These regional institutions also established relations with international agencies in the effort. Among the major international participants in this effort have been UNESCO, UNDP, the German Foundation Frederich Ebert Stiftung, USAID, the U.S. Fulbright Program, the BBC, Deutsche Welle, and the Canadian Broadcasting Corporation. During the period when the socialist model was visible in the Anglophone Caribbean, Grenadian, Guyanese, and Jamaican practitioners went for training in the Soviet bloc.

As a result of these practices, education and training for Caribbean mass communication has taken place at several levels. This chapter will isolate and discuss a selection of those practices.

THE EDUCATION AND TRAINING CHALLENGE

A central idea in Caribbean mass media education and training has been establishing the ideological context. During the colonial period, the goal was clearly to establish British hegemony. As a result, the key tasks during the first decades of the postcolonial period were (a) the decolonization of the mass media and (b) contextualizing the mass media in the realities of developing multiracial Creole societies.

The Caribbean Institute of Mass Communication at the University of the West Indies was developed to provide educational orientation required by Caribbean media practitioners. Through the one-year diploma program, practitioners were exposed to Caribbean history, politics, economics, and culture. There was also a skills component to the diploma program. Sixty percent of the program was related to theory as it relates to development in the Caribbean, and forty percent was skills training. In 1976 there were six courses that "constitut[ed] the one-year, full-time diploma: (1) History, Politics, and Culture of the Caribbean; (2) Principles of Sociology and Economics (with special reference to the Caribbean); (3) Communication Principles; (4) Professional Communication Skills; (5) Broadcast Writing and Production; (6) Writing and Editing for Print Media (Pringle, 1976, p. 24). In 1994, twenty years after the introduction of the diploma program, education represented 75 percent of the program and skills was 25 percent.

Beyond the ideological/educational task, there has been a range of training needs. These needs have been exacerbated by the ongoing "migration" of Caribbean media talent. The low salaries paid to Caribbean media practitioners appears to have encouraged the flight to domestic advertising and public relations agencies or overseas. Entry-level salaries for broadcasters or subeditors range from approximately U.S. $100 per month in Guyana to U.S. $1,000 in Barbados. The high turnover rates and the recent proliferation of new media outlets have led to the presence of many systems staffed with a high degree of inexperienced people. The pattern is more evident in broadcasting than in the print media.

By the mid-1980s, there were clusters of education and training needs shared by the majority of the media systems operating in the English-speaking Caribbean. Table 11.1 provides details.

Recent studies by Hilary Browne and Aggrey Brown have confirmed the continuing presence of these clusters of education and training needs (Browne, 1989, and Brown, 1991). The next section will examine the contributions made by the Caribbean Institute of Mass Communication, University of Guyana, Caribbean Broadcasting Union, Creative Production and Training Center, Frederich Ebert Stiftung, and the School of Continuing Education, University of the West Indies to Caribbean mass media education and training.

RESPONSES

The Caribbean Institute of Mass Communication (CARIMAC)

The Caribbean Institute of Mass Communication was established at the University of the West Indies in September 1974 as a unit of the Faculty of Arts and General Studies. The Institute was a joint project of the "university and the Frederich Ebert Stiftung." The Institute was one of the outcomes of a series of research projects conducted by UNESCO in the late 1960s and early 1970 for the fledgling regional integration movement in the Caribbean (Roppa and Clarke, 1969). As mentioned in earlier chapters, Caribbean leaders at the beginning of the postcolonial era invested much effort in developing regional communication capacity. Along with the Caribbean Broadcasting Union, CARIMAC and the Caribbean News Agency (CANA) were established as key regional communication institutions. Specifically, CARIMAC, which was seen as being responsible for providing regional communicators with "a regional outlook and a solid professional foundation" had the prerequisites for ensuring that Caribbean mass media performed their "enormous development role" (Pringle, 1976, pp. 24–25). Currently, CARIMAC offers "majors" in radio, television, print journalism, and audiovisual (development support) communication.

In the 20 years of its operations, CARIMAC has offered training from the Caribbean, Australia, and Africa. The Institute offers a one-year diploma program, a three-year bachelor's degree, a summer program, and a certificate program through the School of Continuing Education, University of the West Indies in Trinidad and Tobago, St. Lucia, Belize, and Barbados. CARIMAC introduced a M.A. degree program in September 1994. The University of Guyana began offering a diploma in Public Communication in 1975 and now also offers a four-year Bachelor's degree. The University of Guyana program has the same goals as CARIMAC.

Graduates from CARIMAC hold important positions in Caribbean mass media. Graduates have also contributed to the Caribbean mass communication re-

Table 11.1

Education and Training Needs in the English-Speaking Caribbean, circa 1983

Education and Training Clusters	Dominant Training Needs
Management	Planning, Organizing, Financial management, Human resource management, Management information systems, Archiving, Human relations, Labor relations, Client (government, advertisers, and special interest group) relations, International negotiations, Conflict management.
Engineering and Technology	Preventative maintenance, inventory control, Technological compatibility, Research and Development.
Product Quality	The use of English, Writing, Editing, On-air Performance, Care and Maintenance of technology, Media ethics, Optimizing the performance of scarce resources.
Broadcasting	The need to develop a Caribbean style and aesthetic, Production planning, Program exchanges, Coproduction, Marketing and Distribution, Development Support Communication, Grant-writing and Fund-raising

Based on the author's active involvement as a Program Manager who worked closely with the Caribbean Broadcasting Union, the Caribbean Community Secretariat, UNESCO, and the Broadcast Organization of the Non-Aligned Countries (BONAC) during the period from 1981 to 1985.

search literature. The Caribbean long paper requirement has produced important original research. CARIMAC has international recognition as an important mass communication education and training center. There are hopes that the Institute will be elevated to the level of a school in the near future.

The Caribbean Broadcasting Union (CBU)

The Caribbean Broadcasting Union (CBU) was established in 1970 and almost immediately became involved in training activities. CARIMAC emphasized the regional residential training model and CBU has developed the short, on-site model. Over the past 25 years the CBU has taken on the challenge of mobilizing regional and international resources and using those resources to deliver training. Training has been offered in all of the clusters identified in Table 11.1.

The CBU has worked with several international agencies in its training role. These include Germany's Deutsche Welle and the Frederich Ebert Stiftung, UNESCO, and the Voice of America. The relations with the Frederich Ebert

Stiftung (FES) have been substantial. The FES relationship is characterized by a high degree of hands-on work with outcomes aimed at improving production quality. In addition to the applied orientation, the FES/CBU partnership has promoted on-the-job training strategies. The 1989 "training offensive" demonstrated the details of the model in which "two German experts conducted on-the-job training courses in four Caribbean centers. One course was held in Trinidad for production crews from Guyana and Antigua." Other sites includes Curacao, Jamaica, and St. Lucia.[2]

CBU relations with UNESCO have provided a wide range of training for broadcast engineers and media managers. The CBU Annual report for 1990–1991 revealed that these diverse courses were offered to systems that had special needs such as those in the Organization of Eastern Caribbean States (OECS), a subset of the Caribbean Community.

The Creative Production and Training Center (CPTC)

The CPTC was an educational media center developed jointly by the government of Jamaica and UNESCO in the early 1980s. The aim of that facility was to develop educational materials for the Jamaican Broadcasting Corporation. By the end of the 1980s, the agency had expanded its focus to include "hands-on training for media practitioners not only in Jamaica but across the Caribbean." Browne's 1989 market survey of the training needs of the Caribbean media for CPTC underlines their commitment to that objective.

CPTC's orientation is different from CARIMAC or the CBU. Their twin aims are to produce entry-level technicians and use CARIMAC graduates as teachers and producers of media materials for the Jamaican public and private sector (Fowler, 1985).

The Caribbean Publishing and Broadcasting Association (CPBA)

Until 1992, the CPBA represented the privately owned media in the English-speaking Caribbean. The organization became defunct in 1992. During the period of ideological tensions in the Caribbean the CPBA appeared to have been a voice that kept the idea of a free press and transparent electoral politics in the forefront of the region's discourse on democracy. The CPBA was the recipient of funds from international foundations that have been associated with the pro-democracy struggle, such as the National Endowment for Democracy, the World Press Freedom Association, and the Konrad Adenauer Stiftung. As is to be expected, the emphasis of CPBA's training projects in the Caribbean have emphasized print journalism, especially in those areas that supported the development of free market economies and the development of transparent electoral politics. A survey of annual reports for the 1988–1990 period indicated that the organization has organized workshops in financial and economic reporting and "how to cover a general election."

Table 11.2
Projected Mass Communication Education and Training Needs in the Commonwealth Caribbean

Education and Training Clusters	Dominant Education and Training Needs
Management	All of those stated in Table 11.1 plus: International fund-raising, cross-cultural management, and retraining programs.
Product quality	Improved production values, international syndication
Broadcast programming	The development of broadcast niches
Engineering and technology	Utilization of the information superhighway capacity

PROJECTED EDUCATION AND TRAINING CHALLENGES

The next chapter will explore the emerging Caribbean mass communication environment, and will identify some of the implications for policy, regulations, and employment. This section will identify some of the potential training challenges. Table 11.2 will provide the details.

CONCLUSION

The region will have to develop strategic partnerships to execute the current and projected mass media education and training needs. Many of the traditional institutions will lose funding sources. The CPBA has already lost its funding from the National Endowment for Democracy and is currently defunct. It is anticipated that the Frederich Ebert Stiftung will end its financial contributions to the Caribbean Broadcasting Union by 1996. Similar situations are anticipated by the Caribbean Institute of Mass Communication, University of the West Indies and the School of Communication Studies at the University of Guyana.

The demands of the future will require better coordination among the agencies involved in providing education and training for Caribbean mass communication.

NOTES

1. The author recognizes the contributions of Ms. Lisa McClean in the preparation of this chapter. Ms. McClean is a Ph.D. student in the School of Telecommunications, Ohio University, and has conducted research on broadcast education and training in the Anglophone Caribbean in the postindependence era.

2. Based on an interview with Michael Abend, Frederich Ebert Stiftung Consultant to the Caribbean Broadcasting Union, Barbados, November 1990.

REFERENCES

Brown, A. (1991). Regional communication training: The role of UWI/CARIMAC. A paper submitted to the Third Meeting of CARICOM Ministers of Information, Kingston, Jamaica.

Browne, H. (1989). Training needs in Caribbean electronic media: A market survey. A report for the Creative Production and Training Center, Kingston, Jamaica.

Fowler, K. (1985). UNESCO and the CPTC: An attempt at supporting indigenous mass media. Unpublished paper in partial fulfillment of the requirements for the B.A. degree of the Faculty of Arts and General Studies, University of the West Indies, Mona, Jamaica.

Pringle, P. (1976). The Caribbean Institute of Mass Communication. *Combroad, 32* (July–September).

Roppa, G., & Clarke, N. (1969). The Commonwealth Caribbean: Regional co-operation in news and broadcasting exchange, report of a survey mission, November–December 1968. A report for UNESCO.

12 New Technologies, Their Implications, and Special Issues

The future of mass communication in the Caribbean will be determined by a variety of factors. These include: (a) the nature of Caribbean politics, especially the will to operationalize the rhetoric of regional and hemispheric cooperation (Singh, 1994, pp. 16–17; Blades and Evans, 1994, pp. 18–24; Cox, 1994, pp. 16 & 29); (b) the diffusion and application of new communication technologies, (c) the growth of a strong private-sector-dominated communication and information industry; (d) Caribbean popular culture and the role of racial, ethnic, and religious diversity on that development; and (e) the presence of adequately educated and trained human resources and improved coordination among regional communication institutions. Together these interrelated factors will determine the operating environment.

THE NATURE OF CARIBBEAN POLITICS

In 1989 the CARICOM heads of government established the West Indian Commission to develop a plan to "prepare West Indians for the 21st century." The commission was required to "let all ideas contend—political, economic, social, and cultural . . . to let unity of all kinds be appraised, no less than the prospect of disunity . . . let the outpouring of the creative talents of [the] peoples in the region stimulate a process by which [the] region becomes a public forum on the future" (The West Indian Commission, 1993). The report of the West Indian Commission in 1992 stressed that the "community [was] about Communication" (1993, p. 323). As a result, the commission made several recommendations about the importance of developing the communication conditions necessary for the region to participate in the global environment. Specifically, the report recommended to the regional political leadership the need to "commit themselves to developing communication in the region as a necessary element of integration, and to enlarging the process as CARICOM increasingly reaches out into the wider Caribbean.'' This requirement anticipated the establishment of policies, the strengthening of institutions, and strategies to achieve these goals. Among those initiatives will be ''paying special attention to issues of monopoly ownership, whether by Governments or by private individuals, and to the need to minimize opportunities for political interference in the media.'' Other elements include initiatives ''establishing a mechanism to support the production of Caribbean programming . . . more effective information legislation . . . and the matter of training'' (The West Indian Commission, 1993, pp. 325–326).

The establishment of the West Indian Commission was the second in a series of periodic reviews conducted by the Caribbean Community. The first report, published in 1981 and referred to in the first chapter of this section, was clear in its proposition that Caribbean integration was about more than economics; integration was anchored on more than 300 years of cultural similarity. The report therefore required the Caribbean Community to accelerate the process of integration and develop mechanisms to support common external tariffs and a common foreign policy. Those ambitions were constrained by a variety of ideological and structural forces, and by the time the second review had been conducted, new issues had emerged. These included the North American Free Trade Association (NAFTA), the emergence of the Association of Caribbean States (ACS), and the ambition of collapsing both of these economic units into a Free Trade Association of the Americas (FTAA) by 2005.[1]

There is general recognition that the new economic structure will have political and cultural ramifications on the nature and the operations of mass communication in the Caribbean. The emerging economic structures are informed by the conditions of the GATT agreement. Central to this global agreement is ''trade in information and communication services.'' This should facilitate the global flow of information and communication products. There are concerns that GATT will provide additional support for the global media conglomerates that are already poised to dominate the global information and communication industry.

These developments provide the embryonic private sector mass communication industry in the Caribbean with challenges and opportunities. Decisions by Caribbean governments can restrict the emerging industry. Failure to develop responsive legal regimes can put the regional industry at a competitive disadvantage. One regional leader has indicated that the continuing liberalization of the media environment puts Caribbean media operations at a competitive disadvantage as new, external forces are now able to enter the media marketplace and, because of their existing economies of scale, ''outcompete'' national and regional mechanisms.[2] Decisions by Caribbean governments can also facilitate the growth of a vibrant information and communication industry; specifically, those decisions that permit the creation of strategic alliances between Caribbean and international media entities. The recent partnership developed between Trinidad and Tobago's Express Company and Venezuela's Cisneros Company to develop a regional Direct Broadcast Satellite (DBS) service by 1996 is an example of this type of strategic alliance.[3] It is also anticipated that Caribbean governments will curb the external communication (uplink) monopoly enjoyed by the Cable and Wireless Company and other international telecommunications companies.[4] Some Caribbean governments are already permitting or "turning a blind eye" to domestic entities operating satellite uplink facilities that compete with the Cable and Wireless system.[5] This will facilitate the creation of the infrastructure required by Caribbean media industries to participate in the new global communication environment and actualize their competitive advantage in global Africa.

As mentioned elsewhere, the term "global Africa" refers to continental Africa and its diaspora. This cultural and geographic community is becoming an attractive investment site for many of the world's major communication companies. For example, in 1994 AT&T announced the development of "Africa One," a fiber optic network that will encircle the African continent. Major media houses from France, the United Kingdom, the United States, and the Republic of South Africa are currently carving up continental Africa electronically, in a manner reminiscent of the post–Treaty of Berlin era. Global African media entrepreneurs, such as Black Entertainment Television and the World African Network from the United States, are entering this lucrative market. There are, however, expectations that a global African mass communication project can serve to enrich global communication. Some Caribbean media practitioners have already developed expertise in this area. A good example of this trend is the production "Crossing Over." This UNESCO-supported program was produced by Trinidad and Tobago's Banyan Productions and Ghana's National Television and Film Institute. The two-part program explored the West African origins and Caribbean expansion of Calypso music.

THE NATURE OF THE NEW COMMUNICATION TECHNOLOGIES

The communication technologies, especially direct satellite broadcasting, will make a mockery of national broadcasting systems. The arrival of the Wisconsin-based, satellite-delivered GEM Radio in Montserrat and its diffusion in the Eastern Caribbean is making that a reality in radio broadcasting. The earlier-mentioned partnership between Trinidad and Tobago's Express Company and Venezuela's Cisneros Group, along with the new generation of Direct Broadcast Satellites (DBS) will undermine national television in the Caribbean. The broadband capacity now being developed by national and regional telecommunications entities, capable of delivering CD-quality radio and "video dial tone," will further undermine national electronic media systems. The convergence of the media technologies will facilitate the growth of multimedia companies with regional range and scope. Jamaica's Gleaner Company, Barbados's Nation Company, and Trinidad and Tobago's Express Company are examples of the type of company with regional and global ambitions.

THE PRIVATE SECTOR AND A CARIBBEAN COMMUNICATION AND INFORMATION INDUSTRY

Since the early 1980s, there has been dramatic growth in privately owned and operated mass media in the Caribbean. As indicated elsewhere, these companies are acquiring the new communication technologies and are developing regional and international strategic alliances which would make them become important participants in the global mass communication industry. Off-shore, some Caribbean nationals are creating media systems with the new technologies to broadcast to the region.[6]

Regional telecommunications companies are modifying tariffs to facilitate the establishment and growth of the information economies that are emerging in the region.[7] These developments create niche markets that would enable them to be economically viable in the new global communication environment.

In the future, Caribbean political and media leadership will have to address the following questions: Will the Caribbean remain primarily consumers in the global media environment? Or, will the private sector media use the new communication technologies to exploit the climate, geography, flora, fauna, history, and popular culture of the region to carve an important niche in the global communication environment?

THE PERFORMANCE OF CARIBBEAN POPULAR CULTURE

The Caribbean has such centrality in the global imagination that it is virtually ensured of a place in the new global communication environment. To actualize that potential there is the need to create the conditions to allow the full flowering of Caribbean popular culture. At the moment, Caribbean popular music is the laboratory for that potential. Deeper analysis reveals that despite increasing global popularity, there are several constraints to Caribbean popular music in the global market. In October 1994, *CANA Busine$$* asked the question: "How much of a business is Caribbean music?" (Campbell, 1994). In that article the authors reported:

[W]hile some Caribbean singers and musicians are making money, there is substantially more potential than is being realized. Lack of business, professional and legal know-how, the (small) size of the regional market, piracy and fragmentation—lack of unity— are among the obstacles to wider business success.

There is, however, much more to Caribbean popular culture than music. The experiences from the popular culture sector are instructive for other sectors of Caribbean popular culture.

The multicultural heritage of the Caribbean has provided it with a mythology and history that enriches its oral, scribal, and visual expressions that also enjoy international respect.[8] That heritage can be mined to produce media materials for the global media marketplace. Caribbean popular culture, along with attractive locations, exciting fauna and flora, provides the Caribbean with resources to make a valuable contribution to global media programming. This calls for the education and training of practitioners who will be able to navigate the global market, seeking competitive advantages and avoiding the errors of cultural insensitivity associated with international television over the past 20 years. These are the central challenges in the education and training of the next generation of Caribbean media professionals.

ADEQUATELY EDUCATED AND TRAINED HUMAN RESOURCES

Up to now, the mass media practitioner in the Commonwealth Caribbean has performed in an environment that was made up of predominantly state-owned and operated systems. Although these systems operated commercially, they still had the "back stop" of government subventions—license fees and governments grants—to compensate for budgetary shortfalls. This system influenced the output of Caribbean media practitioners, especially broadcasters. It created dependencies on national political and economic elites, resulting in much "talking head" programming and continuing sterile discussions on cultural penetration and cultural domination. The media practitioners, trained on the job through a variety of courses funded through public diplomacy,[9] or at one of the Caribbean training institutions such as the Caribbean Institute of Mass Communication at the University of the West Indies or the Communication Studies Program at the University of Guyana, have been consistently criticized for political bias, arrogance, and lack of creativity. Those who sought new approaches were either frustrated or moved onto careers in advertising and public relations sectors. Poor salaries have been a significant factor in the mobility of Caribbean media practitioners. There has been very little regional program materials exchange among the old-style state-owned and operated systems. Even within national systems there has been little creative reflection of ethnic and linguistic diversity. In short, Caribbean media practitioners have demonstrated ineffectiveness at many levels, including management, programming, and cultural diversity.

The new communication environment in which Caribbean mass communication practitioners will have to perform will be much less "supportive." There will be limited, if any, public broadcasting money. And for any money that is appropriated, there will be demands for it to be used more efficiently and effectively.

The mass communication practitioner of the future in the Caribbean will have to be, first of all, better educated. In the period since the beginning of the independence period, Caribbean media practitioners have been educated in a narrow perspective. In addition to a more diversified general education, there is need for a more contemporary orientation to training. Caribbean media practitioners should develop skills in management, marketing, and computer applications. These areas are central in the new communication dispensation. Going with those skills are needs in the areas of coproduction and the negotiation of strategic alliances. The global marketplace in which Caribbean public and private sector media institutions will have to operate will require linguistic pluralism. The impact of NAFTA, ACS, and the projected FTAA will require competence in French, Spanish, Portuguese, and the many regional Creole languages.

Specific care will have to be taken in the area of technology acquisition. Failure to make reasoned decisions will result in further dependency and marginalization. Central to a relevant education and training program for Caribbean media practitioners will be ethics. Caribbean media practitioners cannot accept that the emerging global contours are immutable and, thus, impervious to Caribbean requirements. They must be conscious of the consequences of their decisions. This requires the presence of an ongoing research agenda. Very little mass communication research has been initiated by the Caribbean mass media (Cambridge, 1991, pp. 81–91). This will have to change. Caribbean mass media institutions must articulate research questions and contribute to the costs of conducting that research.

These challenges for the future will require coordination of the region's mass media education resources. The premier institution, CARIMAC, must be provided with adequate human, technological, and financial resources. Further, there is need to improve coordination among the tertiary institutions. The regional institutions include: (a) The Communication Studies Program at the University of Guyana, (b) the postgraduate diploma in Agricultural Extension at the St. Augustine Campus of the University of the West Indies, and (c) the community colleges in Antigua, St. Lucia, Barbados, Trinidad and Tobago, that offer certificate programs in "Communication Arts" in collaboration with the Mona, Jamaica-based School of Continuing Education of the University of the West Indies. The University of the West Indies Distance Education facilities that link 15 Caribbean locations will be crucial in optimizing the existing resources.

Coordination of these resources will create the conditions for a more unified regional strategy for dealing with the international organizations that have been involved in Caribbean mass media education since the independence period. There is no doubt that the contributions to this project by United Nations agencies such as UNESCO and UNDP, and other agencies such as USAID, the Commonwealth Press Association, and the Frederick Ebert Foundation will continue. A clear vision is needed. Consumers must also be educated. Regional audiences must be involved not only in paying for the new and emerging services, but must become more active consumers. This will be an important step in addressing the real issues of cultural penetration, domination, and homogenization. Regional coordination in media education and training is therefore critical if the Caribbean region is to contribute to the global communication environment.

SUMMARY

The Caribbean mass media have the possibility of becoming key players in the new global communication environment. To achieve that potential, the region will have to make the rhetoric of regional and hemispheric cooperation a reality. The region will have to promulgate media laws and regulation that will give those ambitions substance. In addition, the region will have to make educated decisions on the new communication technologies. The key factor will be the education and training of the next generation of media practitioners.

The new Caribbean mass media environment will be dominated by the private sector. These new companies will develop strategic linkages with other global participants. They have the possibility of drawing upon a rich heritage and contributing to the enrichment and rectification of global communication.

What does this have to do with Afro-media worldwide? The answer may lie in the global African idea. As stated elsewhere, global Africa is a construct whose time has come. It is an idea that recognizes the importance of moving Africa and its diaspora from a marginal position to a more central position. It is about the marketplace as much as it is about identity and the enrichment of the human spirit. Specifically, media practitioners in global Africa will have to respond to the following challenges:

- Development of strategic relationships that will allow global African mass media to be participants in a large and important media market;
- Creation of attractive and internationally valid materials;
- Encouragement of the ambitions of the Pan-African idea;
- Stimulation of global dialogue; and
- Promotion and consolidation of democratic institutions.

The Caribbean has a leadership role to play in this process.

NOTES

1. Among the decisions taken at the recent Summit of the Americas, Miami, December 1994, was the agreement to establish the Free Trade Association of the Americas (FTAA) by 2005. The entity will be a hemispheric mechanism, including all states in the Americas.

2. Based on an interview with Mr. Oliver Clarke, Managing Director, The Gleaner Company, Kingston, Jamaica, December 1, 1994. The Gleaner Company, established in 1838, is one of the oldest media companies in the Caribbean. In recent years the company has acquired a radio license and has ambitions of acquiring a television license. This will make it one of the few multimedia operations in the Caribbean. The Gleaner Com-

pany already has a presence in the Caribbean diaspora in North America and Europe with its daily and special overseas editions of *The Gleaner* newspaper.

3. Based on an interview with Mr. Ken Gordon, Chief Executive Officer, The Express Company, Trinidad and Tobago, December 12, 1994.

4. The Cable and Wireless Company has enjoyed a monopoly in external telecommunications in the Caribbean for almost a century. Currently, Cable and Wireless controls external telecommunications dominance in Jamaica, Barbados, Trinidad and Tobago, and St. Lucia, among others. The U.S. Virgin Islands–based company, Atlantic Tele-Network Inc., controls external telecommunications in Guyana. For a history of international telecommunications companies in the Caribbean, see Marlene Cuthbert's "Communication Technology and Culture: Towards West Indian Policies," *Gazette* 38 (1986), 161–170.

5. Examples of this include the uplink facilities operated by St. Lucia's Helen Television Service and the recent decisions by the government of Barbados that permitted the Caribbean Broadcasting Union and the Caribbean News Agency to operate satellite uplink facilities. The current discussions associated with the CARICOM coordinated Regional Space Segment Agency is another example of that tendency to facilitate external communication competition in the Caribbean.

6. The Miami-based Caribbean Satellite Network, developed by a Jamaican entrepreneur, is an example of that trend. Although the company folded, there is widespread regional recognition that the idea is still valid.

7. BARTEL, the Cable and Wireless–owned Barbados external telecommunications company, recently reduced external communication tariffs, citing the need to support the development of information and communication sectors of the economy.

8. Examples of this international recognition will include the Nobel Laureate Derek Walcott and the Nobel Nominee V. S. Naipaul.

9. This refers to the various training programs offered by international governments. In the Caribbean, the governments of the United States, North Korea, Libya, Cuba, India, Japan, the United Kingdom, France, and so on, have offered short-term training programs. One media manager in the Caribbean identified these as ideological training projects. These short courses should, however, be separated from the longer, more institutionalized contributions offered by organizations such as UNESCO, the Frederich Ebert Stiftung, and USAID to Caribbean media education and training.

REFERENCES

Blades, H., & Evans, E. (1994). The cost of CARICOM membership of NAFTA. *CANA Busine$$* (June/July).

Cambridge, V. (1991). Mass communication research in the Caribbean: Toward a research agenda. *Caribbean Affairs* (April–June), 81–91.

Campbell, H. (1994). How much of a business is Caribbean music. *CANA Busine$$* (October/November).

Cox, R. (1994). The ACS—opening up a new marketplace. *CANA Busine$$* (July/August).

Cuthbert, M. (1986). Communication technology and culture: Towards West Indian policies. *Gazette, 38,* 161–170.

Singh, R. (1994). CAIC, CDB on CARICOM. *CANA Busine$$* (June/July).

The West Indian Commission. (1993). *A time for action: Report of the West Indian Commission.* 2nd ed. Kingston, Jamaica: The Press, University of the West Indies.

IV AFRO-AMERICA

_____ James Phillip Jeter

13 Pre–Twentieth Century Philosophical Contexts

The relationship between Blacks[1] and the mass media is a variation on a basic theme that can be traced to the establishment of America as a British colony. For as long as there has been an ''America,'' black people have been part of it. The black presence in America began involuntarily and coincided with the ''settling'' of the ''New World'' by European settlers in the early seventeenth century. Today, the question of color/race remains one of America's great Gordian knots.

As the largest of the major racial groups in the United States, Blacks have been subject to a long history of economic, legal, and political discrimination at the hands of whites. Consequently, any discussion of the relationship between Blacks in America and the mass media requires that this examination be undertaken in a power context.

PORTRAYAL

The first level of the relationship between Blacks and the power of American media occurs at the portrayal level. For more than 200 years, whites have controlled the definition of Blacks and their cultural image, first via newspapers, literature, and the theater and later, through motion pictures and broadcasting. During this period, there was a linear flow of information, trickling down about and around Blacks.

The theory of America as a melting pot has never truly applied to Blacks. Under the melting pot cliché, persons who immigrated to America would, in a relatively short period of time, lose their identification with the culture and language of their nation of origin and adopt the customs, language, and loyalties of America. As a group, Blacks did not immigrate to America, they were im-

Table 13.1
1991 U.S. Population

	U.S. Population	Percentage
Total	252,177,000	
Blacks	31,164,000	12.3
Hispanics	23,350,000	9.2
Asian Americans	7,996,000	3.1
Native Americans	2,117,000	0.8
		25.4

Source: Statistical Abstract of the United States (113th ed.). Washington, DC: Department of Commerce, 1993.

ported. In addition, the majority of the societal customs, rhetoric, and practices in America were diametrically opposed to allowing Blacks to assimilate. For nearly 350 years the majority of the media did their part in making it clear Blacks had a special place in America. For them, "melting" has been either difficult or fraught with undesirable consequences. This exclusion has diminished since the Civil Rights Act of 1964 but the status of Blacks in America is still problematical.

Unlike the persons of color who are the subject of other sections in this book, the idea of Blacks as a nation is an abstract one. Although the majority of Blacks in America have a common history, origin, culture (i.e., way of life), and, some would argue, language, other elements are missing from the traditional definition of a "nation." Americans of African descent are not a large group of people united for mutual safety and welfare. These Blacks have no definable territorial mass under their control nor do they have a sovereign government in the United States. Consequently, African-Americans are a subculture in the United States.

However, this fact should not obscure the magnitude of the scope and potential of Blacks were they somehow to become a nation of the world. America's black population of approximately 30 million people earned/controlled/spent an estimated $300 billion in 1993 (see Table 13.1). Blacks are and will remain the largest racial minority group in the United States. Although demographers estimate the Hispanic population in America will exceed the black population in the early twenty-first century, Hispanic is not a racial category.

Completing the nation scenario, however, is useful for illustrative purposes. If Blacks could be transported lock, stock, and barrel to a definable land mass and set up their own government, this nation would in 1993 have been the sixth most populous African nation and the fourth largest black nation. The $300 billion that flowed through those black hands would have made the hypothetical nation of ''Black America'' the world's richest black nation and ranked it among the world's 10 wealthiest nations (Kurian, 1991, pp. 11, 68).

BRIEF HISTORY OF MASS MEDIA IN AMERICA

The mass media date back to the founding of America as well and the mass media are often called the Fourth Estate, or fourth branch of government, because of the freedom and power they have under the First Amendment of the Constitution of the United States.[2] Given the historical powerlessness of Blacks in America, it is not surprising that the relationship between Blacks and the mass media has largely been an adversarial one. This friction is perhaps more understandable when one examines American history and the major functions of mass media in America: information, entertainment, persuasion, and socialization/transmission of culture.

FUNCTIONS

Information

The United States has become an information society. The mass media are sources of what Americans have come to believe is reality. Public opinion surveys such as those conducted for decades by the Roper Organization indicate widespread reliance on the mass media by the American people to determine what important things are happening, which people are important, and which events are important. Via its agenda-setting function and information selection and presentation, the media accentuate or marginalize people, places, and events. In this fashion, the mass media are vital to the societal epistemology of any American.

An underlying societal principle is that an informed citizen can be a better participant in the democratic process, yet Blacks were not legally full citizens for nearly the first 150 years of America's colonial history and were second-class citizens for the first 80 years of an independent America's history. Throughout the country's history, the media have helped maintain the subservient relationship between Blacks and the powerful by ignoring the existence of Blacks or, when their existence was noted, offering for the most part caricatures that would not allow them to be taken and treated seriously.

Entertainment

The mass media in America also perform an entertainment function and the line between news and entertainment is blurring. What has developed is the "reality" television genre which has programs that have the appearance of newscasts but are really entertainment. Some television commercials adopt a newscast environment to promote a good or service.

Persuasion

Those who want to create awareness of, change an attitude, or prompt a behavior toward a good, service, or idea have put the mass media to great use. Advertising in America in 1993 was a $130 billion industry. The mass media are integral parts of this industry designed to convince Americans to buy or utilize the goods and services contained in the messages that bombard them through radio, television, newspapers, magazines, and billboards. Political candidates at the national, state, and local levels realize the mass media are increasingly important in their efforts to win election.

Transmission of Culture/Socialization

While performing the previous three functions, the mass media continuously indicate and reiterate that which is American and un-American. Media content explicitly and implicitly indicates notions of beauty and reality. As mirrors of the time, the media reflect current cultural realities and, when they are archived, become a history of society that can be retrieved for examination by future generations. Indeed, when we look at the significant events in twentieth-century America (for example, wars, economic upheaval, the civil rights and women's rights movements, and the deterioration of the American family), the media have been integral parts of the experiences. National sentiment against segregation in the South in the 1960s was, to a certain extent, molded by the sight of civil rights demonstrators being flattened with fire hoses as police dogs nipped at their heels.

As they relay information and opinion, disseminate messages to vote for or against certain politicians, extol the virtues of a bar of soap, amuse us, or let us know what being American means, the mass media are more often than not agents of the power structure reinforcing the status quo. The media are pervasive and consumers are bombarded with messages that say this or that person, action, idea, is beautiful, good, decent, and right while other things are ugly, bad, obscene, and wrong.

These functions have combined to result in a less-than-optimal state of regard for Blacks. For years, critics have chided the media for making Blacks seem less intelligent, less hardworking, less patriotic, less universal, and more violent than they are in reality. While these indictments of the media might be considered anecdotal, a 1990 survey provided empirical data that coincide remarkably with what critics have charged. The survey found that a majority of persons believed that as compared to whites, Blacks were:

- Less hard-working
- Less patriotic
- Less intellectual
- Less universal
- More violent (Duke, 1991)

To realize how it has come to this, an examination of the black experience in America and the development of media serving both are necessary.

THE DEVELOPMENT OF MASS MEDIA IN AMERICA

Influences

Like its judicial system, the immediate influences on the colonial media came from England. The colonies' first publication, *Publick Occurrences Both Foreign and Domestic* (1690), was imitative of the drab, ultraconservative English newspapers. It immediately ran into problems because it was not licensed—printed under the consent of the government.

The colonists proved a rebellious lot and relative freedom of the press began in the 1720s after the *New England Courant* (1721) was published without a license. The trial of John Peter Zenger in 1735 marked another turning point when the concept of truth as a defense against charges of libel was offered. The Zenger trial marked the beginning of a relatively free press and the eighteenth-century newspapers played a significant role in fomenting the colonial rebellion.

Drawing on the work of John Milton's *Areopagitica* and John Locke, Thomas Jefferson was among the most forceful advocates of a free press. In an often-cited phrase from a 1787 letter to a friend, Jefferson, one of the chief authors of the Declaration of Independence and later the third president of the United States, wrote:

The basis of our government being the opinion of the people, the very first object should be to keep that right; and were it left to me to decide whether we should have a government without newspapers, or newspapers without government, I should not hesitate a moment to prefer the latter. (Emery & Emery, 1978, p. 94)

Although the last line is the most quoted of the letter, many fail to note that the caveat of Jefferson's choice depended upon a literate citizenry with accessibility to the media. These qualifications would not apply to Blacks for nearly 100 years.

While much attention has been given in the twentieth century to the concept of objectivity in journalism, the fact remains that partisanship in the American mass media is a tradition that dates back to the founding of the country. In the eighteenth century, the power brokers in America argued for and obtained the right to "publish" without prior censorship, and vigorously defend this right to date.

In the panoply of media theories, the American mass media system skews toward libertarianism, the idea that freedom of expression is a right of citizens and the fact that others or the government may not like what is said is irrelevant. The existence of defamation laws and the requirement to get government licenses in order to broadcast on radio and television stations acknowledge that the right of expression is not absolute. However, one would be hard-pressed to find many more permissive media environments than that which developed and exists to a large extent in the United States. It is against this tapestry that the relationship of Blacks to America and its mass media are explored.

A BRIEF HISTORY OF BLACKS IN AMERICA

Pre-Revolutionary War Era, 1619–1776

The modern black presence in America dates back to the early seventeenth century. In 1619, in exchange for supplies, the captain of a Dutch frigate left 20 black persons in the Jamestown colony—the beginning of the black experience in America. These 20 newcomers did not cause a stir. They were treated like other unfortunate outcasts who were the majority of early newcomers to America. The Blacks became indentured servants—people who could, after appropriate intervals of service, become "free" once their contracts were fulfilled.

The need for labor in the English colonies and the inability of the settlers to exploit Native Americans in the East as farm labor resulted in the use of Blacks as a source of cheap labor. Laws allowed Blacks to be gradually singled out and become trapped in slavery by the mid-seventeenth century where they remained, as a group, largely chattel property for over 200 years. After the colonies' successful revolution secured their independence from Great Britain in the 1780s, Blacks were second-class citizens in the new country by law until the 1960s.

The American Revolutionary War was about freedom, and the media of the day (newspapers and pamphlets) reflected the incendiary revolutionary invective. The colonists decided to break away from Great Britain when the Second Continental Congress convened and adopted the Declaration of Independence on July 4, 1776. This document contained the familiar yet hollow (for Blacks) language: "We hold these truths to be self-evident: that all men are created equal; that they are endowed with unalienable rights and among these are life, LIBERTY [emphasis mine] and the pursuit of happiness."

Revolutionary to Civil War

When the colonies became America via the Declaration of Independence in 1776 and victory in the Revolutionary War that followed, there was a chance to start the slate clean, relative to the status of Blacks in the new country. The new nation's first laws were the Articles of Confederation. These laws governed the nation for more than seven years until they were abandoned in favor of the Constitution of the United States in 1787.

Although Blacks fought in the Revolutionary War and made their contribution to the liberation of America, the country's dependence on slavery for the wealth of the nation proved too great. Although the Declaration of Independence included statements on equality and liberty, the attitude toward Blacks is evident in the infamous "Three-Fifths Compromise" contained in the Constitution of the United States.

The delegates at the constitutional convention in Philadelphia were in a quandary over how to apportion representation in Congress, America's supreme legislative body. If slaves were people, then the slaveholding states would become the most powerful even though these states denied Blacks citizenship rights. What developed was the Three-Fifths Compromise; Blacks would be counted as three-fifths of a person (Native Americans would not count at all).[3] Thus, America, a country founded on the principle of freedom and the idea that people have unalienable rights of life, liberty, and the pursuit of happiness, turned its back on these principles initially relegating Blacks to less-than-full citizenship status.

It had come to this. After over 160 years of a presence in America, black people as a group were not whole people, only a part, less than Americans of European descent. The document whose preamble contains noble words failed to provide liberty and justice for all. Instead, it set up a schism that has yet to be sealed. The dichotomy remains as the nation continues to grapple with the question of color.

Before and since the creation of the Constitution of the United States, this country has exploited Blacks by treating them, at various times, as property, preventing them from acquiring property, limiting their participation in the country's political and social institutions, and exploiting their labor. By the beginning of the nineteenth century, it was clear that the United States was not and would not, in the foreseeable future for Blacks, live up to the language and spirit of the Declaration of Independence.

Although most Blacks were held in abject slavery in the South, there were some free Blacks in the North. They, however, could only watch as events swirled around them, and swirl they did. Some attempts were made to solve the black question by creating a black state in part of what is now Virginia, or send Blacks to Africa. The colonization approach was more than frivolous discussion; some Blacks were settled in Africa in 1822 when Liberia was founded. Liberia, the oldest independent black nation in Africa, was founded by an American charitable society to provide a home for freed black slaves from America. It was with this history and amid this atmosphere that the first black newspaper and, consequently, the first black media vehicle in the United States, was created.

THE DEVELOPMENT OF BLACK MEDIA IN AMERICA (1827–1900)

During colonial and revolutionary times there were no black newspapers. Prior to the establishment of the first black newspaper, Blacks had to rely solely on editors and publishers sympathetic to their quest for full citizenship rights in America to engage their fight in the marketplace of ideas. Newspapers, wittingly or unwittingly, endorsed the social order. For example, many publications routinely carried notices of slave auctions and notices of rewards offered for the return of escaped slaves.

Thomas Jefferson, perhaps the most lauded of the revolutionaries who have become known as America's Founding Fathers, owned slaves and was not above using the newspaper to keep current his inventory of human property. The following excerpt from his ad in a 1769 edition of the *Virginia Gazette* is one example:

Run away from the subscriber in Albemarle, a Mulatto slave called Sandy, about 35 years of age. . . . He is a shoemaker by trade. . . . In his conversation he swears much, and his behavior is artful and knavish. . . . Whoever conveys the said slave to me in Albemarle, shall have 40s. reward. (Curtis, 1988, p. 155)

Jefferson was not alone. George Washington, the military leader of the Revolutionary War and the first president of the United States, owned slaves and kept black men, women, and children in bondage for as long as he lived. Jefferson and Washington are among the most notable examples of the incompleteness of the American Revolution and the weakness of the powerful to make America live up to its creed.

Through books, newspapers, and popular myths, the image/notion of a happy, contented slave was predominant. These images were used to justify the idea of black inferiority because if people in slavery could be happy, this was proof of their inferiority.

Amid this atmosphere, the first black media voices started to faintly make their voices heard. The story of the founding of the first black newspaper is important to an understanding of the relationship between Blacks and the mass media and the philosophy of black media. As with the establishment of the black church, the first black newspaper was founded by Blacks who had been rebuffed in their attempt to participate in an institution. Just as Richard Allen started the black church in 1787 after he was given poor treatment in a Philadelphia church, the black press was born out of similar contempt by a New York City newspaper at the idea of Blacks participating in the discussion of the issues of the day.

New York City was an early city of influence and one of its newspapers, the *New York Enquirer,* had little sympathy for the idea of black rights. Penn (1891, p. 27) described *Enquirer* editor Mordecai Noah as "an Afro-American hating

Jew'' who encouraged slavery and deplored the thought of freedom for the slave. When Samuel Cornish and John Russwurm separately asked for an opportunity to respond to material in the *Enquirer,* Noah turned them down. This affront led Cornish to join with Russwurm to establish *Freedom's Journal* in March 1827. The newspaper carried the credo for black mass media that has passed from generation to generation of black media entrepreneurs. In its first edition, the editors ("To our patrons," 1827, p. 1) wrote:

We wish to plead our own cause. Too long have others spoken for us. Too long has the publick been deceived by misrepresentations in things which concern us dearly (p. 1).

Thus, the first black media vehicle took into account the three major areas of concern. Its raison d'être was the need to counter the characterizations, images (portrayals) of Blacks that had been purveyed by media controlled by whites. It also provided an opportunity for some Blacks to engage in an endeavor they had theretofore been denied. Finally, it allowed Blacks to be the decision makers on what would be published and the angle or slant this information would have. However, as the following chapter indicates, financial success for some enterprises would not come until the twentieth century.

Audience and Support

The low black literacy rate for the first two-thirds of the nineteenth century meant that black newspapers had a small number of readers, many of whom were white, and had to accept donations/subsidies from sympathetic white philanthropists to survive.

Numerous black newspapers were established after *Freedom's Journal* and during the antebellum period. While these publications did voice their opposition to slavery, the other issues the early black newspapers dealt with were racial unity, progress, education, and life for free Blacks in the North. The names of some of the antebellum publications are indicative of their editorial bent, for example, *Alienated American, Mirror of Liberty, The Elevator, Freeman's Advocate, Herald of Freedom,* and *The Journal of Liberty.* Most of these early newspapers were short-lived.

Although *Freedom's Journal* was the first black newspaper, the most prominent and long-lived of the antebellum papers were those associated with Frederick Douglass. Douglass first contributed to *The North Star,* which had begun in Rochester, New York, in 1847. The publication was renamed *Frederick Douglass' Paper* in 1851 to capitalize on Douglass' growing prominence as an abolitionist, to establish the publication's credibility, and to use Douglass' celebrity to help raise or channel funds to the publication. Douglass' (1847) editorial efforts were designed to:

attack Slavery, in all its forms and aspects; Advocate Universal Emancipation; exalt the standard Public Morality; promote the Moral and Intellectual improvement of the COLORED PEOPLE; and hasten the day of FREEDOM to the Three Millions of our Enslaved Fellow Countrymen(sic). (p. 1)

Though it was against slavery, the early white abolitionist press argued for gradual emancipation of Blacks as typified by Benjamin Lundy's *Genius of Universal Emancipation* (Folkerts & Teeter, 1989, 188). It is important to note that *Freedom's Journal* predates the best known of the abolitionist newspapers, William Lloyd Garrison's *Liberator* (1831–1865). The sole purpose of this segment of the American mass media was to demand emancipation of slaves held in the United States. With the Emancipation Proclamation, the Union's victory over the Confederacy in the Civil War, and subsequent passage of the Thirteenth Amendment (outlawing involuntary servitude) to the Constitution, the abolitionist press shut down—its work done. Black newspapers continued to be published.

OTHER ANTEBELLUM MEDIA

Newspapers were not alone in supporting the colonial and antebellum status quo. According to Dates and Barlow (1990), numerous examples of books and plays dating back to 1781 indicated:

Both the popular theater and literature of the antebellum period created standardized images of slaves and their masters. These initial representations were used to rationalize the enslavement of African people. (p. 6)

One form of popular entertainment that developed in antebellum America was the minstrel show. This contained, perhaps, the cruelest of the images purveyed of Blacks. In this "art" form, whites put on tattered clothing, blackened their faces with burnt cork, and exaggerated the size of their eyes and lips with white and red makeup. Although the lampooning of Blacks by whites was a bit more isolated at first, it did not take long for such acts to become widespread. Minstrel shows were popular entertainment by the 1840s and they reinforced the image of the happy, carefree, inferior, idiotic Negro.

Although there were some more genteel depictions of the black experience such as Harriett Beecher Stowe's *Uncle Tom's Cabin* and more militant works (e.g., Stowe's *Dred*, Frederick Douglass' *The Heroic Slave*, and J. T. Trowbridge's *Cudjo's Cave*), the predominant message sent via newspapers, books, and the theater was one of black inferiority. It is not surprising that this antebellum sentiment found its way into law via the Supreme Court's landmark 1854 decision in the *Scott v. Sanford*—more popularly known as the Dred Scott—case. Here the nation's highest tribunal decreed that black men "had no rights or privileges but such as those who held the power and government choose to grant them.''

Civil War to 1900

The abolition of slavery was not the initial goal of the North in the Civil War (1861–1865), but it later became an objective. The victory of the Northern army opened a window of opportunity for Blacks that lasted approximately 30 years. Emancipation brought the end of slavery but the quest then turned to obtaining equal rights and equal protection for Blacks.

Despite the South's loss in the Civil War, it became clear the need for black media continued to exist. The attempt at post–Civil War Reconstruction did not eliminate the need for the black press. While many of the pre–Civil War black newspapers had as their purpose the abolition of slavery, in the post–Civil War era the quest turned to the securing of full citizenship rights, self-determination, and equality under the law for Blacks. Although the need for the black press changed, a need remained nonetheless because of the failure of Reconstruction.

The promises of Reconstruction that could have resulted in the integration of Blacks as full citizens into America were thwarted. As the American power structure coalesced against integration, Blacks saw a society once again becoming institutionally arrayed against them. New laws marked the transformation of Jim Crow into James Crow, Esquire and wiped out the gains of the Civil War and the Reconstruction that immediately followed.

Black newspapers after the Civil War emphasized group uplift and cohesion via church, the lodge, and the black press. In the post–Civil War period virtually any change in the socioeconomic improvement of Blacks as compared to the conditions of slavery was an improvement. Although the country, particularly the South, retrenched institutionally, several factors coalesced to transform black newspaper readers into black newspaper subscribers in the last third of the nineteenth century. According to Pride (1950), Blacks were becoming better educated, freedmen had more money, social service and religious groups gave financial support to the press, a black audience for politically sponsored publications developed, religious organizations entered journalism to advance their views, and the enterprise of journalism could be an influential activity within a black community.

From its inception, the first black medium was a reaction to being excluded or misrepresented by the dominant media. Rebuked by the mainstream media, the only alternative was to take the entrepreneurial route in an attempt to counteract the messages disseminated by the majority media.

The early black newspapers faced tremendous hurdles. In many places in the South, where most of the Blacks lived, it was against the law to teach slaves to read. At the end of the Civil War, approximately 90 percent of Blacks lived in the South and two-thirds of the Blacks who lived in the North were illiterate. One effect of emancipation and Reconstruction was an increase in black literacy.

As a result, the last third of the nineteenth century saw the establishment of approximately 600 black newspapers (Pride, 1950). Although increasing black literacy offered the promise of increased black readership, most of these publications were short-lived. Black newspaper-publishing in the nineteenth century was a tenuous enterprise.

The last third of the nineteenth century also marked America's change from an agrarian republic to one based on industrial capitalism. As this occurred America became an economically and politically oligopolistic society. Each historical period has brought about changes in the roles of Blacks and their status in America.

For 250 years the image of Blacks evolved from one of heathens in a Christian land in the colonial period to the contented slave, happy to be in the servitude of whites in an idyllic antebellum setting. This image abruptly changed after the Civil War to one of incredulity at the thought of Blacks being able to participate in government as voters or officeholders—full citizens.

The post–Civil War period of the nineteenth century is noteworthy for the political maneuvering that negated the victories of emancipation, victory by the North in the Civil War and the Thirteenth, Fourteenth, and Fifteenth amendments to the Constitution. Starting in the late nineteenth century, Blacks were victimized by a blatant and rigid racist ideology which reasserted and encouraged notions of cultural and racial superiority. This ideology promulgated the "Negro as beast" theory for Blacks (Riggs, 1986). These ideas found solace in academe. Anthropological and sociological studies substantiated the inferiority of Blacks. The development of "intelligence tests" legitimized racial superiority theories because these tests were "objective." The practical effect was that if blacks were different—biologically and culturally—then discriminating against them was justifiable. This logic had come full circle to the colonial "Blacks as heathens" rhetoric.

Such ideas, and the practices that resulted from such notions, kept Blacks out of the mainstream and out of positions of power. After the Civil War, the ingenuity of the power/legal/legislative structure concocted literacy tests, poll taxes, gerrymandering (the creation of geographically peculiar voting districts designed to perpetuate incumbents), and "grandfather" clauses (people had certain rights only if their grandfathers had such rights) to deny rights to persons of color.

This attitude culminated in the Supreme Court's 1896 decision in the *Plessy v. Ferguson* case, which established the "separate but equal" doctrine that lasted until the Court reversed itself in the 1954 *Brown v. Topeka Board of Education* decision.

Thus, the nineteenth century had been a roller-coaster ride for Blacks. It had started with Blacks trapped for the most part in that "peculiar institution" of slavery where the only option for relief under discussion was being shipped to Africa. The trap tightened with the Supreme Court's *Dred Scott* decision. Although the Union victory in the Civil War and new constitutional protections marked some progress out of the abyss, the failure of Reconstruction marked another sharp turn to the right followed by free fall in the form of another Supreme Court jolt with its *Plessy* decision.

By the end of the nineteenth century it was apparent that the institutions of power could not be counted on to liberate Blacks and the media were interested in preserving the status quo. By the end of the nineteenth century, the mass media had sequentially treated Blacks as if they did not exist, as childlike simpletons who could not survive on their own, as a problem that had to be dealt with and a threat to society. The media had also established several stereotypic characters that served as shorthand ways to make statements about Blacks. The bulk of literature and news accounts on the happy slave gave America the Sambo (male buffoon), the coon (lazy, good-time-seeking male), the brute (the violent, dangerous young black male), the Uncle Tom (docile, loyal, elder black male), and the mammy (fat, black, asexual, loyal, female servant). Others would be added during the twentieth century.

The beginning of the twentieth century found Blacks in an economic, political, and social straightjacket. The problems of obtaining full citizenship rights would move to a new level.

The Twentieth Century

With the exception of minstrel shows, nineteenth-century mass media in America existed primarily in print form, but other forms and sources of entertainment and information started to develop shortly after the end of the century. Although these new forms competed with newspapers to entertain, inform, persuade, and socialize Americans, they built on the historical patterns of negative portrayals of and discrimination against Blacks in employment, established and practiced by their media precursors. As the next chapter indicates, the repetition of these negative portrayals and employment discrimination forced Blacks into an entrepreneurial mode if they wanted to counter the images and participate in the media industries as managers, publishers, owners, editors, and reporters.

NOTES

1. The term ''Blacks'' refers to those Americans who have West African ancestors who were brought to America for the purpose of being slaves.

2. Congress shall make no law . . . the freedom of speech, or of the press. (First Amendment to the Constitution of the United States of America.)

3. Article I, Section 2. Constitution of the United States of America. This provision was rendered moot by the Thirteenth Amendment.

REFERENCES

Bennett, L. (1993). *Before the Mayflower: A history of black America* (6th rev. ed.). New York: Penguin Books.

Bryan, C. (1969). Negro journalism in the United States before Emancipation. *Journalism Monographs, 12.*

Curtis, L. A. (1988). Thomas Jefferson, the Kerner Commission and the Retreat of Folly. In F. R. Harris & R. W. Wilkins (Eds.), *Quiet Riots: race and poverty in the United States.* New York: Pantheon Books.

Dates, J. L., & Barlow, W. (1990). *Split image: African Americans in the mass media.* Washington, DC: Howard University Press.

Douglass, F. (1845). Narrative of the life of Frederick Douglass: An American slave. In H. L. Gates, Jr. (ed.), *The classic slave narratives.* New York: Penguin Books.

———. (November 5, 1847). Prospectus. *The ram's horn,* p. 1.

Duke, L. (January 14–20, 1991). But some of my best friends are. . . . *Washington Post* (Weekly Edition), p. 7.

Emery E., & Emery, M. (1978). *The press and America: An interpretative history of the mass media.* Englewood Cliffs, NJ: Prentice-Hall.

Folkerts, J., & Teeter, D. L. (1989). *Voices of a nation: A history of the mass media in the United States.* New York: Macmillan Publishing.

Franklin, J. H. (1980). *From slavery to freedom: a history of Negro Americans.* (5th ed.). New York: Knopf.

Jordan, W. D. (1968). *White over black: American attitudes toward the Negro, 1550–1812.* Chapel Hill, NC: University of North Carolina Press.

Kurian, G. T. (1991). *The new book of world rankings.* (3rd ed.). New York: Facts on File.

Penn, I. G. (1891). *The Afro-American press and its editors.* Springfield, MA: Wiley and Co. Reprint, 1969. New York: Arno Press New York Times.

Pride, A. S. (1950). *A register and history of Negro newspapers in the United States: 1827–1950.* (Doctoral dissertation, Northwestern University, 1950).

Prospectus. (November 5, 1847). *The ram's horn,* p. 1.

Riggs, M. (Producer, Director, and Writer) (1986). *Ethnic notions* [Videotape]. San Francisco: California Newsreel.

Snorgrass, J. W. (1989). The sectional press and the Civil War, 1820–1865. In W. D. Sloan & J. G. Stovall (Eds.), *The media in America: A history.* Worthington, Ohio: Publishing Horizons, Inc., pp. 143–162.

"To Our Patrons," (March 16, 1827). *Freedom's Journal.*

Tripp, B. (1992). *Origins of the black press: New York, 1827–1847.* Northport, AL: Vision Press.

Wilson, C. C., & Gutierrez, F. (1985). *Minorities and mass media: Diversity and the end of mass media.* Beverly Hills, CA: Sage.

Wolseley, R. E. (1990). *The black press, U.S.A.* (2nd ed.). Ames, IA: Iowa State University Press.

14 Setting and Philosophical Perspectives in the Twentieth Century

[O]ur basic conclusion: Our nation (America) is moving toward two societies; one black, one white—separate and unequal.
—The Kerner Commission (1968)

The problem of the 20th century is the color line.
—W.E.B. Du Bois

INTRODUCTION

As the twentieth century moves to a close, Dr. Du Bois' and the Kerner Commission's assessments of America have proven remarkably prophetic. Although a cursory glance at the mass media in America today would find more Blacks than ever involved in the newspaper, motion picture, recording, broadcast, cable television, and alternative telecommunications delivery system industries, this visibility may be misleading. As indicated previously, the publication of the first edition of *Freedom's Journal* in 1827 set in motion a tradition of black media activity that survives to this writing. While the current dilemmas faced by Blacks are more subtle than those faced by their eighteenth- and nineteenth-century ancestors, dilemmas nonetheless remain.

The Afro-centric, diversity, and multicultural movements that gained prominence in the United States in the 1980s turn the melting pot theory on its head. These advocates use history to argue that the melting pot idea was/is unrealistic and that instead of expecting America's racial and ethnic groups to lose their differences, such differences should be acknowledged, celebrated, applauded, and preserved. The portrayal battles have continued, and for black media consumers and black media entrepreneurs the twentieth-century question is whether

Table 14.1
Ten Oldest Black Newspapers in the United States

1. Philadelphia *Tribune* (1884)	6. Pittsburgh *Courier* (1905)
2. Baltimore *Afro-American* (1892)	7. Chicago *Defender* (1905)
3. Houston *Informer* (1893)	8. *Amsterdam News* (1909)
4. Indianapolis *Recorder* (1895)	9. St. Louis *Argus* (1912)
5. Norfolk *Journal & Guide* (1900)	10. Kansas City *Call* (1919)

Source: Editor & Publisher International Yearbook 1993, pp. II–85–87.

black media can be economically independent and racially responsible at the same time.

PRINT MEDIA

Newspapers

The twentieth century saw other forms of the mass media develop, and black concern with and activity in them as well. However, the print media—newspapers and magazines—would be the black American media of consequence, importance, influence, and substance until the 1970s. Although characterized by precarious existence, black newspapers have managed to continue to provide a forum for black participation in the discussion of the issues of the day. As indicated previously, approximately 600 black newspapers were started before 1900, yet only four of these newspapers established in the nineteenth century are still publishing (See Table 14.1).

These newspapers provided their readers with information that was excluded from the white-controlled press. It has only been since the 1960s that the white press acknowledged Blacks were born, died, had weddings, distinguished themselves in the service of the country, graduated from college, and so on. In the nadir of the *Plessy* era, the most successful of the black newspapers of the twentieth century were launched. While some were exemplars of the tradition of *Freedom's Journal,* black newspaper owners were not saints. On occasion, they fell victim to internal bickering and manipulation that delayed them from their self-avowed tasks of securing full rights for Blacks.

Black newspapers had ceased to be a novelty at the turn of the twentieth century. As the next millennium approaches, the fact remains that these publications still fill a communications need. Although the publications had lofty goals, the black newspaper became in the twentieth century a business venture, and a hazardous one. Questions of who would advertise in black-oriented/owned media and at what level remain. Over the years, political party patronage and job printing brought in additional revenues.

Of the hundreds of black newspapers that began publication in the late nineteenth and early twentieth centuries, only a few became financially successful. Some of those that did, however, achieved national prominence. This tendency to disappear after being created was not unique to black newspapers but, as is so often the case, these publications experienced failure rates higher than those of their white newspaper counterparts.

Black newspapers had some ignoble moments during the twentieth century. The unstable financial condition of some of the publications made them prey to manipulation. Booker T. Washington, the widely acknowledged "black leader" at the turn of the century, used patronage payments to certain black newspapers to manipulate them in his attempt to mold black public opinion.

The major black media by and large have adopted the economic model of advertiser support. This has come with consequences. Over the years, the publications have carried advertisements for products of questionable value to their readers, such as skin lighteners, hair straighteners, and alcohol and tobacco products.

There is no question of the influence black newspapers had on their readers. Perhaps their most famous legacy is the role the newspapers played in encouraging the black migration from the South to the North in the early twentieth century. To be sure, newspapers were only one factor. The migration was also aided by a combination of the *Plessy* "separate but equal" doctrine, "Jim Crow" laws, southern crop failure, and lynchings. The decline in European immigration and the resultant World War I labor shortage also forced a need for labor that made certain jobs available to Blacks that would not have happened under peacetime conditions.

The effect of this migration was significant. In 1910, 90 percent of Blacks lived in 11 southern states, but by 1920, 10 percent had left for the Northeast, Midwest, and West. Between 1910 and 1950, 3.5 million Blacks left the South. Black newspapers like the Chicago *Defender* and the California *Eagle* were among those which urged Blacks to leave the South. The *Defender* was the best example. Founded in 1905 by Robert Abbott, the *Defender* sounded a clarion call to the North. In becoming a sort of rallying point, the *Defender* took the first steps toward a black press with some kind of national influence. Banned in some cities and discouraged in others, the *Defender* is nevertheless credited with altering the racial landscape of America. Abbott modeled his newspaper after the sensationalist Hearst and Pulitzer newspapers and used this editorial approach to make the paper successful. The *Defender* is noteworthy for being the first unionized newspaper and first black newspaper with a racially integrated staff. The paper's circulation was over 200,000 at one point in the 1940s and published on a daily basis from 1956 to the 1970s.

In addition to the *Defender,* numerous other black newspapers are significant for their impact on Blacks in America and their quest for full citizenship rights.

The *Defender,* along with the *Afro-American* newspapers, the *Amsterdam (Star) News,* the Pittsburgh *Courier,* and the *Journal and Guide* formed the "Big Five." These newspapers had the largest circulations during the heyday of the black press in the 1940s and, consequently, the largest influence.

The *Afro-American* newspapers were founded in 1892 as separate newspapers in Baltimore, Maryland to advertise church news. John Murphy Sr. acquired the publications in 1896, combined them, expanded the focus, and made the paper a financial success. The *"Afro,"* as it is known, was among the early papers that published national and regional editions as well as publishing more than once a week.

The Pittsburgh *Courier* is generally considered the greatest black commercial newspaper in history. The *Courier*'s circulation reached 350,000 during the 1940s with special editions for 15 states and a national edition. The paper was founded in 1910 by a group of 15 Blacks in Pittsburgh who thought the city's 15,000 Blacks needed a voice. The paper ran into financial trouble in 1911 and Robert Vann gradually assumed full control in 1926 and built the publication into national status.

The *Amsterdam (Star) News* was founded in 1909 and is notable for being based in New York City. In addition to being the black publication in, arguably, America's most important city for the first half of the twentieth century, this publication helped provide an outlet for the black cultural expression known as the Harlem Renaissance.

Norfolk, Virginia's *Journal and Guide* was founded in 1909 and guided to prominence by Plummer B. Young Sr. The *Journal and Guide* was noted as one of the most professional black newspapers. Nicknamed "The Black *New York Times*," the *Journal and Guide* eschewed the sensationalism practiced by some of its contemporaries.

The Atlanta *World,* founded in 1928 as a weekly by brothers W.A. Scott and C.A. Scott, deserves mention for becoming the first black daily newspaper in the world in 1932. The Scott brothers pioneered the edition idea among black newspapers and at one point, using the ideas of mass production of shared news, features, and reporting, had 55 black newspapers published under its "World" umbrella.

The most enduring attempt at black newspaper publisher cohesion has been the formation in 1937 of the Negro (now National) Newspaper Publishers Association (NNPA), the trade organization for black newspaper publishers. The other major national black effort relative to newspapers was the development and operation of Claude Barnett's Associated Negro Press (ANP) (1919–1964). Prior to the ANP, most of the stories in the black press came from volunteer reporters. Barnett organized the ANP to facilitate reporting among black newspapers. The concept was simple: Each ANP member paper was the ANP bureau for a city and the members shared their information. What the ANP did was offer increased national coverage to black newspapers via this sharing arrangement. Barnett encountered problems getting publishers to pay for the service on a timely basis. Eventually, ill feeling between Barnett and the leadership of the NNPA resulted in the NNPA setting up a rival news service.

Black papers became more militant during World War II. Abbott's *Defender* and Vann's *Courier* were examples of the black editors and publishers who came to the North from the South and insisted on social equality in education, jobs, housing, and under the law. These editors and publishers were critical of those Blacks who were more cautious than they and expressed concern for the oppressed of all races and all nationalities—a universality not evidenced before in the black press. They looked at problems of people of color all over the world and the impact of race relations on America's image abroad. Lynchings were widely covered, as were Ku Klux Klan rides and race riots in American cities.

Most unions excluded Blacks from membership. Consequently, black newspapers were generally critical of labor unions but defended the Pullman railroad car porters' attempt to organize and exist.

Total black newspaper circulation climbed to two million at one point during the 1940s, largely based on the "Big Five's" national editions. Many of the subscribers were in the South with the papers distributed by black train porters.

Politics

Out of gratitude for emancipation, the black press was generally loyal to the Republican party from the Reconstruction period through the first three decades of the twentieth century. This loyalty started to crack after the Depression and the institution of President Franklin D. Roosevelt's New Deal. Since World War II, most of the major black newspapers have endorsed Democrats who ran for president, although the papers identify themselves as "independent." While Blacks were virtually powerless in the South, where practices such as poll taxes and literacy tests retarded political participation, they became a constituency to be courted in the urban north. Black newspapers were the means by which the sentiment of this constituency could be molded.

More auxiliary agencies formed that improved the quality of the black press. Material from the National Feature Service, Calvin's Newspaper Service, Crusader News Service, Tuskegee Institute Service, and NAACP's Press Service augmented the ANP to provide feature stories and syndicated columns. Some papers had foreign correspondents or New York reporters.

An activist/advocacy press for its entire existence, the late 1930s and 1940s saw black press crusades for elimination of discrimination in defense industries during World War II and for a moral victory in the United States as well as overseas.

The increased activism, circulation, and influence did not go unnoticed. Westbrook Pegler, a nationally syndicated white columnist who was one of the most powerful opinion leaders in America at the time, called the black press traitors for talking about racial problems during the war. Many black newspapers were

Table 14.2
Twentieth-Century Black Population/Economic Growth

Year	Population (Millions)	"Wealth" (Billions)
1940	12.9	$3
1950	15.0	$12
1968	22.0	$30
1978	25.2	$70
1993	29.9	$280

Sources: D. P. Gibson, *$70 billion in the black* (New York: Macon, 1978); *The $30 billion Negro* (New York: MacMillan, 1969); R. Kahlenberg, Negro radio, *The Negro History Bulletin*, pp. 125–129.

investigated by the FBI during World War II on possible sedition charges, but no publication was so charged.

Advertising

Revenues for general circulation newspapers come mostly from advertising with less from subscriptions. For black newspapers, the opposite has been true. Blacks did not become an attractive consumer market until the 1940s (see Table 14.2), and many national advertisers remain skeptical of the effectiveness of advertising in black media vehicles.

By the 1940s, black newspaper publishers were more merchant than militant, as some would suggest. Oak (1948) chided black newspapers for emulating to a fault the "white" press and having become "good business men" but "economic opportunists" (p. 49). A 1949 *Ebony* magazine profile of twenty-three black newspaper publishers concluded that:

Far from being parlor pinks, most Negro publishers are arch-conservatives in their thinking on every public issue with one exception—the race problem. The owners of the biggest newspapers have but two main missions—to promote racial unity and to make money ("Publishers: Owners of Negro Newspapers," 47).

Sociologist E. Franklin Frazier, in his classic work *Black Bourgeoisie* (1957), was very critical of the twentieth-century, pre-Brown decision black press and observed that while the black press was at that time "one of the most successful business enterprises owned and controlled by Negroes . . . (and the) "chief medium of communication which creates and perpetuates the world of make-

Table 14.3
"Big Five" Black Newspaper Population/Economic Growth

Publication	1943* Circulation	1993** Circulation
Pittsburgh *Courier*	190,684	30,000#
Afro-American Group	73,554	13,385
Chicago *Defender*	83,487	30,000#
Amsterdam News	33,748	32,701
Journal & Guide	34,553	25,000#

Sources: *Audit Bureau of Circulation (ABC) figures from *N.W. Ayer & Sons Directory of Newspapers and Periodicals, 1943*, pp. 1221–1222.

**Gale Directory of Publications & Broadcast Media/1993*, pp. 2690–2691. Only *Amsterdam News* and the *Afro-American* have ABC figures.

#—Not ABC audited.

believe'' (p. 174). Black newspaper circulation dropped in the 1950s as the impact of black-oriented radio as an advertising medium for the black consumer market began to take away advertising dollars.

For black newspaper publishers, the Plessy era (1896–1954) ironically gave them a monopoly on the black market. The U.S. Supreme Court decision in the *Brown v. Topeka Board of Education* case overturned the "separate but equal" doctrine established in the Plessy case and started the modern civil rights movement that culminated in the Civil Rights Act of 1964.

Although Congress passed the Civil Rights Act of 1964, there were major riots in some of America's cities in 1965 and 1966. President Lyndon Johnson appointed a presidential commission to study these incidences and the commission (chaired by former Illinois governor Otto Kerner, and more popularly known as the Kerner Commission) provided one often-cited observation: "Our nation is moving toward two societies; one white, one black—separate and unequal." (Report of the National Advisory Commission, 1968, p. 1). The commission went on to blame the mass media for this drift in its portrayal and employment practices.

While circulation of the "Big Five" declined (see Table 14.3) from their World War II highs during this period, the newspapers published by the Nation of Islam (i.e., the Black Muslims) and the Black Panthers took the black newspaper publication lead. The Nation of Islam paper *Muhammad Speaks* was the highest circulation black newspaper in history, reaching nearly 600,000 people in the 1970s, and the *Black Panther* newspaper's 100,000 circulation easily outdistanced their commercial counterparts of their time.

Table 14.4
Geographical Distribution of Black Newspapers

AL - 10	KY - 1	OH - 6
AR - 1	LA - 6	OK - 3
AZ - 1	MD - 2	OR - 2
CA - 43	MA - 2	PA - 5
CO - 1	MI - 7	RI - 1
CT - 5	MN - 3	SC - 9
DC - 6	MO - 7	TN - 2
FL - 15	MS - 2	TX - 15
GA - 14	NV - 1	VA - 6
IL - 11	NJ - 1	WA - 4
IN - 5	NY - 7	WI - 3
KS - 1	NC - 12	

Source: Editor & Publisher International Yearbook 1993, pp. II–85–87.

Current State

Black newspaper circulation has made a comeback of sorts in the 1990s. One trade publication lists nearly 200 black newspapers published in 34 states and the District of Columbia (see Table 14.4) that have a circulation of approximately 3.3 million. The vast majority of the publications are weeklies. Black newspapers with the highest circulation of newspapers are found in Table 14.5.

Magazines

The first black consumer magazine appeared in 1900 with the publication of *Colored American.* Although newspapers would dominate the black press until the 1950s, their national influence has been eclipsed by magazines. The *Black Enterprise* magazine 1994 list of the leading black service and industrial businesses contained no newspaper publishing companies on the entire list. In 1994, there were at least 25 black-oriented magazines. Table 14.6 shows that the circulation of the five largest black consumer magazines dwarfs that of black newspapers, which have evolved into a local medium.

The dominant black magazine publisher is the Chicago-based Johnson Pub-

Table 14.5
Twenty Highest Circulation Black Newspapers, 1993

Audit Bureau of Circulation Newspapers

Title/Location	Circulation
City Sun (New York, NY)	52,600
The Call (Kansas City, MO)	35,000
Los Angeles (California) *Sentinel*	35,000
New York (NY) *Amsterdam News*	30,994
Call and Post (Cleveland, OH)	30,000
Miami (FL) *Times*	18,300
Philadelphia (PA) *Tribune*	12,663
The Sun Reporter (San Francisco, CA)	12,000
Indianapolis (IN) *Recorder*	10,149
Baltimore (MD) *Afro-American*	12,666

Unaudited Newspapers

Central-News Wave Group (Los Angeles, CA)	280,000
Inquirer Group (Hartford, CT)	125,000
Post Group (Oakland, CA)	114,437
San Francisco (CA) *Metro Reporter* Group	111,118
Atlanta (GA) *Voice*	103,000
New York (NY) *Voice*	90,000
New York (NY) *Daily Challenge/Afro Times*	78,000
South Carolina Black Media Group (Columbia, SC)	75,000
Forward Times (Houston, TX)	60,000
Chicago (IL) *Crusader*	55,173

Source: Editor & Publisher International Yearbook 1993, pp. II–85–87.

Table 14.6
Top Fifteen Circulation Black Magazines, 1993

Title	1994 Circulation
ABC Audited	
Ebony	1,791,536
Jet	909,014
Black Enterprise	250,672
Essence	900,350
American Visions	110,000
Non-ABC Audited	
The Crisis	350,000
Dollars and Sense	286,000
Feelin' Good	250,000
Black Family	200,000
Upscale	200,000
Class	187,345
Sophisticate's Black Hairstyles and Care Guide	182,250
Players	175,000
Emerge	130,000
Black Careers	100,000

Source: Gale Directory of Publications & Broadcast Meda/1994, pp. 3083–3085.

lishing company, founded in 1942. Johnson's credo was in part based on the refrain first echoed in *Freedom's Journal*. Disturbed by what he perceived as the general negative portrayal of Blacks in the media, John Johnson decided to emphasize black accomplishment in his publications. The flagship publications are *Ebony* and *Jet*. Published monthly, *Ebony* is the best known, and if circulation is any indication, the most popular of the black magazines. Modeled after *Life* magazine in size, layout, typography, and featuring photographs, *Ebony* pioneered the push for general market advertising to Blacks. Johnson was able to convince many in corporate America that black Americans would be favorably disposed to the products that appeared in black magazines. *Jet,* a pocket-sized weekly newsmagazine, was started in 1951.

Essence magazine was launched in 1970 by three black men, at the prodding of a white Wall Street executive. Initially financed by whites, it has become the premier black woman's magazine. *Essence* fills the gap left by beauty and fashion magazines that for long periods of time failed to feature or carry ads with black models as well as cosmetics for that element of the population. It is published monthly.

Black Enterprise is a monthly specialized publication with primary emphasis on business, although it features some consumer-based articles on travel and technology. The cornerstone of the Earl Graves businesses, *Black Enterprise,* started in 1970.

The *Black Collegian,* founded in 1970, is the only one of the major black magazines that has no white magazine counterpart. Unlike the previously mentioned publications, it has the narrowest potential audience—the 1.2 million black college students. Published monthly, *Black Collegian* is typical of the black magazines that have controlled circulation and are generally not available on newsstands.

There are many other specialized black publications magazines (church, fraternity, sorority, etc.) but their circulation is dwarfed by the magazines listed in Table 14.6. The specialized publications are typically available by subscription, and some accept advertising.

The Black Press in 1995

The end of legal segregation created by the Brown decision, the development of black-oriented radio stations, and the rise of television led to the decline of the influence of black newspapers. The integration movement, prompted in part by white media organizations' attempt to address some of the employment problems identified in the Kerner Commission Report, resulted in a talent raid on the black press by general circulation newspapers. The talent drain and competing media for grudgingly spent black consumer market advertising dollars has resulted in the black press becoming a local medium with little of the national influence once known by the major black newspapers during the highwater mark for black newspaper influence in the 1940s. Although these publications had several or national editions, they were based in specific communities. The last and most serious twentieth-century attempt at a national black newspaper failed when *The National Leader* (1982–1985) ceased publication.

It can be argued that the influence of the black press is not what it was. The questions in 1995 remain what they were at the turn of the century: Can black newspapers get their target audience to read and subscribe to the publications and will enough advertisers deem black newspapers worthy advertising vehicles? The reality is that the readers and the advertisers have different interests and agendas. Advertisers usually want to place their ads in a ''safe'' environment and black readers want their media to deal with the reality of black life in America. The other major question relates to the conflict between social responsibility and maintaining a viable (profitable) business, that is, can black newspapers be economically independent and racially responsible at the same time? As it fights for advertiser support, how critical can the black press be of products such as alcohol and tobacco that have been shown to have detrimental health effects on their intended audience? Arguably, the Nation of Islam paper (now carrying the name *The Final Call*), which does not depend on support from white businesses, is perhaps the most independent black publication in existence in 1995.

The dilemma of the black press is to succeed in making itself relevant to its target audience while not offending the white business interests that support it via its advertising placement.

FILM AND ELECTRONIC MEDIA

Based upon the history of Blacks and the print media, it is not surprising to learn that Blacks experienced similar portrayal, employment, and entrepreneurial "problems" as other forms of the mass media developed. As with the print medium, the issues involving the relationship of Blacks and the motion picture, music, and broadcast industries have centered around portrayal, employment, and entrepreneurship. The issue of the image of Blacks, who creates, presents, and profits from it, has provided a running controversy for most of the twentieth century.

Motion Pictures

Although initially not a mass medium but a popular one, the early motion pictures, when they showed Blacks, borrowed heavily from the minstrelsy tradition. In this "art" form whites would dress up in blackface and entertain crowds that gathered. These blackface traditions were so strong that when Blacks started to perform in minstrel acts, even Blacks had to wear black makeup and exaggerate their lip size by putting on white makeup to conform to what was expected of a minstrel show.

The development of film as mass entertainment in the early twentieth century gave Blacks a new reason to be concerned about their portrayal. The development of the narrative motion picture started in America when *The Great Train Robbery* (1903) allowed the new medium to move beyond being mere novelty. Blacks were part of the early years of motion picture experimentation, as the titles of the shorts *How Rastus Got His Turkey* (1909) and *Rastus in Zululand* (1910) indicate.

The early years of experimentation with the long form of the motion picture culminated in the release of David Wark Griffith's three-hour epic production, *The Birth of a Nation* (1915). Shot for $110,000, the motion picture generated

$18 million in revenues, an 1800 percent return on investment. This film told the story of Southerners, wronged by the North and left at the mercy of carpetbaggers and not-ready-to-govern emancipated slaves, who were saved only by the rise of the Ku Klux Klan.

Birth of a Nation built on the minstrel tradition in that Blacks were an integral part of the story but only white actors were used. Thus, initially the first point of conflict between Blacks and this new medium was again over portrayal and, implicitly, employment. In the film the familiar images of mammies and coons were trotted out again with brute and tragic mulatto characters depicted as well.

It is ironic that one of the most significant of the early motion pictures, *Birth of a Nation,* took as its theme the glorification of the rise of the Ku Klux Klan in the South during Reconstruction. This film contained many nineteenth-century stereotypic characters to make statements about the intelligence, patriotism, industry, and sexual proclivities of Blacks. *The Jazz Singer* (1927), the debut film marking the change from silent to "talking" motion pictures, featured Al Jolson in blackface for a large portion of the film. Unlike newspapers, Blacks attempted to participate in the motion picture industry as it was being established. Among the early black film companies was The Foster Photoplay Company, a Chicago-based company that produced black subject shorts from 1910 to 1916. In response to Griffith's film, the first black motion picture production company, the Lincoln Motion Picture Company, was created in 1916. Based in Los Angeles, Lincoln lasted less than two years. The major black filmmaker of the first half of the twentieth century was Oscar Micheaux. By 1918, Oscar Micheaux had formed the Micheaux Film and Booking Company, based in Chicago. His efforts met with limited success even though he produced films for approximately 40 years.

This early era of independent black filmmaking lasted less than 20 years. On the eve of the debut of talking motions pictures in the late 1920s, a rumor that black voices recorded better failed to materialize in gains in portrayals and employment for Blacks in this industry. The move of the motion picture industry to idyllic Hollywood, the development of the Hollywood studio system, the loss of black-owned theaters, and the Depression proved to be a devastating combination. It would be the early 1970s before any significant flurry of films featuring Blacks would return.

With the ascent and dominance of the major Hollywood studios until the late 1960s, and despite appearing in scores of films, Blacks were relegated to a series of roles film historian Donald Bogle (1973) characterized as "toms, coons, mulattoes, mammies and bucks." Under Bogle's taxonomy, variations of the following black character stereotypes can be found in most American motion pictures produced between 1910 and 1973:

Toms—long-suffering, hard-working, God-fearing black males who were glad to be in the service of whites and knew this was their lot in life.

Coons—superstitious black males who shirked work, liked to sing, drink, gamble, dance, chase women, and were irresponsible.

Bucks (i.e., brutes)—black males who were violent, strong, sexual predators with a penchant for white women.

Mammies—the female counterpart to toms. Mammies were usually dark-skinned, asexual because of their weight, and if married had coon husbands.

Mulattoes—attractive, sexually active, light-skinned women whose blood lines contained enough European traces to make them able to "pass" for white if they so chose.

Looking back over the twentieth century, one can see a pattern of periods where there was a rash of films and then nothing for awhile. As the data in Table 14.7 show, the first commercially successful black star of the post-Brown era was Sidney Poitier. Poitier appeared in each of the films indicated for the 1960s. Richard Pryor held this honor next, appearing in five of the films on the list for the 1970s and 1980s. Eddie Murphy was the black star of the 1980s, appearing in six of the nine films on the list. Although it is perhaps too early to tell, Denzel Washington is shaping up as the black star of the 1990s. Washington won an Oscar for his role in *Glory,* a story about a black Civil War regiment, and had the starring roles in Spike Lee's productions of *Malcom X* and *Mo Better Blues* and costarred in the 1994 films *The Pelican Brief* and *Philadelphia.*

The list of "black" films is misleading in that most films do not necessarily have black themes/storylines but merely featured black characters. A deeper analysis of the roles would show that the black stars were featured in secondary or supporting roles.

In 1995 the debate centers around what exactly is a "black" film. If a "black film" is any commercial, feature-length motion picture that has the black community as its central focus with at least a black producer, director, or writer, many of the films in Table 14.7 would not qualify as such.

There have been two eras of black film since the passage of the Civil Rights Act of 1964. In each case, the catalysts were independent filmmakers, with the major studios quick to jump on the bandwagon. Melvin Van Peebles' *Sweet Sweetback's Baadasssss Song* (1971) and *Shaft* (1971) touched off what became to be known as the "blaxploitation film era" (1971–1979). Shelton (Spike) Lee's *She's Gotta Have It* (1986) started the current era of "black films."

Sweetback was an independent film shot in 19 days for $500,000 that established the black outlaw hero archetype. *Shaft* was released by the MGM studio during a period of financial difficulty. The movie made more money than expected and MGM was able to stay in business, riding the cash flow of a wave of low budget/high grossing black cast films. The *Shaft* soundtrack won an Oscar for black composer Issac Hayes.

Broadly defined, a "blaxploitation" film featured a strong, aggressive black man (usually from the ghetto) who ultimately outsmarted a loathsome white

Table 14.7
Top Earning "Black" Films by Decade

Title/Year Released	Film Rentals* (Millions)
1990s	
Boyz N the Hood (1991)	$26.7
Jungle Fever (1991)	15.7
1980s	
Beverly Hills Cop (1984)	$108.0
Beverly Hills Cop II (1987)	80.1
Lethal Weapon 2 (1989)	79.5
Coming to America (1988)	65.0
Driving Miss Daisy (1989)	50.5
The Color Purple (1985)	49.8
Trading Places (1983)	40.6
Another 48 Hours (1990)	40.1
Harlem Nights (1989)	33.0
Purple Rain (1984)	31.7
Richard Pryor Live on the Sunset Strip (1982)	18.2
Busting Loose (1981)	15.4
1970s	
Stir Crazy (1980)	$58.6
The Wiz (1978)	12.3
Let's Do It Again (1975)	11.8
1960s	
Guess Who's Coming to Dinner (1968)	$25.5
To Sir With Love (1967)	19.1
In the Heat of the Night (1967)	11.1
A Patch of Blue (1966)	6.7
For Love of Ivy (1968)	5.6

*Film rentals are monies actually earned from theatrical release in the U.S. and Canada and reflect actual initial popularity more than anything else. These figures reflect money earned during initial release and are not adjusted for inflation. Foreign rentals and ancillary revenues are not included. For a more comprehensive chart, see *Variety*, October 15, 1990. The box office gross of each film was 2.5 to 3 times the film appeal.

Source: All-time Film Rental Champs. *Variety* (February 24, 1992), pp. 125–168.

adversary and got the money and the girl in the end. Occasionally, women were cast in the lead roles, for example, *Coffy, Foxy Brown, Cleopatra Jones.*

A number of factors led to the decline of the blaxploitation era. First, although black characters were seen more than ever before, the characters shown drew criticism from black organizations such as the NAACP. Among the reasons given were that the movies did not address audience needs in realistic terms, the story lines were unrealistic, or characters were too one-dimensional. The blaxploitation films were also accused of constant depiction of the black lower class often engaging in illegal activities and making fun of the black middle class.

Second, the success of such films as *Star Wars* and *Close Encounters of the Third Kind* added fuel to the "blockbuster" (a high box-office-grossing film) mentality in Hollywood. Since most of the black-cast films were low budget productions, these limited production values also meant these films had a smaller grossing potential. Third, Hollywood seemed to construe the box office failure of *The Wiz* (1978) as an indication that big budget black-cast films had no "crossover" (appeal to whites) potential. *The Wiz* failed to recoup its production and promotion costs of more than $30 million.

Fourth, movie theaters moved from downtown locations to suburban malls. Malls have become a metaphor for white flight to suburban areas from the inner city. In addition to the public transportation problems caused by getting from the center city to the suburbs, several celebrated, isolated incidences of violence associated with the opening of black theme films have made theater security an issue affecting exhibition.

Fifth, there was the perception that the movies were antiwhite. While many of the blaxploitation era films were, many were not, for example, *Sounder, Buck and the Preacher, Let's Do It Again, Lady Sings the Blues.* Finally, there was a perception that there was no aftermarket (revenues from foreign circulation, videocassettes, cable, etc.) for black films.

Despite the resurgence of black-cast films in the early 1970s, by the start of the 1980s Blacks had been reduced to roles of bit players instead of stars. Lee's *She's Gotta Have It* (1986) changed this and earned him a place in the history book alongside Micheaux and Van Peebles.

Again a low budget ($170,000 to produce), quickly made (in 12 days) film that grossed $7 million in initial release set off a rush of black-cast films. *She's Gotta Have It* struck a nerve as an independent fresh film with black appeal. While it is undeniable that black-cast films released since *She's Gotta Have It* usually have a high return on investment, it remains to be seen whether 1991, when the major motion picture studios distributed and marketed 19 black-cast films, will remain the high mark of the latest wave of black films.

At this writing, there are no black "studios" or enough black-owned theaters that would allow for the exhibition of films produced by any black "studio" that might come into being. Black activity is limited largely to the production of motion pictures with very little association with distribution and exhibition, key elements to the success of mass market films. The average motion picture released by the major studios in 1993 cost $20 million to produce and another $8 million was spent on marketing and promotion efforts.

BROADCASTING

Radio

The development of broadcasting trailed slightly the development of the motion picture. After a period of experimentation and regulatory chaos during the first two decades of the twentieth century, by the late 1920s the phenomenon of broadcasting was ready to challenge motion pictures as the premier entertainment medium in America. As with the other media, an aural stereotype of blacks developed. One of the most popular radio programs of all time was the legendary "Amos 'n' Andy" show. In this program two white men, Freeman Gosden and Charles Correll, used an exaggerated black dialect to earn fame and fortune for themselves. At its zenith, more than half of the radio audience would tune in. The program was so popular, many movie theaters delayed their evening programs so that people could hear the show before coming to the theater. The characters' style of butchered English and exaggerated dialect drew heavily on the traditions of minstrelsy and, more importantly, set the tone for Blacks on radio. This pattern of stereotyped characters, which was the rule more than the exception until the early 1950s, reached its most absurd incarnation with creation of the "Beulah" radio character. "Beulah" was a maid in a radio series whose voice initially came from a white male actor utilizing his "black" voice to bring the character to life. Although there were a few shining examples of nonstereotypic programming, such as the radio programs sponsored by some black newspapers and programs like "Destination Freedom," these efforts were short-lived or not national broadcasts such as "Amos 'n' Andy" and "Beulah."

The advent of television forced radio to change. The rise of television had a negative impact on radio audiences and advertising revenues. Radio changed from a medium that featured segmented programming for undifferentiated audiences to one that featured differentiated programming for segmented audiences. This change allowed for the creation of black-oriented radio.

Black-oriented radio made its debut in 1948 when WDIA-AM, a white-owned station in Memphis, Tennessee, converted to 100 percent black programming. This pattern would be repeated across the country as radio station owners—all white—began to devise methods of staving off bankruptcy because television was changing the way audiences used radio.

As this was happening, there was a change occurring in the black consumer market, shown previously in Table 14.2. The quadrupling of total black income from $3 billion to $12 billion from 1940 to 1950 as a result of black participation in the World War II boom increased black disposable income for items like records. By capitalizing on the fact that music could form the basis of radio programming and black music, or (as it was known at the time) "race music," was shunned by many of the general market (a euphemism for white-oriented) radio stations, certain radio station owners were able to attain financial stability by switching to black-oriented formats. In the years that followed, white owners of black-oriented radio stations promulgated a type of programming that was condemned for systematically failing to serve the empowerment interests of the stations' audiences, which were overwhelmingly black. *Newsweek* (Negro Radio, 1967) provided the following characterization of black-oriented radio in the 1960s:

While the money is green, the power is strictly white. Of all the (radio) stations broadcasting to the ghettos, only five are owned by Negroes. There is just one Negro station manager and few top Negro executives. On many of the stations, only the disk jockeys and janitors are black. Whites, for the most part, pick the music. Nor are the majority of the Negro stations responsive to their listeners' needs. They simply present a weary diet of rhythm and blues (music) and "nigger-talking deejays." (p. 113)

Newsweek characterized the result of white ownership:

the angry voice of the ghetto is subdued. Instead, many Negro stations are content to push spelling bees as meaningful public service. A discussion program on WDIA in Memphis called "Brown America Speaks" has drawn request that the title be changed from "brown" to "black" but station officials have refused. Other stations are merely paternalistic.

"We never excite the Negro audience," says the white manager of Baltimore's WWIN. "We have a band of white listeners to protect." (p. 113)

For years the perceived remedy for this programming approach was an increase in the level of black ownership on the grounds that black owners would be more responsive to community needs.

WERD-AM in Atlanta, Georgia became the first black-owned radio station in the United States when businessman Jesse B. Blayton acquired it in 1949. However, black radio ownership was an exception as the *Newsweek* excerpt indicated. As late as 1972, there were only 12 black-owned radio stations in America.

A 1981 study by the author indicated the then new wave of black owners, as trustees of the public airwaves, performed in the public interest, convenience, and necessity equally as well as their white counterparts when sheerly quantitative standards were applied and had superior performance on more qualitative measures. In the 1990s, a controversy has arisen relative to black-oriented radio stations playing "rap" music, particularly "gangsta rap." Its most vocal critics argue that "gangsta rap" celebrates sexual promiscuity, profanity, violence, and misogyny. These critics argue that black-oriented radio does the black community a disservice by giving such material a forum and consequently, access

Table 14.8
Black Broadcast Ownership, 1993

	Total	Black Owned
Commercial AM stations	4,948	110
Commercial FM stations	4,945	71
Commercial television stations	1,153	19

Sources: Black Enterprise (April 1994), p. 16; *Broadcasting and Cable* (January 3, 1994), p. 64.

to young minds. In 1994 a handful of black-owned radio stations indicated they would be more careful about the rap music they played.

Table 14.8 shows the level of black-owned broadcast facilities in 1993. The bulk of the increase in the last 20 years is due to federal government policies that promoted minority, and consequently black, ownership. The Federal Communications Commission (FCC) is the chief federal telecommunications regulatory agency and has three ways it has attempted to increase black broadcast ownership.

First, current FCC policies give Blacks preferences in competing and mutually exclusive license applications procedures. Second, the FCC also issues tax certificates that allow an owner who sells a broadcast station to blacks to defer the taxes on the capital gain for up to two years. Third, owners/licensees who have been designated for FCC review because of policy violations may divest themselves of their station licenses by selling to minorities at a discount.

Television

Television built on the model established by radio in terms of programming and economic support. By being able to bring to the home images as well as sounds, the speed of the diffusion of television into American society remains one of the major phenomena of the twentieth century. Interestingly, television made no attempt at minstrelsy per se. In the early days of television, black actors and actresses were sought to play the "black" characters created by whites on radio for the "Amos 'n' Andy" and "Beulah" television shows.

Although these programs were short-lived for several reasons, both early programs set the pattern for what would largely follow over the years. The genre of preference for portraying Blacks has been the situation comedy. With its laugh track and problems solved within a 30-minute time frame, situation comedies have built on the tradition of Blacks being America's comic relief.

Except for occasional roles, Blacks were largely not seen on television from the early 1950s through the mid-1960s. *Jet* magazine's weekly feature on Blacks on television programs at the time could frequently fit on one 5 × 7-inch page. The Civil Rights Movement of the 1960s forced television producers to stop ignoring Blacks. However, the types of programs that developed and have been the most enduring have been a number of situation comedies which dwarfed the number of dramatic programs featuring Blacks, again adding to the comic tradition of Blacks. Illustrative of the predicament of Blacks on television during the late 1970s and early 1980s was the situation of a series of programs ("Webster" and "Different Strokes") on first-run, commercial television network programming in which no black children were shown being raised by black parents. While critics point out a few examples of what might charitably be termed "positive" programming, few would give the television industry glowing marks for the black images trotted out week after week for the American public. Fifteen of the 17 programs featuring Blacks on the fall 1993 commercial television network schedules were situation comedies.

While there were some strides made in black ownership of radio stations during this period, Table 14.8 shows that the increase in television ownership, although dramatic, is too small to have any real impact on national programming. WGPR-TV (Detroit) became the first television station licensed to Blacks, in 1975, when the International Masons, Inc. acquired a construction permit for and built a UHF television station. As an independent station, WGPR-TV suffered from having no network affiliation at a time when the major television networks (ABC, CBS, and NBC) commanded more than 90 percent of the prime time television audience.

The development of cable television resulted in a significant increase in the number outlets for television programming. Initially an extension of over-the-air television signals, cable television was a passive delivery system from its development in the early 1950s. This mode of operation changed in the mid-1970s with the development of goesynchronous domestic communications satellites that allowed for the development of "superstations," such as WTBS in Atlanta, and cable television programming services, such as the Cable News Network (CNN), Home Box Office (HBO), The Entertainment and Sports Network (ESPN), and the USA Network.

Black involvement in cable television has resulted in few major changes relative to over-the-air television. Only three companies on the *Black Enterprise* magazine 1994 list of top black businesses had any cable franchise (individual system) ownership. In 1995, there were over 11,200 cable television systems in operation that served approximately 62 percent of the 94 million households in the United States. The major black cable programming service is Black Entertainment Television (BET). Started by Robert Johnson in 1980, BET is the only black-owned company that is publicly traded on the New York Stock Exchange. BET in 1995 focuses mostly on entertainment programming, particularly music videos. Ironically, because most of the existing cable television systems were built first in the suburbs and last in the inner city areas, BET is available to more white households than black.

THE MUSIC INDUSTRY

The music recording industry and the broadcast and motion picture industries have become interdependent. Long a staple of radio programming, recorded music and the associated music videos have become a fixture on television. The importance of cross-marketing to the success of motion pictures means that music has become an important component of the success of motion pictures as well.

America is a creative fountainhead for a business that had 1993 worldwide revenues of nearly $20 billion, with Americans accounting for approximately one-third of the market.

Thomas Edison is credited with the invention of the mechanical recording device that evolved into the phonograph at the end of the nineteenth century. As with the other forms of the electronic media that have become commonplace in the twentieth century, Blacks were the subject of some of the earliest recorded music. Shortly after the turn of the century and before World War I, a series of recordings that became known as "coon songs" ("up-to-date comic songs in negro [sic] dialect" (Barlow, 1990, 29) were released. Drawing on the familiar images of Blacks, whites released songs which celebrated and relied upon the time-worn image of Blacks as simple, service-oriented, subservient individuals.

Again the pattern was repeated; white musicians via the "coon songs" or the Dixieland Jass [sic] Band's 1917 recording of "One Step" set the early pattern of Blacks being "portrayed" musically, but in general black performers were not recorded. Bert Williams, the first black vaudeville star, was an exception to this. However, in true minstrel tradition, he performed in blackface. Although some argue his performances added a depth of characterization not found in those of white minstrel performers, Williams's "victories" occurred in the portrayal and employment arenas.

The Jass Band's success provided the archetype of the practice of "covering." Under "covering," white performers would take black music and record it. Aided by the major record companies who could get the distribution necessary to make a "hit," the economic gain went to white artists and the white record companies.

The first black popular music was called blues or jazz. In 1920, Mamie Smith's "Crazy Blues" became the first black popular recording or "hit," selling, to the surprise of Okeh record label officials, 75,000 copies in the first month of its release. Such subsequent recordings by black artists were called "race" music. Although the artists who sang were now black (the employment phase), the entrepreneurial level activity proved much more difficult. Just as the 1995 recording industry is dominated by a series of large corporations (CBS/ Sony, Warner/Elektra/Asylum, PolyGram [sic], MCA, Thorn/EMI, and Bertlesmann), such was the case in the early twentieth century when the big names were Columbia, Okeh, Paramount, and Victor.

The first black-owned record company was Black Swan records, established in New York City in 1921 by Henry Pace and composer W.C. Handy. Other black-owned companies were established later in the decade in Chicago, Kansas City, and Los Angeles. Each was short-lived because of a combination of undercapitalization, inability to get the distribution for their products to compete against the larger white companies, and the cultural bias against "race" music. The larger companies had other product target markets, so their success was not totally dependent on the success of their "race music" components. However, it should be noted that some of the early covers such as Sophie Tucker's "Saint Louis Blues" and the Dixieland Jass Band's recordings sold over one million copies each.

The Depression dampened black business and the market for "race" music was devalued. While certain performers such as Duke Ellington went on to acclaim during this period, Blacks were largely kept off radio and were workers instead of entrepreneurs who had little ability to control, if they *could* record, what material they would record and how the material would be recorded.

The World War II black economic boom rekindled the interest in and the lucrativeness of "race records." The demise of radio's golden age and the development of radio formats built around music forced a market segmentation with race becoming one of those segments. As the economic viability of "race music" became apparent, it was renamed rhythm and blues (R&B). When white teenagers became interested in rhythm and blues, it became rock and roll. The practice of covering became more notorious during the 1950s, with the music eventually being segregated into separate categories of rock and roll and rhythm and blues, which served to isolate black recorded music. During the rise of R&B in the 1940s and 1950s, the black music "industry" was still dominated by white companies. This changed in 1958 with the founding of Motown Records, the most significant black recording company to date.

Berry Gordy, a one-time autoworker and boxer, wrote a song, "Reet Petite," that became a hit but only resulted in meager royalties for him. Realizing that the business end was just as important, if not more so, than the artistic end, Gordy established Motown Records. Utilizing the local talent in Detroit, Michigan, Gordy built a music empire that for years was the number one nonfinancial black business in America. Gordy sold the record company in 1988 to MCA, a major label and a white company. In 1993, only two companies (Rush Communications and Dick Griffey Productions) on the Black Enterprise Top 100 Service & Industrial companies were in the music recording business.

REFERENCES

Barlow, W. (1990). Cashing in. In J. L. Dates & W. Barlow (Eds.), *Split image: African Americans in the mass media.* Washington, DC: Howard University Press, pp. 25–55.

"B.E. Industrial/Services Companies." (June 1993). *Black Enterprise,* pp. 91–98.

Bogle, D. (1973). *Toms, coons, mulattoes, mammies and bucks: An interpretive history of blacks in American films.* New York: Viking Press.

Buni, A. (1974). *Robert L. Vann of the Pittsburgh Courier: Politics and black journalism.* Pittsburgh: University of Pittsburgh Press.

Frazier, E. F. (1957). *Black bourgeoisie.* Glencoe, IL: The Free Press.

Garafalo, R. (1990). Crossing over: 1939–1989. In J. L. Dates & W. Barlow (Eds.), *Split image: African Americans in the mass media.* Washington, DC: Howard University Press, pp. 57–121.

Gibson, D. P. (1969). *The $30 billion Negro.* New York: Macmillan.

———. (1978). *$70 Billion in the black: America's black consumers.* New York: Macmillan.

Harlan, L. R. (1983). *Booker T. Washington: The wizard of Tuskegee, 1901–1915.* New York: Oxford University Press.

Hogan, L. D. (1984). *A black national news service: The Associated Negro Press and Claude Barnett, 1919–1945.* Rutherford, NJ: Fairleigh Dickinson University Press.

Jeter, J. P. (1981). *A comparative analysis of the programming practices of black-owned black-oriented radio stations and white-owned black-oriented radio stations.* Doctoral dissertation, University of Wisconsin-Madison.

Kahlenberg, R. (1965). Negro radio. *The Negro History Bulletin,* pp. 125–129.

Myrdal, G. (1962). *An American dilemma: The Negro problem and modern democracy.* New York: Harper.

Negro radio. (December 11, 1967). *Newsweek,* p. 113.

Oak, V. V. (1948). *The Negro entrepreneur.* Yellow Springs, Ohio: The Antioch Press.

Ottley, R. (1955). *The lonely warrior: The life and times of Robert S. Abbott.* Chicago: H. Regnery Co.

Publishers: Owners of Negro newspapers are hard-headed, farsighted, race conscious businessmen. (1949). *Ebony* (November), 47–51.

Reid, M. A. (1993). *Redefining black film.* Berkeley, CA: University of California Press.

Report of the national advisory commission on civil disorders. (1968). New York: The New York Times Company.

Suggs, H. L. (1983). *The black press in the South, 1865–1979.* Westport, CT: Greenwood Press.

———. (1988). *P.B. Young, newspaperman: Race, politics and journalism in the new South, 1910–1962.* Charlottesville: University of Virginia Press.

Washburn, P. S. (1986). *A question of sedition: The federal government's investigation of the black press during World War II.* New York: Oxford University Press.

15 Education and Training of Media Personnel

> The journalistic profession has been shockingly backward in seeking out, hiring, training and promoting Negroes.
>
> —The Kerner Commission, 1968

INTRODUCTION

The communications industry is one sector of the American economy that has a positive balance of trade. Expectations are that the communications industry will also remain a global growth industry. Interestingly, more than two-thirds of the wages earned in the United States in 1994 came from information sector jobs.

After concerns about the portrayal of Americans of African descent, training and employment in the media is the second major concern for Blacks in their quest for full participation in American life and industry. The role of black labor in American history vividly exhibits the unfavorable relationship Blacks have had with the power structure of the country.

The larger American society has exploited black labor. Although the most egregious and glaring violations occurred during the nearly 250 years of legal and institutionalized slavery, the post-Reconstruction retrenchment on equal rights and protection saw the exploitation continue. The decision to exploit and oppress black workers was a conscious decision and the result was the orientation of an entire race of people toward servitude at the lowest rungs of society. While black workers were used and oppressed, they were also being denied educational opportunities that might have helped them deal with the situations created by white labor and capitalists.

Employment discrimination continues. A 1991 study by the Urban Institute tested contemporary attitudes toward black and white employees. The study matched black and white males for education and background and had them apply for the same jobs in the Chicago and the Washington, DC areas. The white applicants were five times more likely to be able to submit an application for employment, and three times more likely to get a job offer. A study of federal workers for the period ending in fiscal year 1992 found that minority workers were fired at three times the rate of white workers.

The friction between Blacks and whites over labor is not ancient history, as the following anecdote indicates. A television commercial in the closing days of the 1990 campaign for a U.S. Senate seat for North Carolina illustrates how much tension remains. In that race, incumbent Jesse Helms, a white Republican, picked up this old theme in his bid for reelection against Harvey Gantt, the former mayor of Charlotte, North Carolina, who is black and a Democrat. As a television commentator, Helms had been a longtime critic of the Civil Rights Movement in the 1960s. Gantt had desegregated Clemson University to earn his degree in architecture. Helms's commercial showed white hands holding, and then crumpling, a letter saying the reader would not get a job because it had been given to a "minority." The implication was clear and Helms won reelection in the closest race of his career. Failure to get the "angry white male" vote cost the Democrats control of both houses of Congress in the 1994 election.

HISTORY OF BLACK WORKERS IN AMERICA

To understand the situation in 1995, it is necessary to put the black worker into historical context. Black workers did the rigorous labor required by the seventeenth, eighteenth, and early nineteenth century American agrarian economy. Slaves were kept illiterate by laws that, in many instances, provided severe punishments to those who taught slaves to read and write. Consequently, for many years Blacks lacked the requisite skills for media careers and to be print media consumers. Having been among the most ardent fomenters of the American Revolution, journalists and publishers were especially important in the hierarchy of the new society. By and large, Blacks were shut out of this type of employment until the development of the black press in the late 1820s.

The northern victory in the Civil War might have changed the environment for black workers. However, the failure of Reconstruction left Blacks legally free but the old realities returned in another form. After emancipation, inequity in the work force was rampant and mobility was minimal. African-Americans, Asians, Hispanics, and Native Americans (AHANA), by and large had menial jobs in line with their low societal status and historic occupational orientation. When members of these groups worked the same jobs as whites they were paid less (about half the) wages of whites. Organized labor became more powerful but unions often denied Blacks membership. After emancipation, the threat of Blacks as low-wage strikebreakers was often used in labor relations squabbles.

In these situations, white workers had two options. They could blame management and unite in worker solidarity or blame AHANA members. Although whites in the indentured servitude period of the colonies often took the former option, white workers were oriented toward the latter approach. This orientation has been given as one explanation for the wide acceptance/tolerance of the negative black stereotypes that have been promulgated by the media.

The demand for labor in the industrial North during the first two decades of the twentieth century, coupled with a lack of European immigrants to do the work, created the first opportunity for Blacks to leave the southern sharecropper lifestyle approximately 300 years after the first Blacks arrived in the Jamestown colony. Ironically, the "separate but equal" doctrine expanded employment opportunities for Blacks to be reporters, editors, and publishers, albeit almost exclusively on black-owned newspapers. The northern migration created a market for these media products because Blacks had money to spend, but they were still excluded from the general circulation (a euphemism for white) media industry. Limited employment opportunities were also available during this period in the fledgling motion picture industry.

Over a century after emancipation, census data indicate the gap between black and white income is widening. In 1991 (the latest year for which data are available), the median income for black households was 59.62 percent ($18,807 vs. $31,569) of white households. In 1975 the ratio was 66.7 percent. Median household income for blacks and whites has been declining since 1989.

EDUCATION, TRAINING, AND EMPLOYMENT

Education

Many believe education is the key to upward mobility and participation in American society. Kept out of the educational system as a group for over 250 years, Blacks made some progress after the Civil War, but post-Reconstruction retrenchment and the "separate but equal" doctrine produced a system of unequal education that was the law of the land until the Supreme Court's 1954 decision in the *Brown v. Topeka Board of Education* case brought about the beginning of change.

During the first part of the twentieth century, states, and particularly the southern states where most blacks lived, spent multiples more money per pupil on white students than they did on black ones. For many years elementary and secondary education for Blacks was limited or not universal.

The preeminent postsecondary black educator was Booker T. Washington who, as president of Tuskegee Institute from 1881 to 1915, advocated a system of industrial education and manual training for Blacks that would allow them to function, given the societal attitudes then.

Table 15.1

Black Journalism and Mass Communication Education Enrollment and Graduation, 1993

	Enrollment (Projected)	Percentage Black Students (Projected)	Percentage Black Degree Recipients (Projected)
Bachelor's	128,367	13.5	10.1
Master's	10,148	7.0	6.1
Doctoral	1,005	8.0	7.3
Total	139,520		

Source: G. M. Kosicki and L. B. Becker, Undergraduate Enrollments Decline; Programs Feel Budget Squeeze, *Journalism Educator*, *49* (3) (Autumn 1994), p. 12.

Media Education

For many years, the unavailability of jobs and the difficulties in getting training were reasons for the low numbers of Blacks in the mass media. The case of Lucille Bluford describes the mentality of American postsecondary education toward the idea of Blacks as journalists in the pre-*Brown* decision era. Ms. Bluford applied for admission to the School of Journalism at the University of Missouri. To avoid her admission to the all-white school, the state of Missouri created, in 1942, a new and separate journalism program at Lincoln University, the state's college for Blacks, and assigned one teacher to it.

The glamor and potential for influence and prestige of working in the media assures no shortage of personnel in the mass media industries. Enrollment in journalism and mass communication programs fluctuates. Colleges and universities graduated over 16,000 students with degrees in journalism and mass communication in 1992–93 (see Table 15.1).

Although media jobs contain a certain element of glamour and ego satisfaction, aspiring workers deal with low pay and the lack of job security during their initial years of employment. The social value of journalism graduates can be assessed in comparison to other graduates. Table 15.2 indicates the average salaries offered to 1994 recipients of bachelor's degrees.

The value of formal training in journalism and other areas of the mass media is a matter of public debate; formal training does not guarantee success. Despite the instruction in journalism and mass communications programs in over 400 colleges and universities, the need and use of such training is questioned in public forums by journalists such as Ted Koppel. A 1987 study, known as The

Table 15.2
Salary Offers to Bachelor's Degree Candidates, 1994

Agricultural & Natural Resources	$23,003
Computer Science	$31,836
Engineering	
Lowest—Occupational	$24,600
Highest—Petroleum	$38,192
English	$21,581
Finance	$27,246
Health Sciences	$33,117
Marketing	$24,077
Public Administration	$25,094
Sciences	$26,319
Sociology	$22,871
Mass Communications (average)	$21,421
Design/Graphic Arts	$21,223
Media Planning	$22,094
Production	$22,149
Public Relations	$21,156
Reporting	$19,887
Writing/Editing	$22,022

Source: CPC $alary $urvey (July 1994). College Placement Council, pp. 3–4.

Roper Report, found that employers think journalism and mass communication education is not particularly relevant to the personnel needs of media organizations.

Table 15.3 provides Weaver and Wilhoit's 1992 profile of the modal American journalist. By comparison, they found the modal black journalist was a woman, who was not married, had a higher median income although she had

Table 15.3
Profile of American Journalist

Work at daily newspapers	55%
Married	60%
Male	66%
White	92%
Protestant	54%
Has a bachelor's degree	82%
Attended a public college	57%
Did not major in journalism	61%
Works at group/chain-owned organization	65%
Does not belong to a journalism organization	64%
Median news staff	42
Median years worked in journalism	12

Source: D. Weaver and G. C. Wilhoit, *The American Journalist in the 1990s* (Arlington, VA: The Freedom Forum, 1992).

worked slightly fewer years (10 or 11), worked for larger papers, and belonged to at least one journalism organization.

Perhaps the key data from the study are that although 82 percent of the journalists surveyed had at least a bachelor's degree, less than 40 percent had majored in journalism. The Weaver/Wilhoit study shows that white male employees in the media industries with few exceptions have held the decision-making positions. Data from the study confirm that educational credentials are important factors that employers use in assessing job applicants and that there is also a positive relationship between educational and occupational attainment. Employers indicate they desire "qualified," that is, highly educated and highly "talented," Blacks. For this reason, investing in higher education remains a necessity for Blacks.

No formal training in mass media is required for entry to the mass media. Although college educated, John Johnson (Johnson Publishing Company) and Earl Graves (Earl Graves Publishing) launched their black-oriented magazine and broadcast empires without formal training in journalism. High school graduate Berry Gordy was able to make the Motown music recording empire known worldwide. Robert Johnson, who founded Black Entertainment Television, has a degree in public administration. Eugene Jackson, an engineer by training, assembled the Unity Broadcasting group (at one time one of the major black-owned broadcasting groups), started the National Black (radio) Network and is now a principal in the fledgling World African Network, a black-oriented pay cable service. Large black broadcast station group owners Percy Sutton and Ragan Henry came to broadcasting from law. A 1991 study by one of the authors found only 7.6 percent of black broadcast owners surveyed had any experience in broadcasting before becoming station owners.

These entrepreneurial successes notwithstanding, it must be remembered that the occupational orientation of Blacks has been as workers rather than as owners/entrepreneurs. Conventional wisdom assumes that there is a meritocracy and that media applicants who attend an accredited college or university and major in the appropriate mass media subject will, upon graduation, be able to secure a job in the mass media activity of their choice. This approach also assumes that all components (universities, accrediting agencies, industries) are in sync. However, not all colleges are accredited or accredited for their journalism and mass communications programs. Furthermore, journalism and mass communications programs and the media industries continue to wrestle with the question of whether these programs produce graduates who, in the colleges' minds, are intellectually prepared to make American society better, or whether colleges provide the people who will be fodder for the American business activity. The latter defers to producing employees that business wants, but ''is what business wants in the best interest of society?''

In reality, employment in American media industries is secured through personal contacts and influence. People who can convince those who are seeking and hiring mass media industry workers that they can, without formal training in the desired mass media activity, do the job are given opportunities to work and prove themselves. Notable, highly acclaimed black media workers who fall into this category are broadcast journalists Bryant Gumbel, who majored in Russian history at Bates College, and Ed Bradley, who majored in education at Cheyney (PA) State College.

Because of the skills involved, one need not be a college graduate or a telecommunications or journalism/mass communications major to get a job. Indeed, the guidelines for accredited journalism programs stress the need for the bulk (approximately 75 percent) of a student's studies to be in the liberal arts areas. The advice given to most students is to go to college, graduate with a degree in some area, obtain as much practical experience by internships, networking with working professionals, and reading trade publications to get a job in some media organization somewhere.

There are some AHANA training programs, such as those run by the Times Mirror publishing group, the Institute for Journalism Education and the Newspaper Fellowship, an apprenticeship at Syracuse University, that do not lead to degrees but provide some journalism-specific preparation. Such programs are useful to persons who, although lettered, consider the training necessary to give them a competitive edge when looking for work. Many of these programs have a job placement option.

A series of annual studies published in *Journalism Educator* indicates healthy enrollment in journalism and mass communication programs for the past 15 years. The data fluctuate, but the 1993 data estimated that Blacks earned 10.1 percent of the bachelor's, 6.1 percent of the master's, and 7.3 percent of the doctorates (see Table 15.1). Since 1988, the average percentages have been 7.9 percent at the bachelor's level, 5.9 percent for the master's level, and 10.9 percent at the doctoral level. The result is a crowded undergraduate pool for entry-level positions and a diminished number of black students qualified for entry into doctoral programs—the feeder system for future professors—and few Blacks in the pool from which members of the professoriate are sought.

America's historically black colleges came late to journalism and mass communication education. Lincoln University was alone for many years. Hampton (VA) University (formerly Hampton Institute) offered a major in mass media starting in 1967. The journalism program at Florida A&M University (FAMU) in Tallahassee became the first media program accredited by the Accrediting Council on Journalism and Mass Communication (ACEJMC) in 1981, seven years after it became a degree-granting program in 1974.

In 1992, the then three accredited programs (FAMU, Howard, and Jackson State; 3.2 percent of the accredited programs) accounted for 9.9 percent of the AHANA staffers at college newspapers at ACEJMC-accredited programs. These three schools provided 11.7 percent of the AHANA top staffers and were the only schools with Blacks in each of the top five positions. Forty percent of the 94 accredited programs had no minorities in any of the top five staff positions.

In 1990 a group of historically black colleges and universities (HBCUs) offering instruction in journalism and mass communication formed The Black College Communication Association (BCCA) to represent the group's interests within the journalism and mass communication education and industry constituencies. In 1994 there were approximately 40 member institutions. The vast majority of these programs are not ACEJMC-accredited. In 1994 only four schools, Florida A&M University, Grambling (LA) State University, Howard University in Washington, DC, and Jackson (MS) State University, had full AEJMC accreditation. Two other HBCUs—Hampton University and the Southern University campus in Baton Rouge (LA)—had provisional accreditation.

Faculty

According to *The Chronicle of Higher Education,* whites make up 90 percent of the full-time faculty at America's colleges and universities; blacks are 3.2 percent. A 1988 study by David Weaver and G. Cleveland Wilhoit indicated Blacks represented 3.6 percent of the approximately 3,600 full-time journalism

Table 15.4
1992 American Media Employment by Industry

Industry	Employees	Average Hourly Wage (Dollars)
Print		
Newspapers	453,000	$11.71
Periodicals	124,000	12.67
Books	121,000	10.64
Electronic media		
Radio and television broadcasting	226,000	$13.81
Cable television	130,000	11.01
Motion pictures	395,000	12.08
Private sector	------	$10.59

Source: Statistical Abstract of the United States 1993, table 662.

and mass communication faculty. Weaver and Wilhoit noted that although the doctor of philosophy is not yet held by the majority of faculty in journalism and mass communication, they believe it is becoming the standard educational requirement, especially for promotion to full professor. An examination of one 1994 edition of the *AEJMC News,* the newsletter for the largest mass communication education organization, indicated that of the 36 faculty positions advertised, 19 indicated preference for holders of the doctorate, and nine positions *required* a Ph.D. in order to be considered for the job.

Industry Employment

The American media industries employ approximately 1.3 million persons (see Table 15.4).

Despite the gains of the post-Brown era Civil Rights Movement, that is, the Civil Rights Act of 1964 and the Voting Rights Act of 1965, numerous riots occurred in urban areas across America in the mid-1960s, most notably in Detroit, Newark, and the Watts section of Los Angeles. In their wake, President Lyndon Johnson assembled The National Advisory Commission on Civil Disorders (popularly known as the Kerner Commission) to investigate the causes of the riots. The commission's report was one of the most scathing critiques and indictments of the mass media in America for the role they have played in contributing to misunderstanding in American society. The report's most widely cited conclusion was that "America is moving toward two societies, one white, one black, separate and unequal." The report also pointed a finger at the media for being a major contributor to the drift, citing the employment records of the general circulation print and broadcast media as professions that were as much to blame as any American institution for the riots:

The journalistic profession has been shockingly backward in seeking out, hiring, training and promoting Negroes. . . . Fewer than 5 percent of the people employed by the news business in editorial jobs in the United States today are Negroes. Fewer than one percent of editors and supervisors are Negroes, and most of them work for Negro-owned organizations. (Report of the National Advisory, 1968, p. 384)

Since the mid-1970s, the FCC has required broadcast stations to report their equal opportunity employment records for women and minorities. Although black employment in the broadcast industry has increased, the employment benchmarks were so low that any increases would have produced dramatic percentage gains. Although AHANA members were 22.6 percent (Blacks were 9.3 percent) of the 1993 American labor force, their employment in the media exceeds their population in only one industry for which data are available.

Data released by the FCC in 1994 indicated that AHANA members accounted for 18.2 percent of the employees in broadcast stations with five or more full-time employees. AHANA members exceed population parity in the relatively new cable television industry where they are 25 percent of the work force. Employment data for Blacks in the broadcasting and cable industries are shown in Table 15.5. In broadcasting, Blacks were 5.9 percent of the officials and managers with a higher incidence of black females in those jobs compared to black males (956 versus 852 employees). The model category for black males was the service (janitorial, building maintenance category) and for black females it was the office/clerical worker category. If one looks at the categories from a hierarchial perspective, Blacks are concentrated in the lower-level positions.

Despite the fact that minorities have entered the public relations profession in substantial numbers since the late 1960s, they made up only 10.8 percent of the work force (PRSA 1988). Public radio's news work force was 17 percent AHANA in 1988 and the AHANA share of all news employees in commercial radio was only 8 percent (Stone, 1989).

Data indicate that equal opportunity for black workers is not improving. An analysis of data submitted to the federal Equal Employment Opportunity Commission (EEOC) indicated that Blacks were the only racial group to suffer a net job loss during the 1990–91 recession (an explanation for the decline in median household income), losing nearly 60,000 jobs while Asians and Hispanics gained approximately 55,000 and 60,000 jobs, respectively.

The level of AHANA employment at daily newspapers nearly tripled between 1978 and 1994, but as shown in Table 15.6, there is still a large gap between the percentage of workers and the percentage of these AHANA members in the general population. Data from the 1994 American Society of Newspaper Editors (ASNE) survey show that 45 percent of the newspapers in America employ no AHANA members at all. Blacks were 5.4 percent of all newspaper supervisors,

Table 15.5
Black Employment in the Broadcast and Cable Industries, 1993

| | Cable | | Broadcasting | |
Job Category	Black Females (%)	Black Males (%)	Black Females (%)	Black Males (%)
Officials & Managers	3.6	3.5	3.1	2.8
Professionals	4.8	3.5	4.1	4.8
Technicians	1.2	10.4	2.4	9.2
Sales Workers	10.4	8.5	3.0	2.9
Office/Clerical	16.5	3.0	13.9	1.8
Craftsmen	.6	10.7	2.3	4.9
Operatives	.7	14.6	3.0	13.9
Laborers	2.3	16.9	4.7	17.5
Service	1.9	13.3	9.3	27.0
Percentage of All Jobs	7.3	7.3	4.6	4.6

Source: 1993 Broadcast and Cable Employment Report (Washington, DC: Federal Communications Commission, July 26, 1994).

copy editors, reporters, and photographers while 58 percent were employed as reporters. While 17 percent of the black newspapers employees are in management, these workers were 4 percent of all the supervisors.

Since AHANA members are all lumped together under the "minority" rubric, the Kerner Commission report remains a true reminder of the work needed in media employment.

Glass Ceiling

For years the issue for Blacks was getting into media organizations. The affirmative action movement in the wake of the urban riots of the 1960s did improve the numbers and, under the pressure and watchful eye of the federal government, progress was made. However, this pressure lessened during the Ronald Reagan and George Bush presidencies, and the rate of improving black employment, particularly at managerial levels, stalled.

Table 15.6
1994 AHANA Employment in the Newspaper Industry

Category	Total Work Force	Black No.	Pct.	Other AHANA No.	Pct.
Supervisors	12,758	495	4	493	4
Copy editors	9,294	448	5	484	5
Reporters	25,290	1,674	7	1,292	5
Photographers	5,739	273	5	478	8
Totals	53,711	2,890	5	2,747	5

Source: ASNE Bulletin (April/May 1994), p. 21.

While employment and population parity may not be equivalent, it is true that significantly more Blacks are working in the communications industry than in the pre-Kerner Commission days. However, the recent recession underscored the fragile nature of the gains. Part of the employment problems of Blacks during the recession of the early 1990s related to the practice of dismissing the most recent hires (who tend to be minorities) when staff cutbacks are the chosen method of maximizing an organization's resources.

With the increased incidence of black employment has come the additional hurdle of job advancement. Since the 1980s, the concept of a "glass ceiling" has entered the discussion of black employment. The idea is that black and other AHANA members in organizations can see the high-level executive positions but few AHANA members will get top decision-making positions because the corporate culture thinks that white males can either only do those jobs or do them best.

In 1994 no black executive could "greenlight" (approve and commit to production) a motion picture among the major studios. As the previously cited data for the broadcast, cable, and newspaper industries indicate, Blacks have few of the managerial/decision-making positions. In broadcast journalism Blacks were 9.8 percent of the television broadcast news work force in 1992 but only 2.1 percent of the television news directors; for radio, the figures were 7.5 percent and 2.6 percent, respectively. In attempting to interpret the data, Stone (1992) wrote:

For minorities to move into management, they must first get into the (broadcast news) work force and find career opportunities good enough to pursue for a few years at least.

That has not happened nearly as often in the past 15 years as was predicted in the affirmative action years of the late 1960s and 1970s.

On the momentum of the civil rights movement and the FCC's 1969 hiring rule, minority shares of the (broadcast) news work force moved from practically nowhere to substantial levels by 1976. But attrition had set in by the mid-1980s, ground was regained in the late 1980s, and last year (during a recession) saw a return of the status quo. If the past proves a predictor, the diversity of news staffs may look much the same in the year 2000 as in 1992. (p. 27)

Stone's 1994 research found that little had changed.

Thousands of jobs have been lost in the broadcast news business since 1986, when the major commercial television networks were acquired by new owners who were interested in cutting costs. One of the casualties in that process was the CBS minority training program. The job eliminations decreased opportunities for Blacks and increased the competition within organizations for jobs as well as promotions. Issues of socialization within the corporate world confront black workers who wish to "get ahead" in predominantly white organizations, in that organizations have historically promoted people with whom they have a "comfort level." This striving, notes Clint Wilson in his book *Black Journalists in Paradox,* leads to isolation caused by the social conformity of the newsroom, operating on the assumption that because they are black, they were hired for affirmative action purposes and they are really incompetent and are likely to be limited to only certain types of assignments. The result is an "illusion of inclusion" (p. 137). Limited evidence indicates that Blacks are starting to burn out after bumping into the glass ceiling. One 1991 study found that minorities and women are more likely to quit their newspaper jobs than white males.

SUMMARY

The 1990s have marked the dawning of another communications revolution. Much like the first two decades of the twentieth century, a variety of inventions, technological innovations, and convergences promise to change the landscape of the mass media industries in ways that are not yet totally apparent. Newspaper publishers are being urged to abandon newsprint and embrace the electron. Broadcasters are being challenged for audiences and advertising revenues by cable television and a host of other competitors, including the telephone company. Mass media industries are big business and with the increasing concentration of ownership the organizational problems inherent in other industries are becoming apparent.

Many economists believe the new information age will mean tremendous growth for this sector of the American economy over the next 10 years. As newspapers decide how to become electronic, as broadcasters learn to live with more competition, and as technology to produce media products becomes less expensive, the potential for thousands of new jobs exists. Since small businesses are responsible for many of the innovations, it remains to be seen if the new breed of entrepreneurs will engage in hiring practices that depart significantly from history, or if more Blacks will take the entrepreneurial route themselves. The 30th anniversary of the Kerner Commission report in 1998 will indicate how far one generation of media managers and organizations have come in the hiring, training, and promotion of Blacks.

REFERENCES

Barr, S. (February 21–27, 1994). In the line of firings. *The Washington Post National Weekly Edition,* p. 34.

Bennett, L. (1975). *The shaping of black America.* New York: Penguin Books.

Electronic media career preparation study. (1987). New York: The Roper Organization, Inc.

Foote, C. F. (April/May 1994). Minority, total newsroom employment shows slow growth, 1994 survey says. *ASNE Bulletin,* pp. 20–22.

Jeter, J. P. (1991 Summer). Black broadcast station owners: A profile. *Feedback, 32* (3), 14–15.

Kosicki, G. M., & Becker, L. B. (Autumn 1994). Undergrad enrollments decline; programs feel budget squeeze. *Journalism Educator, 49* (3), 4–14.

The nation: faculty and staff. (1994). *The Chronicle of Higher Education Almanac.* Washington, DC: The Chronicle of Higher Education.

1993 broadcast and cable employment report. (July 26, 1994). FCC Public Notice. Washington, DC: Federal Communications Commission.

Opportunities denied, opportunities diminished: Discrimination in hiring. (1991). Washington, DC: Urban Institute.

Opportunities for minorities in public relations. (1988). *PRSA.* New York: Public Relations Society of America.

Placement Service. (March 1994). *AEJMC News, 27* (3). Columbia, SC: Association for Education in Journalism and Mass Communication, pp. 12–16.

Report of the National Advisory Commission on Civil Disorders. (1968). New York: The New York Times Company.

Statistical Abstract of the United States, 113th edition. (1993). Washington, DC: U.S. Bureau of the Census. 1993, tables 289, 662, 672, 711, 1256.

Stone, V. A. (August 1989). Minorities gain in TV news, lose in radio. *Communicator,* pp. 32–35.

———. (August 1992). Little change for minorities and women. *Communicator,* pp. 26–27.

———. (August 1994). Status quo. *Communicator,* pp. 16–18.

Third census of minorities in college media. (1993). Kent, OH: Kent State University School of Journalism and Mass Communication.

Weaver, D., & Wilhoit, G. C. (Summer 1988). A profile of JMC educators: Traits, attitudes and values. *Journalism Educator, 43* (2), 4–41.

———. (1992). *The American journalist in the 1990s* (Advance Report). Arlington, VA: The Freedom Forum.

Wilson, C. C. (1991). *Black journalists in paradox: Historical perspectives and current dilemmas.* Westport, CT: Greenwood Press.

16 New Technologies, Their Implications, and Special Issues

> Our network is not a radical departure for TV. . . . We have not reinvented the wheel, only painted it black.
> —Robert Johnson, founder, chairman, president
> and chief executive officer, BET Holdings, Inc.,
> parent company of Black Entertainment Television

INTRODUCTION

The rise and current status of black media in America have been documented in terms of portrayal and employment with some discussion of entrepreneurship in terms of the traditional media, and a new world/environment is developing around communication technology that is changing the mass media playing field. While patterns of portrayals, employment, and entrepreneurship have been ingrained in the traditional media, the task for Blacks is to not allow history to repeat itself and to become larger players in the developing communications technological environment. One could argue that many of the earlier barriers are becoming less formidable. Oprah Winfrey, Bill Cosby, Michael Jackson, Whitney Houston, and Eddie Murphy had five of the positions on the 1994 *Forbes* magazine list of the 40 richest American entertainers. Houston replaced the artist formerly known as Prince from the 1993 list. Montel Williams, Rolanda Watts, and Starr Jones joined Winfrey as 1994 hosts of their own television talk shows. Broadcast journalists Bryant Gumbel (NBC), Ed Bradley (CBS), Carole Simpson (ABC), and Bernard Shaw (CNN) received regular exposure in 1994 on television news. Black motion picture directors Spike Lee (*Malcom X*), Ernest Dickerson (*Juice*), Matty Rich (*Straight Out of Brooklyn*), and John Singleton (*Boyz N the Hood*) make movies that get major national distribution. Black recording stars Michael Jackson, the artist formerly known as Prince, and Whitney Houston have national and international star status. More Blacks than ever are working for daily newspapers. In 1994 Blacks owned approximately 200 radio and television stations and operated a national television programming service. However, this list of achievements and notable personalities masks the dilemma of Blacks and the emerging communications technologies. The entrepreneurial aspects of the information superhighway and the "new" media and communications services are the focus of this chapter.

MEDIA TRENDS

Several, sometimes contradictory, macrotrends have an impact on the relationship of Blacks and the mass media. First, there is an overall trend toward increasingly larger media organizations through conglomerate growth, with large companies buying each other. A second trend is the globalization of mass media. Both trends have led to subsuming one notable black media institution, Motown Records. Berry Gordy started Motown in Detroit in 1958. For years it was the preeminent independent black record company, until it was bought in 1988 for $61 million by MCA, a large American media conglomerate. MCA sold the company in 1993 for approximately $300 million to PolyGram, a European-based company.

A third trend is a blurring of media distinctions. The term "electronic newspaper" is no longer an oxymoron. Books and magazines are available on CD-ROM. Technological innovations are changing the ability to distinguish easily the new media from each other. A fourth trend is audience fractionalization. In the current competitive environment, many media organizations try to reach specific, targeted audiences instead of large, undifferentiated ones. Finally, the development of the information superhighway, a communications network capable of two-way delivery of audio, video, voice, and data services, could become the pulse of America by the year 2000.

In this environment several realities exist which do not bode well for Blacks. First, the large conglomerates are jockeying for position in the new media age. Second, the new media are more capital intensive than traditional media (see Table 16.1). Third, little black activity is taking place relative to the "new" communications media. There are no black "electronic" newspapers or black magazines available on CD-ROM containing full-motion video clips. Indeed, so much activity is still devoted to level one (portrayal) and level two (employment) for the traditional media that the opportunities for level three (black entrepreneurship) of the new media may be slipping away.

Estimates are that approximately three of every four jobs in service industries deal with the management, production, and processing of information. Because the idea of affirmative action has become part of the American corporate culture, mid- and lower-level black employment opportunities will be likely to materialize, but it remains to be seen if the companies that become the major players

Table 16.1
Alternative Telecommunication Delivery Systems

ATDS	Year Authorized/ Started	Uses Spectrum	Multi-Channel	Regulation	Financial Entry (a)	Technical Requirements (b)	Management Requirements (c)
CATV	1950s	No	Yes	FCC & Local	High	High	Specialized
DBS	1982	Yes	Yes	FCC	High	High	Specialized
HDTV	TBA	Yes	No	FCC	High	High	Specialized
LPTV	1982	Yes	No	FCC	Low/ Moderate	Moderate	Specialized
MMDS	1960s	Yes	Yes	FCC	Moderate/ High	Moderate/ High	Specialized
SMATV	N/A	No	Yes	None	Low	Low	Specialized
STV	1968	Yes	No	FCC	Moderate	Moderate	Specialized

(a) Low (under $500,000)
   Moderate ($500–$2 million)
   High (over $2 million)

(b) Low (No license or personnel required)
   Moderate (Licensed personnel required)
   High (Licensed personnel with specialized skill and education required)

(c) Niche service marketing skills

in the new media age post better black employment records than the traditional media industries. Although management-level black employment might lag below population parity, some Blacks will become mid- and occasionally senior-level managers. The deep and far-reaching implications of developing media forms suggest that Blacks will need to develop strategies for greater participation in the telecommunications industry and take advantage of ownership and employment opportunities. Such opportunities could lead to economic growth and community development if Blacks can control the type of impact that the emerging media have on the social, political, and economic structures within their communities. The developing media rely on local, state, and federal regulations; hardware and software availability; and community acceptance. The new media are or will be able to cover as wide or as narrow a target group as necessary for each different application or service. The technology has the capability to be simple or highly complex and can evolve from one to the other easily. Most importantly, the technology could have a positive impact on local communities through new and upgraded job opportunities. The new media forms require technicians, software producers, media specialists, and system managers.

IMPLICATIONS OF NEW MEDIA FORMS AND TECHNOLOGY

Projections indicate that the global interactive/multimedia world could be a trillion-dollar industry by the early twenty-first century, easily making America's share a multibillion-dollar market. However, if the 1970s and 1980s were harbingers, the future looks bleak for substantial changes in the mass media in terms of portrayal and entrepreneurship for the vast majority of Americans of African descent, and the power to shape the new media environment in a burgeoning industry may elude them.

The major mass media trends have already moved to the new media. We see the impact of the coming communications revolution. Newspapers are urged to embrace the electron to survive, and the media merger mania of the 1980s returned in the mid-1990s. In 1993 alone, several deals were made or attempted. Time Warner Inc. (the world's largest media conglomerate) and US West (one the seven regional Bell telephone operating companies [RBOCs]), completed a $2.5 billion alliance to better position each company for the media/information environment of the future. A planned $33 billion merger between Bell Atlantic (another RBOC) and Tele-Communications, Inc. (TCI) (America's largest cable television system operator) fell through, but industry observers expect each party to form partnerships with other media entities.

Viacom, a diversified media company, paid $10 billion to win a 1994 bidding war with cable home shopping programming service QVC for Paramount Communications, another diversified media company. Undaunted, QVC offered to merge with broadcast giant CBS for $7.2 billion. Less than one month later, QVC was the subject of a takeover bid by Comcast Corporation, another large cable system operator. No architect/major player/principal/chief executive officer in either deal was black.

AN OVERVIEW OF THE ALTERNATIVE TELECOMMUNICATION DELIVERY SYSTEMS

The alphabet soup of alternative telecommunication delivery systems (ATDS) has been with us for some time. The prospect of increased cable television penetration, direct broadcast service (DBS), high definition television (HDTV), low power television (LPTV), multichannel multipoint distribution service (MMDS), subscription television (STV), and satellite master antenna television (SMATV) had the telecommunications environment buzzing in the 1970s (see Appendix 16.1). These and home video and videotext services were widely heralded as the new sources of entertainment and information that would challenge, dazzle, and rival traditional over-the-air (OTA) television. There have been pretenders, but through the mid-1990s cable television has been the only serious competitor that has developed for OTA television. Although DBS started in 1994 on a limited basis, HDTV remains a "phantom" system. Other ATDS on the list, LPTV and STV, have been less than pervasive in their impact. Although many ATDS in the 1970s and 1980s were touted as "new," they had been technically viable for some time. Their "newness" was a result of being possible alternatives to the normal and traditional method of delivering television programming. Many ATDS date back to the late 1940s, when television broadcasting was beginning, while others are scheduled to become realities in the years to come.

The 1994 buzzwords were "interactive" and "multimedia" and the promise was back. It remains to be seen what these developing technologies will ultimately mean for the vast number of black people and where Blacks will fit into the emerging information/telecommunications age. An examination of the future must look at the history of black involvement with financing, implementing, and marketing the current list of ATDS.

BLACKS AND THE CHANGING MEDIA ENVIRONMENT

Because large global corporations control the mass media in America, one measure of black involvement is to look at corporate control, the composition of the boards of directors. A 1994 study found that Blacks had 3 percent of the corporate board seats of the Fortune 1,000 companies and that 63 percent of the Fortune 1,000 companies had no AHANA board members at all. In addition to being in the minority, the sociology of corporate boards (being invited to join after being nominated and found acceptable to a majority of the board members who are white) makes it unlikely that Blacks who are not incrementalists will be selected to serve.

Second, Blacks have few decision-making positions in the major media organizations, as the industry data on management in the previous chapter indicated. Often merged companies "downsize," reducing the work force and duplicated jobs. Consequently, black input on the nature and implementation of strategies for exploiting/utilizing the information superhighway will be minimal or minimized in the face of work force reductions.

There has been a dismal record of black entrepreneurial involvement with the ATDS to date. The author could find no record of any black-owned STV stations or MMDS operations. The FCC keeps no record of black-owned LPTV stations, but a 1990 study found that Blacks held 9 percent of the LPTV licenses compared to 33 percent for Hispanics, 25 percent for Native Americans, and 8 percent for Asians. There is no national black LPTV network. SMATV systems, which are actually closed-circuit cable television systems, serve relatively few subscribers. DBS appears to be the most promising of the ATDS, with two systems, DirecTV [sic] and United States Satellite Broadcasting (USSB), in operation.

Direct Broadcast Satellite (DBS)

Black entrepreneurial involvement with DBS ended in 1983 when Hubbard Broadcasting, Inc., a Minneapolis-based media corporation, bought black-owned broadcast satellite system, Advance, Inc. Hubbard launched USSB in 1994 and will share the same satellite as DirecTV. DirecTV is a subsidiary of the Hughes Corporation which is a subsidiary of General Motors. Both companies will offer multichannel programming for which consumers will pay directly. Both firms are independent, but together they have spent a total of approximately $1 billion to bring these services to market.

The Cable Television Industry as Prototype

Because of the low level of implementation and diffusion of many ATDS, the only ATDS it is possible to examine in terms of patterns and trends is the cable industry. The cable television industry as it existed in 1995 dates back to the late 1940s. Known initially as community antenna television (CATV), cable television was established to bring television to areas that did not have local stations, that were too far from existing stations, or that could not receive OTA signals because of hilly or mountainous terrain.

Cable television existed as a "mom and pop" industry that was no threat to OTA television for many years. In 1952 cable television industry revenues were less than $1 million. The cable television environment changed in the 1970s when FCC rules started to give the industry a freer environment in which to develop. The development of cable "superstations" (broadcast stations whose signals are transmitted nationally via satellite), cable television programming services, and the acquisition of most cable television systems by media conglomerates has resulted in an industry that is now a major player in the mass media environment. The 1994 cable industry consisted of over 11,000 systems, employed over 140,000 persons, reached 63 percent of the television homes in America. Valuing its 58.9 million subscribers at $2,000 each, the cable industry is a $117 billion industry which had 1993 revenues of approximately $21 billion from its multiple revenue streams (regular, premium, and pay-per-view subscribers and advertisers).

Afro-Americans and the New Technology

In the context of the 1990s buzzword of "empowerment," unless these technologies can be used for that purpose the future of the relationship between Blacks and the media will look much like the past, with Blacks attempting to catch up. In addition to coming to the game late historically, the limited participation of black ownership in the traditional broadcast media is because of: (1) not having the money to finance ventures or access to capital markets, (2) a shortage of available properties because most spectrum assignments were made years ago, (3) a lack of training and employment opportunities, and (4) difficulty in attracting advertisers to support operations. ATDS hold potential for new minority communications opportunities that might mean entry and adequate representation as entrepreneurs in the video marketplace. The use or uses of the various forms of ATDS will be shaped by the predominant social, political, and economic forces in America. Although the new media age is a developing one, the landscape already contains the tombstones of several ill-fated black "new" communications technologies media ventures. Several black programming ventures utilizing ATDS were announced in the 1980s; only one (Black Entertainment Television) ever went on the air as announced and was an actual viable service in 1995. The other services were not as fortunate, or were stillborn. The other announced/planned black ATDS programming ventures were:

Apollo Entertainment Television (AETV)

AETV was to be a subsidiary of Inner City Broadcasting Corp., a New York-based company operating radio stations in several major markets, including the successful WBLS-FM (New York). AETV was designed as a national cable network that would feature 10 hours of advertiser-supported programming daily, featuring music and interviews. AETV was to operate out of the famed Apollo Theatre, which was being converted to a production studio. Scheduled to debut in 1982, AETV never made it as anything remotely resembling a full-time network. Inner City experience problems in financing the Apollo Theatre purchase and considered making AETV a pay service rather than advertiser supported. AETV now is the television program production arm of Inner City Broadcasting, with the "Showtime at the Apollo" program as its main effort.

The Channel Black

The Channel Black (TCB) was to be a cable network scheduled to premiere in 1983 with a mix of black-oriented culture, information, and entertainment scheduled to run daily from 7 P.M. to 1 A.M., eastern time. It never made it to air.

The Community Channel (TCC)

The Community Channel (TCC) was scheduled to make its debut in 1982 as a 12-hour-a-day cable programming service offering entertainment, sports, and public affairs programming. This service never started.

Community Television Network (CTN)

CTN was a proposed satellite, interconnected, black-owned network of about 50 low-power television stations in cities ranging from Tampa, Florida, to Seattle, Washington. Reportedly, CTN had capitalization of $60 million at the time of its announcement, but the FCC freeze on LPTV applications in 1980 placed this venture on hold. The FCC's final LPTV rules did not help CTN because many of CTN's applications were for larger urban markets, which were processed last. By the mid-1980s, cable television systems (with their multiple channels) started being built in the major cities. LPTV licenses are not attractive because the stations have limited power (10 watts for VHF [channels 2–13] frequencies and 1,000 watts for UHF [channels 14–82]) and range, approximately ten miles.

These less-than-successful ventures do not mean Blacks have given up attempting to compete in the new communications environment. In 1993 one movie service started and a black-owned pay cable service was announced.

Minority Broadcasting Channel (MBC)

MBC, a Dallas, Texas-based company, launched a movie channel service with 12 hours of daily television programming in March 1993 and planned to go to an encrypted pay television service. At this writing, no subscriber base or audience size could be determined.

World African Network (WAN)

WAN is to be a premium cable channel that was scheduled to begin operation in June 1994, but the launch date has been moved to mid-1995. The principals are Eugene Jackson, who founded the National Black (radio) Network, and Phyllis Tucker Vinson Jackson, who was vice president for children's programming at the NBC Television network for many years. WAN reportedly had $15 million to start the venture.

For all the talk of potential for new opportunities for national impact of the ATDS, what Blacks were left with in 1994 was Black Entertainment Television (BET), a subsidiary of BET Holdings, Inc., as the likely standard by which black success with the ATDS will be judged.

BLACK ENTERTAINMENT TELEVISION (BET) HISTORY

BET is a network which distributes mostly black-oriented programming to cable systems throughout the United States. It is the first black television network in the United States. Robert Johnson was a National Cable Television Association (NCTA) lobbyist before he started BET. He got the idea in 1979 and the service started in 1980. Initially, BET distributed its programming to cable systems that reached 3.8 million subscribers via an arrangement with the USA Network wherein videotapes were sent to the USA Network uplink in New Jersey and distributed over satellite. The USA Network is a general audience cable programming network which carries a variety of sports, children's, entertainment, and infomercial programming. During its first two and a half years, BET's programming consisted of one night of programming a week, from 11 P.M. to 2 A.M. eastern time, on Friday nights, following and preceding other USA Network programming. BET expanded to daily service in 1982, offering programming from 8 P.M. to 2 A.M., eastern time.

Based in Washington, D.C., BET started out as a wholly advertiser-supported service and later charged a monthly subscriber fee to cable systems carrying BET programming, giving the service a dual revenue stream. BET seeks advertisers who want to deliver messages to the black consumer market.

BET experienced some growing pains in the mid-1980s. The speed at which cable systems were picking up or adding BET became a concern. When BET switched to its own transponder and daily service, subscriber homes dropped from nearly ten million homes to two million before rising to three million homes in early 1983. BET faced the possibility of having to refund money to advertisers if the service did not reach five million subscribers by August 1983, but this did not happen.

The company vaulted onto the *Black Enterprise* magazine list of top 100 black businesses at Number 15 in the 1991 list, reporting revenues of $35.8 million. BET Holdings, Inc.—BET's parent company—became a public corporation in 1991, becoming the first (and at this writing the only) black-controlled company on the New York Stock Exchange. BET Holdings, Inc. is a diversified, black-oriented media conglomerate (see Table 16.2). BET Holdings planned to start a jazz channel service in 1995. In 1994, BET programming was available to 39.6 million subscribers (approximately 42 percent of the American television households and approximately 65 percent of the cable homes in America). No data are available on how many of these cable homes were black. BET 1993 multiple stream revenues totalled $74.2 million (see Figure 16.1).

BET's long-term goal is to become the dominant media company reaching the black consumer market and the primary vehicle through which advertisers can reach the black consumer. As a harbinger of black participation in the new communication technology, BET illustrates four areas of concern for black new

Table 16.2
BET Holdings, Inc. Assets

Black Entertainment Television Network	100%
BET Satellites Services, Inc.	100%
BET Productions, Inc.	100%
BET Development, Inc.	100%
BET Publications, Inc.	100%
BET Acquisition Corp.	100%
BET Direct, Inc.	100%
Paige Publications (*Young Sisters & Brothers* magazine)	100%
Avalon Pictures, Inc. (BET Action Pay-per-view)	81%
United Image Entertainment	50%
Emerge Communications, Inc. (*Emerge* magazine)	44%

Source: Standard & Poor's Corporation Descriptions (January 1994), p. 6377.

media ventures: acquisition/ startup financing, product exhibition, programming, and revenue streams.

Financing

Johnson had an idea but little money when he started BET. In exchange for $500,000 in seed money in 1979, Johnson gave Tele-Communications, Inc. (TCI) (America's largest cable system operator) 20 percent of BET. Taft (a major broadcast group owner), invested $1 million in 1982, and Home Box Office (a Time Warner Inc. subsidiary) invested $1 million in 1984. The HBO investment meant that ownership percentages had to be adjusted so that Johnson could retain a majority share. One 1985 report said that TCI, Taft, and the HBO held stakes of 16 percent each, with Johnson having 52 percent ownership.

TCI, under the leadership of John Malone, is known for being an aggressive, cost-conscious company. Some industry critics are harsh on TCI and Malone, who has been referred to as "an industrial buccaneer" in charge of a company known as "the most frugal operators in the (cable television) business" who provide customer service that is "astonishingly bad" (Lublin and Lopez, 1993,

Figure 16.1
BET Revenue Analysis

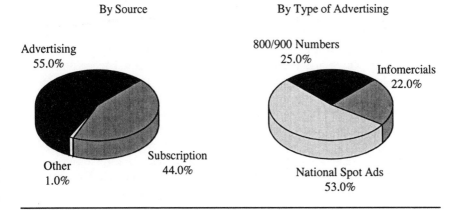

By Source

Advertising
55.0%

Other
1.0%

Subscription
44.0%

By Type of Advertising

800/900 Numbers
25.0%

Infomercials
22.0%

National Spot Ads
53.0%

Sources: *BET Holdings 1992 Annual Report; Hoover's Handbook of Emerging Companies, 1993–94.*

pp. B1 and B10). Malone explained his rationale for backing BET from the beginning:

Bob seemed like the kind of guy you could invest some money with, and he wouldn't embarrass you. When we (TCI) thought of starting this, there was always the concern that this kind of a channel could become something radical, and you wouldn't want your name associated with it. (Smikle, 1985, p. 64)

BET raised $72 million when it went public in 1991; Johnson and his wife control 55.8 percent of the stock. Time Warner retained its interest and in 1994 owned 17.8 percent of the company stock, and Liberty Media Corp. (a TCI subsidiary) owned 21.4 percent. In 1994 BET Holdings, Inc.'s board of directors consisted of three Blacks and three whites (the president of Time Warner Inc.'s cable division, the president of Liberty Media Inc., and Malone). Johnson's investors bought into Johnson's vision of BET as he described it in a *Cable News Network* profile:

You know, all we did was take the TV wheel and paint it black. . . . I didn't get in this business to be the uplifting [*sic*] and to save black America. I got into this business to make money and to return shareholder value and to maximize shareholder wealth and to grow a business. (Pinnacle, 1993, p. 4)

By financial measurements, BET is a successful enterprise. Based on its stock price, BET had a market value of nearly $300 million at the end of 1994.

AN EXHIBITION DILEMMA

Marketing scholars have acknowledged the existence of a black consumer market since World War II. It has grown from a $3 billion one in 1940 to an estimated $300 billion market in 1994. While this market is potentially lucrative, the ATDS question will be, "Is the audience accessible?" Within this context, BET contends with a major marketing problem in its goal to become the major national television network targeted to black America. The reality of cable penetration reveals that BET's market segment for its product—a black-oriented cable television programming service—may not be readily available to its target market, the black people of America.

BET programming faces exhibition challenges that are more subtle and severe than indicated. Table 16.3 paints a reality of cable television for black people that does not exist. The cable penetration levels shown include the suburban areas for the marketers. The inner cities (where most Blacks live) were the last urban areas to receive cable and are still being wired. Cable penetration in the urban areas is approximately 40 percent; the suburban penetration rate is much higher. Cable only came to South Central Los Angeles in 1988; the city of Detroit had only 4,500 cable subscribers in the late 1980s and major cable installation did not begin until 1991. Cable was not available in all parts of the boroughs of New York City in 1994.

The 1994 *Black Enterprise* magazine "List of Top Black Industrial/Service Firms" contained three companies with cable television interests and one company with a national cable programming service (see Table 16.4).

Research/information offices at the National Association of Minorities in Cable (NAMIC), the National Black Media Coalition (NBMC), the National Cable Television Association (NCTA), and BET could not tell this author how many cable systems were black-owned in 1994. A 1992 NCTA convention panel indicated that cable franchising is still an unpredictable process for black entrepreneurs who must battle lending institutions. Historically, city council members or commissioners have frequently treated black entrepreneurs as outsiders and have not looked with favor on cable franchise proposals from them.

A PROGRAMMING DILEMMA

BET, which sought to become the major medium used to distribute movies about Blacks (with black actresses and actors in leading roles dating as far back as the 1930s, as well as musical specials, documentaries, historically black college sports events, and other types of programming), now faces another dilemma. During most of its years of operation as a USA piggyback service, BET programming consisted of a movie or a black college sports event (basketball, football, and tennis). It later added talk shows on teen issues and sports, a gospel program, and "Black Showcase." "Black Showcase" debuted with a black variety review apparently filmed in the 1940s and 1950s or early 1960s. It was

Table 16.3
Cable Penetration in Top Black Market Areas

Rank	Marker	Penetration
1	New York, NY/Newark, NJ	62.4
2	Chicago	53.9
3	Washington, DC	60.4
4	Detroit	61.3
5	Los Angeles/Long Beach	57.9
6	Philadelphia	70.8
7	Atlanta	59.5
8	Baltimore	56.2
9	Houston	49.9
10	New Orleans	67.1
11	St. Louis	47.7
12	Dallas	47.1
13	Oakland/San Francisco	66.5
14	Memphis	56.5
15	Norfolk/Virginia Beach/Newport News, VA	68.5
16	Miami	65.5
17	Cleveland	62.0
18	Richmond/Petersburg	52.9
19	Birmingham, AL	62.1
20	Charlotte-Gastonia, NC/Rock Hill, SC	61.9

Source: Leading 100 metro areas ranked by black population (April 1992). *Spot Radio Rates and Data* and *Broadcasting & Cable Yearbook 1993*, pp. D-71–74.

Table 16.4
Black Cable System Ownership, 1994

Company/Location	Systems/Subscribers
Barden Communication Inc. Detroit, MI	One/114,000
Garden State Cable TV Cherry Hill, NJ	One/186,000
Inner City Broadcasting Corp. New York, NY	One/70,000

Source: Broadcasting & Cable Yearbook, 1993, pp. D–5, D–22; *Black Enterprise*, June 1994, pp. 87–94.

later replaced with a music video program. At various times, BET aired cooking, exercise, children's, public affairs, and informational programming on its schedule. During its early years, BET made it a practice to show at least one film a month with black actors and actresses in leading roles dating back to the 1930s and 1940s. Many of these "classic" films, as BET called them, are public domain films, often with poor soundtracks and print quality. BET no longer carries movies, but movies are carried on its Action Pay-Per-View subsidiary. BET had been acquiring its movies from companies that have long been a part of the Hollywood hierarchy that controls the American film industry and has promulgated a certain type of stereotypic programming featuring blacks. However, it has entered into a joint venture with Baruch Entertainment, a minority program syndicator, to produce more low budget black motion pictures and an agreement with video retailer Blockbuster Entertainment to distribute the joint productions.

Black college sports were initially shown on a videotape delay basis of up to one week. At this writing, BET does not carry a schedule of any black collegiate athletic conference (the Central Intercollegiate Athletic Association, the Mid-Eastern Athletic Conference, the Southern Intercollegiate Athletic Conference or the Southwest Athletic Conference) games or their postseason basketball tournaments. Black college football was not carried in 1994, even though that season Alcorn State University quarterback Steve "Air" McNair was the first player from a historically black college or university to seriously contend for the Heisman Award that is given to the best college player in America.

For most of its existence, BET has resulted in little first-run programming. An author's analysis of BET's 1994 programming one hour before, during, and one hour after prime time found a heavy emphasis on entertainment (music videos, situation comedy reruns, standup comedy, etc.) with nearly 90 percent of the prime time programming in this category and approximately 82 percent of the prime time plus or minus one hour. In 1994, other than one-minute newsbriefs, BET had no news or public affairs programming in prime time and its news show was a weekly program. BET's prime time programming is skewed heavily toward youth/ young adults with music videos and syndicated reruns of cancelled network situation comedies, such as "Roc," "Sanford and Son," "Up All Night," and "What's Happening", and standup comedy shows. BET carried many infomercials (program length advertisements for products or services) which did not feature blacks in prominent roles. In 1994, BET added a black-oriented home shopping program that would be a prototype of a joint venture with the Home Shopping Network.

WHO PAYS?

Since the failure of the CBS advertiser-supported cultural cable programming service in the 1980s, the question remains whether advertiser-supported specialized cable networks are the route to take. One is reminded of the longtime problem of ethnic audience measurement. Although cable advertising has been increasing steadily, advertisers have not yet fully embraced cable television advertising as the preferred mode of television advertising because of the lack of data available on audience size, composition, and viewership. During prime time, when television audiences are at their highest, the OTA television networks (ABC, CBS, Fox, and NBC) accounted for 62 percent of the audience in the 1993–94 television season. Black broadcasters have long raised objections to existing methods of audience measurement and audience estimate reports. It remains to be seen whether ethnic measurement will improve for the ATDS. The trend toward pay-per-view support would provide a much less cumbersome revenue stream. As the AETV experience has indicated, revenues from a per-subscriber base may be preferable to revenues derived from the sale of advertising initially. Consumers have become used to paying for entertainment which is free of advertising. With 500 competitors possible in the new video age, it would seem to make little sense to split the advertising pie even smaller at a time when cost-per-thousand (CPM)—a measure of advertising efficiency—figures are rising and a buy would become more difficult to justify on the basis of cost-per-thousand or ratings points.

THE CHOICE TO BE MADE

This chapter has described the problems faced by black entrepreneurs engaged in and interested in utilizing the ATDS technologies. Obviously, the technology does not exist in a vacuum and is not a panacea. The cable franchise battles fought and lost thus far indicate that blacks and other minorities have had a tough time getting franchises because of the capital-intensive nature of the business and the highly political nature of franchising. One solution may be joint ventures involving two or more well-established black communications firms with strong track records and good access to capital markets. Joint ventures from lesser-known entrepreneurs may remain difficult to fund.

The approximately 200 black-owned/licensed broadcast properties in 1994 constituted only 2 percent of the operating radio and television stations. Most black-owned stations are a direct result of FCC efforts to encourage minority ownership through tax certificates and distress sales policies.[1] These policies were instrumental in bringing about an increase in black station ownership from 17 radio stations in 1973 to approximately 200 radio and television stations in 1994—a 1,176 percent increase. Since the policies were instituted in 1978 and through mid-1994, Blacks have received 66 percent of the licenses transferred as a result of distress sales and 64 percent of the tax certificates issued.

The tax certificate policy has been extended to cable systems and Blacks have been involved in 14 of the 24 deals thus far. The biggest barrier to black participation in the ATDS has been obtaining adequate financing. In general, Blacks have higher credit refusal rates than Hispanics, Asians, or whites. As Table 16.1 indicates, the ATDS with the brightest futures are more expensive than the traditional media.

The minority ownership policies narrowly survived a 1990 U.S. Supreme Court review in the *Metro Broadcasting Inc. v. the FCC* case. However, a 1995 U.S. Supreme Court ruling in *Adarand Constructors, Inc. v. Pena* indicated that the momentum for such government assistance for blacks and other minorities may have peaked. The 1995 ruling said affirmative action policies would now be permitted under limited situations if some "compelling reason" exists.

Programming is another major consideration as Blacks attempt to take advantage of ATDS. Black-oriented radio survives because it can produce a consistent type and volume of programming. There is an adequate amount of new programming (i.e., recorded music) constantly being produced by the recording industry for this market segment. For black ATDS telecommunications ventures to succeed, more black-oriented programming must be produced, but acquiring and producing it is costly; available product is of culturally questionable value, and heavy investment in production capability is difficult to obtain. Thus, the industry cooperation needed to produce the type of video programming fare necessary to fill up the volume of airtime available on a daily basis is lacking. Without new programming, black ATDS ventures will continue to rely on programming which studies have shown to be stereotypic.

POTENTIAL

The ATDS offer the potential for a variety of unique programming formats, particularly in the areas of news, entertainment, and sports. Live programs from a studio or on location before a live audience could be placed on videotape, allowing a library of programming to be established. Weekly or biweekly amateur hour programs could provide national exposure for black entertainers or performers in concert. Production costs could be kept low by using aspiring stars and budding talent.

In the entertainment area, theater departments at historically black colleges could be used on a rotating basis to stage various dramatic productions and the colleges could be compensated or paid on the basis of some amicable agreement between the producer and the colleges, much like the college sports arrangements. Since a news operation can be an expensive undertaking, a fledgling television programming service would be hard-pressed to provide a nightly commercial television network-type newscast; new telecommunications ventures might work cooperatively with black broadcasting networks, such as the American Urban Networks or the Black College Satellite Network to produce news programs. The pooling of resources by black communications organizations, such as black-oriented telecommunications networks, could provide an additional type of programming currently not available to black viewers.

NONBROADCAST MEDIA

The personal communications services (PCS) industry, with an estimated $50 billion in potential annual revenues, is posed for development. PCS are the next generation of wireless communications that will provide two-way cordless/mobile services (telephone, facsimile, imaging, and paging). Because the services will use the electromagnetic spectrum, the FCC must decide who will get PCS licenses. The FCC started to auction the PCS spectrum in December 1994. In an attempt to include entrepreneurial possibilities for AHANA members and women, both groups were given bidding credits and the opportunities to get tax certificates, low- or no-interest loans, and installment payments for PCS licenses (see Table 16.5).

FCC Chairman Reed Hundt has said that these spectrum auctions will be "one of the most important sales of public property since Napoleon sold almost half of the West of this continent to Jefferson's United States" (Hundt, 1994, A-6) and will create "the greatest single (communications entrepreneurial) opportunity made available to women and minorities" (Stern, 1994). The *Wall Street Journal* has viewed the policy differently and called the plan "festooned with special rules for special people," and in a July 13, 1994, editorial said:

More likely the people who will most exploit the FCC's insistence on set-asides (for women and minorities) are fast-buck artists. They can either buy a PCS license and then eventually resell it to a larger company or set up a shell company that can qualify for woman- or minority-owned (status). The FCC knows this. (The 55 MPH, 1994, p. A14)

The auctions carried high participation prices. Potential bidders were required to pay to the FCC an upfront participation fee equal to a percentage of the value of the license sought. For the 10 largest markets/black market areas, this fee averaged $7.5 million. The PCS auction policies were under review at this writing.

Table 16.5
FCC Personal Communications Services Auction Policy

Type of Company	Bidding Credits	Installment Payments	Tax Certificates for Investors
Entrepreneurial Businesses ($40 MM - $125 MM in revenue and less than $500 MM in total assets)	0	Interest only for 1 year; rate equal to 10-year Treasury note plus 2.5% (for businesses with revenues greater than $75 MM, available only in top 50 markets)	No
Small Businesses (less than $40 MM revenues	10%	Interest only for 2 years; rate equal to 10-year Treasury note plus 2.5%	No
Businesses Owned by Minorities and/or Women ($40 MM - $125 MM in revenues)	15%	Interest only for 3 years; rate equal to 10-year Treasury note	Yes
Small Businesses Owned by Minorities and/or Women (less than $40 MM in revenues)	25%	Interest only for five years; rate equal to 10-year Treasury note	Yes

Source: Bidder's Information Package Broadband Personal Communications Services (Major Trading Area Licenses), Federal Communications Commission (September 22, 1994), p. 50.

Only one black firm on the *Black Enterprise* 1994 list of top black businesses—Barden Communications, a Detroit-based company—was involved with PCS. Barden received a license to test PCS technology in 1992, but it did not enter the PCS service bidding. The FCC held an auction for interactive video data services (IVDS) during the summer of 1994 also. IVDS will allow broadcasters and others to provide interactive services through existing television receivers. Since the beneficiaries of these licenses were broadcasters and Blacks hold licenses to only 19 of approximately 1,100 commercial television stations, it comes as no surprise that no AHANA group received any of these licenses. It remains to be seen if IVDS will have a significant impact on black telecommunications involvement. However, one-third of the black-held television station licenses use a commercial shopping format and those owners may be interested in the technology.

CONCLUSION

In 1994, the media conglomeration trend claimed two black players in the electronic media industry. WGPR-TV, the first television station in America licensed to Blacks, was bought by CBS and became the network's Detroit affiliate. Comcast, a top multiple cable system operator, bought Barden Communications' Detroit cable system.

The heyday of the black press in America in terms of influence occurred prior to the *Brown v. Topeka Board of Education* decision. During this era, at least five newspapers (the *Defender,* the *Amsterdam-News,* the Pittsburgh *Courier,* the *Journal and Guide,* and the *Afro-American* group) achieved national status. Two reasons for this success were their advocacy and the fact that they did not depend on advertiser revenues for the bulk of their economic support. The ratio of 80 percent subscriber revenues versus 20 percent advertising revenues gave black newspapers an independence that other black media, and especially black broadcasting, which depends almost entirely on advertiser support, does not.

In 1973, *Black Enterprise* magazine said:

"Community antenna television," better known as CATV or cable TV, is still in its infancy. Any stockbroker will tell you that it is a high-risk industry. Nevertheless, for America's minorities it represents their best (and possibly last) [*sic*] chance to gain a sizeable share of media business and media influence in our society. (p. 36)

History indicates that Blacks missed the cable revolution in terms of share and media business. The sole "success" of BET shows that Blacks may miss out again in the new video age or participate with little independence or any chance at revolutionizing the media business. ATDS raise as many new problems as they provide potential solutions to old problems. It remains to be seen whether the "success" of BET will motivate competitors to take a systems approach to the ATDS, which requires entrepreneurs to assess the ATDS on the basis of its advantages and disadvantages and to evaluate each ATDS on a long-term versus a short-term basis. Whatever method of delivering black-oriented programming or information services by Blacks is used, there need to be concomitant developments in audience research and measurement, exhibition, programming, and program production.

The ATDS are primarily designed as telecommunications distribution systems. Thus, any investments must also consider marketing strategies, software availability, consumer acceptability, and cost-effectiveness of service. Black advertising agencies and market research firms, black production companies, and black-owned local exhibition outlets are all necessary to realize the financial, cultural, and programming potential that the alternative telecommunications delivery systems offer and require.

NOTE

1. The FCC has adopted the following policies to attempt to increase the level of black ownership:

Tax certificates. The FCC will consider granting a tax certificate to the seller of a broadcast station or cable system if the seller sells the station to a minority (AHANA)-owned or -controlled company. This tax certificate enables the seller to defer the capital gains tax realized on the sale for up to two years.

Distress sale. A distress sale occurs when a broadcast licensee has been designated for a FCC hearing at license renewal time because of the station's past practices. A licensee so designated may sell the station to an AHANA company at 75 percent of the station's independently determined, fair-market value.

Comparative credit. The FCC gives comparative merit/credit to AHANA applicants for new broadcast facilities if the AHANA members plan to be actively involved in the management of the proposed station. In reality, most of the broadcast frequencies have been assigned.

APPENDIX 16.1

ATDS Descriptions

Direct broadcast satellite (DBS). High-power geosynchronous satellites that broadcast television signals directly to small receivers at individual homes.

High-definition television (HDTV). Television programming broadcast in wider screens formats/aspect ratios and is really a cosmetic improvement to television.

Low power television (LPTV). Television stations with limited power (10 watts for VHF channels and 1,000 watts for UHF channels). These stations have limited range.

Multichannel, multipoint distribution service (MMDS). Sometimes called "wireless cable," this service broadcasts signals at higher than UHF frequencies. Receivers require special antennas and converters to view the signal.

Satellite master antenna television (SMATV). Closed-circuit cable systems located on private property. Because the equipment is on private property, no franchise from a municipality is required. Signals may be brought in, after payment of proper fees, from cable programming services or DBS companies.

Subscription Television (STV). A conventional, over-the-air television station with scrambled signals that requires a decoder to unscramble the signals. Because of its single-channel limitation, it is not considered a competitive technology to cable.

REFERENCES

The B.E. 100s: Industrial/service companies. (June 1994). *Black Enterprise,* pp. 87–94.

Bidder's Information Package, Broadband Personal Communications Services (Major Trading Area Licenses). Federal Communications Commission (September 22, 1994).

Black corporate directors in the United States. *Business and Society Review, 88*(53) (Winter 1994), 53–62.

Brooks, M., & Havice, M. (December 14, 1990). Low power television 1990 industry survey. (Unpublished report of the Community Broadcasters Association.)

Cable TV offers minorities their last and best chance at the media business. (August 1973). *Black Enterprise,* pp. 36–37.

Hundt, Reed. (April 1994). Address to the superhighway summit. *Emmy,* p. A5–A7.

Lublin, J. S, & Lopez, J. A. (October 14, 1993). Melding of the bold and staid promises a thunderous clash. *The Wall Street Journal,* pp. B1, B10.

Pinnacle. (February 13, 1993). *Journal Graphics,* Transcript #148 (R-#116).

Smikle, Ken. (November 1985). The best BET in cable. *Black Enterprise,* p. 8.

Stern, Christopher. (July 4, 1994). FCC awards PCS advantages. *Broadcasting & Cable,* p. 35.

The 55 MPH information highway. *Wall Street Journal,* July 13, 1994.

Index

Abbott, Robert, 229, 231. *See also Chicago Defender*

Accrediting Council on Journalism and Mass Communications (ACEJMC), 258

Adams, Grantley, 164

Adarand Constructors, Inc. v. Pena, 280

AEJMC News, 259

"Africa One," 205

African Center for the Improvement of Journalists and Communicators, 108, 113, 126

African Council for Communication Education, 40; directory, 40–41

African-Americans, Hispanics, Asians, and Native Americans (AHANA), 252, 253, 257, 258, 260, 261, 262, 269, 281, 282. *See also* Afro-Americans

African National Congress, 15; anti-apartheid broadcasting, 15

African Postal and Telecommunication Union, 47

Afro-Americans: access to cable, 277; attempts to recolonize, 219; attitudes toward, 216–217, 224; consumer market, 215, 232, 243, 276; early history, 218; employment by media industry, 260–263; information superhighway activities, 266, 281; involvement with alternative telecommunication delivery systems, 269–279, 281; journalism degrees earned, 258; media stereotypes, 225, 239–240, 244; median income, 253; nation concept, 214–215; New Deal, 231; non-degree training programs, 257; northern migration, 229; profile of black journalists, 255–256; representation on corporate boards, 269; representation on journalism and mass communication faculties, 258; riots, 259; role in American Revolution, 219; Reconstruction, 223–224; role in labor force, 252–253, 268; U.S. laws regarding, 218, 219, 222, 223, 224. *See also Adarand Constructors, Inc. v. Pena*; *Brown v. Topeka Board of Education*; Civil Rights Act of 1964; *Dred Scott* case; *Metro Broadcasting v. FCC*; *Plessy v. Ferguson*; Voting Rights Act of 1965

—black newspapers: antebellum, 221–222; auxiliaries, 231; "Big Five," 230, 231, 233; criticisms, 229, 232; circulation, 235; and FBI, 231–232; political affiliation, 231, 232; post–Civil War, 223–224; twentieth century, 228–231, 235. Titles: *Afro-American*, 230, 283;

About the Authors

JAMES PHILLIP JETER, Professor and Director of Graduate Studies, Division of Journalism, Florida Agricultural and Mechanical University, has written at length about African Americans and the mass media.

KULDIP R. RAMPAL, Professor of Mass Communication, Central Missouri State University, was a professor in the Communications Program at the National University of Signapore during the 1994–1995 academic year. His research work on journalism education, development communication, press regulation, media ethics, international broadcasting, and international press has appeared in a variety of books and journals. He has traveled to five continents in connection with his research work. In recognition of his publications on Confucianism and press and political liberalization in Taiwan, the government of the Republic of China awarded him the 1993 International Communication Award. A native of India, he worked as a political correspondent for the *Indian Express* before coming to the United States.

VIBERT C. CAMBRIDGE, Associate Professor, School of Telecommunications, Ohio University, has conducted extensive research and written on Anglophone Caribbean mass communication, especially broadcasting history.

CORNELIUS B. PRATT, Professor, College of Communication Arts and Sciences, Michigan State University, has written expansively about communications and the mass media in sub-Saharan Africa.

ISBN 0-313-28400-8

HARDCOVER BAR CODE